PENGUIN BOOKS

PARIS AFTER THE LIBERATION

'This is a beautifully written book about a vast tapestry of military, political and social upheaval. Remarkably researched, wise, balanced, very funny at times ... I was witness to events in Paris in the first desperate, glorious, mad weeks, and this is just how it was' – Dirk Bogarde in 'Books of the Year', *Good Book Guide*

'Technically the book is outstanding: it is also enormously enjoyable to read – exciting, lively, funny, and admirably tolerant and objective in its opinions. It is hard to see how it could have been better done' – Philip Ziegler in the *Daily Telegraph*

'To understand France today you should read this book about France yesterday, a carefully researched and admirably written account ... The book is, however, more than a very competent account of French politics between 1944 and 1949, it is a reminder of how cold the Cold War was, how nearly the communists seized power in France ... compulsive reading' – Mark Bonham-Carter in the *Evening Standard*

'This valuable new book ... a true *vade mecum* of an era' – Paul Ryan in the *Irish Times*

'An entrancing read' – Richard Lamb in the *Spectator*

Antony Beevor wrote his first novel when he lived in Paris for two years. His works of non-fiction include *The Spanish Civil War*, *Crete – the Battle and the Resistance*, which won a Runciman Award, and the highly acclaimed *Stalingrad*, which is also published in Penguin.

Artemis Cooper's work includes *Cairo in the War 1939–1945*. She has just completed *Writing at the Kitchen Table*, the authorised biography of Elizabeth David, which will appear shortly. Her grandfather, Duff Cooper, was the first postwar British Ambassador to Paris, and his private diaries and papers provide one of the previously unpublished sources for this book.

Antony Beevor and Artemis Cooper were both appointed Chevalier de l'Ordre des Arts et Lettres by the French government. They are married and have two children.

Paris after the Liberation
1944–1949

*Antony Beevor and
Artemis Cooper*

PENGUIN BOOKS

For our parents

PENGUIN BOOKS

Published by the Penguin Group
Penguin Books Ltd, 80 Strand, London WC2R 0RL, England
Penguin Putnam Inc., 375 Hudson Street, New York, New York 10014, USA
Penguin Books Australia Ltd, Ringwood, Victoria, Australia
Penguin Books Canada Ltd, 10 Alcorn Avenue, Toronto, Ontario, Canada M4V 3B2
Penguin Books India (P) Ltd, 11 Community Centre, Panchsheel Park, New Delhi – 110 017, India
Penguin Books (NZ) Ltd, Cnr Rosedale and Airborne Roads, Albany, Auckland, New Zealand
Penguin Books (South Africa) (Pty) Ltd, 24 Sturdee Avenue, Rosebank 2196 South Africa

Penguin Books Ltd, Registered Offices: 80 Strand, London WC2R 0RL, England

www.penguin.com

First published by Hamish Hamilton 1994
Published in Penguin Books 1995
6

Copyright © Antony Beevor and Artemis Cooper, 1994
All rights reserved

The moral rights of the authors have been asserted

The acknowledgements on p. 518 constitute an extension of this copyright page

Printed in England by Clays Ltd, St Ives plc

Contents

Preface

Bringing a period such as this to life requires an unusual range of personal memories to put flesh on the bones. We have been fortunate right from the start. Family papers were an invaluable asset. Diana Cooper did not keep a diary, but her regular letters to Conrad Russell contain memorable descriptions. Most important of all was the private diary which Duff Cooper kept every day during his time as British ambassador in Paris. It provides an extraordinary insight into the concerns and issues of the moment, as well as gossip about the major figures of the time – the politicians, writers and artists whom they constantly entertained.

Another valuable unpublished source was the meticulous diary of Brigadier Denis Daly, the British military attaché. He often wrote a page or more each day, recording what people had said about the political situation or the latest scandal. When recreating a period, rumour is just as important as fact established after the event. Such details are absolutely vital, for example, to recreate the deep unease in the spring of 1946 after de Gaulle's resignation, when people expected either a Communist or a right-wing *coup d'état*.

Charlotte Mosley very generously allowed us to go through all of Nancy Mitford's unpublished correspondence from Paris. The diary of the American ambassador, David Bruce, was both delightful as well as instructive on the period of recovery in

1949. This sort of material puts a much richer perspective on the already fascinating foundations unearthed in state archives in Paris, Washington, DC, Moscow and London. A lot of good material is available in the Archives Nationales in Paris, but much still remains firmly locked up. Fortunately, documents and information passed by French officials to foreign embassies at the time fill many of the gaps.

The years 1944 to 1949 cover the joy of the Liberation; the *épuration* (purge) of collaborators with the great trials of the leaders of Vichy; the re-establishment by de Gaulle of the Republic amid the ruins of war; his abrupt departure from office in January 1946; the power of the Communist Party in France; the opening stage of the Cold War, with France on the brink of collapse in the winter of 1947; and the arrival of Marshall Plan aid, saving the country from disaster. The year 1949 provides a fitting end, for many reasons. Communist attempts to destroy the economy had collapsed, as had General de Gaulle's hopes of sweeping back to power. To the surprise of almost everyone, parliamentary democracy had survived. The drama of the Kravchenko trial in Paris provided the first effective blow against the Stalinist myth which had grown out of the Resistance, while the influx of Marshall Plan aid generated an economic recovery which started to lift the country from its wartime misery. There are, of course, overlaps, but in 1950 another age begins with that prototype of the Common Market, the European Coal and Steel Community.

We start the book with a brief prelude to include the collapse of France and the Occupation. All the settling of accounts after the Liberation harked back to those dark times, and one can understand the emotions better with a brief reminder of the reasons for the bitterness between those who followed Marshal Pétain's 'path of collaboration' and those who decided to resist. This inevitably forms the first of the three main issues of the era and of this book.

Another aspect intrigued us right from the start. Almost immediately after the humiliation of the Occupation, and surrounded by the dilapidation and poverty of 1945, Paris rapidly managed to project its sense of cultural superiority. In Saint-Germain-des-Prés, people may have been hungry, but the ferment of ideas after the repression generated an extraordinary excitement. This was the period about which every foreign student still dreams when wandering from the Café Flore or the Deux Magots across the *Quartier Latin* – trying to conjure up existentialists arguing in cafés and Juliette Gréco in a smoke-filled cellar club. Paris was the intellectual Mecca of the world, but a sense of superiority encouraged hubris of a sort when the progressive intelligentsia saw itself as a priestly caste in the cause of left-wing theory.

The third theme, closely linked to the second, is the birth of France's love–hate relationship with the United States. Nobody loves their liberator, but in France the emotions were particularly complex. The young, especially, adored all things American – jazz, films, clothes and the easy manner of the GIs. They represented freedom after the Occupation and the stultifying regime of the old Marshal. But soon both intellectuals of the left and traditionalists of the right began to fear and resent the potentially dominant culture of the United States. This 'recurring fever', to use Jean Monnet's phrase, continues to this day.

A book of such wide scope inevitably depends on the help and generosity of many people. We are very grateful to all those who took the time to talk to us over the last four years and contribute their observations and memories of the period: Susan-Mary Alsop, Richard Arzt, Letitia Baldrige, Lucius Battle, M. le ministre Jacques Baumel, Munir Benjenk, General Pierre de Bénouville, André Bergeron, Sir Isaiah Berlin, Lesley Blanch, Sénateur Édouard Bonnefous, Jean Borotra, William Boswell, Claude Bouchinet-Serreulles, Madame du Bouëtiez, Ambassadeur de France René Brouillet, Evangeline Bruce, John Bruce-

Lockhart, Claus von Bülow, Baron and Baronne de Cabrol, Francis Cammaerts, Comte René de Chambrun, Olivier Chévrion, Sir Ashley Clarke, Professor Richard Cobb, Roger Codou, Ethel de Croisset, M. le ministre Philippe Dechartre, Colonel André Dewavrin, Sir Douglas Dodds-Parker, M. le ministre Pierre Dreyfus, the late Prince Jean-Louis de Faucigny-Lucinge, Magouche Fielding, Maître Max Fischer, Alastair Forbes, Maurice Franck, Jean Friendly, Jean Gager, Martha Gellhorn, Frank Giles, the Hon. G. McMurtrie Godley, Walter Goetz, Juliette Gréco, the Hon. Pamela Harriman, Lady Holman, Maître Jacques Isorni, Joe Kingsbury-Smith, the Hon. Ridgway Knight, Comte Totor de Lesseps, the Hon. Douglas MacArthur II, Alain Malraux, John Mowinckel, the late Henri Noguères, André Ostier, Violette Palewski, Tom Pocock, Odette Pol Roger, Princess Ghislaine de Polignac, Stuart Preston, Baron Alexis de Redé, Comte Jacques de Ricaumont, Sir Brooks and Lady Richards, Sir Frank Roberts, Georges Roditi, Willy Ronis, Baronne Élie de Rothschild, Teresa Lady Rothschild, Jacques Rouët, the late General Comte Jean-Louis de Rougemont, Comtesse de Rougemont, M. le ministre Maurice Schumann, Lord Sherfield, Ambassadeur de France Jean-Marie Soutou, Roger Stéphane, Louis Teuléry, Major and Mrs Desmond Thayre, Denise Tual, Henry Tyler, Ambassadeur de France François Valéry, Mary Vaudoyer, Jacqueline Ventadour-Hélion, Air Vice-Marshal Paul Willert, Tom Wilson, Jean Zinenberg.

We owe an enormous debt to those who so kindly loaned private papers: Letitia Baldrige for her brother's and father's accounts as well as her own letters from Paris; Captain C.P.D. Berrill-Daly for lending us the diary of his uncle, Brigadier Denis Daly, the British Military Attaché; the Duchess of Devonshire and Charlotte Mosley for the unpublished letters of Nancy Mitford; the Comtesse de Durfort for the unpublished memoirs of her father, General Comte Jean-Louis de Rougemont; John Julius Norwich for the papers of Duff Cooper and Lady Diana Cooper.

We have also been extremely lucky with the help and advice which we have received from the curators and staff of archives, institutes and libraries: in France, Mme Chantal Bonazzi, the *conservateur-en-chef* of the Section Contemporaine of the Archives Nationales, and her staff; Henri Rousso and his colleagues at the Institut d'Histoire du Temps Présent; Madame Marie de Thezy of the Bibliothèque de la Ville de Paris; Madame Catherine Trouiller at the Institut Charles de Gaulle; Mme Filloles of the Archives de la Ville de Paris; the staff of the Centre de Documentation Juive Contemporaine; in Moscow, Dr Kyril Anderson, the director of the Russian Centre for the Conservation and Study of Modern Historical Records for his invaluable help; in the United States, the staff of the National Archives and Records Administration; the staff of the Library of Congress; Nelson D. Lankford and his staff at the Virginia Historical Society, which holds the diaries and papers of David K. Bruce; in Great Britain, the staff of the Public Record Office, the British Library and, as always, the librarian and staff of the London Library.

Our constant travels abroad were made possible and vastly more enjoyable by the generous hospitality we received from friends prepared to have us to stay: in France, Jacques-Henri and Cécile de Durfort, Lucy Morgan-Bert, Alexander and Charlotte Mosley, Henri and Sybil d'Origny, the late Commandant Paul-Louis Weiller; in the United States, Susan-Mary Alsop, Jean Friendly, Martin and Julia Walker; in Moscow, David Campbell and Tom Wilson, and Francis and Jill Richards. Work in the Pushkinskaya archives would have been impossible without Olga Novikova, our translator, who subsequently continued research on her own and discovered more valuable material for us.

Historians and biographers have been most generous with their time, their advice and sometimes their own sources: Henry Amouroux, Jean-Pierre Bernard, Jean Bothorel, Philippe Buton, Stéphane Courtois, Jean Elleinstein, M.R.D. Foot, Sabine

Jansen, James Lord, Patrick O'Connor, Patrick Marnham, Bernard Minoret, David Pryce-Jones, Henry Rousso and Philip Ziegler. We are particularly grateful to the documentary film-maker Mosco Boucault, who loaned us tapes of his interviews with leading members of the French Communist Party and provided numerous introductions.

Others who offered advice, material or introductions were Marina Berry, François Claudel, the late Aidan Crawley, Rudi Fischer, Robert and Aliette Gillet, Andrew Harvey, Sir Nicholas Henderson, Alain Malraux, Suzy Menkes, Eric Olivier, John and Yvonne Panitza, Irena Skhondina, Susan Train, Hugo Vickers, Lady Warner, the Hon. Charles Whitehouse.

We cannot thank sufficiently those who read through the whole manuscript or relevant parts of it and made useful criticisms and observations: M.R.D. Foot, Frank Giles, Patrick Marnham, John Julius Norwich and Sir Brooks Richards. Any mistakes which remain are, of course, entirely our responsibility. Translations from works which are listed in the Bibliography in the original French are by the authors. Plays, novels and films translated into English have been given the title under which they appeared in this country; the remaining titles have been left in the original French.

We owe a great deal to our agents, Felicity Bryan and Andrew Nurnberg, and to the advice and help of our editors, Kate Jones at Hamish Hamilton and Jacqueline Kennedy Onassis and Scott Moyers at Doubleday. Finally, we are very grateful to each other, without whom the last few years, although exhausting, would not have been nearly so enjoyable.

Antony Beevor, Artemis Cooper

London, January 1994

Part One
A Tale of Two Countries

1

The Marshal and the General

In the early evening of Tuesday, 11 June 1940, Marshal Philippe Pétain and General Charles de Gaulle caught sight of each other as they were about to enter the Château du Muguet. It was a month and a day since the German invasion of France had begun. They had not seen each other for over two years, and this was to be one of their last encounters. Each would soon proclaim himself the leader of France, and their respective versions of the state would condemn the other as a traitor.

Pétain and de Gaulle had travelled separately along roads encumbered with refugees and dispirited troops. That morning the château, near Briare on the river Loire due south of Paris, had become the temporary residence of General Weygand, the commander-in-chief who had just decided to abandon the capital to the Germans. A conference of the Supreme Inter-Allied Command was assembling to discuss the disaster. The British side, led by Winston Churchill, was expected at any moment. Escorted by a squadron of Hurricanes, the Prime Minister and his colleagues had flown on a circuitous route from England to land at Briare's deserted airfield.

Marshal Pétain, born in the final year of the Crimean War, was now eighty-four. He remained proud of his appearance, especially his flowing white moustache. When he removed his scarlet and gold *képi*, revealing a bald dome, he had the air of a Gallic elder. The only colour left in his marmoreal face came from the eyes which, although watery, remained a startling blue. The '*bons yeux bleus du Maréchal*' were to provide a favourite refrain in the personality cult of his Vichy regime.

Charles de Gaulle was then forty-nine. He was unusually tall and the impression he gave of towering over Pétain was enhanced by his bearing. His body appeared stiffly controlled except when he gestured for emphasis, not just with his hands like most Latins, but with the whole length of his seemingly endless arms. His face was pale and long. The far-seeing eyes were dug in closely on either side of his blunted beak of a nose.

The relationship between Pétain, the defender of the Verdun fortresses in 1916, and de Gaulle, the advocate of armoured warfare and now one of the youngest brigadier-generals in the army, went back a long way. Lieutenant de Gaulle, on passing out from Saint-Cyr two years before the First World War, had asked to be gazetted to Pétain's regiment. But the admiration he had once held had dwindled between the wars. In his view, Pétain, the commander idealized by veterans and politicians alike, had succumbed to the corrupting influence of acclaim and honours. It was not therefore surprising that this meeting lacked warmth.

'You are a general,' remarked Pétain, no doubt eyeing the two new stars on his sleeve. As a Marshal of France, he had seven. 'But I don't congratulate you. What's the use of rank during a defeat?'

'But, Marshal,' de Gaulle pointed out, 'it was during the retreat of 1914 that you yourself received your first stars.'

'No comparison,' was his retort.

The Prime Minister, Paul Reynaud, although determined to resist the enemy, had come under increasing pressure from his *louche* pro-German mistress, Comtesse Hélène de Portes. She shamelessly interfered in matters of state – on one occasion the draft of a top-secret telegram to President Roosevelt had to be retrieved from her bed. But worst of all, she had managed to persuade her lover to appoint several defeatists as ministers. They were to bring him down.

Impressed by de Gaulle's certainty and vigour, as well as by his predictions about the course of events, Reynaud had just made him under-secretary of state for war against much opposition. Yet in mid-May, Reynaud had already felt obliged to recall Pétain from his post as ambassador to General Franco in Madrid, and offer him the post of vice-president of the council of ministers.

Philippe Pétain in old age was still wrapped in the reputation he had made at Verdun. The memory of his rallying cry – '*They shall not pass!*' – was enough to moisten the eyes of veterans. But he had no stomach for this fight and was openly advocating an armistice with the Germans before the French army fell to pieces completely. Already there had been reports of troops refusing to obey orders. Weygand shared his fears. 'Ah!' he is supposed to have sighed, 'if only I could be sure the Germans would leave me enough men to maintain order.'

Neither of them had forgotten the mutinies of 1917 which followed the disastrous offensive on the Aisne. French commanders, alarmed by the disintegration of the Tsarist army and the recent revolution in Petrograd, had repressed the disturbances mercilessly. Pétain had then been given the task of reforming the army and bringing it back to discipline. His admirers saw him as the man who had saved France from Bolshevism.

The conference was to take place in the dark dining-room of the château, where a long table had been prepared. Reynaud, a short man whose intelligent face was a little too well nourished to be described as foxy, called his colleagues together in the hall to greet their allies. The pressure he was under made him nervous and irritable. De Gaulle, one of the most junior members present, stood in the background. He would take his place at the far end of the table when they sat down.

Churchill had left England in a very bad temper and was

dressed in one of his old-fashioned black suits despite the summer heat, yet he entered the room looking rubicund and genial. He was followed by Anthony Eden; General Sir John Dill; Major-General Hastings Ismay, the secretary of the war cabinet; and Major-General Edward Spears, his personal representative to the French government. Spears felt that, despite Reynaud's polite welcome, their presence was like that of 'poor relations at a funeral reception'.

Weygand, at Reynaud's request, gave a description of the current military situation: it was relentlessly pessimistic. He ended with the words: '*C'est la dislocation!*'

Churchill, in a long, passionate speech, full of historical allusions and expressed in his inimitable mixture of French and English, recalled the disasters of the First World War from which the Allies had recovered and won. 'We would fight on and on – *toujours*, all the time – everywhere, *partout – pas de grâce*, no mercy. *Puis la victoire!*' Unaware of Weygand's decision to abandon Paris, he urged the defence of the capital with house-to-house fighting. Churchill's further suggestion of continuing the struggle by guerrilla warfare – one of his pet subjects – horrified Pétain even more. His face briefly came to life. It would mean 'the destruction of the country', he muttered angrily. He was convinced that this loosening of the chain of command would lead to the anarchy that he and Weygand feared so much.

General Weygand, in his baffled anger, was attempting to shift the responsibility for France's humiliation away from the French army. He and his kind bitterly blamed everything they loathed – the Popular Front government of 1936, liberals, Communists, anti-clericalism, freemasonry and now, it seemed, their allies for having started the war. No criticism of the French general staff could be considered.

The commander-in-chief evaded the issue of continuing the struggle by other means. He repeated that they were 'at the last quarter of an hour' of the battle and persisted in demanding every available British fighter squadron. The British were not prepared to transfer any more Hurricanes or Spitfires from home defence, especially when they doubted the will of the French military leaders. Soon it became clear that this refusal would provide the defeatists with an excuse to seek a separate peace with the Germans.

But by no means all the men opposite were *capitulards*. At least eight were firmly opposed to an armistice. The British delegation was particularly impressed by Georges Mandel and de Gaulle. Mandel, the courageous Minister of the Interior − a Jew who was to be murdered in 1944 by members of Vichy's Milice − had ensured that no politician keen on a deal with Germany, in particular the arch-opportunist Pierre Laval, stayed behind in Paris. He also believed in continuing the fight from France's North African colonies should metropolitan France fall. De Gaulle, meanwhile, supported the plan for a last stand in Brittany and left after the meeting to prepare the defence of the north-west peninsula. But against the resolution of such men weighed the scale of the disaster and the shameless manoeuvres of their opponents. When the British Prime Minister and his party flew back to London the following morning, they feared the worst.

The French government moved to Bordeaux two days later, on the last stage of its retreat. Ministers found the city in a state of chaos resulting from both panic and apathy. Those with influence had commandeered rooms in the Hôtel Splendide, the Hôtel Normandie or the Hôtel Montré. They also secured tables at the Chapon Fin restaurant, which maintained its superb cooking despite the acute shortages. Spears and the British minister, Oliver Harvey, looked round at the deputies and senators at other tables. Spears reflected, 'with some annoyance as a Conservative', that the only politicians prepared to continue the fight against Germany were 'in the main Socialists'. But the greatest object of his loathing was the turncoat, Pierre Laval.

The very appearance of the squat Laval, with his toad-like features, decaying teeth and greasy hair, made hatred easy.

Any officials who stepped outside their hotels were mobbed by refugees anxious for news of the German advance or of relatives in the army. Accusations of incompetence, cowardice and even treason rang out, for that mood of '*Nous sommes trahis!*' had started to gain hold. The British consulate was besieged with refugees, including many Jews, desperate to get away. One rumour was not false: German aircraft had dropped magnetic mines in the Gironde estuary, virtually sealing off the port of Bordeaux.

By Sunday, 16 June, Reynaud found resistance to the *capitulards* almost impossible to maintain. It was already hard for a civilian politician to challenge the opinion of military leaders, and he did not have de Gaulle's support at this stage, having sent him on a mission to London. Marshal Pétain had a huge following in the country, and he knew the strength of his position.

Every hope rapidly proved false. An appeal for help to President Roosevelt turned out to have been ridiculously optimistic. Reynaud thought that Churchill's last-minute proposal of an Anglo-French Union, which was backed by de Gaulle, might save the situation. The Pétain faction saw it as a plot by Britain to make France one of her dominions.* One Pétainist minister, Jean Ybarnegaray, exploded: 'Better to be a Nazi province. At least we know what that means.' To which Reynaud replied: 'I prefer to collaborate with my allies than with my enemies.' Pétain himself dismissed the whole idea angrily, describing it as 'a marriage with a corpse'!

Reynaud's opponents then went on to support the proposal of

---

* The idea for the Union in fact came from a Frenchman, Jean Monnet, one of the most influential men of his age. This remarkable economic planner, then in London on an arms-purchasing mission, had already won the complete trust and respect of both Churchill and Roosevelt. He later inspired the Victory Plan in the United States.

another minister, Camille Chautemps, that Hitler's terms should be requested and considered. Chautemps, the Prime Minister in 1933, tainted by the Stavisky scandal, was one of the most notorious of those Third Republic politicians who treated their country 'as if it were a commercial company going into liquidation'. Reynaud promptly offered his resignation to President Albert Lebrun. Afterwards, Pétain went up to Reynaud offering his hand and said that he hoped that they would remain friends. Reynaud was entirely taken in by his manner. He decided to stay in France in case President Lebrun called on him to form another government. The idea that Marshal Pétain would agree to his arrest within a matter of weeks, put him on trial, imprison him and later allow him to be handed over to the Germans was inconceivable.

At ten o'clock that night de Gaulle, who had flown straight back to Bordeaux from London in an aeroplane provided by Churchill, touched down at Mérignac airport still full of hope for the Anglo-French Union. He had not yet heard how things had gone at the Cabinet meeting. An officer waiting for him on the tarmac warned him of Reynaud's resignation. The news that President Lebrun had appointed Marshal Pétain as the next Prime Minister followed half an hour later. The shock can be imagined. De Gaulle was no longer a minister. He reverted, at least in theory, to the rank of temporary brigadier-general. But Pétain's appointment, signalling the victory of the defeatists, removed any doubt from his mind. Whatever the consequences, he must return to England to continue the fight.

To make sure that he left France safely, he had to be careful. Weygand loathed him, both personally and politically. Any attempt by an officer to continue the struggle which the commander-in-chief had been so keen to abandon would be treated as mutinous. Weygand would call for his court martial with the satisfaction which only moral outrage can bring.

Reynaud, in many ways relieved to be free of an appalling burden, encouraged de Gaulle in the idea when they met shortly before midnight. Ignoring the fact that he was no longer Prime Minister, he provided passports and secret funds to provide the knight-errant General with his immediate expenses.

Early the next morning, Monday, 17 June, de Gaulle, accompanied by his young aide Geoffroy de Courcel, met General Spears in the lobby of the Hôtel Normandie. A short time before, a call had been put through to Spears's room. It was the Duke of Windsor, asking for a Royal Navy warship to pick him up from Nice. The former king was told firmly but politely that no warship was available. Surely the road to Spain was open to motor-cars if he did not wish to use the only other ship in the harbour – a collier.

The small party – Spears, de Gaulle and Courcel – drove to Mérignac and boarded the four-seater aeroplane provided by Churchill. It was standing in the midst of what looked like a military junkyard. After an agonizing delay manoeuvring the aeroplane on to the runway, they took off. Soon they were flying over depressing reminders of the military reality below. Ever-widening columns of smoke arose from depots set ablaze and, worst of all, they passed over a sinking troopship, the *Champlain*, which had been evacuating two thousand British soldiers.

This very junior general's decision to resurrect the French battle-flag in defiance of his own government had set him on a path of mutiny. Crossing his Rubicon, the English Channel, constituted both political and military rebellion. Years later, André Malraux asked him about his feelings during that journey on 17 June. 'Oh, Malraux,' he said, taking both of the writer's hands in his, 'it was appalling.'

2

The Paths of Collaboration and Resistance

The announcement that Marshal Pétain was to form a government produced a profound sense of relief in the overwhelming majority of the population. People just wanted an end to the relentless attacks, as if the last five weeks had been an unfair boxing contest which should never have been allowed to start. His address to the country by wireless declaring that 'the fighting must stop' was broadcast on 17 June just as de Gaulle's small aircraft was about to land at Heston, near London.

On 21 June, Hitler stage-managed the French surrender in Marshal Foch's railway carriage in the forest of Compiègne, thus reversing Germany's humiliation in 1918. General Keitel presented the armistice terms without allowing any discussion. The *capitulards* convinced themselves that the conditions were less harsh than they had expected. They, along with the millions who supported their action, also needed to believe that the decision of the British to continue the war alone was madness. Hitler would defeat them too within a matter of weeks, so continued resistance was against everyone's interests.

Once the area of 'unoccupied France' had been defined by the Germans – the central and southern block, excluding the Atlantic coast – Pétain's new government selected the spa of Vichy as its base, a choice partly influenced by the empty hotels available for use as government offices.

There, on 10 July, the senators and deputies of the National Assembly voted full powers to Marshal Pétain and the suspension of parliamentary democracy. They were offered little choice, but the majority seemed to welcome that. A minority of eighty brave men led by Léon Blum opposed the motion. The following day Marshal Pétain's French State came into being, with Pierre Laval as the first Prime Minister. Pétain felt able to congratulate himself that at last the country was no longer 'rotted by politics'.

The most fervent support for Pétain's regime might best be summed up as provincial prejudice. *Vieille France* – that arch-conservative 'old France' symbolized by a ferociously illiberal clergy and a *petite noblesse* that was both impoverished and resentful – still cursed the principles of 1789. A number of them continued to wear a white carnation in their buttonhole and a black tie on the anniversary of Louis XVI's execution, and stuck postage stamps with the Republican symbol of Marianne upside down on their letters. In their eyes, the demonic successors of the French Revolution included the Communards of 1871, all those who had supported Dreyfus against the General Staff, the mutineers of 1917, the political leaders of the inter-war years, and the industrial workers who had benefited from the Popular Front's reforms in 1936. The Right believed that these, not the complacent General Staff, had dragged France down to defeat. This counterpart to Germany's conspiracy theory after the First World War, the 'stab in the back', was also deeply imbued with anti-semitism. On 3 July Britain joined the front rank of Vichy's hate-figures when the French naval squadron at Mers-el-Kebir rejected an ultimatum to sail out of reach of the Germans and was destroyed by the Royal Navy.

In October, the character of the German occupation was defined at the small town of Montoire in Touraine. Hitler's train halted there for a meeting with Pierre Laval, who greeted the Führer effusively. He promised to persuade Pétain to come to Montoire forty-eight hours later. After the Hitler–Laval meeting was over, the train travelled through the night to arrive in Hendaye on the Spanish frontier, where Hitler had a meeting with General Franco.

The train then returned to Montoire, where Marshal Pétain arrived on 24 October, having travelled from Vichy in secret. The contrast between decay and modern military power could hardly have appeared greater. In this little provincial station stood Hitler's special train, a gleaming beast in armoured steel with flak guns mounted on a wagon at the rear. The platforms were guarded by a large detachment of his personal SS bodyguard. Marshal Pétain's *chef de cabinet*, Henri du Moulin de Labarthète, was struck by Hitler's resemblance to his photographs: 'the gaze fixed and severe, the peaked hat too high and too large'. The oblivious old Marshal in a shabby gabardine greeted the Führer, stretching out his hand '*d'un geste de souverain*'.

Pétain felt he had obtained what he wanted from this encounter. France retained its empire, its fleet, and guarantees covering the unoccupied zone. Ignoring the events of the past six years, he treated Hitler as a man of his word. After the meeting at Montoire, Pétain's supporters went further. They persuaded themselves that the old man had somehow managed to outfox the Führer: his principal apologists even called this agreement 'the diplomatic Verdun'. But the 'path of collaboration' on which he had embarked with the occupying power offered up exactly what Hitler wanted: a country promising to police itself in the Nazi interest.

All the self-deception of Pétainism was revealed in a New Year message addressed to '*Messieurs et très chers collaborateurs*' from the Bishop of Arras, Mgr Henri-Édouard Dutoit. This cleric's pseudo-Cartesian formulation only drew further attention to the false basis of his reasoning. 'I collaborate: therefore I am no longer the slave who is forbidden to speak and act, and only good to obey orders. I collaborate: therefore I have the right to contribute my own thought and individual effort to the common cause.'*

This imaginary autonomy described by the Bishop of Arras was so important to the Vichy regime that until 1942 the Germans needed little more than 30,000 men – less than twice the size of the Paris police force – to keep the whole of France in order. Vichy bent over backwards to help the occupier – a policy that was taken to appalling lengths when assisting with the deportation of Jews to Germany.

Pétain's regime had already introduced anti-Jewish regulations without any prompting from the Germans. Exactly three weeks before the meeting at Montoire, a decree had introduced special identity cards for Jews and provided for a census. A Commissariat Général aux Questions Juives was set up. Jewish-owned businesses had to identify themselves clearly, thus allowing the French state to sequester them at will.

The most infamous operation of all was to be the *grande rafle*, the raid in Paris. Reinhard Heydrich visited Paris on 5 May 1942 for general discussions on implementing the deportation of Jews to Germany. Adolf Eichmann came on 1 July to plan the operation. The following day, René Bousquet, the Vichy prefect of police, offered his men for the task. On the night of 16 July 1942 some 13,000 Jews, including 4,000 children whom even the Nazis were willing to spare, were seized in five *arrondissements* by French policemen. They were transported to the Vélodrome d'Hiver, a covered stadium for bicycle races. More than a hundred committed suicide. Almost all the rest later perished in German concentration camps.

One might have imagined that the atmosphere in Paris under

*When the Bishop of Arras was arrested after the Liberation, the British Embassy in Paris reported that 'much surprise was expressed [by the Vatican] at the accusations against the Bishop of Arras since he has had the reputation at the Vatican of holding extreme democratic views'.

German occupation was oppressive, but most Frenchmen found Vichy far more claustrophobic.

The regime's morality was harsh. A woman accused of procuring an abortion was sentenced to forced labour for life. Prostitutes – *'femmes d'une mauvaise vie'* – were rounded up and sent to an internment camp at Brens, near Toulouse. It was not long before the regime had its own political police. The Service d'Ordre Légionnaire, an organization which incorporated Colonel de la Rocque's henchmen from the pre-war Croix de Feu, finally became the Milice Nationale in January 1943. Each member had to take the following oath: 'I swear to fight against democracy, against Gaullist insurrection and against Jewish leprosy.' Officials and army officers had to take a personal oath of allegiance to the head of state, just as in Nazi Germany. Yet the regime which was supposed to put an end to the rot of scheming politics was riven by factional jealousies.

The personality cult of the Marshal depicted him as far above such concerns. Hundreds of thousands of framed prints of his portrait were sold. For a tradesman it was almost obligatory to display one in his shop window. But these prints were not just amulets to ward off political suspicion. They were also hung in thousands of homes as household icons. Adults sometimes coloured in the 'kindly blue eyes' for themselves, as if they had become children once again. Posters of the man who saw himself as the serene grandfather of France proclaimed his simple pieties with the slogan *Travail, Famille, Patrie* – the National Revolution's replacement for the republican trinity of *Liberté, Egalité, Fraternité*.

The idea certainly seems to have formed a psychological barrier against de Gaulle's attempt to rally the French to ignore the armistice and fight on. The twelve-year-old Emmanuel Le Roy Ladurie heard a woman say in outrage: 'This General dares to take exception to Marshal Pétain.'

On 18 June 1940, the day after his arrival in London, Charles de Gaulle made his famous broadcast on the BBC. The British Foreign Office had been opposed to letting him make a speech which was bound to provoke Marshal Pétain's new government while the question of the French fleet and other matters were unresolved. But Winston Churchill and his francophile Minister of Information, Duff Cooper, won the Cabinet round. De Gaulle's brief speech calling on Frenchmen to join him was immensely powerful. Although few people in France heard it, word spread.

De Gaulle was not an easy man and, unlike Napoleon, did little to encourage warmth or loyalty, except in his immediate entourage. Yet this was the source of his strength. His appeal, like Pétain's, evaded the politics and factionalism which had been the curse of France.

Spears had observed that the main defeatists were conservatives, yet not all of *vieille France* had surrendered easily. The defence of the cavalry school at Saumur, when a group of lightly armed subalterns fought off a panzer unit until they ran out of ammunition, was just one example. And many members of the aristocracy were to prove in the next few years by their service under de Gaulle or in the Resistance that they held honour above politics. Such decisions split a number of families.

De Gaulle had accomplished the vital first step: recognition and support from Churchill. On 27 June Churchill summoned him to Downing Street and said, 'You are all alone? Very well, then I recognize you all alone!' The next day de Gaulle received a message through the French Embassy in London – then in a curious state of interregnum – telling him to place himself in a state of arrest in Toulouse within five days. A subsequent court martial in Clermont-Ferrand condemned him to death *in absentia* for desertion and for entering the service of a foreign power. De Gaulle sent back a message rejecting the sentence as null and void. He would discuss the matter 'with the people of Vichy after the war'.

Among the few who joined de Gaulle was André Dewavrin, who soon began to organize the Gaullist intelligence service, the BCRA. It has been said that he was a former member of the Comité Secret d'Action Révolutionnaire, whose members were known as *cagoulards*, or the 'hooded ones'. They were dedicated to the suppression of Communism, by assassination if necessary. The *cagoulards* took the names of Paris métro stations as code-names and Dewavrin's code-name of 'Passy' for his clandestine activities under de Gaulle is cited as evidence for his *cagoulard* past, but this connection is far from conclusive, and he himself has always strongly denied it.

Colonel Passy, as Dewavrin was known, nevertheless recruited two other *cagoulards*, the half-Russian Captain Pierre Fourcaud and Maurice Duclos. (The Cagoule split three ways in 1940, between a pro-Nazi group, an anti-German but pro-Pétainist group, and the small Gaullist splinter.) The presence of *cagoulards*, however few, in de Gaulle's ranks provoked a great deal of suspicion amongst liberals, socialists and, not surprisingly, Communists. And there were many stories, neither fully confirmed nor satisfactorily contradicted, of Passy's subordinates using brutal methods on anyone suspected of attempting to infiltrate the Gaullist organization.

The other important figure to declare his allegiance at this time was Gaston Palewski, later de Gaulle's *chef de cabinet* and most trusted adviser. Palewski, an outstanding young member of Marshal Lyautey's staff in Morocco, had first known de Gaulle, then a colonel, in 1934. The young man was so impressed by this extraordinary soldier that he resolved to serve him as soon as the call came.

De Gaulle's supporters, however much courage and talent they possessed, were still very few in number. The only significant military figure to endorse him in the summer of 1940 was General Catroux, while the troops of Free France amounted to no more than a couple of battalions, mostly evacuees from Dunkirk or from the expeditionary force sent to Norway. A number of officers and sailors had managed to escape metropolitan France, individually or in small groups. Although the trickle of volunteers continued, de Gaulle's only hope of building an army lay overseas in the colonial forces of the Levant, French West Africa and, most significantly, North Africa. The future leadership of France would be decided there.

Like collaboration, the resistance which grew up in France had degrees of commitment and took many forms. Resistance included anything from hiding Jews or Allied airmen, distributing leaflets and underground newspapers, writing poems, minor sabotage or involvement in military action right up to the all-out battles which delayed the Das Reich division in its advance north against the Normandy bridgehead in June 1944.

Men and women in most cases joined because a particular experience or event opened their eyes to the reality of Nazi occupation. Jean Moulin, who was to become the most important martyr of the Resistance, had been Prefect of the department of Eure-et-Loire in 1940. At the time of the defeat, two German soldiers taking over a house in the village of Luray shot an old woman because she had shouted at them and shaken her fist. They tied her corpse to a tree and told her daughter that it was to be left there as a warning. Moulin telephoned the local German headquarters from his office in Chartres to demand justice.

That night, he received a summons to the headquarters. A junior officer asked him to sign an official statement which asserted that a group of French Senegalese infantry had committed a terrible massacre in the area, raping and murdering women and children. Moulin, knowing that he would have heard if any such incident had taken place, demanded proof. He was beaten savagely with rifle butts for his persistent refusal to sign and thrown into a cell. Fearing that he might weaken under further torture, Moulin attempted to kill himself by cutting his throat with a piece of broken glass. A guard found him covered in blood, and the Germans felt obliged to take him to the hospital.

There were numerous Resistance organizations, some dedicated to sheltering Allied airmen and escaped prisoners, others to gathering intelligence for the Allies. 'Colonel Rémy', the *nom de guerre* of Gilbert Renault, a film director who had rallied to de Gaulle, set up a highly successful intelligence network known as the Confrérie de Notre Dame. The Alliance organization, which became known to the Gestapo as 'Noah's Ark' because each member had a bird or animal as code-name, was set up by Marshal Pétain's former military aide, Georges Loustaunau-Lacau, and taken over by Marie-Madeleine Fourcade when the Gestapo arrested him. She had been Loustaunau-Lacau's secretary on his extreme right-wing review just before the war. Under her own code-name of 'Hedgehog', she continued with astonishing courage to build a nationwide network in liaison with Britain's Secret Intelligence Service.

One movement – the French Communist Party – did not lack for clandestine experience, having been proscribed in 1939. It had, however, been deeply disorientated by the Nazi–Soviet pact of August 1939. Twenty-seven members of the National Assembly had resigned from the party. The following year, Communists hardly knew how to react to the invasion of France. Molotov, the Soviet Foreign Minister, sent Hitler a message of congratulation on the fall of Paris, and some party loyalists welcomed the conquerors.

When Hitler invaded the Soviet Union in June 1941, the news came almost as a relief. The Nazis were once again the enemy. But the bitterness did not entirely disappear. A blacklist of party traitors was circulated with orders for their assassination. A number on the list had openly joined the Vichy, but many were fighting bravely in the Resistance: their crime was to have criticized the Nazi–Soviet pact openly in 1939 and 1940. These renegades – falsely accused of being 'agents of the Gestapo' – had to keep looking over their shoulder for the Germans, for the

Milice, and also for killers sent after them by the Stalinist leadership, usually a fanatically loyal young militant, mounted on a bicycle and armed with a revolver.

The Communist resistance organizations were the most difficult for the Abwehr and the Gestapo to infiltrate, partly because of their structure, based on three-man cells. But the most important innovation was a set of ruthless security measures established by the young Auguste Lecoeur, who, like the absent party leader Maurice Thorez, was a tough and intelligent miner from the northern coalfields. One can only guess at the number of innocent men and women killed or sacrificed to maintain Communist security during those years of clandestine existence.

Whether or not the Communists were the first to strike openly against the Germans – the question is still not clear – the party claimed the first casualties. Martyrs were very important for propaganda: the French Communist Party later called itself 'Le Parti des Fusillés' – the party of the executed – with the grossly inflated claim of 75,000 casualties.

The first assassinations of German officers had unpredictable and far-reaching effects. On 21 August, two months after the German invasion of Russia, a Communist militant who later became the Resistance leader Colonel 'Fabien' shot down a very junior officer of the Kriegsmarine called Moser in a Paris métro station. A retroactive decree was passed which effectively made every prisoner, whatever his crime, a hostage liable to execution. To appease the German authorities, three Communists who had nothing to do with the attack were then sentenced to death and guillotined a week later in the courtyard of the Santé prison. Pierre Pucheu, Vichy's Minister of the Interior, who rejected their appeal, was regarded as the prime organizer.

Not long afterwards, another German officer was shot in the streets of Nantes. Twenty-seven Communists were executed on 22 October, and twenty-one were shot at Châteaubriant the following day. On 15 December, the Germans shot a Communist member of the National Assembly, Gabriel Péri. In his last letter he wrote that Communism represented the youth of the world and it was preparing *'des lendemains qui chantent'* – 'tomorrows full of song'. His execution prompted the party's poet laureate, Louis Aragon, to write a fifteen-verse ballad. Péri became one of the leading martyrs of the party, and the phrase *'les lendemains qui chantent'* came to symbolize all the revolutionary hopes that the day of liberation promised.

3

The Resistance of the Interior and the Men of London

Acts of resistance achieved little for as long as the German occupation and the Vichy regime appeared unshakeable. But perceptions began to change dramatically around the end of 1942 when the battle of El Alamein was followed by Operation Torch, the Allied landings in North Africa, and then by the psychologically decisive battle of Stalingrad. The myth of Axis invincibility was broken.

The landings in Algeria and Morocco proved a double blow to Pétain's regime. Vichy lost the North African colonies while the German invasion of the southern zone destroyed the basis of the Montoire agreement. The Marshal's justification for having taken the 'path of collaboration' lay in ruins. Even most of his supporters expected the old man to escape his deceiver by fleeing to North Africa, but he swallowed the humiliation. This lost him the trust and respect of many who had followed him faithfully until then. The only senior officer who attempted to oppose the German takeover was General de Lattre de Tassigny. He had to go into hiding and was later picked up by a Hudson aircraft and flown out to England. Vichy's 'army of the armistice', as it had been known, was disbanded. Many of its officers and men joined the Resistance.

Perhaps the most astonishing aspect of Operation Torch was that it managed to achieve a measure of surprise. For several months, the whole project had been the subject of numerous overtures to Vichy loyalists within the unoccupied zone and in North Africa. Yet, to his fury, de Gaulle and his followers were allowed no part in it.

De Gaulle's relations with Churchill had started to deteriorate rapidly after the ill-fated expedition to seize Dakar from Vichy in September 1940. The British, convinced that information had leaked from de Gaulle's headquarters, refused to warn him of any operations involving French territory. The American government's objective was to avoid the danger of the French colonial army in North Africa resisting the Torch landings. Robert Murphy, Roosevelt's personal representative, had therefore been seeking a leader who would be acceptable to the mainly pro-Vichy officers stationed there. Various leaders, including General Weygand, were considered and approaches made, but with little success. Then an apparently ideal candidate appeared in the form of General Henri Giraud.

Giraud had become a hero in France after escaping from the prison fortress of Königstein in Germany. A good soldier, he proceeded to Vichy to report to Marshal Pétain, but this represented an embarrassment for Vichy's relations with the Germans. The Americans recruited him and he was brought out by submarine.

Admiral Darlan, the commander-in-chief of all Vichy forces, then entered the scene. After being ousted from the premiership by Laval on 17 April 1942, he had made cautious approaches to the Resistance and the American authorities. (The veteran politician, Édouard Herriot, had said of Darlan just after the armistice: 'This Admiral knows how to swim.') Darlan flew to Algiers from Vichy on 5 November, two days before the American invasion, to see his son in hospital. His arrival caused great confusion in the American camp. They did not know whether he would serve their purposes or oppose the landings. Meanwhile their chosen leader, Giraud, then in Gibraltar, started to change his mind at the last moment, causing even greater confusion.

The landings which took place two days later succeeded largely because Admiral Darlan and General Juin in Algiers secured the ceasefire. The deal which the Americans then made with Darlan, who still wanted to remain loyal to Marshal Pétain, was satisfactory from a purely military point of view, but it set off a political storm in the United States and in Britain. The greatest anger, not surprisingly, was among the Free French in London and the Resistance of the interior.

De Gaulle had not been told of the landings on 7 November. He was furious when he heard the news the following morning. 'I hope the Vichy people will fling them into the sea!' he yelled. 'You don't get France by burglary!' When the implications of the American deal with Darlan later became clear – that Roosevelt had no scruples about using unrepentant Pétainists – it looked as if de Gaulle faced political oblivion. The new regime in North Africa was nicknamed '*Vichy à l'envers*' – Vichy back-to-front – because Darlan had hardly changed his coat, let alone his views. He still acknowledged Pétain as leader, the Gaullist cross of Lorraine was still outlawed and Jews had to continue wearing the yellow star. But on Christmas Eve 1942 the balance of power in French affairs was fated to change, when a young monarchist, Sous-Lieutenant Fernand Bonnier de la Chapelle, assassinated Admiral Darlan.

The Shakespearian drama of Darlan's death, with all the elements of treachery and rival ambitions, has long exerted a strong fascination. Conspiracy theories abound, with minutiae disputed. But the overall evidence strongly suggests a Gaullist and royalist plot with a measure of British collusion and private applause in the background from the Office of Strategic Services, which was exasperated by their own president's tolerance of Vichy.

The organizer of the operation was Henri d'Astier de la Vigerie, brother of Emmanuel, the leader of the Libération resistance movement. Henri d'Astier, an officer in military intelligence, was part of a royalist group in close touch with the Comte de Paris, the pretender to the throne of France. In fact he was a monarcho-Gaullist, a combination which was less paradoxical then than it might appear. De Gaulle was seen as a regent who might bring about a restoration of the French royal family.

The knowledge and involvement of de Gaulle's officers, and presumably therefore of the General himself, is hard to doubt. A third Astier brother, General François d'Astier, who had recently rallied to de Gaulle, was found to have left Bonnier's group with $2,000 during a brief mission to Algiers. The notes were traced to a British transfer of secret funds to de Gaulle's Comité National in London. De Gaulle's rather Delphic disclaimer of involvement was most unconvincing, especially when everyone knew that Darlan's death had revived his political hopes.

The only replacement for Darlan acceptable to Roosevelt was the honourable, but infinitely less clever, General Giraud. De Gaulle said little on the subject. He must have sensed that 'the tin soldier', if handled properly, could soon be pushed to the sidelines. De Gaulle never acknowledged that, whatever its motives, Roosevelt's policy may have worked in his own best interests. American support for Darlan and then Giraud had provided two stepping-stones from Vichy to Free France, thus averting the danger of civil war in French North Africa.

The German invasion of the unoccupied zone had changed things in other ways. When Vichy's 'army of the armistice' was disbanded, large quantities of weapons suddenly became available to the Resistance. Many of its officers joined or set up groups belonging to the ORA – l'Organisation de Résistance de l'Armée. Reluctant to support de Gaulle, they were prepared to acknowledge General Giraud.

The most important effect, however, was moral. Laval's open support of Nazi Germany, with the dispatch of French volunteers in Wehrmacht uniform to the Russian front, stood out even more as an act of treason. Yet the worst form of vassalage was the Service de Travail Obligatoire. This destroyed the last shreds of the argument that Pétain's 'path of collaboration' had saved France from the same fate as other occupied countries. Those due for military conscription were sent to Germany to work as forced labour in terrible conditions. Thousands evaded this draft by going into hiding or swelling the ranks of the Resistance.

The Resistance already contained a remarkable political and social mixture – in some groups regular officers, socialists, students both left-wing and Catholic, and Spanish Republicans all fought alongside each other – but as the prospect of liberation approached, and with it the political implications of a post-war order, the thinking of the main movements became more defined. De Gaulle strongly disliked the idea of political consciousness and party activity. Power struggles at the time of liberation might well lead to disturbances or even civil war, giving the Americans and British the excuse to impose their military government on France.

Such a danger could only be averted by uniting the different Resistance movements and bringing them under his own apolitical command; this unity was achieved largely through the efforts and personality of Jean Moulin.

In 1941, Moulin had decided to go to England to see de Gaulle after conferring with Henri Frenay, the leader of the Combat resistance movement. He had made his way in disguise via Spain and Portugal. Unlike many early members of the Resistance, Moulin did not fear de Gaulle as a future military dictator. He saw that without the unifying figure of de Gaulle, the Resistance would become '*démietté*' – would break into crumbs.

After landing in Bournemouth, Moulin was swept off by Maurice Buckmaster, the Head of SOE's Section F, who wanted to recruit him as a potential coordinator for his groups in France; but Moulin insisted on reporting to General de Gaulle.

Passy saw him first, and realized that Moulin was the ideal man to bring the Resistance together under Free French control. Passy was already planning his organization, the Bureau Central de Renseignements et d'Action (BCRA), a Free French version of Britain's SOE. Reports from Gaullist networks such as Rémy's had convinced him that the Resistance groups of the interior could be just as important in the struggle as the conventional Free French forces outside. They would also play an important role in the political struggle which was bound to follow the Liberation.

On New Year's Day 1942, Moulin and a small liaison team, armed with de Gaulle's authority and a radio set, parachuted into Provence from an RAF Whitley bomber. Moulin made his way to Marseilles to meet Frenay. Frenay's initial enthusiasm at the idea of a coalition cooled once he studied the instructions from London more closely. De Gaulle and Passy seemed to be expecting the Resistance groups to fall into neat ranks and snap to attention. But on balance, Frenay acknowledged that it must be right for the main movements of the centre and centre-left – Combat, Libération and Franc-Tireur – to unite where possible.

As part of his attempt to create an effective umbrella organization, Moulin recruited Georges Bidault, a Catholic of the centre-left, to be the head of the Resistance's public information branch: the Bureau d'Information et de Presse.

Another of Moulin's initiatives was to set up a sort of constitutional think-tank, the Comité Général d'Études, to prepare the governmental structure of post-war France and its relationship with the Allies. Members of this body, almost all lawyers, included several future ministers: François de Menthon and Pierre-Henri Teitgen, the first two Ministers of Justice of liberated France, Alexandre Parodi, and Michel Debré, a future Prime Minister.

The most important of these developments came in September 1942, when the military wings of Combat, Libération and Franc-Tireur joined to become the Armée Secrète. De Gaulle immediately gave it his blessing. In his eyes the Secret Army was a vital step towards bringing the Resistance within the framework of a reconstituted regular armed service. That many French Resistance groups had worked with the British from early on was, in his eyes, akin to treachery.

The British, on the other hand, were relieved that the Resistance had grown up in three different ways: the groups backed by SOE and the Secret Intelligence Service, the Gaullist groups and the Communists. This, they felt, reduced the chance of a civil war between Gaullists and Communists. The British were able to provide radio sets as well as transport, whether by Lysander landings on moonlit nights or by parachute drops; so the misunderstandings, suspicions and exasperation, all of which were bound to develop between *les gens de Londres* and *les gens de l'intérieur*, never led to an irretrievable breakdown of relations. The greatest resentment felt towards the London Gaullists by those who had stayed behind was the implication that remaining in France in 1940 had represented a lapse of duty.

In November 1942, the possibility of Communists and Gaullists working together was greatly improved by their common anger at the Americans' deal with Darlan. Neither Bogomolov, Stalin's ambassador to the exiled governments in London, nor the old Comintern controller, Georgi Dimitrov, considered the decision of the French Communists to sign an agreement with the Gaullists 'a good idea'. But since Stalin expressed little interest in France, and since communications into enemy-occupied territory were far from easy, Dimitrov left things as they were.

Soon afterwards, the Communist Party's military organization, Franc-Tireurs et Partisans Français, decided to associate itself with the Secret Army, thus acknowledging, at least in theory, General de Gaulle's military authority. For the Communists, it was also the only way to receive British arms drops, and their insistence on this point led to many wrangles.

*

At the Casablanca conference of January 1943 the Americans, influenced by Churchill, promoted a 'shotgun wedding' between de Gaulle, 'the bride', and Giraud, 'the bridegroom'. Roosevelt, however, was only interested in acknowledging a symbolic military leadership. As far as he was concerned, France did not exist as a political entity until elections were finally held in the whole of its territory. He still suspected de Gaulle of harbouring dictatorial ambitions.

Roosevelt, and also Churchill, had failed to realize how far things were changing within occupied France. The dramatic shift in de Gaulle's favour was confirmed on 10 May 1943, the third anniversary of the German invasion, when the National Council of the Resistance was established, acknowledging de Gaulle's leadership.

General Giraud, proud of his cavalry moustache and well-cut uniform, was devoid of personal ambition. His basic political education was taken in hand by Jean Monnet, sent by Roosevelt to strengthen his hand against de Gaulle. But Monnet, one of the few Frenchmen Roosevelt trusted completely, was much more of a realist than the President. He did all he could to prepare an orderly transition of power to de Gaulle.

De Gaulle arrived in Algiers on 30 May. Giraud, with a band playing the Marseillaise, was waiting to receive him on the runway. The American and British representatives remained in the background. But the next few days would be marked by furious manoeuvres: there were even rumours of coups and kidnap plots. The scheming prompted General de Bénouville to remark that 'nothing was more like Vichy than Algiers'.

Once again, de Gaulle's inflexibility, rooted in his implacable sense of mission, proved indomitable against anyone with a lesser will. On 3 June, the Comité Français de la Libération Nationale was set up. Its constitution was almost entirely dictated by de Gaulle. Giraud found himself having to concede on almost every decision. One of the most significant was the legalization of the Communist Party. This dramatic change acknowledged their importance in the Resistance and led to their recognition of de Gaulle as leader of the government-in-waiting.

When the newly legalized Communist Party in Algiers heard that their arch-enemy, Pierre Pucheu, had turned up in Morocco, they could hardly believe his foolhardiness and their luck.

Pucheu had retired from Vichy politics after Admiral Darlan was replaced by Pierre Laval on 18 April 1942. A year later, he decided to join the 'repentant Vichyists' in North Africa – what one Resistance leader described as '*Vichy à la sauce américaine*'. Giraud gave him a safe-conduct on condition that he stayed out of politics. Pucheu accepted, utterly failing to understand the hatred he had generated as Minister of the Interior, and how dramatically the balance of power in North Africa had changed since Darlan's assassination.

On 14 August, he was arrested. In the following months new legislation was passed to deal with members of the Vichy government. Giraud, who had signed Pucheu's *laissez-passer*, found himself attacked from two directions. The right-wing colonists, who had supported Vichy, demanded what was the value of Giraud's signature on a safe-conduct if it did not save you, while the Communists called for Giraud's head for having been Pucheu's protector.

Pucheu had a further value for de Gaulle: his condemnation would also serve as the condemnation of the Vichy government. In March 1944, Pucheu was put on trial for his life and the Marshal's reputation. Proving a regime's criminality, as this trial sought to do, did not necessarily prove its illegality, but it was a useful act of psychological warfare. In Paris, Simone de Beauvoir overheard two collaborators in a café talking of the trial. 'It's our trial,' said one. His companion agreed. It brought home to many others, notably the writer Pierre Drieu la Rochelle, that the side they had backed was now liable to lose.

Pucheu, the first collaborator to face the official justice of the victors, died in defiance. He insisted on giving the orders to the firing squad himself. But documents discovered after the Liberation proved without doubt that he had been guilty of designating hostages to be executed.

Operation Torch, coming after Alamein and followed by Stalingrad, gave a tremendous encouragement to the early Resistance groups, both *'les gens de Londres'* – the London-based Gaullists – and *'les gens de l'intérieur'*, who endured the whole Occupation. But during 1943, severe setbacks soon followed inside France where the fight between the Gestapo and the Milice on one side and the Resistance on the other became increasingly violent.

Jean Moulin, having achieved his aim of unifying the Resistance in May, sensed that the Gestapo was closing in. He had already warned the BCRA in London that somebody should be ready to replace him. In answer to his request for a deputy, General de Gaulle's military assistant, Claude Bouchinet-Serreulles, volunteered and parachuted in. Serreulles made contact with Moulin in Lyons on 19 June. But two days later, Moulin fell into a trap laid by the Germans in the hillside suburb of Caliure. The circumstances in which Klaus Barbie's network of agents and traitors managed to catch the head of the Resistance have been fiercely debated for many years and are still not fully resolved. Moulin died after severe torture supervised by Barbie.

Serreulles, although finding himself in an almost impossible position, quickly re-established contact with the leaders of the different movements making up the Secret Army.

De Gaulle's most pressing concern was not the Resistance, but his relationship with the two Anglo-Saxon leaders. Roosevelt, still advised by Admiral Leahy, his former ambassador to Vichy, that Pétain was the only man to unite the country, went ahead with preparations for the administration of French territory as if neither de Gaulle's government-in-waiting nor the Resistance existed. Already officials were being trained in Charlottesville, Virginia, for the acronym which Gaullists feared and loathed most: AMGOT – Allied Military Government for Occupied Territories.

De Gaulle, in spite of his anger, did not lose his ability to calculate the odds. He threatened to withdraw all cooperation if AMGOT was imposed on liberated France. Americans in the European theatre, including Eisenhower, knew that any attempt to introduce military government against the mass of the people would be disastrous.

Three days before D-Day, on 3 June 1944, the French National Liberation Committee in Algiers proclaimed itself to be the provisional government of the French Republic. De Gaulle and his staff then flew to England, arriving the next morning to hear that the Allies had entered Rome and that the invasion of France was imminent.

Churchill, although determined to be magnanimous towards de Gaulle, was in a state of subdued frenzy waiting for the invasion. With a disastrous lack of tact, he told de Gaulle that he had sent for him to broadcast to France. Even the more diplomatic Eisenhower, under renewed pressure from Roosevelt, reverted to the American position that de Gaulle and his colleagues counted for nothing until elections were held. On the morning of the invasion, Churchill heard that de Gaulle had refused to broadcast to the French people or to provide liaison officers to accompany the Allied forces. All his resentment and frustration burst forth. He accused de Gaulle of treason to the cause and raged about sending him back to Algiers in chains. American and British officials were horrified that the volatile chemistry between national leaders should have exploded at such a moment. 'It's pandemonium,' a senior French diplomat noted in his diary. Finally Eden calmed Churchill while Viennot, de Gaulle's ambassador, and Duff Cooper persuaded de Gaulle to send liaison officers.

On 14 June 1944 de Gaulle crossed the Channel in the French

destroyer *Combattante*. His party included Gaston Palewski, the ambassador Pierre Viennot, and Generals Koenig and Béthouart. One of them, hoping to lighten their leader's mood, said to him: 'Has it occurred to you, General, that four years ago to the day the Germans marched into Paris?'

'Well! They made a mistake!' came the inimitable reply.

De Gaulle relaxed only after the party had landed and visited General Montgomery in his caravan. He then went on to meet civilians on French soil for the first time since 1940. These rather dazed citizens all knew his voice from the nocturnal radio broadcasts, but nobody recognized his face: Vichy had never allowed the publication of his photograph. News spread rapidly. The local *curé*, Father Paris, came cantering up on his horse to reprove the General for not having shaken his hand. De Gaulle climbed out of the jeep he was in. '*Monsieur le curé*,' he said, opening his arms, 'I do not shake your hand, I embrace you.' Two gendarmes then appeared on bicycles which wobbled as they tried to salute. They were sent on ahead to Bayeux, prophets of the General's coming.

Here the emotional reaction to de Gaulle's appearance was unstinted by the usual Norman reserve. One old woman, however, became confused in the enthusiasm of the moment, and cried out, '*Vive le Maréchal!*' De Gaulle, on hearing this discordant note, is said to have murmured, 'Another person who does not read the newspapers.' Gaston Palewski, when told of the approach of the Bishop of Bayeux and Lisieux to greet the Liberator, was certain they had finally won: 'the clergy does not take risks'.

The sub-prefect appointed by Vichy, wearing his red, white and blue sash of office, welcomed de Gaulle's party. But the change of regime had been too abrupt for him. He suddenly remembered the portrait of Marshal Pétain in the *salle d'honneur* and dashed off to take it down. It was four years and three days since the General and the Marshal had met on the steps of the Château du Muguet.

4

The Race for Paris

On 31 July, General Patton's Third Army began the breakout from Normandy at Avranches. Encircling the Germans from the west, his right hook brought the Allies to Argentan, 167 kilometres from Paris.

For General de Gaulle, there was only one formation which merited the honour of liberating the capital of France. This was the Deuxième Division Blindée, the French second armoured division, always known as the '2e DB'. Its commander was General Leclerc, the *nom de guerre* of Philippe de Hauteclocque.

Much larger than most divisions, the 2e DB was 16,000 strong, equipped with American uniforms, weapons, half-tracks and Sherman tanks. Its core consisted of men who had followed Leclerc from Chad across the Sahara, besieged the Italian garrison at Koufra, and went on to join the British. In its ranks served regulars from the metropolitan army, including cavalrymen from Saumur, Spahis, sailors without ships, North African Arabs, Senegalese, and French colonials who had never before stood on the soil of France. One company, the 9th, was known as '*la nueve*' because it was full of Spanish Republicans, veterans of even harder battles. Appropriately, the battalion itself was commanded by Major Putz, the most respected of all the battalion commanders in the International Brigades. Leclerc's division was such an extraordinary mixture, with Gaullists, Communists, monarchists, socialists, Giraudists and anarchists working closely together, that General de Gaulle formed an over-optimistic vision of how post-war France could unite under his leadership.

When de Gaulle returned to France from Algiers on 20 August, he was faced with deeply unsettling news: a rising, largely inspired by the Communists, had begun in Paris. The Allied armies were in no position to come to its support.

On 15 August, the decision of the German authorities to disarm part of the Paris police force provoked a strike. News of the Allied landings on the Mediterranean coast round Saint-Tropez was announced on the radio at noon, and strengthened resolve. The Communists, who wanted to increase the pressure towards an uprising, had begun to infiltrate and recruit among the police as rapidly as possible. Since many policemen were embarrassed at their record of subservience to German orders, a Communist Party card offered a good insurance policy. The same day, a call for '*l'insurrection populaire*' appeared in *L'Humanité*, the party newspaper.

Two days later the National Council of the Resistance and the COMAC (the Comité Militaire d'Action) debated the call to arms. Although presided over by Georges Bidault, a Christian Democrat, the National Council of the Resistance was dominated by the Communists, as was the military committee. The twenty-nine-year-old Gaullist Resistance chief, General Jacques Chaban-Delmas, had returned from London the day before, having accomplished the last part of the journey through the German lines on a bicycle. The purpose of his clandestine journey to England had been to warn the Allies that a premature insurrection in Paris was inevitable. Yet he returned with the vain instruction from General Koenig, de Gaulle's chief of staff, that there was to be no uprising without his order. Koenig had been appointed commander of all the Forces Françaises de l'Intérieur (FFI), known both affectionately and disparagingly as '*les fifis*', but so far his authority was purely theoretical.

Chaban-Delmas had told the military authorities in London that against the 16,000-strong German garrison, which might be reinforced by another division, the Resistance in Paris had fewer than 15,000 FFI volunteers and only enough weapons for 2,000. Even that seems an optimistic figure. The best the Resistance in Paris could hope for were some army rifles hidden since 1940, shotguns and revolvers often stolen from arms shops, a few sub-machine-guns parachuted elsewhere in France by the Allies, and weapons taken from the Germans by force. A Communist youth group in the 18th *arrondissement*, for example, used to send their female comrades to pick up German soldiers round Pigalle, then entice them into an alley, where young male comrades were waiting to club them down and take their weapons.

A group of Communist Francs-Tireurs et Partisans (FTP) also managed to seize a ton of explosive from the Poudrerie Sevran. But very few of the volunteers had much experience either of the army or of the Resistance. Colonel Rol-Tanguy, the Communist who commanded the FFI of Greater Paris, admitted to Louis Teuléry, a major in the Service B (the Communist counter-intelligence service) that despite all the propaganda the FTP had numbered only 600 men in the whole of the Greater Paris area before the Normandy landings. The real rush to join came afterwards.

Thirty-five young resistants fell headlong into a trap when they were promised a consignment of weapons by an *agent provocateur* working for the Gestapo. When they arrived at the rendezvous they were rounded up, brutally interrogated at Gestapo headquarters in the rue des Saussaies, and executed.

Yet Colonel Rol-Tanguy was unimpressed by calls for caution. That day the FTP gave the order to seize vehicles and prepare them with armour-plating, as if Paris in 1944 was comparable to Madrid or Barcelona in July 1936. The following day, flyposters across the city called for a general strike and '*l'insurrection libératrice*'.

On 17 August, Charles Luizet, de Gaulle's appointee as

Prefect of Police, arrived in secret. He became part of the skeleton team of administrators, of whom Alexandre Parodi, de Gaulle's delegate general, was the most senior.

That day also saw the exodus of Germans and collaborators in increasing numbers – what the inimitable diarist Jean Galtier-Boissière described as '*la grande fuite des Fritz*'. The immensely tall Galtier-Boissière, with his military moustache from the First World War, straw hat in the style of a Victorian traveller and ivory-handled umbrella, was a curious figure, full of contradictions. A funny and endearing anarchist of the *grande bourgeoisie*, he had started his satirical publication *Le Crapouillot* (the slang for a trench-mortar) as a corporal in the front-line. Now he noted the traffic jams of departing vehicles directed by German *feldgendarmerie* with their disks on sticks. 'Along the rue Lafayette, coming from the luxury hotels around the Étoile, sparkling torpedoes pass by containing purple-faced generals, accompanied by elegant blonde women, who look as if they are off to some fashionable resort.'

Overruling the objections of Pierre Laval, the German ambassador, Otto Abetz, ordered the evacuation of the Vichy administration to Belfort, a few miles from the German border. Laval's attempts over the last few days to convene parliamentarians, such as Édouard Herriot, the President of the National Assembly, had only managed to enrage General Oberg, the chief of the SS in France.

The Germans, preparing to leave, were stared at openly and scornfully by groups of Parisians who for the last four years had pretended not to see them. But when a detachment of soldiers on the Boulevard Saint-Michel was mocked – Sylvia Beach, the founder of the bookshop Shakespeare & Company, described the Parisians cheerfully waving lavatory brushes at them – they opened fire into the crowd.

In many cases, packing up included some last-minute looting. The Gestapo broke into the apartment of Gertrude Stein and Alice Toklas on the rue Christine. A neighbour rang the police, and twenty appeared. Backed up by half the population of the street, they demanded to see the Gestapo's authorization. The Gestapo officials, uttering threats, were forced to leave.

A group of soldiers, probably on the order of a senior officer, loaded the contents of the wine cellar of the Cercle Interallié, a large private club, on to lorries. Other military and civilian vehicles, including even ambulances and a hearse, were piled with anything which might be of value: Louis XVI furniture, medicines, works of art, pieces of machinery, bicycles, rolls of carpet, and food.

Odd bursts of firing seemed to break out on all sides on Friday, 18 August, after Communist posters had appeared. The next day, the tricolor reappeared on several public buildings, most notably the Préfecture of Police on the Île de la Cité. Since seven in the morning, policemen on strike over the German move to disarm them began to arrive in ever-increasing numbers following a summons by their Resistance committees. The Gaullists, led by Parodi, by now had no alternative but to accept the direction of events and join the rising. Charles Luizet slipped into the Prefecture of Police and took over the office of his Vichy predecessor, who had been arrested by one of his own subordinates.

Any Parisian rash enough to hang a tricolor from a balcony in imitation of those which had appeared on public buildings might receive a fusillade through the window from a passing German patrol. At lunch-time, German tanks and trucks of infantry arrived to crush the rebellion in the Prefecture of Police, but the tanks had only armour-piercing shells, which made holes without breaking down walls.

Heavy bursts of firing broke out in other parts of Paris, with Wehrmacht vehicles ambushed, and their occupants replying. On the left bank opposite the Île de la Cité the fighting was particularly heavy. Altogether that day, forty Germans were killed and seventy wounded, at the cost of 125 Parisians killed and nearly 500 wounded. The Resistance had started with so little ammunition that by evening it was almost exhausted.

The situation within the besieged Prefecture was critical. The Swedish Consul-General, Raoul Nordling, arranged a truce with General von Choltitz, the German commander of Greater Paris.

The truce was not respected, partly due to the chaotic lack of communications, but it somehow held for two days, thanks to the tolerance or complaisance of General von Choltitz. This in itself was regarded by the insurgents, with dangerous optimism, as a proof of victory. The continuing attacks did not come just from over-eager groups of young Communists. The Gaullists, in the interests of restoring 'Republican legality', needed to take over as many symbolic buildings as possible. On 20 August, leaders of the National Council of the Resistance took over the Hôtel de Ville, in an operation that deliberately excluded Communists.

Over the next four days, the Germans peppered the walls of the Hôtel de Ville with machine-gun fire, but never mounted a determined attack; fortunately, since the insurgents had only four machine-guns and a handful of revolvers.

On 21 August the National Council of the Resistance met to discuss the truce. It was a tense and bitter meeting and the Communists prevailed. The Council decided to rescind the truce the following day. Once again the Gaullists were forced to follow the Communist lead to avoid civil war.

Since the first news of the rising in Paris two days before, General Leclerc had found it hard to contain his impatience and frustration. His American commanders showed no willingness to advance on the city. Eisenhower meant to leave Paris in German hands for a few weeks longer. That would allow Patton to follow the defeated Germans across northern France, and perhaps even to push right through to the Rhine while they were still disorganized. If the Americans were to relieve Paris and thus become responsible for feeding the city, he would have neither the fuel nor the transport to support Patton's push. But for de Gaulle and Leclerc Paris was the key to France, and they feared that a Communist-led rising could lead to another Paris Commune. The Americans would then step in and impose their AMGOT on France.

The first call to insurrection by French Communists in Paris had come two weeks after General Bor-Komorowksi had launched the ill-fated Warsaw uprising on the approach of the Red Army. Yet the rush to revolution in France in the summer of 1944 was a spontaneous reaction in Communist ranks, not Kremlin policy. The regular political leadership of the French Communist Party had no control over events. Maurice Thorez was in Moscow, and his deputy, Jacques Duclos, hidden in the countryside, exerted little influence over the party's fighting arm, the FTP. Hamstrung by difficult communications and the Communists' own draconian security measures, Duclos found himself unable to control Charles Tillon and the other leaders of the FTP who, like most of their followers, wanted to carry resistance through into revolution.

Leclerc, at his headquarters near Argentan, eventually decided to send a small detachment towards Versailles on the evening of 21 August. He did so without the permission of his American corps commander. This minor act of military insubordination strengthened the suspicion among a number of American officers that the Gaullists were fighting their own war for France, not the Allies' war against Germany.

Leclerc had not managed to contact de Gaulle, who had only returned from Algiers the day before, but wrote, impressing upon the leader of the provisional government that Eisenhower must be persuaded to change his plans without any further delay. A series of messengers from Paris, all bearing warnings that the city would be destroyed if the Allies did not capture it quickly, had achieved little success.

The Communist FFI commander for Greater Paris, Colonel Rol-Tanguy, re-launched the fighting the next morning, 22 August. Posters across the city proclaimed his battle-cry – '*Chacun son boche!*' This was followed a short while later by an even more atavistic call to battle – 'TOUS AUX BARRICADES!' – recalling the failed revolutions of the nineteenth century, and the old myth of Paris as the Red Jerusalem. He ordered the whole population of Paris, men, women and children, to barricade every street they could to prevent the Germans from moving, a lesson learned in Barcelona at the outbreak of the Spanish Civil War.

Hardly any barricades were erected in the fashionable districts – the 7th *arrondissement*, the 8th, and the 16th; the greatest number were in those quarters around the north and east of the city, which had voted overwhelmingly for the Popular Front in 1936. The most effectively sited were in the south-eastern part of Paris, where the FFI was commanded by Colonel Fabien, the Communist who had assassinated the young German naval officer three years before.

Teams formed spontaneously from street or neighbourhood. The young and strong uprooted cobblestones, while a human chain, mostly women, passed them back to those building the barricade with railings, iron bedsteads, a plane tree chopped down across the street, cars turned on their sides, and even, in one case, a *vespasienne* public urinal. A tricolor was usually planted on top. Women meanwhile stitched white FFI armbands for their menfolk, usually with just the initials in black, or with patches of red and blue to make a tricolor. Paris at this time was a city of rumours. No one knew how far away the Allies were, or whether German reinforcements were on their way. This created a tense atmosphere, affecting defenders and onlookers alike.

'I arrive at a small FFI position near the Place Saint-Michel,' wrote Galtier-Boissière in his diary. 'A machine-gun is placed on the pavement, covering the Saint-Michel bridge; a tall, fair-haired and well-dressed young man is the gunner. On both sides of the boulevard there are about ten young men in shirt sleeves, with a *brassard* round their biceps, carbine in hand or brandishing little revolvers. Some wear army helmets. These combatants are surrounded by about fifty lookers-on waiting for something to happen. As soon as a vehicle appears on the bridge, all the lookers-on rush back into nearby doorways.'

People helped as they could. The bravest were the stretcher parties, collecting hundreds of wounded from bullet-spattered streets, with only a Red Cross flag to protect them. Professor Joliot-Curie, Nobel prize-winning physicist and devoted Communist, set up a production line making Molotov cocktails in the Sorbonne. Between Saint-Germain-des-Prés and the Place Saint-Michel, Zette Leiris, who ran a well-known gallery, started a canteen for FFI members in the rue Saint-André des Arts. Concierges swabbed blood from the paving-stones.

As Galtier-Boissière observed, fighting was much more civilized in the city than in the countryside, because you could go off for lunch with your rifle. There was another advantage: 'The whole neighbourhood is watching you from their windows and applauding.' A number of people, however, ignored the firing around them. Some sunbathed on the stone embankment of the Seine, while urchins dived in to escape the heat. Odd figures sat immobile on little canvas chairs, fishing in the river while German tanks attacked the Prefecture of Police, a few hundred metres away on the Île de la Cité; a perch from the Seine represented a free meal. Provisions were so short that when a horse was killed by stray bullets, housewives rushed out with enamel bowls and began slicing steaks off the carcass.

Paris being Paris, cultural landmarks counted for as much as ministries and police headquarters when it came to a revolution. For the acting profession, the first place to be liberated (not that there were any Germans there) was the Comédie-Française. Yves Montand, who had recently established himself in Paris as a singer, appeared for sentry duty; an actress had rung

Edith Piaf, his lover and mentor for the last two weeks, to say that they needed more volunteers. The twenty-three-year-old Montand gave the secret knock to gain admittance to Molière's theatre.

Actors and actresses greeted each other as if this were the greatest first-night party of their lives. Julien Berthau, appointing himself their leader, made a rousing speech, ending with the cry of the moment: '*Paris sera libéré par les Parisiens!*' The whole company in a surge of emotion sang the forbidden Marseillaise, standing to attention. But there was something of an anti-climax when Berthau gave the order to distribute weapons. A few hundred metres from where they stood, German tanks waited for the first sign of trouble. To oppose them the Comédie-Française could produce just four shotguns and two stage revolvers.

The day was memorable as a day of collective bravery, as infectious as collective cowardice. Already bands of young men in the 17th *arrondissement*, with only a handful of weapons between them, had fought several German patrols. Those who were wounded refused to be taken to hospital, and as soon as they had been bandaged insisted on returning to their barricade. There were numerous attacks on German convoys by *corps-francs* of the FFI, especially on the Left Bank. Some were ambushed from rooftops or windows with Molotov cocktails and stick grenades. Several groups also attacked Wehrmacht ration trucks coming from the Gare d'Austerlitz.

Any German soldiers rash enough to go out singly or in pairs were picked off or surrounded. The prime objective was to seize more weapons and vehicles. One daring young man made off with the German ambassador's Horch convertible from outside the embassy at 78 rue de Lille.

Attacks often prompted heavy-handed German reaction. Five German armoured vehicles, supported by infantry, sallied forth from the Palais du Luxembourg up the rue Soufflot to attack the *mairie* of the 5th *arrondissement* in the Place du Panthéon.

Shows of strength occurred elsewhere, but on the whole the Germans were effectively deterred from moving around the city.

Father Bruckberger, the Dominican chaplain-general of the Parisian FFI, rode from one area of fighting to another on his bicycle, 'his white habit dirty from the smoke of battle' as he supervised medical care for the wounded and attention to the dead. Coffins were piling up in churches, so heavy were the casualties among civilians. Burials were impossible in the circumstances, so as a defence against the August heat some bodies were kept in the meat-freezers at Les Halles, now empty of food.

The Champs-Élysées were ominously empty. The sidewalk cafés where the Germans in their field-grey uniforms had been sitting *en masse* only a few days before, drinking their *bocks*, were now deserted. For the German tanks on the Place de la Concorde, the gentle incline to the Arc de Triomphe offered a perfect field of fire. But this part of Paris gave a misleading impression of calm. Elsewhere, confusion was compounded by rumours springing from either hopes or fears: the Americans were approaching from the south-west; a fresh panzer division had arrived from the north; there was no ammunition left; the Germans had mined every building in central Paris; the *fifis* had managed to cut the wires to the detonators. Nobody knew for certain what was happening.

On this day, 22 August, a new wireless station, Radiodiffusion de la Nation Française, came on air. It was to act as the voice of the Resistance. Proclamations from various bodies were read out, often followed by the Marseillaise, which had been banned for the last four years. People would turn up the volume and open their windows to make sure everybody in the street could hear it too.

The new station was soon warning people to avoid certain areas. The rue de Seine in Saint-Germain-des-Prés was particularly dangerous because the Germans had a line of fire from their strongpoint in the Palais du Luxembourg. The Place Saint-Michel at the bottom of the boulevard was so dangerous that it was known as '*le carrefour de la mort*'. But however invaluable the broadcasts, people could only listen during the short periods when the electricity supply was restored.

That evening the firing died away. 'Fritz and *fifis* went off for supper,' remarked Jean Galtier-Boissière. And sightseers soon emerged to inspect the damage.

The Germans continued to improve their principal strongpoints in the centre of Paris: the Prinz Eugen barracks near the Place de la République, the Palais du Luxembourg (the Senate), the Palais Bourbon (the National Assembly), the École Militaire, the Invalides, and the Hotel Majestic on the Avenue Kléber. The Hotel Meurice on the rue de Rivoli, which was General von Choltitz's headquarters, was less heavily fortified.

There, the commander of Gross-Paris received the formal order from Hitler's headquarters to defend Paris to the last man and turn the city into 'a pile of ruins'. Choltitz, to the lasting gratitude of its citizens, had no desire to carry it out, but needed the Allies to arrive soon so that he could surrender to regular forces. If they did not come in time and Hitler discovered the degree of procrastination in following his instructions, he would order in the Luftwaffe.

Finally, that evening, there was a change of heart in the Allied camp. A messenger managed to convince General Eisenhower's staff officers that failure to move on Paris immediately would lead to a terrible massacre and possibly the destruction of the city. Eisenhower, who had turned down de Gaulle's appeal two nights earlier, was now convinced. Shortly before nightfall, Leclerc received the order from General Omar Bradley to advance rapidly on Paris. The exultant yells of '*Mouvement sur Paris!*' provided an electrifying charge of fierce joy.

At dawn the following morning, Wednesday 23 August, the 2e DB, in two columns following parallel routes, pushed eastwards out of Normandy as fast as it could through heavy rain towards the Île de France. The hot weather had broken at the worst moment, and their tanks and half-tracks slithered on the slippery roads. Leclerc went ahead. He had over 140 kilometres to go to Rambouillet, which lay close to a very ill-defined front line.

The officers of Leclerc's division found a curious collection of irregulars at Rambouillet when they arrived in the afternoon, of whom the most colourful was Ernest Hemingway. Officially, Hemingway was a war correspondent for *Collier's* magazine, but he was more interested in playing the professional soldier. He was surrounded by some locally recruited and heavily armed ruffians, and seemed to be making up for lost opportunities in Spain seven years before.

Based in the Hotel du Grand Veneur, waiting for the 2e DB to advance the last stretch to Paris, were Colonel David Bruce of the OSS, who in 1949 became the United States ambassador to France, John Mowinckel from a field unit of the Secret Intelligence Staff, and a senior member of the Gaullist intelligence service, Michel Pasteau, whose *nom de guerre* was 'Mouthard'.

Hemingway and his group of *fifi* irregulars had been reconnoitring the routes into Paris over the last few days, but their methods were unsubtle. A pathetic little German soldier, a straggler seized a few kilometres down the road, was brought back to the hotel in triumph, his hands tied behind his back. Hemingway asked Mowinckel to help bring the prisoner up to his room where they would interrogate him at ease while drinking another beer. 'I'll make him talk,' he said. Once in the room, Hemingway told Mowinckel to dump him on the bed. Then he said: 'Take his boots off. We'll grill his toes with a candle.'

Mowinckel told him to go to hell, and the little soldier was released. Hemingway did, however, lend 'Mouthard' an automatic pistol to execute a traitor.

Another arrival was Major Airey Neave of MI9, who wanted to get into Paris as soon as possible on a mission of retribution. He was after a British army sergeant, Harold Cole, who had deserted in northern France in 1940, had later joined the French Resistance, then betrayed its largest escape line. As a result of his treachery the Germans arrested 150 people, of whom around a third had been executed. After this great coup for the Abwehr, Cole was transferred to the Gestapo in Paris, where he was still managing to trap other Resistance workers.

Irwin Shaw, the author who later wrote *The Young Lions*, turned up with his combat camera detachment of the Army Signal Corps. Shaw had introduced his lover, Mary Welsh, to Hemingway not long before D-Day, an encounter which led to her becoming the fourth Mrs Hemingway. (The third Mrs Hemingway, the journalist and writer Martha Gellhorn, had infuriated her husband by getting ashore in Normandy well before him.)

A group of American war correspondents arrived next. They were piqued to find Hemingway acting as the local commander of Rambouillet. When the Chicago journalist Bruce Grant made a disobliging comment about 'General Hemingway and his *maquis*', the object of the remark strode over and knocked him to the ground.

At six o'clock that evening, General de Gaulle joined Leclerc at the Château de Rambouillet, a former residence of the kings of France. While the soldiers of the 2e DB cooked their rations in the woods, and, on the assumption that they would be in Paris the next day, shaved with ritualistic care, their commander explained his plan of attack to the head of the provisional government in one of the salons of the château. When he had finished, de Gaulle reflected for a short while, then agreed with his proposals. 'You are lucky,' he said, thinking of the glory ahead.

On the following morning, Thursday 24 August, while the two columns advanced to make contact with the enemy, Paris began its last day under the Occupation. Several key figures in the future administration received the call to report for work.

Jacques Charpentier, the leader of the French Bar, set off on the very uncertain journey across a barricaded and enfiladed city to the Palais de Justice on the Île de la Cité. He encountered a twelve-year-old urchin proudly showing off an automatic pistol and boots taken from a dead German officer. The boy then acted as his guide from barricade to barricade, on a complicated but effective route.

The courage shown over previous days did not slacken. People responded at once to an announcement on the radio that the *mairie* of the 11th *arrondissement* was under heavy attack by the Germans and that the defenders were almost out of ammunition; anyone with a weapon should go to their aid. Thanks to the unflagging work of telephonists on the central exchanges, people were able to pass news back and forth. Some soldiers in Leclerc's advance units, as they drove through villages or outer suburbs of the capital, asked bystanders to ring their families in Paris to tell them that they were about to arrive. Inhabitants in one district kept friends in another up to date on events with a running commentary. Windows had become theatre boxes, albeit dangerous ones. Many watchers were mistaken for snipers or killed by stray bullets. Often, if they had been living alone, their bodies lay on the floor undiscovered until the smell of decomposition alerted a neighbour.

The Resistance fighters in Paris could now hear Allied tank guns. Captain Dronne's group, a troop of Shermans from the 501st Tank Regiment and the half-tracks of '*la nueve*' had reached the suburb of Fresnes, from where they could see the Eiffel Tower. But the fighting had been heavy, with well-concealed anti-tank guns (unidentified by Hemingway's scouts) ambushing Leclerc's Shermans, and causing many casualties.*

After knocking out the German detachment holding the prison of Fresnes, Dronne was ordered by his column commander

---

* That day Leclerc's division lost 71 men killed and 225 wounded; 35 armoured vehicles were destroyed, along with 117 other vehicles.

Colonel Billotte to withdraw, and rejoin the main axis of advance. Dronne was furious as he led his much reduced group back. On the way, he encountered General Leclerc.

'Dronne, what the hell are you doing here?' Leclerc demanded.

'*Mon général*, I'm following the order to pull back.'

'No, Dronne, head straight for Paris, enter Paris. Don't allow yourself to be held up. Take whichever route you want. Tell the Parisians and the Resistance not to lose hope, that tomorrow morning the whole division will be with them.' Dronne quickly briefed his vehicle commanders – he was down to three Sherman tanks and eleven half-tracks – and set off.

That same afternoon, Leclerc's American commander (furious to find that the French division had changed the main thrust of its advance over to the right, where the US 4th Infantry Division was supposed to be advancing in support) passed on General Omar Bradley's order that the American troops were to force on into Paris, whether or not the French had got there first. Clearly, neither de Gaulle nor Leclerc wished to acknowledge the fact that the 2e DB was under Allied orders.

Dronne, having been given *carte blanche* by Leclerc, and now guided by Parisian resistants who had reconnoitred the routes into the city, was able to advance rapidly via a network of back streets, avoiding all German strongpoints. In an hour and a half – just before half past nine – the little column of Shermans, half-tracks and jeeps reached the Place de l'Hôtel de Ville. Dronne climbed out of his jeep to look around. He was seized by the exultant defenders of the Hôtel de Ville and, amid cries of '*Vive La France!*' and '*Vive de Gaulle!*', was carried inside in triumph, to be embraced by the president of the National Council of Resistance, Georges Bidault.

Even before Dronne crossed the Pont d'Austerlitz to the right bank of the Seine, cyclists had started to spread the news of his arrival. The radio broadcast an appeal to priests to begin ringing their church bells. One group of ringers started to toll the great bell of Notre-Dame. Others joined in, one after another, until bells were pealing out right across the city. After four years of silence, this for many people was the most memorable sound of the whole war. With the occasional boom of a heavy gun and the constant refrain of the Marseillaise, both broadcast on the radio and sung spontaneously in the street, the Liberation of Paris started to sound like the 1812 overture.

In the more fashionable districts, the joy was less spontaneous: and not just in the apartments of Pétainists who awaited the future in grim silence, nor in the shuttered hiding-places of those advocates of the New European Order who had decided to stay behind, and now listened to the rejoicing outside, wondering what fate awaited them. There were also those who had continued to live their lives much as before, caring little for politics. If they had consorted in various ways with Germans during the Occupation, their motives had been purely social, and they had thought little of it.

General von Choltitz, on hearing the bells, telephoned his superior, General Speidel, and held the receiver to the open window so that Speidel knew what had happened.

While the bells rang out, Albert Camus, in the offices of the Resistance newspaper *Combat*, surrounded by 'enormous disorder and enormous gaiety', worked on an editorial which became famous: 'The greatness of man,' he wrote, 'lies in his decision to be stronger than his condition.'

For many people, that night was spent in excited anticipation. Women curled their hair and pressed their dresses. Most planned to wear the tricolor in some form or other, either in panels on their skirts, or even on earrings. Others sewed flags out of old clothes to greet their French and American liberators the next morning. A friend of the writer Julien Green worked through the night on an American flag, which, she said, 'gave her a lot of trouble because of the stars which she had been obliged to cut out from a dress'.

*

Early on the day of Liberation, Friday 25 August, crowds began to gather at the Porte de Saint-Cloud. The beautiful weather had returned. A detachment commanded by Major Jacques Massu had secured the Pont de Sèvres the night before, soon after Dronne reached the Hôtel de Ville. All was ready for Colonel Paul de Langlade's advance up through the 16th *arrondissement* to the Place de l'Étoile and the German administrative headquarters in the Hotel Majestic.

Colonel Billotte's group was the first to enter Paris and headed for the Prefecture of Police. Meanwhile Colonel Dio's group was heading for the Porte d'Orléans. Its objectives were the strongpoints of the École Militaire, the Invalides and the Palais Bourbon, which housed the Chambre des Députés.

When people first sighted the olive-green Sherman tanks, half-tracks, jeeps and GMC trucks, they assumed that the soldiers in them were American. Then they saw that the vehicles were marked with the cross of Lorraine set in an outline map of France, and although some of the soldiers had American helmets, others wore *képis*, black French berets, leather tank helmets and midnight-blue sidecaps. The old and the ill were brought out from hospitals so that they too should not miss the Liberation. Children were held aloft to see and remember the day. While the crowds waved from the pavements, young girls climbed on to vehicles to kiss their liberators. In many cases, the columns were brought to a virtual standstill, so afraid were the drivers of crushing civilians under their tracks. In any case, the crews saw no reason to refuse kisses or the bewildering array of alcohol offered in celebration.

Soon after nine o'clock, Jean Galtier-Boissière, in his bookshop on the Place de la Sorbonne, was suddenly told that Leclerc's troops had arrived. He ran outside with his wife. 'A vibrant crowd surrounds the French tanks draped in flags and covered in bouquets of flowers. On each tank, on each armoured car, next to crew members in khaki mechanics' overalls and little red caps, there are clusters of girls, women, boys and *fifis* wearing armbands. People lining the street applaud, blow kisses, raise clenched fist salutes, call out to the victors their joy at liberation!'

When the vehicles halted on the *quai*, more young women climbed up to kiss the soldiers. Shortly afterwards, the time came to launch the attack on the German strongpoints round the Palais du Luxembourg. A whistle blew. There was a shout: '*Allons les femmes, descendez . . . On attaque le Sénat.*' The young women climbed down, tank gunners and loaders dropped back inside the turrets of their Shermans, and the column set off up the Boulevard Saint-Michel. A crowd of spectators followed the tanks and watched them take up position. Meanwhile, from the other direction, Captain de Boissieu, commanding the divisional headquarters defence squadron, advanced from the Port Royal métro. He was joined by the 'Fabien battalion' of the FTP who volunteered to act as his infantry. Boissieu, a young cavalry officer who seventeen months later married one of General de Gaulle's daughters, had never imagined finding himself in command of a Communist unit. He had little time to consider the paradox. Mortar fire from the Jardin du Luxembourg landing on the Boulevard Saint-Michel had to be stopped. Evidently, the Germans had an observation post in the clock tower of the Senate. Two tanks traversed their guns on to it, and a moment after they fired, he saw the German observers hurled into the air, then fall on to the roof.

At a quarter past two on the right bank of the Seine, as Colonel de Langlade's armoured column came clanking and grinding up the Avenue Victor Hugo in the 16th *arrondissement* towards the Place de l'Étoile, Paris firemen hung a huge tricolor from the Arc de Triomphe. Crowds gathering to watch the attack on the Hotel Majestic on the Avenue Kléber yelled their support. Yves Montand and Edith Piaf were among those who had to throw themselves flat on the ground or shelter behind trees when the firing began.

The assault on the Majestic was almost perfunctory, although still confused. The defenders were hardly élite troops, but like most of the Gross-Paris garrison, soldiers 'abandoned by their officers to a suicidal task'. There was confusion over the surrender. The Protestant leader, Pastor Boegner, saw four German soldiers, bareheaded, their field-grey tunics unbuttoned, hands raised and clasped behind their necks, led at gunpoint to the Place de l'Étoile. One of them was alleged to have shot a French officer after the white flag had been hoisted. All four were shot. '*Chose atroce!*' the Protestant clergyman recorded, powerless to save them. Shortly afterwards, Edith Piaf stopped a young *fifi* from throwing a grenade into a lorry full of German prisoners.

After the Majestic had fallen, catching fire in the process, the crowd gathered at the Arc de Triomphe under the firemen's tricolor to sing the Marseillaise. The fighting and the impression of a 14 July celebration 'were mixed up together in a hallucinating way', Boegner noted.

Many of Leclerc's soldiers were returning home after four years far from their families. One young woman suddenly spotted her husband on a half-track, but emotion made her dumb. Fortunately, he caught sight of her, but clearly he hardly believed what he saw. Husband and wife threw themselves into each other's arms, while his comrades, equally filthy and unshaven, crowded round to share in the joy of their embrace.

The most important objective was to force General von Choltitz's surrender. Only then could the fighting in other parts of Paris come to an end. Choltitz had refused to accept a message demanding his submission.

At about the same time as Colonel de Langlade's troops began their attack on the Majestic, Colonel Billotte's group moved against the Hotel Meurice. Five Shermans and a force of infantry set off along the rue de Rivoli towards the Meurice, near the gilt statue of Jeanne d'Arc in the Place des Pyramides. As they got closer to their objective, they began dodging forward along the rue de Rivoli colonnade. Crowds cheered on the attackers in a carnival atmosphere, but as soon as the fighting started, the mood changed abruptly. The German tanks in the Tuileries gardens and on the Place de la Concorde were dealt with at the cost of four Shermans. After a brief battle, resistance ceased. Two French officers went up to General von Choltitz's room and demanded his surrender.

The crowd surged forward, some spitting, when he was driven off to sign the surrender with General Leclerc at the Prefecture of Police. Other German soldiers coming out of the headquarters with their hands up were attacked by a crowd, mainly of women, who tore at their clothes, spectacles and watches.

The formal act of surrender took place in the billiard-room of the Prefecture in the presence of the military leaders of the Resistance. Colonel Rol-Tanguy announced that as commander of the FFI in Paris he wished to sign the document with Leclerc. Rol's request was supported by the other leaders, including the non-Communists, Chaban-Delmas and Colonel Lizé, so Leclerc felt obliged to agree. Due to a confusion, Leclerc's signature came below that of Rol.

After the ceremony, Leclerc, accompanied by most of those who had been present, including General von Choltitz, moved to the railway station of Montparnasse, where he had arranged to meet de Gaulle. The head of the provisional government arrived around four o'clock, while Choltitz's orders to cease fighting were prepared to be sent off to the last German strongpoints. De Gaulle was angry when, shown the act of surrender, he saw that not only was Colonel Rol-Tanguy's signature on the document, but it came first. He was irked not so much by the fact that Rol-Tanguy was a Communist, but that he had no official position in the provisional government or its armed forces. But this did not stop de Gaulle from congratulating Colonel Rol on the achievement of his men. He knew full well the value of the myth that the rising had created.

For de Gaulle, on this victorious afternoon, symbolism was of paramount importance. He did not hurry to meet Bidault and the leaders of the Resistance at the Hôtel de Ville. After Montparnasse, his first visit was to the Ministry of War in the rue Saint-Dominique, his own fief in 1940 before the Pétainist usurpation intervened. His memoirs describe how little the place had changed: 'Not a piece of furniture, not a tapestry, not a curtain had been altered. The telephone was still in the same place on the desk and exactly the same names were to be seen under the buttons.'

Then he went to the Prefecture of Police to see Alexandre Parodi and Charles Luizet. He was greeted by a huge crowd and a band of the Parisian fire brigade led by its drum-major, playing patriotic anthems. Finally, just after eight in the evening, he crossed to the right bank, to the Hôtel de Ville, where Georges Bidault and the National Council of the Resistance awaited him.

There, in the great hall, he made one of the most emotional speeches of his life. 'Paris. Paris outraged, Paris broken, Paris martyred, but Paris liberated! Liberated by herself, liberated by her people, with the help of the whole of France, that is to say of the France which fights, the true France, eternal France.'

Yet many members of the Resistance felt that in one way the General had not been emotional enough. 'One would have liked more understanding,' wrote one of them in his journal. 'And this speech . . . short, authoritarian and spotless. Very good, perfect, but all the same, he should have said thank-you to the CNR and to Alexandre [Parodi], who had given so much of themselves.'

When de Gaulle had finished, Bidault asked him to proclaim the Republic to the crowds waiting below, but de Gaulle refused. Largely as a result of his deliberate *hauteur*, this exchange has often been described as a cruel snub to Bidault and the leaders of the Resistance. Even Bidault himself later contributed to the myth of a great clash.

In reality, de Gaulle simply wished to re-emphasize his view that Pétain's regime had been an illegal aberration. René Brouillet, Bidault's *chef de cabinet*, who was standing just behind the two men when the request was made, had a clear memory of the exchange. 'The request of Georges Bidault was the request of a history professor, who had a strong memory of the proclamation of the Republic from the balcony of the Hôtel de Ville, in 1848 and 1870. And as a result [he] asked General de Gaulle in the most natural way, and the General, in no less natural a way, replied, "But why should we proclaim the Republic? She has never ceased to exist."'

De Gaulle nevertheless agreed to make an appearance. The 'balcony' of the Hôtel de Ville is more of an imposing balustrade, adding to the importance of the principal window. De Gaulle got up on to the balustrade and raised those endless arms in a victory sign to the crowd below. The response was tumultuous.

General Koenig, the new military governor of Paris, invited officers of the 2e DB to dinner at the Invalides. Before they went in, Koenig stopped Captain de Boissieu in the courtyard, and made a sweeping gesture, saying: 'Look, Boissieu, it is extraordinary to have liberated Paris without having destroyed its wonders; all the bridges, all the great buildings, all the artistic treasures of the capital are intact.'

The last guest to arrive was Major Massu, still filthy in oil-stained battledress. He shook out his napkin, laid it carefully over the seventeenth-century tapestry seat, and sat down to eat.

All over central Paris, liberators were sitting down to celebration dinners. When Colonel David Bruce and Ernest Hemingway, followed by the private army, entered the Ritz lobby, the hotel appeared deserted, but soon Claude Auzello, the manager, appeared. He recognized both Hemingway and Bruce from pre-war days. The forty-six-year-old Bruce, a Princeton friend of F. Scott Fitzgerald, had spent much of his youth in Europe, from military service in France at the end of the First World War until 1927, when he returned to the United States.

The 'imperturbable' Monsieur Auzello asked what he could do for them. Hemingway and Bruce glanced back at the mob behind them for a rough head-count and answered that they would like fifty martini cocktails. The Martinis 'were not very good, as the bartender had disappeared,' Bruce recorded in his diary, 'but they were followed by a superb dinner.'

For once in history, soldiers seem to have had a better time that night than their officers. What Simone de Beauvoir described as a *'débauche de fraternité'* during the day became a *débauche tout court* after dark. Few soldiers were to sleep alone that night.

Major Massu, on returning from the dinner at the Invalides to his battalion camped around the tomb of the unknown soldier at the Arc de Triomphe, wrote later that he preferred to draw a veil over what he found there. In fact so widespread was the love-making that a Catholic group began distributing hastily run-off tracts addressed to the young women of Paris: 'In the gaiety of the Liberation do not throw away your innocence. Think of your future family.'

Not everybody, however, was out on the streets to savour a new era of freedom. Through an open widow, Pastor Boegner saw a neighbour, an old lady, sitting at her table playing patience, just as she did every evening.

5
Liberated Paris

Paris on the morning after the fighting had a strange air of calm. For those who went out early on a tour of inspection – mainly the older generation since the young were sleeping off the excesses of the night before, as well as the accumulated fatigue of the last week – the traces of fighting amply testified to the reality of events.

During the battle for the Hôtel Meurice, some of the huge columns had been shot down from the great façade of the Ministry of Marine on the north side of the Place de la Concorde. In the expanse of the Concorde, even the burnt-out tanks looked small. Just beyond, in the Tuileries gardens, the carbonized hulk of a Tiger tank was still smoking.

Across the river, outside the Ministry of Foreign Affairs, yet another scorched carcass of a tank – this time a Sherman of the 2e DB – had written on its side in chalk: '*Ici sont morts trois soldats Français*'. Flowers had already been laid on its blackened hulk. Other flowers soon appeared on street corners or outside *portes cochères* where victims had failed to reach safety. Passers-by often paused, then stepped round them carefully, as in a cemetery. They were reminded of all those who had not lived to see Paris free again.*

---

*Estimates of the number killed vary greatly. Many seem too high. The archives of the Ville de Paris record 2,873 Parisians, including inhabitants of the inner suburbs, killed during the month of August.

Many other areas had also suffered in the fighting – the Palais du Luxembourg and its surroundings, the Champ de Mars, the Palais Bourbon, the Île de la Cité, and the Place de la République. But as General Koenig observed, they were incredibly lucky that the destruction of monuments had been so limited. The Grand Palais, that beached whale of the *belle époque*, was reduced to little more than a skeleton, but all the other major buildings could be repaired.

In the cafés on the Boulevard Saint-Michel, glass with starred holes from bullets was left unreplaced for reasons of pride as well as economy. Shop windows broken in the fighting had been quickly boarded up, and yet people were already beginning to remove the lattice-work of sticky tape from their own windows in the belief that the threat of bomb-blast had disappeared, though the Germans were still within artillery range out at Le Bourget.

Most people, certainly the liberators of the day before, were light-headed either from love-making or the drinking of relentless toasts. David Bruce recorded that it had been impossible to refuse the bottles thrust at them which had been hoarded almost religiously for the moment of liberation. 'The combination was enough to wreck one's constitution,' he wrote. 'In the course of the afternoon, we had beer, cider, white and red Bordeaux, white and red Burgundy, champagne, rum, cognac, armagnac and calvados.'

If the day of Liberation had belonged to the FFI and Leclerc's men, Saturday, 26 August was to be de Gaulle's triumph.

A discordant note was struck by General Gerow, Leclerc's American superior. Still furious at the way the French had ignored his orders over the last few days, Gerow sent an instruction forbidding the 2e DB to take part in any victory celebrations. Yet with the city not yet fully clear of the enemy, de Gaulle needed Leclerc's men to provide security and preserve public order. Vichy *miliciens* were not covered by General von

Choltitz's ceasefire, and there was always the possibility that other German forces might counter-attack from the north.

In the early afternoon, huge crowds converged on the centre of Paris by foot, many coming from the outer suburbs, in some cases a distance of a dozen kilometres or more. Well over a million people gathered in the sunshine on both sides of the route from the Arc de Triomphe to Notre-Dame.* To obtain better views, people crowded at the windows of buildings over-looking the route, and the young climbed trees or lamp-posts. There were even people lining the rooftops. Paris had never seen such crowds. Many carried home-made tricolors.

At three o'clock, de Gaulle arrived at the Arc de Triomphe, where all the principal figures awaited him: Parodi, Luizet, Chaban-Delmas, Bidault and the other members of the National Resistance Council, Admiral d'Argenlieu and, of course, Generals Juin, Koenig and Leclerc.

The leader of the provisional government took the salute of the Régiment de Marche du Tchad, standing in their vehicles drawn up across the Place de l'Étoile. Under the Arc de Triomphe, he relit the flame over the tomb of the unknown soldier which had been extinguished in June 1940, when the Germans marched into the city. Then, preceded by four of Leclerc's Shermans, he set off on foot down the Champs-Élysées towards the Place de la Concorde.

Behind the official party, swelled by numerous officials who wished to establish their credentials, came a throng of FFI militia and onlookers who decided to join in, singing and embracing as they went.

From time to time, de Gaulle raised his arms to acknowledge the cheering, which at a distance sounded like the roar and booming of a sea crashing on rocks. 'There took place at that

---

* In the first opinion poll carried out since before the war, IFOP found that 56 per cent of its sample in Paris claimed to have been present that day. '*C'est un plebiscite*' was a widespread comment.

moment,' he wrote in his memoirs, 'one of those miracles of national conscience, one of those gestures of France herself, which occasionally, down the centuries, come to illuminate our history.'

Not everyone, however, was yelling for de Gaulle, the man. There must have been Pétainists cheering in the crowd: there had certainly been enough people cheering the Marshal only four months before. Meanwhile, Communists could not resist the odd '*Vive Maurice!*' in honour of Maurice Thorez, still in Moscow, where he had remained ever since deserting from the French army on Stalin's orders at the start of the war. Simone de Beauvoir, who had gone to the Arc de Triomphe with Michel Leiris, was later careful in the way she described her approbation that day. 'Mixed in the immense crowd, we acclaimed not a military parade, but a popular carnival, disorganized and magnificent.' Jean-Paul Sartre was waiting much further down the route to watch from a balcony of the Hotel du Louvre.

With police cars well in front, then the four tanks, de Gaulle's escort increased with largely self-appointed groups of FFI. At the Place de la Concorde, a platoon of the 'Jewish army' resistance group joined in, wearing captured Milice uniforms (their provenance countered with tricolor armbands). Shortly after de Gaulle had climbed into an open car to drive the last two kilometres to Notre-Dame, shooting broke out. To this day, nobody knows whether this was a serious assassination attempt, a provocation, or simply the result of too many tense and inexperienced people with weapons.

In the Place de la Concorde and the rue de Rivoli, the crowds threw themselves flat on the ground or sheltered behind groups of armoured vehicles from the Leclerc division. One man lifted his bicycle over his head as a shield. Nobody knew where the shooting came from, and the result was panic. The *fifis* began firing at rooftops and windows. Jean-Paul Sartre, on his balcony outside the Hotel du Louvre, was shot at by a trigger-happy *fifi*, who mistook him for a *milicien* sniper. (Jean Cocteau, watching from a window of the Hotel Crillon, claimed less convincingly that his cigarette was 'cut in half' in his mouth.) The most senior official in the Ministry of Finance was shot dead at his office window. At least half a dozen people were killed around the Place de la Concorde and the rue de Rivoli.

For the rest of the day, black *traction-avant* Citroëns, daubed with the FFI initials on the roof and sides, charged around self-importantly at breakneck speed, stopping only to shoot at rooftops and windows. Other vehicles requisitioned by the Resistance had men armed with rifles lying on the mudguards, or standing on the running-boards. 'The heroes multiplied,' wrote Galtier-Boissière. 'The number of last-minute resistants, armed from head to toe and covered in cartridge belts in the Mexican style, was considerable.'

De Gaulle, meanwhile, affected not to hear the firing. His open car continued down the rue de Rivoli to the Hôtel de Ville where the band of the Garde Républicaine was drawn up in review order outside. After a brief stop, he crossed the Pont d'Arcole to Notre-Dame.

Outside the cathedral Mgr Suhard, the cardinal-archbishop of Paris, was conspicuously absent from the welcoming party. He had wanted to be present, but there was little to recommend him in Gaullist and Resistance eyes. In August 1942, he had insisted on giving the absolution in the service of blessing for the Legion of French Volunteers off to fight for the Wehrmacht in Russia. In April 1944, he had welcomed Pétain on the latter's visit to Paris; and only two months before the Liberation he had dignified the funeral of Philippe Henriot with full pomp and ceremony. Henriot, assassinated by the Resistance, had been Vichy's minister of information and a pro-Nazi propagandist.

Shooting broke out again just as de Gaulle entered Notre-Dame. Outside, FFI groups began firing at the towers. The members of the Jewish platoon concentrated on the north tower. Inside, policemen and soldiers trying to protect de Gaulle aimed up into the recesses and vaulting of the cathedral. Some shots brought down chunks of masonry. Members of the congregation, who had thrown themselves flat, then tried to hide behind pillars, or even under chairs. De Gaulle, disengaging himself from the mêlée, walked forward up the aisle towards the high altar where the service was due to begin.

Malcolm Muggeridge, a British intelligence officer who had reached Paris late the night before, described the whole event. 'The effect was fantastic. The huge congregation who had all been standing suddenly fell flat on their faces. There was a single exception; one solitary figure, like a lonely giant. It was, of course, de Gaulle. Thenceforth, that was how I always saw him – towering and alone; the rest, prostrate.' There were others, such as Alexandre Parodi, who remained upright, but with all eyes fixed on de Gaulle, he alone appeared majestic, fearless and untouchable.

The incident confirmed de Gaulle in his determination to disarm the FFI at the earliest opportunity. There could be no further doubt that they represented a bigger danger to public safety than the rump of any 'fifth column' of *miliciens*. Disturbances presented a double threat. 'Public order is a matter of life and death,' he told a visitor to the rue Saint-Dominique a few days later. 'If we do not re-establish it ourselves, foreigners will impose it upon us.' The American and British forces now appeared to be seen as 'foreigners' rather than allies.

At half past eleven, during a second night of celebration, the air-raid sirens sounded. The Luftwaffe had arrived on a revenge attack, bombing at random. A hospital was seriously damaged. So too were the spirit warehouses of Les Halles des Vins. The orange glow against the night sky could be seen from all over Paris.

On the day of Liberation, it seemed as if almost every French Communist had converged on party headquarters at 44 rue Pelletier, always known as 'le 44'. Those released from prison turned up at the six-storey building in search of news, and most had gone into one of the nearby cafés in the hope of discovering who had survived the terrible years and who had not. The entrance was protected by sandbags, a legacy from the building's last occupants, the Milice.

Six days later, Jacques Duclos, Thorez's deputy and stand-in, summoned a meeting of the party's central committee. Only some twenty members met that night, including Professor Joliot-Curie, the scientist who had made Molotov cocktails in the Sorbonne. Four tables had been arranged in a rectangle, 'like a marriage feast'. The veteran Communist Marcel Cachin presided. Behind his head a proclamation decorated ostentatiously with tricolor flags listed the members of the central committee who had 'died for France'. From another wall, a photograph of Stalin watched over them.

Duclos's fellow members of the French Communist Party's wartime triumvirate were Benoît Frachon, who was to prove a skilful leader of the Communist trades-union movement in the post-war years, and Charles Tillon, a hard and resourceful man who had been the real leader of the Communist resistance during the Occupation. Duclos feared his influence, and soon arranged for him to be one of the Communist ministers in de Gaulle's government. This would restrict his freedom of action, and also remove him from the real centre of power within the party itself.

Duclos, when he faced his colleagues, was in an embarrassing position. We now know that it was he who had directed the approach to the German authorities in 1940, invoking the Nazi–Soviet pact, to arrange for the reappearance of the party newspaper *L'Humanité* and the release of Communist prisoners. In exchange he had offered to put France back to work. Tillon had ridiculed the idea that French Communists would thus receive preferential treatment. 'For shit's sake, do you really think that in Paris the Germans will see you as Russians?'

Duclos was a little man, almost risible in the eyes of someone like Tillon. His round face with round glasses made him look like a complacent *petit-bourgeois*; but the impenetrable smile and the clever little eyes hinted at why he was such a formidable survivor: for he knew that the faithful follower of the party line would come out on top, and Stalin did not want a revolution launched on the back of the Liberation.

Duclos could not assert party discipline until de Gaulle granted Thorez an amnesty for his desertion at the beginning of the war and allowed him to return from Moscow. For the moment, the General did not even bother to reply to Thorez's telegrams, only passing a message back by his representative in Moscow that any delay was the fault of the British.

The reason for Stalin's non-revolutionary policy in France was simple. He wanted no trouble with the Americans and the British whose material support to the Red Army remained vital until Germany was finally crushed.

While Tillon and his followers wanted to maintain the Resistance in arms as a force for political change, Duclos accepted the Kremlin line, of avoiding clashes with de Gaulle and the Allies. The party, however, could still increase its power by installing its own candidates in key positions wherever possible. One way was to lead the call for popular justice against traitors and then, during the ensuing purges, denounce anti-Communists as collaborators and replace them with their own people. More and more reports arrived from all over France of last-minute massacres carried out by the Germans. There had also been incidents of German officers who let political prisoners go, but they received less attention at a time when most news was so grim.

On 1 September, the French and foreign press was given a tour of the Gestapo's torture chambers in the rue des Saussaies, just behind the Ministry of the Interior on the Place Beauvau. In a relentless campaign, *L'Humanité* did all it could to exploit stories of massacre and torture to their utmost. The implication was that Vichy and its officials had been involved in every crime: directly, indirectly or by association.

*

New arrivals in liberated Paris were seeking out old friends. One of Hemingway's first visits was to Sylvia Beach at 12 rue de l'Odéon. He was sad to find that in 1941 the Germans had forced her to close down her bookshop, Shakespeare & Company, so this part of expatriate Left Bank life was over. But at least she had survived, having spent six months in an internment camp.

In the cafés of Saint-Germain-des-Prés, people discussed their different wartime experiences, or heard about events from which they had been separated by censorship or distance. Raymond Aron described the bombing of London. Far worse tales had also begun to emerge, like that of the Warsaw uprising, and the first rumours of the death camps.

Some people resurfaced in astonishing new roles. Right-wing anti-semites appeared full of stories of the Jews or Communists they had saved from the Gestapo. Among the members of what was mockingly known as the 'RMA' – the resistants of the month of August – there were characters who, having denounced fellow citizens to the Germans, now denounced fellow collaborators with such venom that people dared not speak out against them.

It was a time for making new friends. Camus introduced Sartre and Simone de Beauvoir to Father Bruckberger, the FFI chaplain, whom they found in his white Dominican habit, smoking his pipe and drinking corrosive punch in the Rhumerie Martiniquaise. They also met the writer Romain Gary, and Lise Deharme, a poet whose salon was frequented by the rump of the Surrealist movement. Black American soldiers were greeted in Saint-Germain by Parisians starved of jazz, and the warmth of the welcome prompted a number of them to wonder whether to stay there instead of returning to the States.

It was a time of debate, ideas and conversation. Jean Cocteau and his friends held court in the bar of the Hotel Saint-Yves in the rue Jacob, where Cocteau, like Picasso, was famous for his monologues. For Cocteau, 'the spoken word was his language and he used it with the virtuosity of an acrobat'.

It was also a period of feast and famine. Tobacco hunger, only partially assuaged by packets of Camel thrown from passing jeeps, was far more noticeable than a skinny rib-cage. People dug out cigarette-holders from the 1920s so as to be able to smoke their cigarettes down to the last drop of nicotine. Brassai's photograph of Picasso's wartime muse, Dora Maar, shows the ash burning to within a millimetre of the holder. The black market boomed. At night the métro station of Strasbourg-Saint-Denis was 'packed full of types who whispered out of the corner of the mouth as you passed: "Chocolate? Tobacco? Gauloises? English cigarettes?"'

In spite of the destruction of Les Halles des Vins, a miraculous supply of cheap alcohol somehow remained available, and a frenzy of parties followed the Liberation. *Les Lettres Françaises*, the counter to the right-wing takeover of France's great literary magazine, *La Nouvelle Revue Française*, gave a cocktail party presided over by the Communist 'royal couple', Louis Aragon and Elsa Triolet. Éditions de Minuit, which had won such admiration by underground publication of books like *Le Silence de la mer* by Vercors and François Mauriac's *Cahier noir*, gave a party at Versailles with a play by La Fontaine. Few guests were very smart, as much out of necessity as taste. Simone de Beauvoir had a single black suit for grand occasions, but Sartre seldom changed out of his worn lumber jacket.

For the GIs, however, the young women on bicycles with short skirts billowing were the most enduring memory of Paris. Galtier-Boissière noticed how 'the short lampshade skirts generously uncovered pink thighs'. These short, loose dresses for bicycling were made out of patchwork, though even patchwork could differ in quality. Simone de Beauvoir observed that '*les élégantes* used luxury silk scarves; in Saint-Germain-des-Prés we made do with cotton prints'.

Long hair, piled high above the forehead, was one answer to the shortage of electricity. Constant power-cuts made coiffeurs resort to a lot of back-combing. Lee Miller took a photograph of a pair of male cyclists furiously pedalling a tandem linked to a dynamo, to provide current for the dryers upstairs. Most ingenious of all were the wooden-soled shoes, with an articulated sole to avoid the rigidity of clogs. (The Germans had requisitioned all stocks of leather for the Wehrmacht.) The noise of those shoes clacking on pavements was one of the most evocative sounds of the war years. One of Maurice Chevalier's songs was entitled '*La Symphonie des semelles de bois*'.

Maurice Chevalier put all his efforts at the Liberation into the song '*Fleur de Paris*', an air of sentimental patriotism, which he clearly hoped would help him '*se dédouaner*' (get him through 'customs' in the form of purge committees) for having sung on the German-run Radio-Paris, among other accusations. Chevalier, Charles Trenet and the singing nightclub owner Suzy Solidor were all blacklisted, and Tino Rossi was locked up in Fresnes prison. Suzy Solidor went round to visit the editors of newspapers, claiming she had worked for the Resistance and that the only accusation against her was to have sung 'Lili Marlene' at a time when it was a great hit with British troops.

Even Edith Piaf was suspect for a moment, having, like Chevalier, gone to sing for French prisoners in Germany; but she had never supported the Pétainist regime: unlike Chevalier, who had taken off his boater and had drunk a bottle of Vichy water as a show of loyalty to journalists – the most ill-judged photo-opportunity of his career.

One singer whose Resistance credentials were impeccable was Josephine Baker. General de Gaulle even wrote the preface to the book about her exploits by Commandant Jacques Abtey, *La Guerre secrète de Josephine Baker*. De Gaulle also attended her first concert in Paris after the Liberation. Josephine Baker had returned to France with General de Lattre's 1st Army and came up to Paris to see old friends and prove that the reports of her death were premature. She gave a gala concert for the French air force charity at the Paramount in November, when she sang

'Paris chéri', one of the last songs written for her by Vincent Scotto. Jo Bouillon's orchestra provided the music and, soon afterwards, she married him.

Malcolm Muggeridge went in uniform with a brother officer to a very different cabaret on the Left Bank, packed out and thick with tobacco smoke. 'There were only flickering candles to light the tiny stage, where a man, completely bald, with a large, sad clown's face, was intoning a soliloquy, in which he recalled all the terrible things that had happened to him since the Germans came to Paris. "*Et maintenant*," he concluded, with an expression of infinite woe, through which he struggled to break into a wry smile – "*Et maintenant, nous sommes libérés!*" The audience roared their approval, looking quizzically at Trevor and me. Somehow it seemed the most perfect comment on the situation.'

6

The Passage of Exiles

The resounding acclaim which greeted de Gaulle at the Liberation helped create the impression that Vichy's version of France
had evaporated, almost as if it had never really existed. This
was the fairy-tale finish to a disturbing story. It helped soothe
the deep wounds in national pride and aided the notion of
Republican legitimacy.

The lingering death of Pétain's regime was the grotesque
fruition of its self-deceit. Patriots who had supported the old
Marshal in 1940 found by 1944 that his path of collaboration
had been the path of dishonour and humiliation at the hands of
the occupying power; while the feuding Germanophile factions –
those of Pierre Laval, Marcel Déat Jacques Doriot and Joseph
Darnand, the head of the Milice – finally discovered that they
were far from equal allies in the New European Order. The
Nazis had despised them, simply using them for their own ends.
As the Allied armies broke out of Normandy, the exodus of
those vulnerable to Resistance reprisals matched the departure
of German officials on 17 August. The collaborationist newspaper *Je suis partout* became known as *Je suis parti*.

The mutual hatreds and suspicions on the extreme right, both
French and German, became more poisonous as the defeat of
Nazi Germany approached. One of the first victims was Eugene
Deloncle, the head of the pre-war Cagoule. On 7 January 1944,
the Gestapo arrived at his apartment to arrest him. Deloncle

assumed they were Resistance 'terrorists' who had come to assassinate him. He fired at them and the Gestapo gunned him down immediately; then, while some looted the apartment, others arrested his family. One son was beaten into a coma. Deloncle's wife and his daughter Claude were driven off to Fresnes prison, to be locked up with members of the Resistance.

In August 1944, Joseph Darnand, head of the Milice, ordered his scattered groups of *miliciens* to withdraw eastwards. In Paris, Jean Galtier-Boissière watched the *miliciens* leave the Lycée Saint-Louis in a convoy of lorries.

Fearing reprisals, *miliciens* from many parts of France fled towards an increasingly embattled Germany with their wives and families. Those from the south-west had to cross a large stretch of hostile territory in small, vulnerable groups.

The old Marshal formally protested at the order for him to leave Vichy. He was escorted by Otto Abetz's deputy, the minister von Renthe-Fink, to Belfort on France's eastern frontier; then, on 7 September, he reached Sigmaringen, the castle and small town designated by Hitler as the capital of France in exile.

The castle of Sigmaringen on the Danube was supposedly the cradle of the Hohenzollern dynasty. As the setting for the *Götterdämmerung* of French fascism, its position, history and even quasi-Wagnerian name seem fittingly ironic. But the reality was far from grand opera. If anything, the claustrophobic squabbling sounded more like a parody of the ante-chamber of hell in Sartre's play *Huis clos*, which had opened in Paris some ten days before D-Day. That brilliantly crazed writer, Louis-Ferdinand Céline, with his unfailing eye for the grotesque, was the perfect chronicler of Sigmaringen. In *D'un Château à l'autre*, he described the vain rivalries as '*un ballet de crabes*'.

Pétain was a privileged prisoner. He benefited from special menus – the Germans allotted him sixteen ration cards – and escorted walks in the countryside. His suite was on the seventh floor. The hierarchy, as Henry Rousso describes in his book, *Un*

Château en Allemagne, descended floor by floor. On the sixth floor, Laval and ministers were lodged. Laval complained about his four-poster bed – '*Je suis un paysan, moi!*' He spent the first part of each morning in a study lined in blue silk preparing and practising his defence for the day of temporal judgement, when he would face de Gaulle's new Haute Cour de Justice on charges of treason. Laval had brought out 20 million francs of the government's petty cash, but German banks refused to change it.

The nominal leader of Sigmaringen's equally nominal administration was Fernand de Brinon, a failed aristocrat whose Jewish wife had been made an 'honorary Aryan'. Brinon had been Vichy's ambassador to Paris, an extraordinary yet significant paradox for Pétain's French state. The tricolor was raised over Sigmaringen to a roll of German drums and a *milicien* guard of honour presenting arms. The French state exchanged ambassadors with that other puppet-theatre of the absurd, Mussolini's Salo republic.

General Bridoux, the equivalent of Minister of War, was put in charge of recruiting French prisoners to fight in the SS. The 'minister of information' was Jean Luchaire, a newspaper magnate, who was accompanied by several mistresses and his three daughters, one of whom was the film star Corinne Luchaire. In the library, intellectuals of the arch-right, such as Alphonse de Châteaubriant and Lucien Rebatet, met and squabbled. Céline managed to avoid them. He had found lodgings down in the town with his wife Lucette, and there he reverted to his profession of doctor.

News of the Ardennes offensive in December produced an outburst of almost hysterical optimism in the castle. Some people declared that they would follow the German army back into Paris by the New Year, not knowing that Field Marshal von Rundstedt's tanks had run out of fuel. When the scope of the disaster was finally revealed, the only hope left was the promise of Hitler's secret weapons. For the more realistic, their nightmare was of falling into the hands of French colonial troops, the Senegalese or the *goums*. Céline, despising all around him, set off northwards with his wife, a journey through the terrifying death throes of Nazi Germany, until they reached Denmark, where he was imprisoned.

As for the wives and children of the *miliciens* who had sought refuge in Germany, their fate was little better. Far from being treated as allies, they were locked up in conditions comparable to the worst internment camps. At Siessen, sixty children died of malnutrition. The least fit of the men were transported for forced labour. The remaining 2,500 were transferred to the grandly designated Charlemagne Division of the Waffen SS. Sent to East Prussia in February 1945 to fight under Himmler's Army Group Vistula, a third of the French contingent was lost to the Russian onslaught in their first encounter.*

The ghastly story was dragged out to the end. The remnants of the Fenet Battalion, less than a hundred strong, was transferred to Berlin. In April 1945, along with some Danes and Norwegians from the Viking Division, they faced the Red Army's final assault in the unrecognizable landscape of what had been the Unter den Linden. On 29 April, the eve of Hitler's suicide, a brief candlelit ceremony took place in an underground station while the battle still raged overhead. SS General Krukenberg presented the Knight's Cross of the Iron Cross to former *milicien* Eugène Vanlot for having destroyed six Soviet armoured vehicles. Few of these last defenders of the New Europe returned to their homes.

The British, not having suffered the divisive effects of occupation, had few traitors to deal with. Yet two of the most famous, John Amery and Harold Cole, were in Paris in August 1944.

John Amery, the son of the Secretary of State for India and

---

*Altogether some 8,500 Frenchmen served in German uniform, a much lower proportion per head of population than other occupied nations of northern Europe.

Burma, Leo Amery, had developed an infatuation for the Nazi regime. He had made broadcasts from Berlin urging Britons to fight for Hitler, and the Nazis used him to lead the Legion of St George, the British contribution to the New Europe. Only sixty-six volunteers emerged, which did not make a centuria let alone a cohort or a legion. Amery, arrested in Paris at the Liberation, was flown back to London for trial. He was hanged on 19 December 1945.

Sergeant Harold Cole, the British deserter whom Airey Neave was hunting, came into a different category. With his ginger hair and close-set cunning eyes, he had the quick wits of an inveterate confidence trickster. He had disappeared with the funds of the sergeants' mess in his unit, to lie low during the German invasion of France. A year later, he introduced himself to a nascent French Resistance group in Lille as Captain Cole of the British Secret Service. In the course of three months he escorted thirty-five Allied escapers over the demarcation line into the unoccupied zone. RAF pilots returned with stories of his daring and ingenuity.

In London, MI9 did not quite know what to make of this unexpected volunteer. Checks of army records did not show any Captain Harold Cole, but Scotland Yard rapidly identified the Sergeant Cole who had deserted in April 1940 as a housebreaker and con-man with a string of minor convictions. Room 900 in the War Office, the headquarters of MI9, was uneasy, but it was decided to give Cole the benefit of the doubt. Officers in London could not bring themselves to believe that an Englishman would turn traitor.

Cole at this time was not a traitor, but an embezzler. He had mistresses in several different towns, on whom he spent the secret funds destined for the network in Lille. In December 1941 he was accused of fraud by the senior member of the network in a safe house in Marseilles. But he escaped, and went straight to the Abwehr to denounce every member of the network in northern France. He even betrayed the relations of the young French girl he had married, and then stole their jewellery.

Safe houses and cover names had to be changed, and the order was spread that Cole should be shot on sight. But he was never sighted by anyone who knew of his treachery before he left for Germany with Sturmbannführer Kieffer of the SD.

There was no further trace of Cole until the end of the war. In May 1945, he walked into the headquarters of a US cavalry regiment in Bavaria and introduced himself as Captain Mason, a British secret agent. He even brought his former controller with him and said that Kieffer had been secretly helping the Allies. The American officers believed him and provided Kieffer with a safe conduct as Cole requested. Cole, in an even more dazzling display of confidence trickery, then persuaded senior American officers to appoint him as a captain in their Counter-Intelligence Corps, interrogating captured Nazis.

In Paris, Neave had followed up every lead on Cole, interviewing all those who had known him. It looked as if he had disappeared for good. But then in the summer of 1945, one of Neave's colleagues in Paris received a visit from a former mistress of Cole's. To prove that her lover was not a traitor, she produced a boastful letter he had written from Germany describing his life as an intelligence officer with the Americans. A British officer and a French officer from the BCRA went as fast as they could to the American zone, and when they reached the base they found Cole hosting a cocktail party. He was arrested and brought back to Paris to face court martial and almost certain execution. But in the cell block attached to Eisenhower's headquarters, he managed to trick his guards and slipped out of the camp in the uniform of an American sergeant. He then rented a room above a bar in the rue de Grenelle.

For three weeks the BCRA searched for Cole all over the city, but his downfall was brought about unexpectedly. On 9 January 1946, he was discovered by two gendarmes who were looking for deserters from the French army. Cole was armed and wounded one of them, but the other gendarme shot him dead. One of the leaders of the lifeline he had betrayed, a survivor of

Dachau, and in fact the man who had confronted him in Marseilles, came to identify the body.

The other Englishman in Paris whom the British authorities wished to interview was no traitor, but simply the victim of his own unworldliness.

One of the first jobs given to Major Malcolm Muggeridge on his arrival in Paris was to keep an eye on P. G. Wodehouse, who was still at the Hotel Bristol where he had been installed by the Germans. Arrested with his wife at their villa at Le Touquet in 1940, he had been interned in the Silesian lunatic asylum of Tost. Released shortly before his sixtieth birthday, he was asked by the Berlin representative of CBS to make a broadcast to the United States. Not realizing that this would be used by German radio for their own purposes, Wodehouse made the broadcast in his typically jolly way, making light of his imprisonment and giving the impression that life under German domination was not too bad.

This story emerged at a bad moment in Britain. Wodehouse's failure to hate anybody at this time of total war was incomprehensible to most people who had endured the Blitz, and some of his throwaway remarks – the most notorious was 'whether England wins or not' – provoked great anger. The worst onslaught came in a broadcast by the journalist William Connor, 'Cassandra' of the *Daily Mirror*. This was personally authorized by Duff Cooper, the Minister of Information, who had overridden the objections of the BBC.

Just over a week after the Liberation, Wodehouse wrote to the Home Secretary in London, 'hastening to report to you my presence here':

> This is not the occasion for me to make a detailed statement, but may I be allowed to say that the reports in the Press that I obtained my release from internment by agreeing to broadcast on the German radio are entirely without founda-

tion. The five talks which I delivered were arranged for after my release, and were made at my own suggestion.

That it was criminally foolish of me to speak on the German radio, I admit. But the only motive in doing so was to give my American readers a humorous description of my adventures, as some response to the great number of letters which I had received from them while I was in the camp. The five talks covered the five phases of my imprisonment, were purely comic in tone, and were designed to show American listeners a group of Englishmen keeping up their spirits and courage under difficult conditions.

The British authorities could not make up their mind what to do, so left Wodehouse where he was. On the night of 20 November, however, an Englishwoman at dinner with the Prefect of Police announced that Wodehouse, who had broadcast from Berlin, was living openly in Paris at a hotel. Luizet wasted no time. Four leather-jacketed policemen armed with submachine-guns were promptly despatched to bring him in.

Malcolm Muggeridge went round to the police station where Wodehouse was held. Ethel Wodehouse had been brought in as well, with her pekinese Wonder; the police inspector in charge was only too relieved to be rid of its hysterical yapping, so 'Mme Wodenhorse' was allowed to leave. All that remained was to convince the French authorities that 'M. Wodenhorse' was ill and that he should be transferred to a sanatorium under the guard of Major Muggeridge. On 1 December, Duff Cooper saw Wodehouse's stepson-in-law, Peter Cazalet. They agreed 'that the best thing that could happen would be if the French would agree to get him moved out of Paris and allowed to live quietly in the country'.

When George Orwell came to Paris, Muggeridge took him round to introduce him to Wodehouse, a meeting which stimulated Orwell to write an article in Wodehouse's defence. It is hard to imagine a more dissimilar pair. Plum thought Orwell 'a gloomy sort of chap'. Orwell, on the other hand, recognized that Wodehouse, who lived in the fantasy world of his own creation, made an ideal whipping-boy in the demagogic atmosphere of war socialism.

After a brief sojourn near Fontainebleau, the Wodehouses moved back to Paris. They were left undisturbed, feeding their meat ration to Wonder, until they finally left for the United States in 1947.

7

War Tourists and Ritzkrieg

In the weeks following the Liberation, Paris experienced an Anglo-Saxon influx which far surpassed the days of the Versailles peace conference. The very first arrivals included intelligence officers, counter-espionage experts and journalists. Within a week or two, the proportion of those simply 'wangling a joy-ride' from London – including the wives, or future wives, of men already there – gathered pace.

A more permanent population began to assemble during the middle of September, with officers posted to the city on official business, either attached to embassies or to SHAEF (Supreme Headquarters Allied Expeditionary Force). British staff officers, with red bands round their service dress caps, were sometimes – to their furious embarrassment – mistaken for Soviet officers by French Communists, who acclaimed them with clenched-fist salutes and fervent expressions of admiration for the Red Army.

The first British officer to enter Paris was Lieutenant-Colonel Lord Rothschild. Victor Rothschild, in his wartime role of bomb-disposal expert, slipped into Paris ahead of his unit and went straight to the Rothschild town house on the Avenue de Marigny. He wanted to make sure that he requisitioned it for his own counter-sabotage team before the Americans took it over.

His group's first task was to locate booby-traps and demolition charges left behind by the Germans, and make them safe. The rest of the unit, which included his future wife, Tess Mayor, arrived soon afterwards to work with the French Deuxième Bureau, hunting for arms and caches of explosives which might be used by a fifth column.

Muggeridge joined Rothschild at the Avenue de Marigny, since the Services Spéciaux to which he was attached had not yet set up shop. After a very good lunch, they decided to make their position official with the British military authorities, and set off for the Roger & Gallet building in the rue du Faubourg Saint-Honoré, where they had heard that a British Force Headquarters had been established. The brigadier to whom they reported, immaculate in service dress with red tabs, took this very scruffy pair for impostors. As soon as he realized that he was talking to Lord Rothschild, however, he became positively deferential. It was the sort of behaviour that Rothschild loathed.

Victor Rothschild was a man of many parts and many paradoxes. Scientist, academic, and government adviser by profession, he was also, in his private capacity, a socialist, a millionaire, a jazz pianist, and a peer who both hated privilege and enjoyed it. The servants at the Avenue Marigny, headed by Monsieur Félix, the *maître d'hôtel*, were well aware of his foibles. They could not believe how meagre British army rations were, and since Victor Rothschild refused to eat better food than his soldiers, Muggeridge had to go off and scrounge K rations from the Americans.

The German occupiers had looked after the house on the Avenue Marigny very well. The heavy furniture and decoration in the '*style Rothschild*' of the 1860s were untouched. Muggeridge asked Monsieur Félix why he thought the Luftwaffe general who had occupied the house had behaved so well. 'Hitlers come and go, Monsieur,' came the reply, 'but Rothschilds go on for ever.'

Few of the journalists then starting to pour in knew Paris better than Lee Miller. She had been the muse, lover and apprentice of the Surrealist photographer Man Ray between 1929 and 1932. Now she had come in the splendidly original role of war photographer for *Vogue*. In her US war correspondent's uniform, she went straight to the Place de l'Odéon. There she found the painter and theatre designer Christian Bérard and his lover, Boris Kochno. They took her to see Picasso in his studio on the rue des Grands Augustins. Picasso, for whom she had sat before the war, embraced her, declaring that she was the first Allied soldier he had seen, and that he wanted to paint her again, this time in her uniform. They went to Picasso's local bistro in the same street, Le Catalan, and Lee handed over her K rations to augment the lunch. Over the next few days she tracked down other friends from Surrealist days, including Jean Cocteau, and Paul Éluard and his wife Nusch, who was looking skeletal.

'Paris was liberated,' Picasso later said to his friend Brassaï, the photographer, 'but I was besieged, and I still am.' It seemed that everyone wanted to visit him in his studio.

Cleve Gray, a young American painter serving in the US army, longed to meet Picasso. Summoning up his courage, he went to the door of Picasso's studio and knocked. Jaime Sabartès, Picasso's friend and general factotum, stuck his head out of an upstairs window and peered down. He was very short-sighted. 'Who's there?' he called. 'I'm an American painter,' Gray shouted back, 'and I want to meet Picasso.'

It was late morning, but Picasso was just getting out of bed dressed in nothing but his underwear. The room had no pictures on the walls. The scene that followed was a Bohemian version of the *lever du roi*. Picasso stood by the side of the bed holding a copy of the Communist newspaper *L'Humanité* in one hand while he held out the other for Sabartès to thread it through a shirt sleeve, then he transferred the newspaper to the other hand while Sabartès pulled on the other sleeve. Picasso was just about to join the Communist Party.

Then Daniel-Henry Kahnweiler, Picasso's dealer, walked in.

This was their first meeting for four years. The two men greeted each other with great warmth and effusion, though Kahnweiler was evidently irritated to find somebody else there.

They all trooped upstairs to the studio, a large, long room with heavy old beams and a floor of well-worn hexagon tiles covered by the odd small rug. Paintings finished during the Occupation were propped against the wall, including all those which Picasso was about to exhibit in the first post-liberation salon. The collection of frames, easels and a large stepladder, with a platform and pulpit for working on large canvases, gave the impression of a lumber room. Almost as fascinating as Picasso's sculptures was his huge cast-iron stove with bulbous pipes ascending in pillared layers, like a Jain temple.

Picasso pointed to Gray's boots and said, 'Look at them. Aren't they extraordinary?' Gray did not know what to do. Should he follow the Arab custom, and take them off immediately to present them as a gift? Picasso might even render them immortal with a study. But if he did, how could he explain their disappearance on return to his unit? They were government property, and he might face serious charges for selling them.

Charles Collingwood, the famously good-looking reporter for CBS radio, toured Montparnasse with Pamela Churchill, who had come to set up a club for British troops on leave. Collingwood, however, was feeling rather bashful, and certainly hoped not to be recognized. To scoop his rivals, he had made a pre-recorded report announcing the liberation of Paris, but this had been broadcast by mistake forty-eight hours before Leclerc's troops reached the city. Parisians had listened in anger and disbelief to the reports of worldwide celebration while fighting continued all around them.

Almost everyone in London with a good excuse made sure of a trip to Paris as soon as possible after the Liberation. Like many from the OSS office in London, Evangeline Bruce, a future ambassadress but at that time responsible for creating personal histories for the false papers of secret agents, hiked a pillion ride on the back of an OSS motorbicycle for a tour of central Paris.

Mary Welsh, who had worked for the London bureau of *Time*, *Life*, and *Fortune* throughout the war, managed to reach Paris in time to cover de Gaulle's triumph down the Champs-Élysées. Once she had filed her reports, she went round to the Place Vendôme and straight up to Hemingway's room in the Ritz.

Marlene Dietrich also used a room at the Ritz as her Paris base while she travelled back and forth to the front singing to American troops. Hemingway had known her for ten years, and they were still close – she used to wander into his bathroom in the Ritz and chat to him while he shaved – but he emphasized that he had never slept with her.

Hemingway did not stay only at the Ritz. He also used the Hotel Scribe near the Opéra, which had been taken over as a centre for war correspondents. The lines of olive-green US army staff cars and jeeps with large white stars made the place look like a headquarters, an impression reinforced by the cluster of Allied flags over the entrance. The Parisians were envious of its privileged rations. Simone de Beauvoir, who visited the Scribe with a French journalist on *Combat*, wrote disapprovingly: 'It was an American enclave in the heart of Paris: white bread, fresh eggs, jam, sugar and Spam.'

The Hotel Scribe rapidly became a subject of folklore. The rooms were full of military impedimenta – jerrycans of petrol, ration packs, waterbottles, weapons and ammunition. One visitor recalled seeing in every window of the central light-well a journalist in an army shirt with a cigarette hanging out of his mouth, tapping away furiously.

During the course of that autumn and winter, the Scribe's inhabitants included Robert Capa, William Shirer, Bill Paley, Sam White, Cy Sulzberger and Harold Callender of the *New York Times*; William Saroyan; Helen Kirkpatrick of the

Chicago Daily News; Janet Flanner, the *New Yorker* diarist for
Paris since 1925; Virginia Cowles, who had covered the fall of
France in 1940, and her friend Martha Gellhorn.

George Orwell, a much later arrival, was delighted to be in
Paris in uniform. Having heard that Hemingway, whom he had
never met, was also at the Scribe, Orwell went to his room and
knocked on his door.

'I'm Eric Blair,' he announced hesitantly.

Hemingway was packing. He looked up, displeased at seeing
a British war correspondent: he was going through a strongly
anti-British phase. 'Well, what the ying hell do you want?'

'I'm George Orwell.'

'Why the zing hell didn't you say so?' bellowed Hemingway.
He pushed the suitcases aside, bent down under the bed and
emerged with a bottle of Scotch. 'Have a drink. Have a double.
Straight or with water, there's no soda.'

Orwell had more in common – including the same tutor at
Eton and a love of Dickens, Kipling and Hopkins – with the
philosopher A. J. Ayer, who was also in Paris at the time.
Freddie Ayer, the author of *Language, Truth and Logic*, had been
an SOE officer and had a roving commission reporting on the
liberated areas of France. For this task, he had acquired a large
chauffeur-driven Bugatti in which he installed his army radio
transmitter. He had now returned to Paris to work as an attaché
at the British Embassy, where he impressed important guests by
being able to explain what existentialism was.

In January 1945, Hemingway was visited by Sartre and
Simone de Beauvoir. They found him in bed with a heavy cold,
wearing a green newspaperman's eyeshade.

Hemingway promptly grabbed Sartre by the hand enthusiasti-
cally. '*Vous êtes un général!*' he exclaimed, embracing him. '*Moi,
je ne suis qu'un capitaine: vous êtes un général.*' Bottles of Scotch
were produced, and the drinking began. Sartre later admitted
that it was one of the few occasions when he had passed out
from alcohol. Around three in the morning, he recovered; and,
opening one eye, watched in astonishment as Hemingway tip-

toed round the room collecting up the empty bottles to hide them from members of the hotel staff.

Allied officers benefited from what might be termed unofficial privileges in Paris. Establishments, including all the *bonnes adresses* of the Occupation, were compulsively generous to senior Allied officers. They were allowed to dine free at the Tour d'Argent, they were given scent for their wives by Guerlain, and shirt-makers fell over each other to offer them prices so special that they were almost free. Even the grandest institutions were not averse to political insurance in these uncertain times.

The Jockey Club, at 2 rue Rabelais, quickly offered member-ship to a number of senior American and British officers. The British military attaché, Brigadier Denis Daly, received 'the impression that members of the Jockey Club had very probably supported the Pétain régime' and that they felt it would be 'wise to have the support of the British and the Americans during the months to come'. At lunch, the Duc de Doudeauville plied Daly with questions about the menace of the Red Army. When Daly said that there was no doubt that the war could not have been won without the Russians and that from a 'realistic point of view' the Allies should therefore be grateful, Doudeauville ap-peared 'considerably shaken'.

This highly advantageous state of affairs for Allied officers was soon somewhat curtailed. For example, British officers were no longer allowed into restaurants in uniform, since most of the good ones depended on black market produce. To circumvent this inconvenience, Maxim's in the rue Royale was taken over as an officers' club, and Albert, the *maître d'hôtel* who had bowed to their tables almost every German officer from Reichsmarschall Goering down, was soon doing the same for their enemies. The French army, not to be outdone, took over Ciro's as an officers' club, and Charles Trenet and Edith Piaf went to sing there.

With a large number of British and American officers avid for Parisian cooking, restaurants reopened with startling speed. For the richer officers, Prunier and the Méditerranée in the Place de l'Odéon were soon serving fresh seafood in a triumph of black market enterprise over appalling communications. Lucas Carton in the Place de la Madeleine, perhaps the greatest of all Parisian restaurants, possessed an outstanding advantage over its rivals. Having bricked up its wine cellars (which run right under the Place de la Madeleine itself) just as the Germans entered Paris in 1940, it could still offer the very best vintages.

Parisian night-life was in great demand, especially among those on leave from the front. At least 60 per cent of the audience at the Folies Bergère were in uniform. Soldiers were attracted to the *bals publics* or dance-halls, which, having been banned throughout the Occupation, reopened with the Liberation. The most popular were the establishments on the rue de Lappe near the Place de la Bastille and the numerous *bals musette* around the edge of the city. The musicians were amateurs, working part-time, who gave rousing versions of popular songs on accordions and percussion instruments.

The next tier up – *les dancings* – included the more sophisticated dance-halls and night-spots from the Moulin de la Galette to some of the smarter places on the Champs-Élysées, employing almost all the capital's 1,500 professional *musiciens de danse*. At the top were places like Monseigneur in the rue d'Amsterdam, an ornate and expensive establishment, heavily White Russian, with tzigane violinists serenading the diners. You went to Monseigneur, remarked one of Martha Gellhorn's characters in her collection of short stories, *A Honeyed Peace*, only if 'beginning a romance'.

The revival of public dancing was short-lived. At the end of October the provisional government banned it again, this time in response to a press campaign claiming that too many families were in mourning to permit such levity. On 16 January, cabarets and nightclubs were also closed.

The Syndicat des Artistes Musiciens de Paris denounced the measure as 'a prudery out of touch with the virility demanded by the war'. Dancing, they argued, had never been forbidden in London throughout the Blitz or the V1 rocket attacks, because the authorities realized how important it was for morale. Dance-halls used less electricity, because their customers did not like too much brightness, and gaiety must be kept up in the capital: '*Afin que PARIS reste PARIS!*' But protests were in vain. Dancing in public places was not permitted again until April 1945, just before the German surrender, and even then organizations representing deportees and prisoners of war objected.

Many of the most expensive nightclubs ignored the January ban, but they received a shock the night after it came into effect. The police raided six establishments and took a total of 300 customers off to unheated cells in police stations. One of the clubs targeted was the Monseigneur. Those unfortunate enough to have picked Wednesday 17 January to begin their romance got off to a chilly start.

8

The *Épuration Sauvage*

Whenever the Allies liberated a town or village during the advance across northern France, they often found that the first victims of what became known as the *épuration sauvage* – the unofficial purge – were the most vulnerable members of the community. 'At Saint-Sauveur-le-Vicomte yesterday,' David Bruce wrote in his diary, 'the inhabitants had shaved the heads of twelve women who had been sleeping with German officers and soldiers. They must henceforth slink about the village. The Frenchmen with us think it is a very fitting and salutary punishment.' Six weeks later, he discovered that a production line for head-shaving had been established in the Prefecture at Chartres as soon as the last Germans had been rounded up.

Among the accused were married women whose husbands were in Germany as prisoners or conscripts of the STO. In their case, '*collaboration horizontale*' seemed like a double betrayal. Yet sleeping with a German might have been the only way to keep children from starvation.

Some women were subject to even greater degradation. There are photographs of women stripped naked, tarred with swastikas, forced to give Nazi salutes, then paraded in the streets to be abused, with their illegitimate child in their arms. There are also reports in some areas of women tortured, even killed, during these barbaric rites. In the 18th *arrondissement*, a working-class area, a prostitute who had served German clients was kicked to death. Victims were not just working-class women. Pastor Boegner recorded the shaving of women's heads in the 7th *arrondissement*, and there were a few cases of women of fashion receiving similar treatment, including the wife of one prince, and the daughter of another – Jacqueline de Broglie, whose mother was Daisy Fellowes, and whose Austrian husband, Alfred Kraus, had been accused of betraying members of the Resistance.

Head-shaving is said to have been inflicted on a well-known French count who had fallen for the martial attractions of the conquerors. He had earlier been arrested by the *feldgendarmerie* for having enticed German soldiers to indulge in *Unzucht zwischen Männern*, but when the prisoner replied that his sexual tendency was not only honoured by the ancient Greeks but practised by the Führer himself, his captors threw him back on to the street in consternation.

A number of Resistance leaders tried to stop head-shaving. The Communist military commander, Colonel Rol-Tanguy, had posters run off and pasted up which warned of reprisals against any further incidents. Another leader, René Porte, respected in his *quartier* not least for his strength, bashed the heads together of a group of youths he found shaving a woman's head. One woman is said to have shouted at her shearers, 'My ass is international, but my heart is French.'

A volatile mixture – moral outrage, suppressed fear, jealousy and guilt – seems to have produced a hysteria which was quickly spent. In too many cases the women were made scapegoats for the whole community. Whether men who had collaborated escaped more lightly as a result, remains a difficult question to answer.

Most Allied soldiers seem to have been shocked or sickened by incidents of head-shaving, but in the battle zone the execution without trial of traitors provoked far fewer objections. There was a strong feeling among American, British and Canadian forces that, not having suffered the trauma of defeat and occupation, they had no right to sit in judgement on France's private agony.

Political passion rejects shades of grey, yet during the four years of occupation France had witnessed every paradox imaginable, from anti-semites who saved Jews to *bien-pensant* anti-fascists who betrayed them, from black marketeers who helped the Resistance to Resistance heroes who pocketed 'expropriations'. There were also examples of saintly self-sacrifice as well as cases of the blackest evil, but these two extremes represented tiny minorities and were seized upon by extremists to demonstrate their point.

The philosopher Isaiah Berlin, who visited France many times during the immediate post-war period, came up with an informal, but useful, definition of acceptable conduct during the Occupation. To survive, you might have needed to do business with the Germans, whether as a waiter, a shoemaker, a writer or an actor, but 'you did not have to be cosy with them'.

For many there was no such thing as a good German, and, for the Communist Party especially, the notion of a good Pétainist was treason in itself. All the crimes of the Germans in France were heaped upon Vichy, clouding an already complicated issue still further. The Communists' anger was both genuine and artificial. Their strength of feeling over Vichy's selection of Communist hostages for execution, or over its close cooperation with the Gestapo and the dispatch of French workers to slave labour in Germany, cannot be doubted. Yet there was a deliberate political purpose behind their condemnation of Vichy. The greater the purge of every part of the administration which had continued to work under Vichy, from the police to the post office, the greater the opportunity for Communist control after the war.

One can define acceptable and unacceptable behaviour under enemy occupation, but to decide degrees of guilt or fitting punishment in the strong emotions of the period is difficult. However, it seems to have been generally agreed that the denunciation of fellow French men and women to the Germans was a shooting offence.

News of last-minute massacres of political prisoners carried out by German forces just before they retreated, and details of barbaric Gestapo tortures, filled the Resistance press and fuelled the strong desire for vengeance.

Morever, the Resistance did attract ill-educated youths who were prepared to join any group, no matter what its ideology, as long as it gave them a gun. It also attracted many last-minute conversions: collaborators trying to efface a dubious record by being *plus résistant que les résistants*, as well as opportunists who saw the chance for plunder. Although a despicable minority, their crimes, along with the excesses of some genuine resistants, tarnished the reputation of the movement as a whole. One of the most notorious gangs of brigands, a hundred and fifty strong, operated in the Loire valley, where Michel Debré had been appointed Commissioner of the Republic. They had collaborated with the Germans, then fought against them at the Liberation. In the early autumn of 1944 they continued to loot and kill until their leader was arrested, largely thanks to the efforts of Debré.

In addition to head-shaving and summary executions, the *épuration sauvage* included sentences handed out by FFI military tribunals and by Comités de Libération; looting under the guise of searches; and the lynching of prisoners set free by conventional courts. Many of those executed had committed appalling crimes. But since the Germans and most of the *miliciens* responsible for the worst crimes had departed, people who were only marginally guilty, as well as some hapless innocents, were killed out of rage and frustration. In a number of cases, both German soldiers and collaborators were saved by French veterans of the Great War who, with considerable courage, told the would-be executioners that they had no right to kill anybody without a trial.

The provisional government's efforts to put a skeleton administration into place to restore law and order were impressive, but a new Commissioner of the Republic could not hope to exert authority from the first moment. However much the Gaullists wished to maintain the fiction that they were simply reintroducing 'Republican legality', the system, in many places, had to be rebuilt almost from nothing. Often, the local Liberation Committees simply ignored the authority of representatives of the provisional government.

On 26 August, the day that General de Gaulle marched down the Champs-Élysées, a group of FFI arrested the consul-general of the Republic of San Marino at his house and took him off, without any explanation, to their improvised headquarters at the Lycée Buffon. It is possible that the FFI militiamen had confused the ancient Republic of San Marino with Mussolini's puppet Republic of Salo. In any case, they took the consul-general's money, jewels and car. He was then transferred to Fresnes prison and released on 7 November without any charges having been brought against him.

Malcolm Muggeridge was invited by an FFI group to accompany them on their nightly purges. They were 'very young, with that curious hunted animal look that street-life gives'. He was taken to their base, an apartment on the Avenue Foch which had been occupied by the Gestapo, as the 'empty champagne bottles and discarded erotica' showed.

They boasted about their executions, took cigarette-cases, jewels and money, which were recorded and locked up in a strong-box to be handed over later. But what became of the booty afterwards was never revealed. 'Considering their youth,' wrote Muggeridge, 'they behaved with horrifying callousness, arrogance and brutality.' He was not surprised to hear later that their leader had been arrested and found to have a record of collaboration.

The most notorious false resistant was Dr Marcel Pétiot. Between 1942 and 1944, Pétiot set up his own escape line. Jews, members of the Resistance, even gangsters being hunted by the police, were directed to the doctor, who said he could arrange safe passages to Argentina. On the pretext that the Argentinian authorities demanded inoculations, he gave his clients a lethal injection of cyanide, then watched them die in agony. Pétiot disposed of the bodies efficiently, at least at the start of his grisly career: they were dissolved in quicklime, and what was left was incinerated in the boiler.

Rough justice, in the form of severe beatings, was another form of reprisal. French railwaymen, known as *cheminots*, had played a courageous and important role in the Resistance, sabotaging German rail movements. Many were members of the Communist Party and a considerable number had been shot for their activities. It is not surprising that the treatment of colleagues suspected of collaboration was brutal. During the autumn of 1944, seventy-seven managers, stationmasters and senior engineers were 'made incapable of working'. None, however, is recorded as killed.

It was not just the FFI who mistreated captives. The old Brigades de Surveillance du Territoire, which remobilized themselves at the Liberation and purged the police, were controversial in their methods. Even women were said to have been tortured in the camp of Queueleu near Metz. 'The BST of Metz,' according to one lawyer's report, 'were unashamed of using methods for which the Gestapo was condemned – prolonged ducking in a bath – freezing – the plank torture – bastinado, etc . . .'

In Paris, those accused of collaboration by Resistance groups, or denounced anonymously by a neighbour or concierge, were usually arrested early in the morning before they had a chance to dress.

A group of FFI burst into the apartment of the writer Alfred Fabre-Luce to arrest him, but he managed to slip out of the service entrance. (Fabre-Luce was doubly unfortunate: although a Pétainist, he had been imprisoned by the Germans for an anti-

Nazi book he wrote.) The *fifis*, not finding their intended captive, took his old butler away instead.

Fabre-Luce's wife Charlotte rang her brother, Prince Jean-Louis de Faucigny-Lucinge. He rushed round to 42 rue de Bassano, where an impromptu revolutionary tribunal had been established. Lucinge spotted the butler through a glass-panelled door, and also the Duchesse de Brissac, her hair dishevelled, wearing a fur coat which had been thrown on over her underclothes.

As soon as Alfred Fabre-Luce heard that his butler had been taken in his stead, he went straight to the rue Bassano to give himself up. The duchess, whose romantic friendships with German officers had become too well known, was taken off to the Conciergerie 'like Marie Antoinette'. Lucinge telephoned her husband to warn him what had happened. The duke thanked him, but never mentioned the episode again. Most of those accused, however, were taken to police stations or the town hall of the *arrondissement*. The pianist Alfred Cortot was released after three days and three nights on a police-station bench.

The next step was transfer to the Prefecture of Police on the Île de la Cité. Many arrived at the Prefecture literally shaking with fear. Others were unbowed. Comte Jean de Castellane, younger brother of Boni de Castellane, the great *fin de siècle* swell described in his heyday as 'rotten with chic', proved worthy of his family's traditions. One of the guards told Castellane to remove his shoelaces and braces, the normal procedure to stop prisoners hanging themselves. He regarded the man with a thunderstruck expression: 'If you take away my braces, I will leave immediately.'

After a length of time which could vary from a couple of hours to a few days, prisoners were taken across to the ancient Conciergerie of blackened stone and pepperpot towers on the Quai de l'Horloge. From the Conciergerie, after a few hours, days, or even weeks, some prisoners were transferred to the holding camp at the Vélodrome d'Hiver, that stadium of dreadful memory where the Jews had been taken after the 'Great Round-up'. Then they would be sent either to Fresnes prison, or to the camp at Drancy, the former staging-post for Jews before they were forced on to cattle trucks bound for Germany. A number of women prisoners were sent to the fort of Noisy-le-Sec. Many prisoners were also held at the Santé prison – ill-named, since it possessed only twelve showers for a population which now numbered nearly 3,000 prisoners.

Drancy was completely run by the FFI for the first few weeks after the Liberation, to the frustration of the authorities. The Prefect of Police had no control at all, and visitors were not welcome. Pastor Boegner, who finally managed to gain entry to Drancy on 15 September, discovered cells that measured three and a half metres by one and three-quarters, holding six people, with only two mattresses between them. Luizet at least achieved one objective, quite rapidly. On 20 September, Drancy was 'liberated' from the *fifis* and returned to the regular prison service.

The main prison for those accused of collaboration was Fresnes. It held so many celebrities that one inmate, a 'trustie' who helped with the catering, used to take his autograph book with him on meal rounds. There were many members of 'le Tout-Paris de la collaboration', like the film-star Arletty and the actor-playwright Sacha Guitry, who had met either at the receptions of the Luftwaffe General Hanesse, or in Otto Abetz's salon. Albert Blaser, the head waiter at Maxim's, was also briefly in Fresnes, as were the singer Tino Rossi and the publisher Bernard Grasset. Rossi was never in danger of execution, but that did not stop one of his female fans from offering to be shot in his place.

In Fresnes, Jean de Castellane was pleased to see Sacha Guitry. Castellane was something of a chatterbox, and since Guitry possessed a similar taste for *jeux de mots*, the two men made running jokes on the unsavoury conditions in the prison and on their own likely fate. Guitry later observed that beds which had been occupied by unexpectedly released prisoners were thought lucky, and people clamoured to take them over.

Many inmates tried to depict themselves as victims of a second Terror. But savage as the *épuration* was in some places, this was hardly September 1793. Outraged at their treatment, few asked themselves what the camps and prisons had been like under the Vichy government. One well-dressed woman, given a palliasse to sleep on, asked for another. When told that prisoners were only allowed one each she replied that it would be needed for her maid, whom she wished to summon to look after her. Daisy Fellowes's daughter, Emmeline de Casteja, served five months in Fresnes locked up with prostitutes. Their chief amusement, she told a friend later, was to jiggle their bare breasts at the men in the block opposite.

Before the war, Fresnes had no more than one prisoner for each of its 1,500 cells. Now there were 4,500 inmates. The *bloc sanitaire* was even more crowded than the *bloc pénitentiaire*, because many were unfit for the rigours of prison life. A considerable number were elderly, and unaccustomed to a diet of dried vegetables and noodles.

At the beginning, prisoners had no right to a lawyer. Whenever they wrote letters, the guards usually read them and made sure they were never delivered. The only contact with the outside world was established through four representatives of the French Red Cross. These four ladies were swamped with work. Whenever possible, they obtained the address of each prisoner and a telephone number where they could contact the family to inform them. In many cases the families had had no news and had been left destitute when the breadwinner was arrested.

The work of the French Red Cross was greatly encouraged by the Prefect of Police, Charles Luizet, who was very keen to bring Fresnes back under control. He had managed to get the FFI guards out of Drancy three weeks after the Liberation, and wanted to purge the 'auxiliary' guards in Fresnes. It is alleged that in the early days of the Liberation a number of prisoners were taken out in the middle of the night and shot, and a few beaten to death; but since there were no reliable records of who had been arrested, and since the guards refused to release the names of those they held, the number of cases is impossible to assess.

Partly prompted by a campaign in the Communist press claiming that traitors were living in style, the Ministry of the Interior commissioned a report on the prison. 'It must be acknowledged,' wrote the inspector-general of prisons, 'that the auxiliaries have let us down badly.' Jewels and money had been stolen from prisoners, and a flourishing black market existed. The guards charged prisoners 300 francs for a packet of cigarettes, 3,000 for a bottle of alcohol, and sold extra clothes when the weather turned cold. They also took bribes for turning a blind eye during lawyers' visits.

Escoffier, the director of the prison, tried to appeal to the better nature and patriotism of the guards, but his efforts clearly did little good, 'because trafficking continued just as before during the following months'. The Prefect of Police then sent in some of his men in disguise, but they were quickly spotted and had to be withdrawn before they could do anything useful. Altogether only ten guards were arrested in over six months.

The chaotic state of records and dossiers meant that many people were held for several months and then released for lack of evidence. 'Many of the dossiers were empty,' recorded the jurist Charpentier. 'Others only contained anonymous denunciations. The worst thing was to have no dossier at all.' Without a dossier, you could not even see a *juge d'instruction* to have your case heard.

On 21 September, General de Gaulle told Boegner that there had been 6,000 arrests in Paris, but that may well have represented only those processed through the Prefecture of Police. Altogether in France, around a third of a million dossiers were opened on the basis of accusations. It would appear that the main backlog of untried prisoners, particularly of people who should never have been arrested in the first place, began to be cleared by the end of 1944. Pastor Boegner was struck by the decline in the numbers of prisoners in January 1945. But release did not necessarily represent the end of the affair.

Some stories are so terrible that they are hard to believe. Roger Codou, a Communist veteran of the International Brigades, reached Lyons in October 1944. He had been summoned back by the party from Algeria, officially to work in the Cabinet of the Communist minister, Charles Tillon, but also to help set up a secret factory in Paris for manufacturing false papers. In Lyons, a Communist major from the FTP looked after him. During their time together he took Codou out to the military airfield of Bron. In August, the Germans had massacred 109 prisoners from Montluc prison on the runway, now used by French bombers flying over enemy territory ahead of de Lattre's 1st Army. One of the pilots asked: 'Have you got any customers for us tonight?' The major then explained to Codou that, as a fitting punishment for traitors, any Vichyist prisoners acquitted by the courts in Lyons were kidnapped, bound and gagged, then taken to the airfield after dark and put in the bomb-bay of an aircraft on top of the bombs. They were then dropped on 'their friends' during the next sortie. Nearly fifty years later, Codou still did not know whether this was a ghastly revelation or told only to shock.

The scale and nature of the *épuration* is bitterly contested to this day. The wildest figures – 100,000 to 120,000 victims during the Occupation and after the Liberation – have long been discredited. Yet although the difference between the estimates has now narrowed considerably – approximately 10,800 according to the Institut de l'Histoire du Temps Présent, and around 14,000 to 15,000 according to Henri Amouroux – strong disagreements remain. They reflect the conflicting attitudes of two generations

– the older one which experienced the dilemmas and sought to justify many of the compromises; and the younger one which refused to condone Vichy's assistance in deporting Jews to Germany.

There is, however, a general agreement that some 30,000 French were executed during the Occupation. Out of that figure, the Milice probably killed between 2,000 and 3,000 – a tenth of the total, or less. The Milice was without doubt responsible for a large proportion of the other deaths, having in many cases provided information. Yet nobody can yet give an accurate idea of how many French men and women were betrayed to the Germans by the French of Vichy, or simply by neighbours with a grudge.

The battle lines of the debate have tended to concentrate on how many people were killed by the Resistance. This turns on the huge problem of defining the whole process. Do you include the settling of private accounts? Do you include the victims of criminal gangs who operated under Resistance colours?

The figures in certain areas are still contested. The *département* of the Seine, with the city of Paris, had the greatest population. Yet the Institut d'Histoire du Temps Présent lists a total of only 208 killings by members of the Resistance during the war, of which 57 took place after the Liberation. And while it is true that there were no mass killings in the capital, there were countless deaths in suspicious circumstances in the sixteen months following the Liberation. For example, from September 1944 there was a very marked increase in the number of deaths listed as 'violent death of undetermined nature'. From August 1944 until the end of the year they amounted to 424, while in the five months before the Liberation there had been only 259 cases. Murder by firearm more than doubled, from 42 cases in 1943 to 107 in 1944.

How, for example, does one classify the case of the blacklisted publisher Denoël, who had brought out Céline's *Voyage au bout de la nuit* in 1932, and more recently the work of the pro-Nazi polemicist, Lucien Rebatet? Denoël, a Belgian, was found killed beside his car in December 1945. This may well have been a common crime, for there were many that particular winter, but one cannot rule out the possibility that the motive was political.

The *épuration sauvage* throughout France was not a phenomenon which burnt itself out within a couple of months of the Liberation. There was another surge of killings in January and February 1945, perhaps influenced by the fears raised during the Ardennes offensive. A larger wave, however, occurred in June 1945 following the shock of the deportees returning from the prison, labour and concentration camps. Many returning prisoners had scores to settle. Almost any Vichy official was at risk, however indirect his involvement in the policy of sending workers or prisoners to Germany. Others were frequently regarded as guilty simply for having supported a regime capable of sending French men and women to such a fate.

According to the less than comprehensive files of the Renseignements Généraux, the number of assassinations '*de caractère politique*' did not begin to tail off until the second part of August 1945. Between 3 July and 13 August there had been 410 killings in a total of twenty *départements*. A small revival was recorded later in October. The most striking statistic, however, is revealed in the detailed figures for the week of 13 August 1945. Out of 37 killings, 33 were carried out by explosives. Unfortunately, this is the only week for which such a breakdown is provided. One must of course be extremely wary of reading too much into it; yet perhaps it sheds light on the curiously high number of people listed as dead from 'gas explosions'.

In the Archives de la Ville de Paris, figures for causes of death in the metropolis are scrupulously broken down, even if the categories are not always consistent. From September 1944 the casualties from gas explosions increase dramatically. In 1942, 184 people died in gas explosions during September, October and December. In 1943, 183 died during this period. But in 1944, no fewer than 660 died. Even allowing for pipes fractured during the fighting and the frequent interruptions of supply, it is hard to explain such a massive rise. The possibility must be acknowledged that a portion of the German demolition charges, discovered at the time of General von Choltitz's surrender, might have been used for 'popular justice' or private revenge, with the explosions listed in the most convenient category by officials later.

Alfred Fabre-Luce wrote that 'France is a country where, in revolutionary times, hysteria is tempered by corruption'. Although partly true of many upheavals, this view is unduly cynical in the case of France in 1944. The restraint on hysteria came almost entirely from examples of physical and moral courage, men and women standing up and daring to say that it was wrong to punish people without a proper trial.

The real argument in the historical debate is essentially a question of degree. How brutal was the *épuration sauvage* in its context? If the reaction after the occupation of France is compared with those of the other occupied countries of north-western Europe – Belgium, Holland, Denmark and Norway – 'the *épuration* in France was moderate', according to Jean-Pierre Rioux. His colleague Henry Rousso has argued, on the other hand, that if one compares the number of executions with the number of French who served in German uniform, then it was much harsher than elsewhere. Accurate atrocity figures are of course vital, but the debate they inspire can quickly turn into a moral quagmire.

Part Two
L'État, c'est de Gaulle

9

Provisional Government

The euphoric welcome accorded to General de Gaulle when he marched down the Champs-Élysées appeared to confirm his authority as unchallengeable. But the relationship between the provisional government and the Resistance was still unresolved. French Communists had rightly suspected during the Occupation that his policy, aided by the British, was to 'deform' the popular nature of the Resistance and 'prevent at any price a true national insurrection'. They even tried to claim that the Allies had held back from Paris in August 1944, in the hope that the Germans would crush the largely Communist-inspired insurrection. This was a shameless attempt to counter criticism of the Red Army's deliberate failure to come to the aid of Polish nationalists during the Warsaw uprising.

De Gaulle was convinced that the Communists had wanted to seize power just before Leclerc's troops reached the city. 'De Gaulle,' wrote Georgi Dimitrov in a briefing for Molotov and Stalin, 'is afraid of the French Communists and considers their activity a threat to his authority, but he is obliged to take into consideration their power established during the clandestine struggle.'

Even after the triumph of the Liberation, the provisional government's authority remained tenuous, especially in the provinces, cut off from the capital by the destruction of roads, bridges and railway lines. De Gaulle also knew that if France was to have any claim to a seat at the conference table alongside the Americans, British and Russians, then all her available troops, both regular army and freshly brigaded FFI contingents, had to make a conspicuous contribution to the war effort by continuing the advance on Germany. He therefore could not hold back regular troops to assure law and order. This also meant leaving in place the rest of the FFI and 'patriotic militias', which often contained the least reliable elements.

Travelling across France was not easy, even for a government official with car, petrol coupons and every *laissez-passer* imaginable. At towns and villages, vehicles would be stopped by militiamen or a sort of 'committee of public safety'. who would not only study the documents of all passengers in laborious detail but often subject them to an examination in patriotism. Paris, like Madrid in 1936, may have had great symbolic importance, but decrees issued there carried little weight in the countryside, especially in the south-west.

Well before the invasion of Normandy, General de Gaulle and his entourage had foreseen the main problems they would face. Several months before D-Day they had begun to select men to take over from Vichy officials in the provinces and re-establish Republican legality before it was usurped by revolutionary committees.

The provisional government could never hope to produce a fresh and untainted state apparatus to drop into place all over France. It had to work with existing institutions, most of them compromised. To curb the excesses of popular justice, gendarmes, even if they had worked with the Germans, were needed on the streets. The vast majority of magistrates who had sworn allegiance to Marshal Pétain would have to return to their court-rooms. Civil servants who had loyally served the Vichy régime were required back at their desks. And to revive the pulverized economy, factories had to be re-started with managers who had in many cases collaborated with the Germans. The instruments charged with this difficult programme, each responsible for a region, were called Commissaires de la République.

Their first priority was to provide food and essential services for the population. Claude Bouchinet-Serreulles, who remained with the Ministry of the Interior as Commissaire de la République at large, emphasized that food was the key to almost everything. Without it, public order would collapse.

Neither law nor order existed in many areas during the first few months of the *épuration*. In November, some twenty former members of the Resistance broke into a prison. They seized a colonel who had commanded a reprisal expedition against the *maquis* and, contemptuously ignoring the fact that he had been spared the death sentence by de Gaulle, shot him in a nearby field. Louis Closon in the north of France had to cope with 30,000 liberated Red Army prisoners of war who had 'a provoking attitude, considering themselves to be in conquered territory'. But probably the most chaotic situation in the whole of France existed in the south-west, around Toulouse.

'At the time of the Liberation,' wrote the philosopher A. J. Ayer, on a semi-official tour of the south-west for SOE, 'the whole of the area was in the hands of a series of feudal lords whose power and influence was strangely similar to that of their fifteenth-century Gascon counterparts.'

One of the most powerful of these modern barons was Colonel George Starr, the senior SOE officer in the south-west of France. Starr was an immensely tough man, a mining engineer who had proved a strong military leader and whose popularity had been immeasurably increased when he was able to arm most of the *maquis* in south-west France with air drops from England. Another was Colonel Serge Ravanel, an Alpinist, a Communist and a graduate of the École Polytechnique, who by the age of twenty-five had proved himself one of the most inspired warriors of the French Resistance.

In Toulouse itself, there were many armed bands which

included large numbers of foreigners: mostly Spanish Republicans, but also Georgian deserters from General Vlassov's renegade army. The Spanish Communists meanwhile were plotting an invasion of the Val d'Aran, which took place in October. Some 3,000 men organized in twelve guerrilla brigades crossed the frontier, hoping to stir a national rising across Spain, but they did not last long once the Spanish Foreign Legion had been let loose after them.

'Toulouse was the soukh for all sorts of adventurers,' remarked Jacques Baumel of the Combat resistance movement. Not all the groups were left-wing. A colonel of extreme anti-Communist views tried to seize the border area and link up with General Franco's forces. He was reputed to be the main organizer of the '*maquis blanc*', which owed allegiance to the Comte de Paris.

Pierre Bertaux, Commissioner of the Republic for the region, knew the area well, having been a professor at the university before the war. He found himself sitting in an empty Prefecture, ignored by everyone except a few *naphtalinés* – mainly Pétainist army officers who had earned the name by joining the Resistance at the eleventh hour, in uniforms reeking of mothballs. When Colonel Starr came to see him, it was to make the point that he took his orders from the Allied chain of command, not from an as yet unrecognized provisional government.

In the middle of September, de Gaulle went on a tour of regional cities – Lyons, Marseilles, Toulouse, Bordeaux – to establish his authority in the wake of liberation. He clearly regarded Toulouse as the place for his showdown with the Resistance.

De Gaulle's aircraft, bearing the cross of Lorraine, landed at the aerodrome of Blagnac on the morning of 16 September. It was very late, and the reception committee of *maquis* leaders, some 150 strong, had become impatient in the cold wind. They cheered up when the aircraft door opened, expecting a little speech of warm congratulation for all they had done towards the liberation of France. But all they received were some brief handshakes, cold nods and a rapid departure. The General's entourage had arranged formidable security precautions, with escort cars and motorcycle outriders.

Pierre Bertaux accompanied de Gaulle into Toulouse. The young Commissioner of the Republic made the mistake of trying to amuse de Gaulle with an account of how Colonel Starr had come to his office and announced that with his 700 armed men he had only to bang on the table to sort out any problems. De Gaulle flew into a rage and asked why he had not arrested this Englishman. Bertaux had to admit that not only had he failed to arrest Starr, but he had invited him to lunch that day to meet the head of the provisional government. De Gaulle told him to cancel the invitation.

As they reached the outskirts of Toulouse, de Gaulle ordered the driver to stop the car. He intended to walk to the Prefecture. In this city of trigger-happy guerrillas, he would once again demonstrate his authority, as he had during the fusillade at Notre-Dame. He made no secret of his conviction that this young Commissioner of the Republic badly needed a lesson in the art of leadership. But to Bertaux's relief there were neither shots nor even enthusiastic crowds when de Gaulle began striding along. The exercise having proved a severe anti-climax, the General decided to waste no more time and allowed Bertaux to call up the cars and motorcycle escort.

Starr received the message that his invitation to lunch had been withdrawn and that de Gaulle wished him to report to the Prefect's office that afternoon. He had half expected it, but it did not improve his mood. Ravanel, the head of the *maquis*, fared little better, even though he had been appointed by General Koenig. He had travelled in the other car with André Diethelm, the Minister for War, who refused to acknowledge his presence. Ravanel was included in the lunch; yet de Gaulle's attitude towards him and his officers was one of conspicuous disdain. He asked each member of this '*belle brochette de colonels*' what their real rank had been during their military service. This degradation of Resistance rank by a career officer was reinforced during his speech to the populace, when he spoke only of the achievements of regular French forces, without mentioning the Resistance.

When Starr appeared in his British uniform in the Prefect's office, the General's fury re-ignited at the thought of an Englishman being so influential on French territory. He even said that Starr and his followers were no more than a band of mercenaries. Starr, restraining his temper, pointed out that a number of his subordinates were regular officers of the French army. This made de Gaulle even angrier and he ordered him to leave Toulouse immediately. Starr retorted that he came under the orders of Allied Forces Headquarters, not the provisional government, and that he would not abandon his post until instructed. If General de Gaulle wished to arrest him, then that was his decision.

The silence which followed was unbearable. De Gaulle was finally forced to acknowledge the reality of the situation. Starr's popularity in the region was such that news of his arrest could lead to serious disorder, to say nothing of further problems with the Allies. De Gaulle, mastering his own emotions, had the sense and good grace to stand up, walk round the desk and shake the British officer's hand.

Starr was still obliged to leave Toulouse shortly afterwards, but de Gaulle later agreed that he should receive the Croix de Guerre and the Légion d'Honneur for his services.

De Gaulle's confrontation with the Resistance in Toulouse, although partly symbolic, was also an experiment before attempting his decisive move of abolishing the patriotic militias which had sprung from the Resistance. The *maquis* of the south-west were among the most volatile in the country.

On 24 October de Gaulle played his trump card. He had ignored the Communist Party's heavily orchestrated campaign of rallies and marches demanding '*le retour de Maurice Thorez*', just as he had ignored Thorez's telegrams from Moscow. Thorez was de Gaulle's hostage, and now the time had come to make an exchange (just as Thorez had suspected, according to a letter to Dimitrov exactly three weeks earlier). On 28 October de Gaulle's representative in Moscow informed Thorez that he would receive an amnesty, but he must say nothing until the decree was published in the *Journal Officiel*. Dimitrov immediately sent a memorandum to Stalin informing him of the development.

That day, de Gaulle summoned a council of ministers. Everyone present knew that de Gaulle was about to demand payment for allowing the return of Maurice Thorez. A proposal for disbanding the patriotic militias was put to each member in turn, but all eyes were on the two Communist ministers, Charles Tillon, the Minister for Air, and François Billoux, the Minister for Health. They were trapped, both by de Gaulle and by the Kremlin's opposition to revolution in France. As a result even Charles Tillon, the great leader of the FTP, raised no objections when his turn came to speak.

The mass of French Communists, who had no idea of Stalin's policy, were shaken at this blow to the Resistance. Over the next ten days the party went through the motions of protest, with rallies and rousing speeches; but there was never any question of confrontation with the government. Duclos and the other Communist leaders were far from happy with the situation, but, as with the Nazi–Soviet pact, they had to accept that the interests of the Soviet Union always came first.

The rank-and-file were determined not to hand over their weapons, often seized at huge risk during the Resistance, for they had received few parachute drops from England. All over France, weapons of every sort were oiled lovingly, and wrapped in oilcloth to be buried in gardens or under floors. The quantity concealed can only be guessed at. In December, the gendarmerie detachment at Valenciennes discovered one arms cache. It contained three aircraft machine-guns, two rifles, three anti-tank rifles, one revolver, eight grenades, fifteen stick grenades, two boxes of detonators, 19,000 rounds of ammunition and six cavalry saddles. Former members of the FTP incorporated into the army at the Rouzier barracks nearby promptly threatened to attack the gendarmerie if there were any more searches.

In many parts of the country, members of the *maquis* refused to bow to the order from Paris, and the local Commissioner of the Republic decided to bide his time, whatever the Ministry of the Interior might decree. But the move had been made, and it was only a question of time before the state re-established its monopoly of force everywhere.

De Gaulle's speech in Toulouse had revealed his dislike of irregular warfare, and his text was imbued with his almost monarchical view of legitimacy and succession. The Liberation was a restoration, not a revolution, and Charles de Gaulle was not so much a head of government as a republican sovereign. The Communist leader Jacques Duclos used to refer to him as Charles XI.

The selection of his pre-war office at 14 rue Saint-Dominique, part of the Ministry of War, demonstrated de Gaulle's determination to rebuild France upon elements of the past. The army was a sure foundation. He did not, however, feel the same about industry. His speech at Lille on 1 October, on the second leg of his post-Liberation tour of France, promised a programme of nationalization in terms that could have come straight from the mouth of a *dirigiste* socialist, if not a Communist.

De Gaulle seemed able to relax only with trusted members of his staff. Claude Bouchinet-Serreulles, who was one of his young aides in London before parachuting into France to join Jean Moulin, never forgot his '*grande courtoisie*'. The General would always rise to shake hands when he brought in the dossiers first thing in the morning. He never ate alone, usually taking one of his young colleagues to eat with him, and used the opportunity to formulate his ideas to an audience. In those wartime days, he always talked of the future, never of the past, although he had a deep knowledge of history. But with the Liberation the future had arrived, and it was not comfortable. One of the main problems was his very limited circle of companions when the breadth of problems to be discussed was so great.

Close associates, often lacking specialist knowledge, were the only people able to influence him, since with ministers his mind was usually made up in advance. His *chef de cabinet*, Gaston Palewski, whose job was to control access to an already overburdened de Gaulle, inevitably made the most enemies. He was particularly resented by senior French army officers. The myth of Palewski's power spread to such an extent that people used to say that the initials GPRF (Gouvernement Provisoire de la République Française) on official cars stood for 'Gaston Palewski Régent de France'.*

Members of the government constituted in the second week of September were to suffer many surprises – often with their appointments. Georges Bidault was the first to admit that he was an extraordinary choice for Minister of Foreign Affairs. 'This adventure was unexpected,' he wrote, 'and strongly tinged with paradox.' Having led a clandestine existence during the Occupation up to his time as head of the National Council of Resistance, he had not the slightest idea of what had been going on in the outside world.

Pierre-Henri Teitgen, erstwhile professor of law at the University of Montpellier and member of the Resistance's Comité Général des Études, found to his astonishment that he had been

---

* One of Palewski's bodyguards remarked that he had 'more nicknames than a boules club in Marseilles'. The bodyguards knew him as '*la lavande*' from the overpowering strength of his eau de toilette. In the *Canard enchaîné* he was known as 'Lodoiska' – the nickname given to the censorship; politicians called him '*l'Empereur*', while the female secretaries, of whom the vast majority had no doubt received his energetic attentions, referred to him ironically as '*le beau Gaston*'.

appointed Minister of Information. He commandeered a fine building on the Avenue de Friedland which the Wehrmacht had converted into a cinema. He asked one man he knew and trusted to be his secretary-general and another to be his *chef de cabinet*.

Starting from scratch, Teitgen faced fewer difficulties than some of the more well-established ministries. The burnt-out tank was still blocking the entrance to the Ministry of Foreign Affairs when de Gaulle's senior diplomats, René Massigli and Hervé Alphand, arrived on 29 August. They discovered bloodstains on the main staircase and strips of German army shirts torn up to clean rifles in corners of its empty, echoing reception rooms. Eventually a few timid officials who had served the Vichy regime put in an appearance, not knowing whether they would be shot, imprisoned, or given back their old jobs.

Apart from the handful who rallied to de Gaulle, the Quai d'Orsay was still, as Alphand wrote, '*peuplé de Vichy*'. In 1940, the majority of officials had continued to work for what they thought was the government of France. This almost certainly prejudiced de Gaulle against the Quai d'Orsay as an institution. Two days before D-Day, de Gaulle had confided to Duff Cooper that Roland de Margerie – who had been Vichy's representative in Shanghai – was the man he found it hardest to forgive. 'He could have helped me so much, saved me from many of the mistakes I made. If he had come then he would be Minister for Foreign Affairs now.'

Alphand's most vivid memory of those first weeks in the Quai d'Orsay was the lonely figure of Georges Bidault, hugging himself in an overcoat in front of a wood fire in an immense and empty reception room. The Germans had taken all the important files back to Berlin when they retreated, as well as most of the typewriters and filing cabinets. This booty was then shipped back to Russia in 1945 after the fall of Berlin.

Most of the other ministries were in a similar position. Writing-paper was in such short supply that they had to use up the remaining batches of Vichy letterhead, striking out 'État Français' at the top and typing in 'République Française' underneath. In some departments this embarrassing practice had to continue until the trial of Marshal Pétain the following summer.

It was not just government ministries which were short of essential equipment. Hospitals lacked thermometers as well as drugs and bandages. In the terrible winter of 1944–5, there was little plaster of Paris left to mend the bones, brittle from malnutrition, which broke so easily in falls on the icy streets.

The cold spell which started during the Ardennes offensive at the beginning of January and continued throughout most of the month was one of the worst that France had suffered for a long time. On 20 January 1945, the American ambassador sent the following telegram to Washington: 'There has been snow on the ground for 17 days; previous record 10 days. It is still snowing – water frozen to hydro-electric plants – ice-breakers unable to smash thru 8"–12" ice on canals from coalfields, so 70,000 tons of coal stuck in barges, ice-bound. Daily arrivals have dropped by a third down to under 5,000 tons for whole of Paris. Sixty-six trains frozen fast.'

But even before this, the government's greatest concern remained the food supply. White bread had appeared just after the Liberation, thanks to flour provided by the Americans, then disappeared again as soon as the provisional government was left to its own resources. Shortages became so acute that people were saying they had been better off under the Germans. Such complaints overlooked the fact that the transport system had been destroyed in the fighting. Several main lines were impassable for many weeks after the Liberation; and after the Germans had withdrawn, taking most vehicles with them, road transport depended on a very limited number of charcoal-burning *gazogène* trucks. The fundamental problem, according to the Sûreté Nationale, lay with peasant farmers resisting *la Collecte*, the compulsory purchase of foodstuffs at fixed prices. The reactionary peasantry of the Vendée was apparently the worst. In

October 1944, no more than four tons of butter in the whole *département* were handed over. During the same month, the Pas de Calais, with only a few more dairy cattle, produced 355 tons for the official market.

Money in these times seemed to have no politics. The Duc de Mouchy was mayor of Mouchy, a village whose peasant farmers mainly voted Communist. He was liked and trusted, to the point that one old farmer asked him to buy a diamond ring for his daughter the next time he was in Paris. The duke bought a ring as requested. But when he returned with it, the farmer promptly said that it was not nearly big enough. So the following week the duke went to Chaumet, the jewellers in the Place Vendôme, with 350,000 of the farmer's francs in a paper bag, and bought a huge ring. This time the farmer was delighted, reassuring the duke that he still had seven million francs tucked away in his cupboard.

François Mauriac wrote that the government's efforts against the black market resembled those of 'the child St Augustine saw on a beach who wanted to empty the sea with a shell'. Paul Ramadier, the Minister of Supply, demanded that the Sûreté Nationale initiate '*la plus active repression*'. Ramadier bore the brunt of the government's unpopularity for the lack of food. He was soon known as 'Ramadan' and the daily rations as '*Ramadi- ète*'. His ministry became the target for demonstrations by committees of housewives, usually organized by the Communists. At the Hôtel de Ville, 4,000 women chanted 'Milk for our little ones!' And at a mass meeting at the Vélodrome d'Hiver, the crowd yelled '*À mort!*' every time Ramadier's name was mentioned.

The Prefect of Police received orders to crack down. In the second week of March checkpoints were put up on all roads leading into the city, an operation that was quickly dubbed 'the Siege of Paris'. But the first priority was to cut the traffic in provisions, brought in by 'suitcase-carriers' who purchased food directly and illegally from Norman farmers. Ripening Camembert, twenty to a suitcase, and the blood from joints of freshly slaughtered animals dripping from the luggage racks, made such a sickly and overpowering smell in trains that even the normal French obsession about draughts was overcome and the carriage windows left open.

Over two days, Luizet mounted a large-scale operation with his police at the Gare Montparnasse to search the suitcases of all travellers returning from the rich agricultural regions of north-western France. But the travellers were so angry that a virtual riot developed. 'In the circumstances,' Luizet reported to the Minister of the Interior, 'I felt obliged to give the order to my men to stop this sort of control operation.'

While the day-to-day struggle for food continued in the towns and cities, France's task of reconstruction was overwhelming for a bankrupt economy, and was kept afloat only by heavy American aid and loans. Factories had been destroyed or stripped by the Germans, the major ports bombed into rubble and twisted steel. There were still millions of mines to clear. SHAEF reported that 1,550,000 buildings had been destroyed, almost exactly twice as many as at the end of the First World War. There was also a severe lack of building materials and timber, much of the available stock having been used up by Allied forces.

The shortage of coal was so serious that well before the winter started urgent telegrams began arriving at the Ministry of the Interior from prefects, warning of the consequences. On 29 October a signal reached the Place Beauvau stating that Rouen had less than four days' supply left. The train due had not yet arrived, and even when it did it would take three days to unload it. There was suspicion in the provinces that Paris was receiving privileged treatment. 'We are most unhappy,' the mayor of Rouen wrote to the Minister of the Interior, 'to see Paris with theatres, cinemas and métro running long after working hours while Rouen suffers in its ruins without any help.'

One of the most striking items in the mass of data provided by opinion polls during the period following the Liberation was that its sample rated the confiscation of illicit profits as the top priority for ministers to tackle. It even topped the issue of food supply.

Communists, working on the Stalinist theory of sabotage – that every setback must be the work of a fifth column – had no doubt where the fault lay. 'The insufficient purge has left the controlling levers of industry and government departments in the hands of people who collaborated with fascism before and during the Occupation.' Even the government, while needing to keep experienced administrators in their posts, was privately forced to acknowledge that injustices remained. The minister initially responsible for reconstruction admitted that the government faced '*un problème délicat*'. The companies which had worked with the Germans were the best equipped – in finance, manpower and raw materials – to tackle the daunting tasks faced by France. Many of the larger construction companies had not even existed at the start of the war; now they assumed '*une importance anormale*'. Meanwhile, 'patriotic' companies which had refused to work with the Germans were very weak.

The Communist Party's threats of reprisal against collaborationist industrialists had begun well before the Liberation, and were repeated in *L'Humanité* as the Allies approached Paris. 'The directors of the Renault factories must be made to pay for the lives of Allied soldiers killed as a result of their enthusiasm to equip the enemy.' Louis Renault was arrested and sentenced on 23 September for having sold over six billion francs' worth of material to the German army. The sixty-seven-year-old industrialist died a month later in Fresnes prison. His wife claimed he had been murdered; the doctors said it was a stroke. Marius Berliet, head of the truck manufacturers, and his sons were imprisoned in Lyons without trial, but they were hardly the worst offenders. Renault, Citroën and Peugeot had between them manufactured nearly 93,000 vehicles for the Wehrmacht, while Berliet had produced only 2,239. The banker Hippolyte Worms was another important figure to be arrested. But the vast majority of industrialists who had worked for the Germans, including the builders of the Atlantic Wall, escaped untouched.

Companies were confiscated and nationalized, some because they had genuinely collaborated, others because unavoidable collaboration provided the excuse to nationalize key industries. The Communists, once Charles Tillon became Minister for Air, were determined to have a fully nationalized aircraft and transport industry.

Surrounded by revolutionary rhetoric and the threat of nationalization, French industrialists' and employers' groups, known generically as *le patronat*, sent a memorandum to de Gaulle complaining about the campaign. It insisted that it had 'fulfilled its duty to the nation by keeping the means of production on French soil while carrying out managerial resistance on an unrecognized scale. It must protest against the myth that France was saved by the working class alone.' But such arguments were disingenuous. Only a distinguished minority of managers sabotaged the work and the justification for maintaining production implied that France's long-term interests lay with a continuing German occupation rather than eventual liberation.

In the climate of the moment, with the right seen as morally bankrupt after Vichy and the Occupation, there was a strong tide of opinion in favour of change for the sake of change. The achievements of the Resistance and the fraternity of the Liberation should be pushed forward into peacetime, to create a more equitable society. This political instinct or emotion was described as *progressisme* – a word which was convenient for Communists who did not want to alarm potential fellow-travellers or right-wing socialists who feared Communist plans, but did not yet dare say so openly.

For those across Europe who had lost so much, *progressisme* seemed to offer the only way forward, leaving behind both the moral ambiguities of the war and the misery of the depression in the 1930s. But conservatives and political free-thinkers who questioned such assumptions saw it as a slide towards Communism. Aldous Huxley, viewing a destroyed Europe from the United States, expected a *Pax Sovietica* to spread across the whole continent. He, like many, feared that it would be impossible 'to put Humpty Dumpty together again' except in a 'nightmarishly totalitarian and pauperized form'.

10
Corps Diplomatique

General de Gaulle's anger in Toulouse against Colonel Starr had really been an explosion of resentment against the Allied leadership. His obstinacy and readiness to take offence had not been eased with the triumph of the Liberation. The French *en masse* had acclaimed him as their leader, yet the Allies continued to delay formal recognition of the provisional government. At Roosevelt's insistence (and almost certainly on the advice of Admiral Leahy, his former ambassador to Vichy), this delay extended for nearly two months after the Liberation of Paris. The fact that the ambassadors of the 'Big Three' were already in place only irritated de Gaulle more.

The British ambassador, Duff Cooper, whom de Gaulle already knew from Algiers, landed at Le Bourget airport in a Dakota on 13 September, having been escorted across the Channel by no fewer than forty-eight Spitfires. A police motorcycle escort swept his motorcade to the Arc de Triomphe, where he laid a wreath on the grave of the unknown soldier. He then joined the advance party of his staff in the Berkeley Hotel. The British Embassy, Pauline Borghese's palace in honey-coloured stone on the rue du Faubourg Saint-Honoré, was undamaged; but there was no water or electricity, and its reception rooms were still piled with the furniture of families who had fled Paris in June 1940.

Next morning, Duff Cooper went to see Bidault at the Quai

d'Orsay, and recorded their meeting in his diary: 'He seemed curiously young and somewhat overcome by his responsibilities, admitting himself that he knew nothing, and had had no experience. On the whole I liked him, but whether he will prove a big enough man for the job I am inclined to doubt.'

It was not long before Duff Cooper found himself in a position he knew well from Algiers: being ground between the millstones of Churchill and de Gaulle. One of the first messages from the Foreign Office warned that Churchill wanted to pay a visit in about three weeks. Back went the reply that the Prime Minister must not think of coming until he had recognized de Gaulle's government, and received a proper invitation from the General himself. Churchill still saw France as part of the Allied war zone and not as a sovereign country.

The United States government was equally tactless. Duff Cooper was told privately by the Quai d'Orsay that the Americans had nominated an ambassador to France, without even asking for the provisional government's *agrément*, and that Bidault was deeply offended.

Until Roosevelt was prepared to recognize his government officially, de Gaulle would not see either the American ambassador, Jefferson Caffery, or Duff Cooper, even though his own ambassador in London, René Massigli, had been received by the King and had been to stay in the country with Churchill. De Gaulle was holding up the process of recognition by refusing to agree to a temporary division of France between a war zone, which came under the authority of SHAEF, and a zone of the interior.

Eventually, after a last-minute flurry of confusion, the final barriers were removed, and at five o'clock in the afternoon of Monday 23 October the United States, Great Britain, Russia and Canada simultaneously recognized the provisional government. 'At *last*!' noted the head of the Foreign Office, Sir Alexander Cadogan. 'What a fuss about nothing! Due to that spiteful old great-aunt Leahy. Hope he's feeling pretty sick!'

That evening, Duff and Lady Diana Cooper were invited to dine with the General. The Coopers took Beatrice Eden, the wife of the Foreign Secretary, with them. Other guests at the General's residence in the Bois de Boulogne included Bidault, General Juin, François Mauriac and Gaston Palewski. The atmosphere remained resolutely gloomy, with very little conversation. De Gaulle refused to reply when Duff Cooper mentioned the recognition of the provisional government; and when the ambassador persisted, saying that he hoped the General was glad the whole process was over, de Gaulle shrugged and said that it would never be over. Duff Cooper sat next to Madame de Gaulle, who never took her eyes off her husband and said nothing the whole evening.

This 'extremely frigid and dreary party, worse even than his entertainments usually are ... should have been a gala evening,' wrote Duff Cooper in his diary, 'but gala is not a word included in the vocabulary of General de Gaulle'. On their way home in the car afterwards, Beatrice Eden observed that usually the things that one dreaded were not as bad as one expected, but this had proved far worse. When Duff saw Massigli in London a few days later and described the evening, his counterpart roared with laughter. As they both knew well from experience, de Gaulle was at his most churlish when nursing his wounded pride. It also did not help that he clearly believed small talk to be a vice. Perhaps the key to this, as a senior member of the Quai d'Orsay pointed out to Duff, was his excessive shyness.

De Gaulle was forced to take some part in social life, but it was alien to his nature. Diana Cooper had already found in Algiers that dinner conversation with the General 'flowed like glue'. She and Duff Cooper called him Charlie Wormwood – as in wormwood and gall. De Gaulle's household was famously austere, and embassy wives dreaded the experience of having tea with Yvonne de Gaulle, who had even less small talk than her husband. 'Tante Yvonne' was notoriously strict. Just the thought of meeting a divorced woman was said to give her a migraine.

The American ambassador, Jefferson Caffery, who arrived on 12 October, was not helped by the 'discouraging' accounts circulated by other Americans about him. Caffery was not a born diplomat, and often looked ill at ease. He was always extremely well-dressed, though he walked stiffly, with the aid of a cane. At times he was almost inarticulate due to a speech impediment, at others forthright and brusque, yet when relaxed he could be excellent company. Courageous and generous, he was a discreet homosexual; although his lover, one of his own staff in the embassy, was slightly less careful to preserve the secrecy of their relationship. His wife Gertrude was older than her husband and could be very *protocolaire*, but at heart she was kind. She clearly did not enjoy entertaining any more than her husband, but made a determined effort. Their absence at diplomatic receptions, however, was frequently noticed.

Although Caffery had little experience of France, several members of his staff made up for this deficiency. His political counsellor, Douglas MacArthur II (nephew of the general, and son-in-law of a former vice-president), had been in the Paris embassy before the war and then on Admiral Leahy's staff at Vichy. Ridgway Knight, who had been one of Robert Murphy's vice-consuls in North Africa, proved one of the best-informed members of the embassy, thanks to his contacts: he had been brought up in France and was completely bilingual. On the intelligence side, there was Charles Gray, a rich polo-player and man-about-town who had lived in Paris before the war, and Captain David Rockefeller, who held the official position of assistant military attaché, that internationally recognized fig-leaf for intelligence work.

The relaxed and charming Gray, who was a member of both the Travellers' and the Jockey Club, had little in common with his ambassador. One day in the Travellers' after lunch, Gray looked up from the backgammon board to find two members of the Jockey Club in white gloves, standing to attention. They had come to deliver a challenge to a duel on behalf of a friend, who felt that Gray had insulted him. Monsieur Gray had the choice of weapons. Would he please communicate his answer later?

News of the challenge spread so rapidly that Charlie Gray found, on his return to the embassy, a message summoning him to the ambassador's office. Caffery told him in the severest terms that any member of his staff involved in a duel would have to resign on the spot. Gray was despondent. He loved his job, but if he declined to fight he would never again be able to hold up his head in Parisian society. The solution came to him just in time. He wrote a note accepting the challenge, and informed the seconds that his choice of weapon was tanks – at any range they cared to select.

The diplomatic corps reassembling in Paris, perhaps inevitably for such a place and such a time, seemed to divide automatically between hedonists and puritans. The Canadian ambassador, General Georges Vanier, was an incorruptible Catholic. He at first stayed in the Ritz while the embassy was made ready, but, according to his military attaché, he 'left in disgust, as it appeared to be full of war profiteers drinking champagne by the bucket'. Vanier also refused to have his office heated, as the French had no fuel for their homes, so he sat at his desk in his army greatcoat.

The Papal Nuncio, Mgr Roncalli, the future Pope John XXIII, was not a soldier-monk like Vanier. The food and wine at his little lunch parties were always good, but these gatherings were very discreet. He explained to Jacques Dumaine, the *chef de protocol* at the Quai d'Orsay, that he thought it wise to keep a low profile, though Georges Bidault and other Catholic ministers made de Gaulle's government much less hostile to the Church than many in the past.

The Swiss ambassador, Carl Burckhardt, had been League of

Nations commissioner in Danzig, then President of the International Red Cross during the war. His legation was the Hôtel de l'Abbé de Pompadour, at 142 rue de Grenelle. It had come into Swiss hands in the late eighteenth century, having belonged to Besenval, the captain of Louis XVI's Swiss Guard and an entertaining diarist of court life.

Burckhardt, the humanist historian, was a worthy, albeit more serious, successor to Besenval. Tall and good-looking, his conversation could be highly intellectual – 'I'm always in an agony of not understanding', wrote Diana Cooper, with whom he had had an affair in the late thirties. The Coopers and the Burckhardts remained firm friends; and he regaled her with all the wild stories which circulated about her and the British Embassy.

The British Embassy was decidedly unaustere, not so much with luxury, although the food and drink were always good, but in a refusal to take petty moral stands. As far as Duff Cooper was concerned, what was past was past. He would not invite any notorious collaborators – guest-lists were privately checked with Gaston Palewski – but he had no time for poisonous and often ill-informed whispering campaigns. Writers of the Resistance such as Vercors and the Communist Paul Éluard did not object to lunching with Cocteau and Louise de Vilmorin, who were much criticized after the Liberation. Even bitter political enemies accepted the advantage of meeting on neutral ground. The Communist poet Louis Aragon did not walk out on finding an increasingly right-wing André Malraux present.

Diana Cooper had a way of mixing guests recklessly and getting away with it. On one occasion she threw Daisy Fellowes and the Marchioness of Bath, two of the most *mondaine* women imaginable, into a lunch party for Tito's ambassador and Marcel Cachin, the doyen of the French Communist Party. The fact that Daisy Fellowes, who had long been regarded as the most beautifully dressed woman in the world, sat opposite Madame Cachin who was 'looking like an old concierge' caused no unease on either side. Madame Cachin, who 'proved to be highly cultured with a great knowledge of art', was a pronounced success.

The Russian Embassy in the rue de Grenelle had been a beautiful building until iron doors with peepholes and every other security device imaginable had been bolted on to it. Receptions took place in gilded rooms ablaze with powerful electric light, and in the place of a string orchestra, a wireless blared from the sideboard. It was a suitable setting for Stalin's representative, Sergei Bogomolov, the most hedonistic ambassador of all – if measured by alcohol consumption.

One evening, after the ambassadors of the Big Three had presented joint notes at the Quai d'Orsay, Bogomolov asked Caffery and Duff Cooper back to the Russian Embassy. 'There were two tables,' Duff Cooper recorded in his diary, 'one for the three Ambassadors, and another for the three secretaries, Eric [Duncannon, later Earl of Bessborough], MacArthur and Ratiani.' Dishes with slices of sturgeon, pots of caviare, eggs and sardines were placed in the middle of the table, to help the drinking. Bogomolov began by proposing some fifteen toasts, all being drunk in vodka. The other two ambassadors were expected to follow suit.

The first to succumb was Bogomolov's own secretary, Ratiani, who was sick on the floor. It was not long before the other diplomats present had to be helped to their cars. Neither Caffery nor even Bogomolov himself was seen until the late afternoon of the following day. Both Duff Cooper and MacArthur were really ill, and had to stay in bed for several days.

On another occasion, a *diner à quatre*, Madame Bogomolov fortunately put a stop to 'the vodka struggle' when her husband began to propose more and more 'ingenious toasts so that one seemed ungallant or unpatriotic and ungrateful or churlish to refuse'. She even reproved him for interrupting their guests, but that did little good. While Stalin's representative 'issued a monologue of statistics – how many women had matriculated in each

Soviet republic – and boasted of Soviet scientists and astrono-
mers', Madame Bogomolov confided to Lady Diana Cooper
that she had not seen a bar of soap for weeks. The Soviet soap
crisis was rectified by messenger the next day with several
tablets as a thank-you present.

The 7 November celebration of the Russian Revolution
proved neither very proletarian, nor egalitarian. 'The traffic in
the rue de Grenelle was completely out of control,' Duff Cooper
observed. 'It took about half an hour to approach the house.
All the members of the Embassy were in their smart uniforms,
and Madame Bogomolov was in full evening dress. There were
lights everywhere and cinema operators. Everybody was photo-
graphed as they went in and again upstairs while shaking hands
with the Ambassador and the Ambassadress. I was conducted
by a junior member of the staff to a special room set apart for
the more privileged guests, where there was any amount of
vodka and caviare, the others being allowed only inferior sandwiches and hardly any drink.' For Duff Cooper, however, the
evening, when he did manage to fight his way out through the
crush in the outer room, proved to be memorable in other
ways: it was the night he fell in love with the writer Louise de
Vilmorin.

While Duff Cooper had diversions whenever de Gaulle proved
particularly intractable or rude, Georges Bidault bore the brunt
of his unpredictable head of government. De Gaulle, who seldom
consulted his Foreign Minister or even kept him informed of his
private *démarches*, made policy 'uneasy to conduct or even
formulate'.

Over the next fifteen months, Bidault was constantly apologiz-
ing in private to the British and American ambassadors for de
Gaulle's provocations. They had much sympathy for his difficult
position. Caffery reported a series of Bidault's complaints against
de Gaulle, and remarked that the Foreign Minister had added
'that there is absolutely no one else in sight and that it must be

admitted that de Gaulle loves France, even if he doesn't like Frenchmen'.

Under the strain, Bidault began drinking too much – in diplomatic circles, he soon acquired the nickname of 'In Bido Veritas' – and in November, de Gaulle nearly refused to take him on an important mission abroad.

Bidault's life was not made easier by the distinctive and unusually slow character of the French diplomatic service. The Quai d'Orsay had still not caught up with the change in the balance of world power. While three diplomatic bags a week went to London, only three a month went to Washington. French diplomats were also noticeably out of touch with what was going on in their own country. But nobody could dispute their erudition. It was a service in which the elegant composition of a report seemed to be of far more concern than its contents.

The Quai d'Orsay has always had a close and distinguished relationship with literature. Alexis Léger, who wrote poetry of exotic meditation under the name of Saint-John Perse, had been an ambassador and secretary-general at the Quai d'Orsay before the war. He was stripped of all rank in 1940 by Pétain. Yet during his subsequent exile in the United States he remained viscerally opposed to de Gaulle, and refused to return to France until 1958, two years before he received the Nobel Prize. Paul Claudel had served since the 1890s as a consul and then as ambassador across the world from South America to his last appointment in Tokyo before the war. And the playwright Jean Giraudoux used to leave his hat and walking-stick hanging in his office to camouflage his absence while he worked on his plays at home. Paul Morand had been Vichy's minister in Bucharest, before moving to Switzerland; Jacques Maritain, a religious philosopher, was appointed ambassador to the Holy See in 1945.

François Mauriac feared later that the literary constellation of 'Claudel, Alexis Léger, Giraudoux and Morand has created a kind of cerebral cramp with the result that after them the diplomatic machine has suffered from intellectual anaemia, to be cured only by blood transfusions from the École Normale Supérieure'.

After the Liberation, key administrative posts were given to the handful of career diplomats of outstanding talent who had not served Pétain, such as Hervé Alphand. The junior ranks were purged and repopulated with those who had a good war record, like Romain Gary, a Free French aviator and novelist.

Foreign ambassadors were much encumbered by the social round. Official and semi-official lunches took up most of the middle of the day, since they could run to seven or eight courses, even at a time of desperate shortage. At one interminable meal Duff Cooper agreed with his neighbour, Jean Monnet, who 'was most indignant about the length of the menu, and said that it was feasts like this that gave people passing through Paris such an entirely false idea of the true position'.

In the autumn of 1944, the visitor who preoccupied Duff Cooper most was Winston Churchill. Once again, he was horrified to hear that the Prime Minister proposed to arrive in Paris without a word to de Gaulle beforehand. He even had to beg Churchill not to visit General Eisenhower at SHAEF, because without an invitation from the provisional government his arrival on French soil would be taken as yet another insult. Finally, with the help of Massigli and Bidault, de Gaulle was persuaded to accept a visit from the British Prime Minister on 10 November, so that Churchill would be in Paris for the First World War commemoration of 11 November.

Churchill arrived in fine form at Le Bourget, where he was met by the Communist Minister for Air, Charles Tillon, and then taken to the apartments reserved for state guests at the Quai d'Orsay. The British Prime Minister was thrilled to find that he had a gold bath, while Anthony Eden's was only silver.

Churchill's presence in Paris had been kept secret, but news spread with astonishing rapidity on the morning of Armistice Day as he drove in an open car from the Quai d'Orsay to meet de Gaulle. Churchill was well buttoned up against the cold in an RAF greatcoat, and beaming from under the uniform cap. After the two leaders left the rue Saint-Dominique for the Arc de Triomphe, 'the reception had to be seen to be believed', Duff Cooper wrote in his diary. 'It was greater than anything I had ever known. There were crowds in every window, even in the top floors of the highest houses and on the roofs, and the cheering was the loudest, the most spontaneous and the most genuine.'

As Churchill and de Gaulle laid wreaths on the grave of the unknown soldier, members of their entourage glanced up at the umbrella of Spitfires circling over Paris to guard against any marauding German fighters. The crowds were more than ten deep when the two men began their walk down the Champs-Élysées to the dais from where they would take the salute. They all chanted: 'Vive Churchill! Vive de Gaulle!' De Gaulle raised both arms, Churchill made the V-sign, unleashing further roars of approval. They presented 'a curious pair,' observed Malcolm Muggeridge, 'the one so rotund and merry, the other so tall and grave; like Mr Pickwick and Don Quixote.'

The march-past was led by General Koenig, with a band from the Brigade of Guards playing 'The British Grenadiers'. There were also kilted Canadian pipers, *goums* from the Atlas mountains, a detachment from the Royal Navy and the Garde Républicaine in their cuirassier uniforms on black chargers.

Almost as important as the public enthusiasm was the relaxation of tensions between the two leaders. Both de Gaulle and Churchill were 'in the happiest of humours'. After a lunch for sixty people at the rue Saint-Dominique, they went upstairs for discussions. De Gaulle, Palewski, Massigli, and Coulet and Chauvel from the Quai d'Orsay sat on one side of the table, facing Churchill, Eden, Duff Cooper and Alec Cadogan of the Foreign Office on the other. The conversation lasted 'for about two hours – Winston talking most of the time in his uninhibited and fairly intelligible French. He speaks remarkably well, but understands very little. There was not an unpleasant word said, although nearly every subject, including Syria, was covered.' Yet despite moments of real warmth – almost affection of the sort an estranged couple shows in the relief of making things up – de Gaulle was about to make advances in a different direction.

Three days before Churchill arrived in Paris, de Gaulle had told Bogomolov that he would like to visit the Soviet Union to discuss relations with Marshal Stalin. De Gaulle knew that the Americans and the British would soon be discussing a post-war settlement with the Russians, and he did not want France to be left out.*

On 24 November 1944, the day after General Leclerc's 2nd Armoured Division entered Strasbourg amid scenes like those in Paris the previous August, Charles de Gaulle took off by plane for Moscow. His party included Gaston Palewski, Georges Bidault and General Juin, together with a number of senior officials from the Quai d'Orsay.

Their slow progress along North Africa and across the Middle East to Baku represented its own form of humiliation. The head of government's obsolete two-engine aircraft broke down with embarrassing frequency. De Gaulle's party left their aircraft in Baku, mainly because of the bad weather. Allotted the old-fashioned train of the Tsarist commander-in-chief, Grand Duke Nicholas, they then embarked on an even slower journey north across the steppes to Moscow. They were banqueted at every stop amid appalling misery and war damage. In the ruins of Stalingrad the Russians were still digging corpses out of the frozen ground two years after the battle. One day, in the compartment of the train, after glancing out at the endless

* De Gaulle's right-wing opponents who claimed he was a Soviet puppet at this time were much mistaken. The detailed briefing document for this visit, prepared by Dimitrov for Molotov and Stalin, leaves no doubt. 'Although his outward attitude towards the [French] Communists is correct, he was prepared to use all possible means of hidden struggle against them.'

winter landscape, de Gaulle observed dryly that the journey was taking so long that he hoped there would not be a revolution in his absence.

Descriptions of Stalin at this time focus on his sloping rectangular forehead, his pale complexion, and large, slanted, gleaming eyes. The way his skin was stretched tightly over his cheeks when he smiled increased the impression of a mask. De Gaulle summed him up memorably as a 'Communist dressed up as a field marshal, a dictator ensconced in his scheming, a conqueror with an air of bonhomie'.

The main banquet in the Kremlin, with its conspicuous display of luxury, was not a cheerful occasion. There were some forty Russian officials, the French delegation, the British chargé d'affaires and Averell Harriman, the American ambassador. Stalin proposed endless toasts, first of all complimentary ones to his guests, followed by some thirty more to his Russian subordinates – Molotov, Beria, Bulganin, Voroshilov and on down the hierarchy.

Each time he raised his glass at the end of his little speech, he said 'Come!', and the designated recipient of the honour had to hurry round the table to clink his glass with Stalin's. The rest of the company sat in frozen silence. The Marshal's voice was disconcertingly soft as he raised his glass to the chief of the Soviet air staff, then threatened him in a brutal display of hangman's humour.

At one point that evening, Stalin turned to Gaston Palewski and said with a malicious smirk, no doubt because the French delegation had ducked the question of recognizing his puppet government for Poland, 'One never ceases to be Polish, Monsieur Palewski.'

One of the main objectives of de Gaulle's journey was to revive the traditional Franco-Russian alliance against Germany – his sense of history never let him forget that Russia had saved France in 1914 – but equally important, he wanted an alliance with Stalin as a counterbalance to Roosevelt and Churchill. He also needed to make sure that the French Communist Party behaved itself.

De Gaulle's sense of injustice at the hands of Roosevelt and Churchill should not be underestimated. His outrage at the lack of consultation had been so intense in 1942 that he had even considered breaking off all relations with Churchill and Roosevelt. In London, he had requested the ubiquitous ambassador, Bogomolov, to discover the conditions that Stalin might impose in return for recognizing the Free French. In early 1943, a Free French fighter group went to Russia to fly in support of the Red Army, and distinguished itself as the 'Normandie-Niemen' regiment. A number of its aviators, although Gaullists rather than Communists, were made Heroes of the Soviet Union.

De Gaulle clearly had far fewer illusions about Stalin than did Churchill and Anthony Eden, who showed an astonishing readiness to believe in his good faith. Yet from the beginning, de Gaulle had shown a restraint towards the Soviet Union which he had seldom demonstrated towards his Anglo-Saxon Allies. He had never openly criticized Stalin, the French Communists or even the Nazi–Soviet pact. De Gaulle had a good reason for keeping quiet on this last point.

Stalin despised the French. The fall of France in 1940 had undermined the major purpose of his pact with Hitler. He had hoped for a prolonged war of attrition in the west between Nazi Germany and the capitalist democracies. But Marshal Pétain's armistice had allowed Hitler to turn on the Soviet Union with undiminished strength and increased mobility, thanks to the mass of French army transport captured. At the Teheran conference in 1943 Stalin declared that 'France must pay for her criminal collaboration with Germany'.

Stalin was much more suspicious of the Americans and the British. Eisenhower's deal with Admiral Darlan in 1942 so convinced him that the British and the Americans would come to some sort of compromise with Germany that Roosevelt and Churchill were forced to reassure him with a declaration that they would accept only unconditional surrender. Stalin still did not believe them. De Gaulle's view, on the other hand – that Germany should be split into tiny states and deprived of its industrial capacity – showed no sign of wavering. He thus offered the only thing of possible interest to Stalin – a wild card within the Western alliance.

Stalin eventually got round to the subject of Maurice Thorez's return to France. He must have appreciated the subtlety of de Gaulle's move to create an invisible link between Thorez's return and the disbandment of the Patriotic Militias. But de Gaulle did not hide his irritation when Stalin tactlessly brought up the subject of Thorez directly. 'Don't take my indiscretion amiss,' he told de Gaulle in a confidential tone. 'I want only to say that I know Thorez and that, in my opinion, he's a good Frenchman. If I were in your place, I wouldn't put him in prison.' Then Stalin's eyes narrowed in one of his smiles. 'At least not straight away!'

'The French government,' replied de Gaulle haughtily, 'treats its citizens according to what it expects of them.'

Thirty-six hours before Thorez left for Paris, Stalin had summoned him to the Kremlin for only the second audience granted to the leader of the French Communist Party in five years. His parting advice, after warning Thorez against de Gaulle's reactionary and dictatorial nature, was to remind him that the overriding priority in France must be national unity to bring about the downfall of Hitler. The underlying message was clear. And Thorez, totally subservient, did not miss it.

Stalin was not simply afraid of the United States cutting off supplies to him if the French Communists caused trouble. A Communist revolution in their rear might also give the Americans an excuse for making a separate peace with the German general staff, or even – the worst nightmare of all – a military alliance against Soviet Russia.

*

The Franco-Soviet agreement was finally signed at four in the morning after a compromise formula had been reached over Stalin's puppet government for Poland. Bidault, having collapsed from alcohol at the banquet, was hastily revived. With Stalin and de Gaulle standing behind, the two Foreign Ministers signed. '*Il faut fêter cela!*' Stalin insisted, and more food and vodka were brought in.

There had been several gaffes during the visit to Moscow, such as de Gaulle's mention of Pierre Laval's pact with Russia in 1935. There were also several taunts from the Russian side. Ilya Ehrenburg, almost certainly on Stalin's instructions, presented de Gaulle with a copy of his novel about the collapse of 1940, *La Chute de Paris*. Yet on the delegation's return to Paris a week before Christmas, everybody seemed to consider it a great success, even though, to the amusement of Hervé Alphand, accounts differed wildly.

De Gaulle was more sanguine. The agreement signed in Moscow might not have had a great effect on the international stage, and he had failed to achieve support for French claims to the west bank of the Rhine, but he could hardly have hoped for a better domestic insurance policy. Maurice Thorez, having reached France in his absence, was not calling the French Communist Party to the barricades, but demanding blood, sweat, increased productivity and national unity. The Communists of the Resistance could hardly believe their ears, but next day the party press confirmed his words, emphasizing the Kremlin line.

The notion of revolution in France became even less likely over the next two weeks. On 17 December, the day de Gaulle returned from Moscow, news of Field Marshal von Rundstedt's offensive in the Ardennes reached Paris.

Much of the panic came from stories of English-speaking German commandos causing chaos far behind the lines. Identity documents were not sufficient at checkpoints. Anyone in

American uniform was asked about baseball, while those in British uniform were challenged with 'How much is a pint?' or 'What does LBW stand for?'

In the expectation of parachute attacks on Paris, troops arrived to defend public buildings and a curfew was imposed from eight in the evening until six in the morning. Wild rumours spread that Strasbourg had been re-taken, even that the Germans were beyond Sedan, a name with terrible echoes of 1870. For the French, the fear of another German invasion was not so much for their own safety – although some refugees left Paris – but anger at the prospect of collaborators getting away with it. The rejoicing in Fresnes prison among the pro-German element who believed they would soon be liberated was very rash. There were many – not just former members of the FFI – who were determined that collaborators would not live to welcome the Germans to Paris again.

Christmas 1944 was not joyful: three million men and women were either dead, missing, or still in German prison camps. 'Paris is lugubrious, cold, as if empty and without a soul,' wrote Hervé Alphand. 'It reminds me a little of Vienna at the end of the last war, a magnificent setting without people or lights.'

De Gaulle, quite understandably, was horrified to hear that Eisenhower considered withdrawing from the recently liberated city of Strasbourg to straighten his line. Fortunately Churchill, who was in France, joined de Gaulle and Eisenhower at SHAEF headquarters at Versailles on 3 January, and supported a compromise solution that two French divisions should be left to defend the capital of Alsace. De Gaulle was so relieved at the outcome of this conference that he wanted to issue a vainglorious communiqué. Palewski brought the draft round to the British Embassy first. Duff Cooper told him that it would not help matters at all. 'It suggested that de Gaulle had summoned a military conference which the PM and Eisenhower had been allowed to attend.'

Even when the German offensive collapsed, with Strasbourg

saved, de Gaulle had little to be optimistic about. France was virtually brought to a halt by freezing cold. It was so cold in that January, without fuel, that Pastor Boegner wrote in his diary: 'I felt my brain slowing down. A strange sensation not to be able to choose one's words with the usual speed.' But for de Gaulle, the worst blow was that France was not invited to take part in the discussions at Yalta during the first half of February.

Roosevelt had not abandoned his old antipathy to de Gaulle. Nor had Stalin's attitude been changed by the agreements in Moscow. The Kremlin view of France was that it was the Americans and British who had 'chased out the Germans and liberated the country, not French armies'.

The performance of British leaders at this time was far from their finest hour. Eden especially seemed almost morbidly afraid of irritating Stalin in any way. Yet all the most infamous agreements, from Churchill's 'percentage agreement' with Stalin in October 1944 to the betrayal of Poland, have often been taken out of context. And the idea that de Gaulle's presence at Yalta might have saved central Europe from nearly fifty years of tyranny is hopelessly misguided. It ignores the fact that the Yalta agreement was in many ways the political seal placed on the military reality established as a result of the strategy decided at the Teheran conference. And no Western government, after all the praise for the sacrifice of the Red Army, could have asked soldiers eager for demobilization to prepare to take a stand against the Russian ally.

French resentment that Europe was being carved up without a single Continental representative was understandable, although misdirected. Unfortunately, the situation was made far worse when President Roosevelt invited de Gaulle to Algiers on his way back from Yalta to tell him what had been agreed. De Gaulle was furious that Roosevelt could treat Algiers, which was French territory, as if it were his own property, and promptly refused. Word then leaked out that Roosevelt had called him a 'prima donna', and this inflamed the situation further.

French emotions, however, underwent some change in the early spring of 1945, as the Red Army advanced at a breathtaking rate. 'The French authorities are frankly frightened,' Caffery reported to Washington. Bidault had exclaimed: 'Who is going to stop Attila? He is covering more territory every day.' Even de Gaulle acknowledged that France very much needed the friendship of the United States. Caffery could not let the opportunity pass. 'I remarked,' he wrote, 'that some officials of the French government do not always act as if they shared that view. He retorted by listing grievances against us, and I retorted in kind. In the end, however, we both agreed that this is definitely no time for bickering.'

De Gaulle had a wonderful sense of history, but found it hard to stomach the vulgar fact that, without money, you could not be a major power. The greatness of France and the greatness of Britain were as doomed as their empires, which had carved up much of the world between them in the previous two centuries. Now two different superpowers were about to dominate the continent of Europe. The prospect was a bitter humiliation which he and the majority of his countrymen refused to accept. It had a disastrous effect, making them doubly determined not to give up colonial possessions. It also made them sensitive to what at times appeared like a new occupation of France, this time by the United States army.

11
Khaki and the Tricolor

For some time after the Liberation and even the end of the war, white-helmeted military policemen used to halt the traffic on the Place de la Concorde to give priority to US vehicles approaching the American Embassy.

Eisenhower, the Supreme Commander, was no thick-skinned autocrat, yet even his relationship with the provisional government suffered from the distrust which had grown up between President Roosevelt and de Gaulle during the war. The plan to install Allied rule as if France were conquered enemy territory was bound to poison any alliance.

Allied forces came ashore in Normandy comprehensively prepared. The 'France Zone Handbook No. 16, Part III' ostensibly dealt with 'Local Information and Administrative Personalities', but was in fact a guide to Parisian brothels, *arrondissement* by *arrondissement*. Prepared in May 1944, presumably from information supplied by Allied intelligence services, it warned that the list was 'not necessarily exhaustive' and that 'owing to the shortage of all medical supplies' there had been 'a very great increase in the number of VD cases in the country'.

Whether or not foreknowledge of the brothel known as 'Aux Belles Poules' in the rue Blondel, or the unnamed establishment at 4 rue des Vertus ('street of the Virtues') or the 'House of All Nations' in the rue Chabanais hastened the American advance on the capital is hard to judge. But clearly American troops made good use of the information so liberally provided by their commanders, because within a year US military authorities felt obliged to print barrack posters which proclaimed: 'Gonorrhea. Do you want a *Family*? 12% of all men who contract Gonorrhea become STERILE. Keep fit to go home.'

The puritan General Montgomery put brothels out of bounds to British troops and posted military police in red light districts. This did not put a stop to business. In spite of all the summer storms, the fields next to bivouac areas were used instead.

To the dismay of French patriots, the exuberance of the Liberation was rapidly tarnished by pilfering or dabbling in the black market. For many people it was a question of survival, as it had been during the Occupation. Even Yves Farge, later the Minister of Supply, admitted that there were those 'condemned to traffick or perish'. Yet the black market was at first seen as a French disgrace, both by the Allies and by the French themselves.

Early posters issued by the provisional government concentrated on the threat to French patriotism: 'French people do not have the right to make their fellow citizens go hungry' ... 'Officers and soldiers of our Allies are astonished at the prices charged in certain shops and restaurants'. It soon became apparent, however, to both civil and military authorities that members of the Allied forces were profiteering just as shamelessly. In fact many people suspected that the black market had moved into a higher gear with the rackets operated by certain quartermasters and young entrepreneurs determined to make a fortune before they returned to the States.

Since French shops were virtually bare, almost all the items provided by the American military cornucopia – coffee, gasoline, tyres, cigarettes, boots, soap, ammunition, morphine, Spam or whisky – were resold on the black market, thus flaunting a wild capitalist streak at a government trying to introduce an effective war socialism.

On 13 January 1945, newspapers carried a proclamation by

the military governor of Paris to the population: 'Anyone found in possession of gasoline, arms, munitions, equipment or war material will be tried by court martial.' But such warnings did little good. The theft and sale of fuel supplies in jerrycans even started to endanger the attack on Germany.

Colouring the gasoline did little good. Even the court martial of American soldiers, several of whom received extremely severe sentences, made no difference. The profits to be made were so easy and so large that French drug-dealers moved in on the racket, sometimes in alliance with American servicemen. It was above all the effrontery of the black marketeers which drove the government almost to despair. On one occasion, the Minister of Supply issued an order to 'seize three French trucks transporting food, travelling with papers signed Eisenhower'.

To the exasperation of the French government, there were other ways for American soldiers to make a killing at its expense. All US forces were exempt from French exchange controls and import duties. This meant that servicemen were allowed to convert their pay in French francs back into dollars at the official rate of exchange. Many of them promptly sold their dollars for francs on the black market at a great profit. Another money-making activity at the expense of the French government emerged later. 'I am told,' Caffery reported to Washington, 'that a large number of New York firms are mailing American cigarettes and nylon stockings to [Army Post Office] addresses here. Much of this merchandise is illegally bartered or sold by American purchasers enjoying benefits of APO exemption from French customs control.'

The nylon stockings may not have been destined for the black market. For American soldiers, they were the most obvious bait to persuade young Frenchwomen to go out with them. Overall, exploitation was probably evenly balanced between the two sides. 'Lise's main sport since the Liberation,' wrote Simone de Beauvoir of a young woman who lived in the same hotel, 'was what she called "hunting the American".' This meant charming them into parting with cigarettes and rations, which she then resold.

For attractive *midinettes* (the young Parisians who worked in the fashion industry and shops) there was no shortage of American soldiers on seventy-two hours' leave from the front, with dollars saved up, and eager to see Paris. The GIs were bowled over by the *midinettes*, who were brilliantly inventive in their clothes and especially their hats, piled high in Carmen Miranda-like fantasies. 'The hats in Paris are really terrific,' one young soldier wrote in a letter home, 'very high, usually like a waste basket turned upside down with feathers and flowers all over them.'

The welcome for the young soldiers had been quite genuine at first, largely because of what they represented. 'The easy-going manner of the young Americans,' wrote Simone de Beauvoir, 'incarnated liberty itself . . . once again we were allowed to cross the seas.'

Young Frenchmen, however, would not have agreed with the US Embassy euphemisms which described their troops as 'ardent and often very enterprising' in the pursuit of women. Many reports, in fact, suggest that within a few months of the Liberation, certainly by the spring of 1945, American ardour was no longer appreciated by most Parisian girls, who did not like the arrogance that went with it. Summoned by a whistle and a proffered packet of 'Luckys', one girl earned the cheers of French onlookers by taking a cigarette from the GI, dropping it to the ground and grinding it under her foot.

This coolness was accompanied by another development which embarrassed and shocked the American military authorities. According to a SHAEF report, very young girls had begun to loiter in large numbers outside US army camps, offering themselves to GIs. It is hard to tell whether this was juvenile prostitution driven by hardship, or thrill-seeking by children disturbed by the war. The Americans put forward various suggestions, including the imposition of a curfew for girls under sixteen and an increase in the age of consent to sexual intercourse from thirteen to fifteen, but the French government reacted frostily to any hint of interference from its ally.

With few young Frenchwomen prepared to go out with soldiers, the behaviour of servicemen began to provoke trouble. The conduct of US airborne troops in Nancy, a designated rest area from the front, led to a rash of complaints. What American officers regarded as the natural high spirits of their men was more often seen by the French as insulting behaviour.

The Hotel Meurice was the Paris officers' mess for SHAEF. Staff were also billeted at the Crillon, but those in the Meurice remember the smell in cupboards from the thick, greased leather of Wehrmacht boots. Morgan's Bank in the Place Vendôme was taken over as SHAEF's offices in Paris, but the bulk of Eisenhower's swelling military court was out at Versailles.

SHAEF was dominated by the Americans, with General Walter Bedell Smith as Eisenhower's chief of staff, but the British were also well represented. Bedell Smith's deputy was General Freddie Morgan, the chief planner of D-Day. But the two main administrators were General Lewis and his British counterpart, General Dixie Redman. Redman lived in some style, having taken over the apartment of Lady Mendl, best known as the decorator Elsie de Wolfe. There he entertained, with a limitless supply of whisky, gin and sandwiches made from NAAFI bread and tinned salmon.

SHAEF almost inevitably represented a state within a state, and Duff Cooper's concern was that 'all the Generals at SHAEF are violently anti-French except Morgan'. General Kenneth Strong, Eisenhower's chief intelligence officer, was prepared to show the British and American ambassadors intelligence reports only on condition that they did not show them to the French. Clearly, diplomats were suspected of being too sympathetic. Strong told even British colleagues that American officers at SHAEF 'did not have a high opinion of Mr Caffery', and that the ambassador was 'likely to be subordinated to General Eisenhower as long as the latter is in France'.

SHAEF used the fact that it was fighting a war to do whatever it pleased, ignoring Allied diplomats and the French provisional government. In the autumn of 1944 it obstructed the return of French officials from Algiers to Paris and British journalists coming over to France. The British also complained that Paris was 'full of American businessmen dressed in uniform', while British businessmen were refused permits to travel.

SHAEF's worst demonstrations of bloody-mindedness were reserved for the end of the war. It suddenly decided to destroy all the German equipment which the Americans did not need and refused to give any to the French. 'It seems hardly believable,' wrote Duff Cooper, when he heard. A month later SHAEF went further, ordering the French to hand over all captured enemy arms and equipment for destruction. 'The French have very sensibly refused,' wrote Duff Cooper in his diary on 13 June.

American diplomats appear to have had much more sympathy for France's predicament. When the American ambassador made 'a quiet and unostentatious visit to some of the so-called "red banlieus" of Paris' he was 'shocked and disturbed by the misery' he saw there and was surprised at the calm way their inhabitants regarded the terrible destruction from Allied bombing attacks on the marshalling yards. Over a thousand people had been killed in one area.

'It is clear that they expect pertinent help from the US,' he reported to Washington. Yet even telegrams from the American Embassy expressed one exasperation after another.

The French, on the other hand, felt belittled by the American attitude to their war record. Senior French officers had begun to complain openly that 'the US is supplying inferior and semi-obsolete tanks and other material to the French forces'. A far greater cause for French resentment, however, was the generally justified suspicion that the Americans preferred the Germans. In France, Americans claimed to hear only complaints and excuses; while in Germany they found a population grateful for having been saved from occupation by the Red Army.

Even military parades and celebrations of victory produced bad feeling among the Allies. During the spring and early summer of 1945, de Gaulle held no fewer than five major parades in just over three months. Allied diplomats and officers, especially the Americans, became increasingly exasperated at having to stand for hours watching 'their' tanks trundling past on victory parades, using their gasoline when the French were complaining about shortages of fuel.

After the victory celebrations in May came the biggest parade of all on 18 June – the anniversary of de Gaulle's broadcast from London – with a march-past by 50,000 men, led by the whole of the 2nd Armoured Division. It was a tremendous display, with the French air force flying low overhead in the shape of the cross of Lorraine. 'One couldn't help thinking,' wrote the usually sympathetic Duff Cooper, 'how all these [planes and vehicles] and most of the equipment was of Anglo-American origin. Not a single English or American flag was shown. There was no evidence of an ounce of gratitude and one felt throughout that France was boasting very loud, having very little to boast about.'

SHAEF had another reason for disapproving of the celebrations with the extra national holidays announced by the government. Coal production in France fell 80 per cent during the week of VE Day, just at the time when France was demanding more coal from the Ruhr on top of the 50,000 tons already allocated. 'They do not seem to be taking any very active steps to put their own house in order,' the SHAEF report concluded. Inevitably, another unfavourable comparison was made with the German determination to get back to work.

*

The French Communist Party was quick to exploit the reservoir of anti-American feeling. Some of the rumours spread were ludicrous, yet gained a measure of credence. The Communist minister, François Billoux, claimed that during the fighting the United States air force had bombed heavily 'in a premeditated plan to weaken France'. Another rumour even claimed that the Americans had been so angry about the Franco-Soviet pact signed in Moscow that they had allowed the German Ardennes offensive to penetrate into France purely to give the French a fright. Other rumours, rather closer to the truth, concerned a wave of crime by American servicemen and deserters.

Galtier-Boissière wrote, 'it appears that they are American deserters, who, with sub-machine-guns in hand, are playing at Chicago movies'. The Germans had been the '*Fridolins*'; now the Americans became known as '*Les Ricains*'.

At a dinner at the British Embassy, General Legentilhomme, the military governor of Paris, painted a terrifying picture to the Englishwoman beside him. American servicemen were 'barbarians, worse than the Russians, you simply cannot imagine, *chère madame*, how appalling the situation is'. Coincidentally, a British diplomat, driving back with his wife from a dinner party, found a street cordoned off by men armed with sub-machine-guns ready to rob the occupants of any car which passed. Reacting quickly, he accelerated, forcing them to jump for cover.

There is no way of telling whether these hold-ups were carried out by military personnel, or by civilians who had got hold of uniforms. Military police apparel was the most sought after. Clearly, French deserters and former *fifis* were also involved in some of the attacks. The director-general of the Sûreté Nationale described this 'increase in armed attacks' in a strong letter to the Minister of the Interior. On one evening alone, seven armed robberies had been carried out in the capital, two of them by American soldiers.

The generosity the French displayed towards the Americans and

British had been unstinted in the early days, going far beyond the bottles of champagne hidden until the Liberation. 'We've been waiting for you for so long,' they had said over and over again, with genuine emotion. But then, as Malcolm Muggeridge observed, everybody ends up by hating their liberators. The writer Alfred Fabre-Luce wrote of 'an army of drivers, with no indication of rank, who threw cigarettes to onlookers as if to an African crowd'.

The French indeed felt themselves very poor relations. The quantity of vehicles alone was a painful reminder of the French army in 1940, trudging to war after being delivered to a rail-head in cattle-trucks. The US army seemed to run not just on gasoline, but also on baked beans, coffee, cigarettes and packets of almost everything imaginable; not just cookies, candy and condoms, but also sachets of stew and mashed pota-toes, permanganate to sterilize the water, tins of peanut butter and condensed milk, doughnut-making machines mounted on army trucks, and, of course, K rations. French children swarmed round their vehicles begging for chewing-gum. Soon the drivers of trucks painted on their tailboard: 'No Gum Chum'.

The American influence in Paris became unmistakable. Some typically French bars were transformed, in an attempt to attract the rich liberators. Windows were darkened, iron chairs changed for comfortable upholstered ones, and the waiters in their black waistcoats and long white aprons were replaced with smiling girls. As a final touch, these new venues were given names like 'New York', or 'The Sunny Side of the Street'.

Many disliked the way French youth appeared infatuated with all things American – detective stories, films, clothes, jazz, bebop, Glenn Miller. This fascination represented both a yearn-ing to escape from the poverty and dilapidation around them, and a preference for American informality after the stuffiness of Vichy. But it also struck a deeper chord, the legend of a new world offering a vision to the old. 'America symbolized so many things!' wrote Simone de Beauvoir. 'It had stimulated our youth. It had also been a great myth – an untouchable myth.'

12
Writers and Artists in the Line of Fire

When the Allies disembarked in Normandy, Alfred Fabre-Luce saw their landing-craft as Viking ships in a new invasion. Along with other right-wing writers, journalists, actors and artists likely to be accused of collaboration, Fabre-Luce had to decide whether to stay or flee, but he appeared more relaxed than most. At a literary funeral during the uneasy interregnum of that summer, when writers of the intellectual Resistance were moving back to Paris, he noted that 'one could see side by side François Mauriac "already returned" and Drieu la Rochelle "not yet departed"'.

The tension increased during late July and early August. The actor and dramatist Sacha Guitry, like several others at risk, began to receive scribbled death threats. The Spanish ambassador, José Lequerica, at a dinner on 17 August, offered Guitry a visa for Spain. He made a similar offer to Drieu la Rochelle, but both declined: Drieu because he felt his fate awaited him in Paris, not in exile; and Guitry because he believed his popularity would protect him. (His optimism was excessive, if one goes by an IFOP opinion poll: 56 per cent of the sample wanted him punished.)

As well as writers such as Céline and Lucien Rebatet who escaped to Sigmaringen, a few sought shelter elsewhere. The elderly Alphonse de Châteaubriant, who won the Prix Goncourt in 1911, elected to live out a hermit's existence in a forest of the

Austrian Tyrol. He was on the Resistance's wanted list because he had been a member of the central committee for the recruitment of the Legion of French Volunteers. Charles Maurras, the arch-reactionary demagogue of Action Française, hid under a false name in Lyons. Georges Simenon, the Belgian-born creator of Inspector Maigret, feared arrest because two or three of his books had been filmed by the German film company Continental. He was placed under house arrest in January 1945 for three months, but released without charges being brought.

The majority of compromised writers chose to lie low and stay in the capital, despite the threat issued by the Resistance that all those who had contributed to enemy propaganda would be brought to justice. This justice was undefined, but the assassination on 28 June of Philippe Henriot, the Minister of Propaganda in Laval's last government, provided a clear warning that words as well as deeds could constitute a capital offence.

Drieu la Rochelle and Jacques Benoist-Méchin were among those who stayed behind. Benoist-Méchin had the most to fear. He had not simply written in support of the New European Order; he had served as a junior minister in the Vichy administration and been passionately involved in raising the anti-Bolshevik legion for the Russian front.

Drieu had signed the diehard declaration of right-wingers on 9 July 1944, which called for a new government and heavy penalties, including the death sentence, for all those who encouraged civil war or compromised 'the European position of France'. This would have been enough to execute him, but many would have pleaded for mercy in his case. Thanks to his charm and his talent, he had many friends on the left despite his views.

Obsessed since adolescence with death and suicide, Drieu made an unsuccessful attempt to kill himself the day before the church bells rang out in Paris. 'He failed with his death as he failed with his life' was the verdict of the Resistance newspaper *Franc-Tireur*. It took two more attempts before he finally succeeded in the following year. Drieu's old friend, Aldous Huxley, wrote after his death: 'The moral of the whole distressing story is that the majority of intellectuals at the present time recognize only two alternatives in their situation, and opt for one or the other, with results that are always bad, even if they happen to choose the victorious side.'

Others who stayed behind in the capital were Jean Giono, Fabre-Luce, Henry de Montherlant, Paul Chack and Robert Brasillach, the latter an exultant fascist and former editor of that virulent publication, *Je suis partout*. Hidden in various apartments behind closed shutters, all they could do in that last week of August was to listen to the sounds of the Liberation and wait for a hammering on the door.

On 14 September, after twenty-eight days concealed in an attic room, Brasillach gave himself up. After taking a last look at the banks of the Seine opposite Notre-Dame – 'Paris is beautiful, when one is about to leave it,' he wrote later in prison – he presented himself in the afternoon at the Prefecture of Police, and was conducted without handcuffs across to the Conciergerie on the Quai de l'Horloge.

Prominent figures in the performing arts were more visible targets than writers, but few of them had been carried away by the sort of dangerous idealism which had infected Brasillach. These members of the demi-collaboration were not guilty of treason, but of wanting to continue their lives as if nothing had changed. Jean-Louis Barrault argued that continuing to work and ignoring the Germans was a positive attitude, and all that could be done if one were not an active member of the Resistance.

This was perfectly valid as far as it went, but many people found it difficult to remain morally upright throughout the Occupation. It was also tempting for people in the performing arts to look on the Germans in Paris as no more than a new, cultivated élite. Otto Abetz was an ardent francophile and those who attended his parties at the German Embassy in the rue de Lille found it hard to remember that this was the civilized face of a brutal and oppressive enemy.

The superficial glamour of the Occupation was perhaps best illustrated at the parties given by General Hanesse of the Luftwaffe, who had taken over the Rothschild town house in the Avenue de Marigny as his official residence. There he gave magnificent receptions, for Goering amongst others, which attracted a number of stars from the French stage. Arletty had a stronger reason for going. Her lover, with whom she lived in the Ritz, was one of General Hanesse's officers. His guests were not only film stars. On his return from prison camp, Baron Élie de Rothschild remarked to the old family butler, Félix, that the house must have been very quiet under General Hanesse's occupation.

'On the contrary, Monsieur Élie. There were receptions every evening.'

'But . . . who came?'

'The same people, Monsieur Élie. The same as before the war.'

Sacha Guitry, whose talents both as a dramatist and an actor suggest comparisons with Noël Coward, was arrested early one morning before he had a chance to dress. He was hustled out of his house in yellow-flowered pyjamas, jade-green crocodile pumps and a panama hat, and taken to the *mairie* of the 7th *arrondissement*. When asked by the examining magistrate after his arrest why he had agreed to meet Goering, Guitry replied '*par curiosité*'. He said that he would have been just as interested in having dinner with Stalin, which was probably true.

Guitry recorded in his memoirs that as Leclerc's troops approached the city Arletty had telephoned him in great agitation: she was an obvious target for *épuration*. When she was arrested early in September, a terrible rumour ran round Paris that her breasts had been cut off. This was a grotesque invention, but she may well have had her head shaved. Her hairdresser clearly remembers her turbanned head and having to make a wig for her. Arletty is said to have yelled at her accusers: 'What is this government which is so interested in our sex lives!' Her own account plays down the event of her arrest: 'Two very discreet gentlemen came to fetch me.' There was a car and no handcuffs, she said. From prison, she was allowed out under escort to make the final re-shoots for *Les Enfants du Paradis*. It came out on 15 March 1945. One of her lines ran: 'I am the victim of a miscarriage of justice.'

Gabrielle Coco Chanel was born poor like Arletty, but rose to become the founder of one of Paris's most successful fashion houses. She too had made her way up from nothing, and was contemptuous of what people thought. 'France has got what she deserves!' Chanel declared at a lunch party on the Côte d'Azur in 1943. Prince Jean-Louis de Faucigny-Lucinge's wife, Baba, was so shocked that on meeting Coco the next day, she turned her back. (Shortly afterwards, when police came to arrest Baba Lucinge as a Jew – she was born d'Erlanger – Johnny Lucinge suspected that Chanel had tipped off the German authorities.)

The most striking similarity between Arletty and Chanel was that both had taken German lovers and lived in the Ritz. Arletty had her '*beau fridolin*' from the Luftwaffe, as Galtier-Boissière called him. Chanel – then aged sixty – was with a handsome German called Hans Gunther von Dincklage, known as Spatz, who may or may not have been an Abwehr spy.

As an insurance policy at the Liberation, Coco Chanel is said to have given away hundreds of *flacons* of Chanel No. 5 to GIs, from her establishment in the rue Cambon. But when she was arrested at the Ritz early in September no American troops came to her support. She was, however, released soon after. She claimed that she had been involved in a secret mission to Spain, to bring the Allies and the Axis to the peace table, and hinted that Winston Churchill – a friend from her days as the mistress of Bendor, the 2nd Duke of Westminster – had intervened on her behalf. But whatever the reasons for her release, she left Paris in a bitter mood. She and Spatz, who had got out of France before the Liberation, were reunited in Switzerland; and Chanel made only odd visits to France over the next eight years.

Colette had supplemented her income during the Occupation by writing for the collaborationist paper *Le Petit Parisien*, and even produced an article for the pro-German *La Gerbe*. On the other hand she was hiding her Jewish husband, Maurice Goudeket. After his escape from prison camp, he did not leave their apartment in the Palais Royal until the Liberation.

Colette's neighbour in the Palais Royal, Jean Cocteau, exaggerated the insults and blows he received from fascists during the Occupation as an avant-garde writer and a homosexual. As a persecuted minority, he stood a better chance of effacing his appearances in Otto Abetz's salon at the German Embassy.

Serge Lifar, Diaghilev's protégé, who during the Occupation had been the Vichy-appointed director of the Paris Opéra and had toured in Germany, was initially banned for life from the French stage but was then let off with only a year's suspension. He protested that he should have been honoured, not condemned, for having saved the Opéra from the Germans, but Lifar was seldom in touch with the real world.

Collaborators in the plastic arts numbered those who had attended the opening of the exhibition of Nazi-approved sculpture by Arno Breker at the Orangerie in May 1942, and those who had accepted an official tour of Germany sponsored by Berlin.

The Breker exhibition, in aid of Wehrmacht charities, was opened by the sculptor Aristide Maillol, and the occasion attracted most of the demi-collaboration. Guitry even argued in his memoirs that because Breker had asked Maillol to open his exhibition, and introduced him to a line of saluting Wehrmacht generals as '*Mon maître vénéré*', the whole event represented France's supremacy in the arts over Germany, and thus washed away the defeat of 1940. Guitry did not mention that a year later 'degenerate works' by Max Ernst, Léger, Miró, Picabia and Picasso were publicly destroyed outside the Jeu de Paume.

Among the painters who had been on the sponsored tour of Germany were Paul Belmondo, André Derain, Dunoyer de Segonzac, Kees van Dongen and Vlaminck. Vlaminck, a friend of Simenon and bitter enemy of Picasso, went into hiding at the Liberation. But the sanctions against the painters were mild. The Beaux-Arts recommended that they should each be made to create a major work for the state as punishment, and their works were excluded from the Salon de la Libération.

'It is clear,' wrote Galtier-Boissière in his diary two weeks after the Liberation, 'that the majority of our stars are more or less tainted ... but in the campaigns which are gathering steam, there is a strong whiff of jealousy.' Even after Arletty's death in the summer of 1992, letters were published in newspapers objecting to the fulsome obituaries. They did not complain about her '*collaboration horizontale*' with a German officer, but about the fact that she had been dining at the Ritz while the rest of France was eating so badly.

Most of the directors and stars of the cinema had worked with the German-controlled company Continental. Henri-Georges Clouzot was the director of *Le Corbeau*, considered one of the most remarkable films of the war years. The Germans were very dubious about *Le Corbeau*, in which a series of poison-pen letters throws the inhabitants of a village into a turmoil of mutual hatred and suspicion. Many people saw it as a veiled indictment of the Occupation; but after the Liberation, Clouzot was banned from working in France. As soon as the decision was announced he left for Hollywood.

Robert Brasillach reached Fresnes prison a week after Benoist-Méchin, but at first neither of them knew of the other's presence, even though they were colleagues in an alien world, with echoing sounds of footsteps, keys jangling and iron doors clanging.

Benoist-Méchin described the image of shivering figures in its foggy penumbra as 'a queue of the damned waiting to cross the river Styx'.

In the rare moments they found for conversation, usually in the exercise space, they discussed their lawyers, their examining magistrates, but not their own prospects of acquittal, only those of others. The trials of writers and propagandists began that autumn.

The last day of October marked the trial of a fanatical old scribbler of pamphlets, Comte Armand de Chastenet de Puységur, who described himself professionally on his visiting cards as '*anti-sémite, anti-mason, anti-bourgeois, anti-capitaliste, anti-communiste, anti-democrate et anti-républicain*'. When he heard the death sentence read out, he gave the fascist salute and shouted, '*Vive la France!*' The anti-semites of *vieille France* had forgotten nothing and forgiven nobody. When Charles Maurras, the leader of Action Française, was condemned to life imprisonment a few months later, he cried from the dock, 'It's the revenge of Dreyfus!' Maurras lost his chair at the Académie Française.

Céline, imprisoned in Denmark, was accused *in absentia* of collaboration under Article 75. His retort, predictably sarcastic, was that he had hardly sold the plans of the Maginot Line. He also sent the following diatribe from Copenhagen: 'I never set foot in the German Embassy. I never met Otto Abetz before the war. Abetz always detested me. I met Abetz during the war two or three times for a few minutes. I always found the political activities of Abetz grotesque and disastrous and the man himself a creature of terrible vanity, a cataclysmic clown.'

The purge of writers was not only a judicial affair. It became a matter of professional conscience, or politics. During the Occupation the Comité National des Écrivains – the National Committee of Writers – had been established as an association of intellectual resistance. Its mouthpiece was *Les Lettres Françaises*, the literary review of the Resistance, established by Jacques

Decour (later executed by the Germans at the fort of Mont-Valérian) and Jean Paulhan, the writer and editor at Gallimard. *Les Lettres Françaises* was a defiant challenge to Drieu la Rochelle's takeover of *La Nouvelle Revue Française*.

On 9 September, two weeks after the Liberation, the first non-clandestine issue was published. It contained not only articles by Mauriac, Sartre and Paulhan, but also a 'Manifesto of French Writers' signed by some sixty leading intellectuals. This contained a demand for 'the just punishment of usurpers and traitors'. The next issue had a blacklist from the CNE containing ninety-four names. An expanded list of 156 names was included in the issue of 21 October.

Jean Paulhan – '*Paulhan le Juste*', as Galtier-Boissière called him – became first uneasy, then strongly opposed to the calls for retribution. Like Paulhan, Galtier-Boissière distrusted and disliked the rush to accuse. 'The Nazis,' he wrote, 'have left us an imprint of authoritarianism and persecution.'

Louis Aragon, the Surrealist turned Stalinist, with his silver hair and icy looks, was the Robespierre of the intellectuals. He attempted to extend the attack to writers hated by the Communist Party. But he was not as bloodthirsty against his right-wing colleagues as has often been made out. He stood up for Drieu la Rochelle and for his former publisher, Robert Denoël.

The trials of journalists and writers continued in December and into January 1945. This rapid rhythm was explained by Pierre-Henri Teitgen, who became de Gaulle's next Minister of Justice: 'these "intellectuals" had provided the prosecution case for their own trial during the Occupation. It was only necessary to reread their articles and other published work to establish, without any argument, the indictment they deserved before sending them in front of the court.' The result was that writers were tried while the clamour for vengeance was at its peak.

On 29 December, however, when Henri Béraud, the editor of

Gringoire, was condemned to death, people were shocked. Béraud was right-wing, anti-semitic and hated the British, but he had never written in favour of the Germans. Many suspected that jealousy had played a part. Béraud had been the best-paid journalist in France, earning 600,000 francs a year. And when the secretary of Jean Hérold-Paquis (the announcer of Radio-Paris, who had been executed in October) was condemned to forced labour for life, even the Resistance press was outraged.

Two days later, on 4 January, François Mauriac published his article, 'About a Verdict', in *Le Figaro*. There were no grounds for condemning Béraud for intelligence with the enemy, he argued.

This intervention almost certainly persuaded de Gaulle to commute the sentence. In his campaign in *Le Figaro* against the imbalances of the *épuration*, Mauriac even went so far as to say that people should be allowed to have made the wrong political choice – a brave position to hold at the time, and one that made him many enemies. The satirical weekly, *Le Canard enchaîné*, baptized this outspoken Catholic writer *'Saint-François des assises'* – St Francis of the assizes. Camus argued in *Combat* that mercy for killers removed their victims' right to justice, and that the crimes of fascism must be discouraged for ever. Mauriac replied in *Le Figaro*; and so began a great tennis-match of moral argument.

Even before it opened on 19 January 1945, there was a feeling that Robert Brasillach's trial was to be the apogee of the intellectual purge. François Mauriac and Paul Valéry both provided submissions on his behalf. And the reaction of his fellow inmate at Fresnes, Jacques Benoist-Méchin – 'one doesn't kill a poet' – revealed an instinctive belief that a poet was sacrosanct, almost a secular priest. It was the feeling which had swept Europe in 1936 when the Nationalists executed Federico García Lorca. The fact that Brasillach was on trial, not for his literature, but for his denunciatory journalism made little difference.

The morning of the trial was intensely cold. Paris had been under snow for sixteen days. There was no fuel for heating since coal-barges were ice-locked on canals. In the ill-lit court-room, the breath of a speaker condensed in the freezing air.

The issues, apparently clear at first, were hammered in and out of shape by both sides. Brasillach's counsel, Maître Jacques Isorni, who became famous as Marshal Pétain's most eloquent defender seven months later, claimed that an error of political judgement did not constitute treason. If Brasillach had supported the Germans, it was his way of wanting a stronger France.

The crucial question lay in his articles in *Je suis partout*. Here Isorni was on more difficult ground. Brasillach's words were there on the page, and what Isorni called his '*erreurs tragiques*' went beyond most people's idea of collaboration. He had supported the German invasion of the unoccupied zone in November 1942 on the grounds that it reunited France. He had called for the death of politicians such as Georges Mandel, Reynaud's Minister of the Interior in 1940, who was murdered by *miliciens* shortly before the liberation of Paris. Although he had not denounced anybody directly, he had denounced people in print. Brasillach, like Drieu, had signed the call in the summer of 1944 for the summary execution of all members of the Resistance. But perhaps his most telling statement was: 'We must get rid of the Jews as a whole and not keep the children.' Brasillach claimed that, although anti-semitic, he had never advocated collective violence against the Jews. Probably he did not know about the death camps when he wrote those words; yet even if he was thinking of mass resettlement in Eastern Europe, they are still horrifying.

Despite the weight of the case against him, Brasillach confidently dissected the prosecution case in the interests of historical accuracy. He defended himself 'with eloquence and skill', wrote the apprentice film-director Alexandre Astruc, reporting the case for *Combat*. The jury, however, took only twenty minutes to reach their verdict. '*C'est un honneur*' was Brasillach's only comment on the death sentence, after some of his supporters had cried protests in his favour.

Mauriac decided to try to save Brasillach's life. Meanwhile, a petition demanding mercy was organized. There were a few genuine resistants who signed, many neutrals, and a number of writers and artists who were already under a cloud. Some, like Jean Cocteau, signed because they felt that writers were being made the scapegoats for other leading collaborationists, especially industrialists, who, it could be argued, had killed many more people by helping the German war machine.

But the petition for mercy racked many consciences, Camus suffering most of all. A number of writers feared that if they signed, they would appear to condone what Brasillach had done.

On 3 February 1945 at midday François Mauriac was received by de Gaulle at the rue Saint-Dominique with great courtesy; but that, as he realized, was not a reliable indication of the General's thinking. Isorni received a much clearer idea that night at de Gaulle's private residence in the Bois de Boulogne, where he was taken in an official car, through heavily guarded barriers. De Gaulle, despite all Isorni's arguments, decided to reject the appeal.

Isorni believed that de Gaulle did not want to be attacked by the Communists for softness. There is also a phrase in Gaston Palewski's memoirs which revealed his influence: 'Personally, I regret that I did not insist on a reprieve for Robert Brasillach.'

Brasillach was executed on 6 February. It was the eleventh anniversary of the right-wing riot and the attempt to storm the National Assembly across the Pont de la Concorde, an event which led, two years later, to the Popular Front government. On 20 April 1945, as the Red Army fought towards the centre of Berlin, Brasillach's coffin was moved to the cemetery of Père-Lachaise.

His friend, Jacques Benoist-Méchin, did not face trial for over two and a half years. The delay undoubtedly saved him. He was condemned to death on 6 June 1947, but his sentence was quickly commuted to forced labour for life. He was freed in 1954, having acquired a fascination with the world of Islam through prison reading. This extraordinary man amassed such a knowledge of his subject that de Gaulle, after he became President in 1958, used him discreetly as a special adviser on Arab matters.

Céline, finally tried *in absentia* in 1950, received a sentence that would have been unimaginably light five years before – a year in prison and a heavy fine.

The *épuration* only increased political tensions in the world of letters and the arts. According to that redoubtable chaplain of the FFI, Father Bruckberger, he and Camus resigned from the National Committee of Writers because of the increasing Communist grip exerted by Aragon and Elsa Triolet. Mauriac, who did not resign, later buttonholed Camus in an attempt to persuade him to return.

'Why did you resign?' he asked.

'It's for me to ask you why you didn't resign,' Camus replied. 'And I'll tell you why you didn't: because you were afraid.'

'You're quite right,' Mauriac admitted.

Mauriac was too honest to have any illusions. At a dinner with Pastor Boegner, he described the National Front – a Communist-dominated organization of which he was a member – as 'the screen behind which Communism carries out its business. I know because I'm part of it.'

Jean Paulhan raged the most against the takeover of *Les Lettres Françaises*. He openly scorned the more-resistant-than-thou fellow-travellers and the National Committee of Writers, which Aragon and Triolet wanted to turn into a writers' union closely allied to the Communist Party.

Aragon's plan, no doubt elaborated at party headquarters, was the classic Stalinist tactic of extending the purge to include critics of the Communist Party. On 25 November, in *Les Lettres Françaises*, he launched an attack on André Gide, comparing him to Hérold-Paquis, the fascist propagandist from Radio-Paris. His real target was not the Gide who had, for a short period, written for Drieu's *Nouvelle Revue Française*, but the unrepentant author of *Retour de l'URSS*, the book most reviled by Stalinists at the time of the Spanish Civil War. Gide's friend, Roger Martin du Gard, was disgusted with 'the bad faith and the dishonest motives of Aragon', and he warned Gide in Algiers to take care on his return to France. 'Think carefully about reaching Paris: the ground is mined!'

The party also sought to destroy the reputation of Paul Nizan, a novelist and Sartre's oldest friend, who had been killed on the retreat to Dunkirk in 1940. Nizan had been a loyal Communist until the Nazi–Soviet pact in August 1939. When his very short and simple letter of resignation was published, the enraged party circulated malicious allegations and Maurice Thorez described him as a 'police spy'.

After the war Louis Aragon, as part of a renewed whispering campaign against Nizan, repeated the allegation to Sartre, a fellow member of the National Committee of Writers. Sartre prepared a statement of protest against the vilification and persuaded André Breton, Albert Camus, Jean Paulhan, Julien Benda and François Mauriac to sign as well. Sartre was powerful enough to stand up to the Communist anger directed against him, but the lies lingered on for years.

Politics were also complicated for those in the literary establishment who had something to hide. The veteran Catholic poet, Paul Claudel, presented a poem to the glory of General de Gaulle, which was read at a gala for the Resistance at the Comédie-Française some ten weeks after the Liberation. But the following morning, unkind tongues reminded people that

Claudel had written a strikingly similar work in 1942, dedicated to the glory of Marshal Pétain.

Several publishers faced even more delicate problems. A week after the Liberation, the Resistance press demanded the blacklisting of publishers accused of collaboration, among them Gaston Gallimard, Bernard Grasset and Robert Denoël. Grasset was arrested and taken off to Fresnes prison, but Gallimard was left untouched. Gallimard had allowed Drieu la Rochelle to take over the *Nouvelle Revue Française*, but since he had also helped Jean Paulhan launch its Resistance counterpart, *Les Lettres Françaises*, he had covered himself brilliantly. 'Not stupid, the old man!' commented Galtier-Boissière in cynical admiration.

Gallimard had another strong suit. His publishing house, which dominated French literature, boasted many members of the National Committee of Writers. He had been scrupulous, even generous, in the dispatch of royalty cheques during the lean Occupation years, so it would have been a very churlish writer who was not grateful. Even Aragon was about to have his next novel, *Aurélien*, published by Gallimard, having forsaken Denoël.

It was no secret that Gaston Gallimard had cooperated with the Germans. He had respected the 'Otto List' (named after Otto Abetz) of works proscribed by the Germans; he had exercised self-censorship in the books he published during the Occupation, and he had attended receptions at the Deutsche Institut. Nobody said anything, but André Malraux did not forget. To obtain revenge on Jean-Paul Sartre some four years later, he was to blackmail Gaston Gallimard, threatening to expose his wartime record.

13
The Return of Exiles

The steady stream of exiles returning to Paris in 1944 and 1945 came from all classes and several nationalities. Many workers and their families, who had been close to starvation in the city, had sought shelter with peasant relatives. Hitching rides in different sorts of wood-burning vehicles, or on trains once the tracks were repaired, they returned with their few possessions in cardboard suitcases. Wherever possible, they brought a sack or two of flour back with them, either to sell or to keep them through the months ahead. Few took much notice of their arrival in the upheaval of the times. But the exiles whose return Parisians remembered for the rest of their lives were the *déportés* who arrived back from Germany in the spring of 1945.

The term *déporté* was loosely used to cover three different categories of prisoner: Jewish and other racial minorities sent to extermination camps, members of the Resistance sent to concentration camps, and conscripts sent on forced labour by the Vichy government from 1943. The prisoners-of-war from the defeat in 1940 were treated no differently from their British, Dutch and Belgian counterparts.

In April 1945, the advancing armies found themselves liberating one camp after another. The commanders, their attention focused on finishing the war, were unprepared to cope with the problem of feeding and caring for hundreds of thousands of civilians, many of whom were close to death. All too often, they were given ration packs and told to fend for themselves until the fighting was over.

Relatives waiting for news in Paris found the mixture of hope and fear very hard to bear. It often produced a feverish nausea. Sleep was impossible. The novelist Marguerite Duras sat by the telephone, convinced that her husband Robert Antelme had been among those executed at the last moment by the SS before the Allies arrived. Whenever it rang, the caller turned out to be a friend asking, 'Any news?'

Even when transport was finally organized for repatriation, the process was still slow. The journey back to France could take five days. (As soon as the war ended in May, the Americans allocated the bulk of their transport aircraft to ferrying back prisoners, and the whole procedure speeded up immeasurably.) Some passed through Switzerland via Geneva, where Pierre de Gaulle, the General's brother, was consul. The depth of his sympathy was in no doubt. Pierre Daix, a young Communist who had survived Mauthausen, found himself spontaneously embraced.

On 14 April 1945 at the Gare de Lyon, an official reception committee, which included General de Gaulle, Henri Frenay, François Mitterrand and the two Communist leaders, Jacques Duclos and André Marty, waited to welcome back the first group of 288 women.* Well-wishers carried lilac blossom to present to them and women brought lipsticks and face-powder to distribute. They expected the returning prisoners to look thin and tired from their experiences, but not much more. France had been partially shielded from the appalling truth. The French ministry with responsibility for prisoners, deportees and refugees had been trying to suppress information about the camps, just when General Eisenhower was calling for every available jour-

---

* De Gaulle, however, was seen as relatively uninterested in the fate of the deportees. Marguerite Duras could not forgive him for having said on 3 April, 'The days of tears are past. The days of glory have returned.'

nalist to be brought in to Germany to report on their horrors.

Few had imagined the reality of virtual skeletons dressed like scarecrows. 'Their faces were grey-green with reddish brown circles round their eyes, which seemed to see but not to take in,' wrote Janet Flanner, the American journalist. Galtier-Boissière described deportees as having 'a greenish, waxen complexion, shrunken faces, reminiscent of those little human heads modelled by primitive tribes'. Some were too weak to remain upright, but those who could stood to attention in front of the welcoming committee and began to sing the Marseillaise in cracked voices. Their audience was devastated.

Such scenes were repeated many times. Louise Alcan, aged thirty-four, a survivor of Birkenau and Ravensbrück, described her own arrival: 'Gare de l'Est. Eight in the morning. A crowd behind the barriers. We sing the Marseillaise. The people look at us and burst into tears.'

The few French Jews who returned from the death camps aligned themselves with their compatriots. Vichy had stripped them of their nationality and handed them over to the Germans, but they were no less French for that: they too sang the Marseillaise and the '*Chant du départ*', that battle anthem of the French Revolution. Only a tiny percentage of almost 80,000 'racial deportees' returned: over a quarter of the entire population of French Jews had perished. Vichy had also handed over another 40,000 foreign Jews who had sought refuge in France. In addition there were around 100,000 political prisoners and the 600,000 conscripts on forced labour, many of whom had worked and died while constructing factories underground to escape Allied bombing. Out of a total of 820,000 French deportees, some 222,000 are estimated to have died.

The first processing point was at the Gare d'Orsay. General Dixie Redman took his military assistant Mary Vaudoyer there, having told her: 'You must see this, and you must never forget it.' They stood looking out of a window into a huge space, where hundreds of men were walking, completely naked, covered in de-lousing powder and DDT, such was the fear of typhus.* Their faces were cavernous, their heads bald, either shaved or with alopecia from malnutrition, their eyes downcast. None spoke. Both Redman and his assistant were appalled that they should be obliged to undergo yet one more humiliation. When they were deemed to have been disinfected, they were dressed in surplus British battledress, coarse, hot and often several sizes too big for them, and heavy ammunition boots.

From the Gare d'Orsay, the deportees were taken to the Hotel Lutetia, which had been the Abwehr headquarters during the Occupation. The whole block was surrounded by relatives desperate for news. Newspapers were full of little advertisements seeking information on missing relatives, or announcements of deaths at last confirmed. Such was the confusion and the scale of the task that some families had to wait several more months.

Marguerite Duras's husband was saved by a miracle and by determination. François Mitterrand, the leader of Antelme's resistance group, was part of a semi-official French mission sent to Germany. He managed to get into Dachau, which had been sealed off by the US army to prevent the spread of typhus. A voice called out, 'François!' He did not recognize the living corpse. It was his companion who recognized Robert Antelme, and then only by his teeth.

Mitterrand rang Duras in Paris. He told her to send two members of the group to his office, where he had organized passes and three uniforms. Using a car and petrol obtained by Mitterrand, the two friends drove through the night, reaching Dachau the next morning. They dressed this virtual skeleton in the spare uniform which they had smuggled into the camp and carried him out, held upright between them, past the guard post. Fortunately, the American sentries were so afraid of infection that they all wore gas-masks and could not see very clearly.

* In fact there were only 91 cases in Paris, and only 77 Parisians died of it that year, half the figure of twenty years earlier.

The concierge who had decorated the entrance to welcome him home shut herself in her *loge* to cry in anger.

The concierge who had decorated the entrance to welcome him home shut herself in her *loge* to cry in anger.

Antelme was laid on the back seat of their car and driven back to Paris. The return journey took three times as long. None of them expected him to survive it. But when they finally reached the rue Saint-Benoît, he was still alive. Despite all the warnings of how he had changed, Duras herself nearly suffered a nervous breakdown and had to be revived with rum by a neighbour. The concierge who had decorated the entrance to welcome him home shut herself in her *loge* to cry in anger.

Everything possible was done for the deportees at the Luttia. By right of suffering, they were known as 'the best of the French'. Nothing was too good for them: veal, cheese and real coffee, obtainable only on the black market, were produced. But often the best intentions did not effect the right treatment. Deportees needed the simplest food in tiny quantities. Their stomachs were so unprepared for the change that they were violently ill. They also needed peace and quiet, not the pandemonium around the Luttia. 'We really felt like Martians,' wrote Daix.

Some had survived their ordeals in the most astonishing way. Among those flown in from Germany was the Comtesse de Mauduit, an American who had hidden Allied airmen in her château in Brittany until a maid denounced her. Bessie de Mauduit arrived from Ravensbrück 'still dressed in the striped uniform of prisoners, yet still very elegant'. She told her story to Jean and Charlotte Galtier-Boissière: 'I never cried once in two years of captivity,' Bessie de Mauduit concluded, with a proud smile, 'but I cried on seeing Paris again.' A few days later Galtier-Boissière learned that Bessie de Mauduit had managed to look so elegant in her camp uniform because a forewoman from Schiaparelli, a fellow prisoner, had re-fashioned it for her.

The resistants survived best in the long run, while '*kapos*' and collaborators – with what might be seen retrospectively as moral justice – had the lowest survival rate. Those who had tried to obliterate their own individuality in an attempt to make them-

selves invisible to *kapos* or SS guards may have survived better
in the short term; but turning off a psychological switch to
become an apathetic automaton – they were known as 'musulmans' in the camps – made it almost impossible to recover
afterwards. Altogether 6,000 deportees died soon after their
return, of whom 'musulmans' made up a significant proportion.

The difficulty of returning to their old lives was common to
all. They were unable to sleep in a soft bed. They suffered from
nightmares and a lack of confidence. Worst of all, in a way, was
the disappointment in homecoming: their families found it very
hard to cope with their depressions, caused largely by survivor
guilt. 'Joy did not come,' wrote Daix, 'because we had brought
too many dead back with us.'

Their whole relationship with the normal world had been
completely distorted by their recent submersion in the nightmare
of the '*univers concentrationnaire*'. Charles Spitz, a *résistant-déporté*
who had worked in the Dora tunnel, found that the habits of the
prison camp died hard. Two months after his return to Paris, his
wife suggested they go and have dinner in a restaurant. 'She
had bought me the whole panoply of civilized man, including a
wallet and purse. But, without her knowledge, I still kept in my
pocket a little wooden box which a comrade from Dora had
made for me. It contained some bits of string, pins, and other
treasures which were precious in the camp . . . When it came to
pay the bill, to everybody's stupefaction, I automatically opened
my box and emptied its contents on the table.'

The prisoners-of-war were processed at the Rex and Gaumont
cinemas. One prisoner, just arrived from Germany, when asked
where his home was in France, replied that he was from Ora-
dour. The person in charge of interviewing him fainted, unable
to tell him that the village and almost all its inhabitants had
been destroyed by the SS Das Reich division.

There were many tragedies awaiting them, both great and
small. In a number of cases, a prisoner reached his apartment to

be told by a neighbour that his wife had gone to live with another man. One arrived home to find a child of whose existence he had never been told. His wife was not there, having slipped out to the shops. The man's jealousy exploded after five years of prison camp and he killed the child. He then went off to surrender to the police. But the child was not his wife's by another man. She had just been acting as a child-minder, to earn a little money.

Special Operations Executive (SOE), whose captured agents had been sent to concentration camps, devoted great efforts to finding them in the crowds at the Gare d'Orsay. Teams of FANYs (the young women of the First Aid Nursing Yeomanry attached to SOE) worked in relays trying to spot survivors who had changed almost out of all recognition. The task was so distressing that one or two of them had nervous breakdowns.

SOE had already set up a base in Paris by taking over the Hotel Cecil in the rue Lauriston, and was doing all it could to help its agents, their families and those who had helped in other ways, with food from US army bulk ration packs. This had to be done discreetly because it was strictly against regulations. They were all invited to eat at the Cecil, then encouraged to take away as much as they could afterwards.

Apart from its own refugees, France found itself responsible for over 100,000 displaced persons from forty-seven nationalities by July 1945. They included 30,000 Russians, of whom 11,800 were prisoners-of-war, 31,500 Poles and 24,000 Yugoslavs.

Since long before the First World War, Paris had been the haven for refugees from all over Europe, fleeing autocracy, pogroms and violent nationalism. Bolshevism and then fascism in all its forms vastly increased the flow. Since 1900 foreign communities had swelled in Paris, with Armenians escaping the Turkish massacres; White Russians escaping the Revolution and civil war; Poles, mainly Jewish, fleeing Pilsudski's regime. Political fugitives arrived from Mussolini's Italy and the Balkan dictatorships; then Jews, left-wingers and liberals from Hitler's Germany and other countries subsequently occupied by the Nazis. Finally, in 1939, came the largest wave of all when over half a million defeated Spanish Republicans crossed the Pyrenees, fleeing Franco's execution squads.

The largest Jewish ghetto had been in the 20th *arrondissement*, '*le village Yiddish de Belleville*' just north-west of Père Lachaise. The oldest was in the Marais; but the Jewish professional classes were spread all over the middle-class districts of Paris. People who had undergone the most appalling tortures and humiliations had to re-learn how to be doctors, teachers, lawyers and businessmen. The only way they could do this was to lock away the past at the back of their minds, and never to refer to it. Richard Arzt, who grew up in a French Jewish family in the late 1940s, said that in his house the Holocaust and the sufferings of the Jews were simply never mentioned. When a female cousin became engaged to a German many years later, Arzt was astonished at the depths of rancour and pain that the announcement aroused.

Other returning foreign exiles seemed to inhabit a completely different world, whether on the Left Bank or in the *beaux quartiers*. Gertrude Stein and Alice Toklas, apparently protected by their innocence or a guardian angel, had managed to live out the war in the Alpine foothills of Savoie. They had never imagined that they were in danger as Jews. German soldiers had been billeted on them but had not realized that Stein and Toklas were not French, and they had gazed blankly at the Picassos on the wall. Fortunately, the friendly mayor had kept their name off the register.

Their return to the rue Christine was an emotional moment. 'All the pictures were there, the apartment was all there, and it was all clean and beautiful. We just looked, and then everybody came running in, the concierge, the husband of the laundress downstairs, the secretary of our landlord, the bookbinder, they all came rushing in to say how do you do and to tell us about the visit of the Gestapo; their stamp was still on the door.'

While Gertrude Stein found that her apartment had been protected, Nancy Cunard returned to a scene of devastation. She had known Paris from the days of the Surrealists in the Café Cyrano on the Place Blanche, when Louis Aragon had been her lover. Her greatest achievement was the Hours Press which published original works, mainly poetry, by Ezra Pound, Richard Aldington, Robert Graves, Harold Acton and Samuel Beckett.

Nancy Cunard reached Paris at the end of February 1945, and embraced a rather bewildered porter in blue overalls, the most accessible representative of the city's working class. Over the next few days, she walked back and forth across the city, looking and remembering, and saw friends from the past, such as Janet Flanner and Diana Cooper, whom she had known before the First World War. But when she returned to her house at Réanville in Normandy she found that it had been looted and defiled, not by the Germans but by neighbours she had considered friends. The Hours Press was badly damaged, along with all her primitive statues. She was left in no doubt of how much the locals had secretly disapproved of her left-wing causes and her lovers, especially her black lover, Henry Crowder.

Samuel Beckett returned from his hiding-place in Provence where he had often listened to music composed by Henry Crowder, played on an upright piano. Nancy Cunard thought he looked like 'an Aztec eagle' and that he had a 'feeling of the spareness of the desert about him'. Peggy Guggenheim, with whom he had a brief affair shortly before the war, described him more prosaically, but no less accurately, as 'a tall lanky Irishman of about thirty with enormous green eyes that never looked at you'. He was so modest that after the war very few people knew that he had been awarded the Croix de Guerre and the Médaille de la Résistance.

Others took longer to return home. Julien Green booked his passage back across the Atlantic on the *Erickson*, a former troopship which had lost little of its discomfort, but the poems of John Donne took his mind off it. Even if the danger of submarines was over, mines still floated in the English Channel. But what struck him most was the advice he received on reaching Paris when he asked after friends: 'It's better not to ask after this person or that.'

André Gide, whom he went to see, was scarcely more encouraging from another point of view. He told Green that he would die of cold and hunger in Paris. To escape such misery, he himself was off to Egypt.

Foreigners returning received a slightly different impression; not one of external dilapidation, but of an internal decay while the exterior remained untouched. Isaiah Berlin wrote to a friend, 'Paris seemed terrifying to me – so cold and abnormally clean and empty and more beautiful than I have ever seen a city to be – more so than Leningrad, and I cannot say how much that means – but empty and hollow and dead, like an exquisite corpse; the metaphor is vile and commonplace, but I can think of nothing else.' And Susan Mary Patten, the wife of an American diplomat, wrote that 'it was like looking at a Canova death mask'.

But the city's empty elegance soon began to be filled with those who regarded it as the most civilized setting for their entertainment. The shortages of food did not cause them suffering, only the expense of the black market.

'The Ritz,' noted the British ambassador, 'looked exactly as it did pre-war with Mrs Corrigan sitting in one corner of it.' Laura Corrigan had reappeared, having left Paris in 1942. She had made generous efforts to help French soldiers in 1940, and for her work she had received the Legion of Honour from Pétain's administration; but this award, like all similar ones, was automatically cancelled by the Gaullist government. She was virtually *persona non grata* mainly because she was said to have offered Goering her apartment, the most sought-after in the Ritz, and also sold him an emerald ring for £50,000.

One of the grandest exiles to return found her property in good order, but not her family. Daisy Fellowes – born Marguerite Séverine Philippine, daughter of the 4th Duc Decazes and married first to Prince Jean de Broglie – was acclaimed as the most elegant woman of the age. The news of her arrival at the end of April 1945 unsettled many women, above all Louise de Vilmorin, who was in love with Daisy's old lover, the British ambassador. 'It is remarkable,' commented Duff Cooper, a touch ingenuously, 'how other women fear Daisy even now when she is fifty-five.'

Daisy Fellowes's property was safe, mainly because she had arranged for Brigadier Daly, the British military attaché, to live in part of her house. It would have been in danger of expropriation otherwise, because her daughters Jacqueline and Emmeline de Broglie had lived there during the Occupation, and both of them were in serious trouble. Jacqueline, the one who had her head shaved, was married to an Austrian, Alfred Kraus, accused of having betrayed many people to the Gestapo.

Emmeline's war, on the other hand, had started well. She had fallen in love with an American woman working for British intelligence, and had smuggled her several times across the Swiss border; but when this agent became involved with another woman, Emmeline betrayed her in a fit of jealousy.

Daisy Fellowes, it must be said, was hardly an ideal mother. Her comments about her daughters were famous – 'If only I knew who their fathers were' was a favourite remark. Of her lesbian daughter, Emmeline, she is reputed to have said in her presence: 'She's just like her father, only a little more masculine.' Yet when her daughters were in trouble, Daisy did not abandon them. After Emmeline's arrest in July 1945 she went to see Duff Cooper, on a visit to London for consultations, to beg for his intervention. He warned her that there was nothing he could do, except through regular channels.

On his return to Paris, Duff Cooper took Daisy Fellowes to see her daughter. 'Daisy hasn't succeeded in getting to the judge,' wrote Diana to Conrad Russell, 'yet she goes and sees the monstrous daughter through bars and minds very much, I think.' Emmeline was not released until late December.

The most famous couple of that milieu, the Duke and Duchess of Windsor, reached Le Havre on the liner *Argentina* on the morning of Saturday, 22 September 1945. Their first concern was to smuggle ashore their little Cairn terrier, Pookey, who had been brought on to the ship with the help of an American general. Now they needed to get him past the French authorities. 'H.R.H. asked me to smuggle Pookey ashore,' wrote Brigadier Daly in his diary that night, 'as I was the most unlikely person to be caught. I hope nothing is ever heard of it.'

The Duke spoke to the large group of waiting newspapermen of the terrible damage around them, and the Duchess said that she hoped to join a relief organization for helping war victims. Finally, after the 134 pieces of luggage and packages had been dealt with, the Windsors climbed into the British Embassy Daimler with Daly. Their staff – the Duchess's secretary, a maid, and their black butler Sydney, – were put in the car behind. Meanwhile the drivers of an American military escort in five jeeps revved their engines impatiently. The British military attaché was still far from relaxed at breaking the law. 'There was a terrible moment when Pookey was in the car safely ashore and the journalists crowded round for a final cinematograph show and photographs. The little beast kept quite quiet in his covered box shaped like a suitcase – he must have known he was a stowaway.'

Within a couple of days of the Windsors' return to their rented house at 24 Boulevard Suchet, Adrian Holman, the minister at the embassy, had a talk with the Duke of Windsor – still referred to as 'Edward P' from his signature when Prince of

Wales. Holman warned him that things had changed since his departure from the Côte d'Azur in 1940. French politics had moved sharply to the left, and he and his wife must recognize the new state of affairs. They should also be careful to avoid French people who were not *bien vus* – the safest course would be to stick to British and American friends for the time being – and they should not patronize the black market. But it was clear that the Duke and his wife, whatever her pronounced intentions to work for war victims, had not emerged from their egotistical cocoon. The Duchess remarked that Paris now offered 'the most expensive discomfort she had ever known'.

There was no shortage of people ready to provide their luxuries. Count O'Kelly, a member of an Irish expatriate family who had a well-established wine business in the Place Vendôme, was able to provide much more than just wine. Nor was there a shortage of guests. 'The house was looking extremely well, with masses of flowers,' wrote Daly in his journal after a party there. 'One of the best dinners we have ever had in Paris in a private house.' Others were curious to see at close quarters this famous couple, rather less than fairy-tale, but still unreal. 'At fifty,' recorded Jacques Dumaine, 'the Duke remains the royal Peter Pan . . . his wizened jockey's face, his fair hair and his debonair appearance contribute towards his persistent youthfulness and make one understand the note of novelettish sentimentality in his abdication.' Janet Flanner observed that the lines on his face were the result of too much sun, and not too much thought.

Duff Cooper's greatest problem was that the Duke was 'so anxious to do right'. The ex-king was still angling for an official position, preferably in the United States. The Duke asked him whether he should pay calls on General de Gaulle and Bidault. Duff Cooper found it sad that he still hankered after public life.

The Duke's next preoccupation, however, was the Communist menace in France. It does not seem to have occurred to him that events like his meeting with Hitler offered perfect material to promote Communist Party propaganda. But the Communists evidently felt they had better targets. They pointed ceaselessly to the extermination camps, with the argument that only an international Communist order could prevent such horrors happening again.

14
The Great Trials

Early in 1945, with Nazi Germany disintegrating, France knew that it could not face the post-war world until accounts had been settled with Marshal Pétain and Pierre Laval; but both men were still in Germany.

In the meantime the trial of traitors who had betrayed the Resistance provided a false assurance that the basic issues were clear. Most of the public eagerly followed court proceedings in the press. The trial that preoccupied everyone for the first eleven days of December 1944 was that of the notorious Bonny–Lafont gang, otherwise known as the 'Gestapo Française'.

Lafont, a petty criminal before the war, lost no time in making himself useful to the German occupiers. He became a member of the Gestapo, and took German nationality in 1941. His right-hand man was an ex-policeman called Bonny, who had been involved in several pre-war scandals. With their henchmen, they formed one of the most hated gangs in Paris. Employed and protected by the Gestapo, to whom they acted as informers, they rounded up and denounced hundreds of people and grew rich on blackmail, robbery, racketeering and terror. In their headquarters in the rue Lauriston, they tortured and sometimes killed their victims.

In the murky society of collaborationist Paris, Lafont became a person of some consequence. He acquired a town house in Neuilly where he entertained his well-connected friends and mistresses, and among his guests was Bussières, the Prefect of Police whom Luizet replaced at the Liberation. He mixed with the journalist Georges Suarez, and Jean Luchaire, the press baron and later 'Minister of Information' at Sigmaringen. Maurice Chevalier was said to have been another friend, but Chevalier quickly issued a statement saying he had met him only once. Lafont even boasted that he had acted as intermediary between Laval and Otto Abetz.

He was betrayed at the Liberation by one of his own followers, a certain Joanovici, who joined the Resistance at the eleventh hour to save himself, even providing weapons for the police defending the Préfecture on the Île de la Cité. Joanovici, who allied himself with the new Communist element in the Paris police, was to cause their undoing two years later, when the government fought back against their encroachment.

The twelve principal members of the 'Gestapo Française' were tried simultaneously. The charges against them ran to 164 pages, and took three hours to read. At one point during the trial, Lafont complained about being beaten up in custody – which earned the police a rousing cheer from the court-room. All but two of the gang were sentenced to death. Muggeridge, who had interviewed him, fantasized about the guillotine slicing off 'his neat, sallow head with the blunt Mediterranean back to it' like a thistle's. In fact Lafont faced a firing squad on 26 December, watched by his defending counsel, and arrogant to the end.

Of the other traitors brought to trial, their motives varied, but not very widely. Jacques Desoubrie, a fanatical Nazi-sympathizer who betrayed the 'Comet' network in Paris in June 1943, proclaimed his belief in National Socialism at the Court of Justice in Lille, and was executed. But most traitors did not have the courage of any conviction. Prosper Desitter, the German-recruited spy known as 'the man with the missing finger', and his mistress Flore Dings were also sentenced to death for helping the Gestapo destroy the 'Comet' network. The

1. The Resistance plans the rising against the Germans in Paris.

2. Pulling up the tarmac in the Place Saint-Michel to strengthen a barricade, 22 August 1944.

3. The cast of Picasso's play, *Desire Caught by the Tail*, in his studio: (in front) Sartre, Camus, Michel Leiris and Jean Auber; (behind) Cécile Eluard, Pierre Reverdy, Louise Leiris, Zanie de Campan, Picasso, Valentine Hugo and Simone de Beauvoir.

4. The lean, sad Christmas of 1944. Père Noël distributes leeks on behalf of a Resistance charity.

5. French Communist leaders – Duclos, Thorez, Frachon and Marty at the funeral of Colonel Fabien, 3 January 1945.

6. What Communists called the 'new occupying power' – US Military Police in Paris.

7. 'I am the victim of a miscarriage of justice' was one of Arletty's lines in the film before she was imprisoned for '*collaboration horizontale*'.

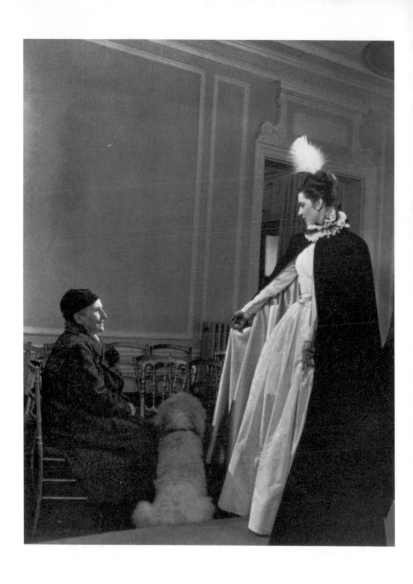

8. Gertrude Stein at the show of Pierre Balmain, with whom she had made friends during the Occupation.

9. De Gaulle, bare-headed in the rain, gives his speech against the indiscipline of party politics at Bayeux, 16 June 1946.

10. The New Look – Dior's triumph.

night before his execution, Desitter was said to have howled with terror in his cell.

'The purge trials preoccupied us all that year,' wrote Susan Mary Patten, 'and the incoherence with which justice was meted out did much to cause the *crise morale*, or crisis of conscience among the French.' The mood of the populace was not the only obstacle to a fair trial for those accused of collaboration at that time. The *Cours de Justice* set up by the provisional government were, in a sadly ironic way, a new form of the *Cours Spéciales* of Vichy. The problem was that nobody had ever envisaged one version of France putting another version on trial for treason, so the principal law used against collaborators was Article 75 of the Penal Code, which covered 'intelligence with the enemy'.

In the eyes of the provisional government, it was better to have juridical imperfections than no courts at all. As one of de Gaulle's entourage put it, 'it was not possible to administer justice serenely' in the situation which existed after the Liberation. If collaborators were not judged and sentenced, people would simply take the law into their own hands, with revolutionary tribunals and lynchings. But the Minister of Justice should never have permitted a jury system in which the jurors were members of the Resistance and relatives of those who had been in camps in Germany.

The trials of journalists and writers had shown that timing, just as much as the evidence, could play a decisive part in a prisoner's fate. The lack of chronological logic in the trials of senior Vichy officials was even more flagrant. 'One sees more and more,' wrote Pastor Boegner in his diary during the trial of Admiral Esteva in March 1945, 'that the trial of the Marshal should take place before those of men who only obeyed him.' This question of following orders revealed fundamental flaws in the new legislation. Article 3 of the decree of 28 November 1944 acknowledged that no crime had been committed if the accused had followed orders – '*la stricte exécution exclusive de toute initiative personelle'* – but another piece of legislation stipulated that any order coming from the 'so-called government of the État Français' had no validity.

The spring of 1945 began beautifully, with wistaria, chestnut blossom and lilacs out early. Yet almost every foreigner in Paris at the time was struck by the unhappy, haunted and often bitter faces they saw in the streets. The sight of the first deportees and prisoners to return from the camps in Germany had created a profound sense of shock. This was then augmented by film footage of liberated death camps such as Belsen and Dachau, shown in cinemas. Pierre-Henri Teitgen, the Minister of Justice, recorded that crowds stormed two jails, those of Dinan and Cusset, and lynched several collaborators.

The sense of shock was renewed whenever a deportee was seen in Paris. They were instantly recognizable: Liliane de Rothschild recalled how pathetically hunched and thin they were. Their teeth were black with decay, their skin sallow, clammy, and constantly sweating. In the métro, even the most elderly lady rose 'silently to surrender her seat when one of the skeletons entered the carriage'. The change in mood since the Liberation had been gradual but striking. In September 1944, no more than 32 per cent of IFOP's sample had expressed a belief that Pétain should be punished. Only 3 per cent wanted the death penalty. By the time Pétain's trial started eleven months later, the proportion demanding punishment had more than doubled to 76 per cent, and those wanting the death sentence for the old Marshal had risen from 3 per cent to 37 per cent.

The Communist Party, knowing that it could tap this anger and that the other parties would be forced to support it, began an intense and sustained campaign, demanding the Marshal's execution. Meetings with star speakers like Louis Aragon were called ostensibly to commemorate the Resistance, but the true purpose was clear.

*

Proceedings were started against Marshal Pétain in his absence in Germany at the beginning of April 1945. Pétain, hearing of this on the wireless at Sigmaringen, wrote to Ribbentrop, demanding to be allowed to return to France to face his accusers. He received no reply.

On 20 April, General de Lattre de Tassigny's 1st Army reached the Black Forest. The next morning, before dawn, Pétain was taken from the castle of Sigmaringen to Wangen, and then on to another castle to escape the advancing armies. His German escorts acknowledged that the only sensible course was to take him over the frontier into Switzerland at Bregenz, and decided to act on their own initiative.

Pétain reached the border with joy and relief. The Swiss authorities allowed him to enter the country and then to cross to France to surrender to the jurisdiction of the High Court. On 26 April, after taking the salute from a Swiss guard of honour, Pétain crossed into France at Verrières-sous-Jougne in a limousine. The reception committee awaiting him on the French side of the border included General Koenig and the local Commissioner of the Republic. Pétain offered his hand, but Koenig remained rigidly at the salute for forty-five seconds and refused to take it, despite the Marshal making two more attempts.

The Marshal, impervious to all these signs, talked on quite casually, congratulating Koenig on his war record. Koenig was 'furious with de Gaulle for sending him to meet Pétain' – particularly since the Resistance press was outraged that he had saluted the Marshal at all.

There was also considerable bitterness over the fact that the Pullman carriage in which the new prisoner was brought back to Paris was given priority over the far less luxurious wagons repatriating the deportees, who had been sent to Germany in cattle-trucks. But any comfort which the Marshal may have enjoyed was disturbed by demonstrations along the way, organized by the Communist Party. At Pontarlier, a crowd of two thousand threw small stones at the carriage and shouted: 'Shoot the old traitor! Pétain for the firing squad!'

On arrival, Pétain was taken to the fort of Montrouge on the perimeter of the city. A suite of cells had been hastily prepared for him and his wife. As a petty touch of humiliation, a portrait of General de Gaulle surrounded by tricolor ribbon had been hung in his main cell.

The *bâtonnier*, Jacques Charpentier, the head of the Paris Bar, received a request that he should choose a defence counsel for the trial. So Charpentier came to discuss the matter. Pétain appeared completely lucid on banal matters, but when it came to the question of his defence, he was clearly out of touch with reality.

'Why do you not plead my case?' Pétain suddenly said.

'Because I took a position against your government,' Charpentier replied. Pétain was astonished. He could not believe that a reasonable man could have done such a thing. Charpentier found Pétain's armour of complacency, strengthened by an old man's facility for blocking out the world, breathtaking.

Pétain's return caused deep unease in Paris, acting as an uncomfortable reminder that the mass of the population had considered him their saviour in 1940. His presence now was seen as a direct threat to national unity. The centre-right and right feared that his trial would be used as a stick by the Communists to beat conservatives of every hue, while left-of-centre Resistance papers such as *Franc-Tireur* saw Pétain's return as Germany's secret weapon against France. The majority feared the washing of dirty linen that was about to begin. Only those who thirsted after 'popular justice' showed any relish.

The torrent of abuse in the Communist press campaign never slackened. But the incident which best demonstrated the mood occurred in the third week of June 1945 at the congress of the Communist-dominated Union of French Women. A resolution demanding the death of Pétain was proposed, to fervent applause. But when it came to the vote, a handful of Catholic women from the Christian Democrat MRP voted against it.*

'The assembly exploded in anger,' Comrade Popova, the leader of a delegate of Soviet women, reported to the Kremlin a few weeks later. 'It demanded that the women who were against the motion should go up on the podium and explain why they voted that way – whether it was their own opinion or that of their delegation. One of these women was dragged by force on to the podium. "Pétain is old," she said. "What is the point of killing him? He is not the only guilty one and as I am a Catholic, I am against killing him." The assembly was outraged. Only when somebody began to sing the Marseillaise did things calm down again.'†

On 23 July, in debilitating heat, the trial of Marshal Pétain opened in the Palais de Justice. Several hundred policemen were on guard in and around the building. The court-room had room for only six hundred people, not nearly enough for those who wanted to attend, so cafés in the neighbourhood were packed. The jury consisted of twelve members of the Resistance and twelve members of the National Assembly who had refused to vote full powers to Pétain in 1940.

The ninety-year-old prisoner, accompanied by guards, entered in uniform to emphasize that he was still a Marshal of France. He wore only one medal, the Médaille Militaire. The marmoreal face, according to Galtier-Boissière, 'makes one think of his wax effigy in the Grévin Museum'. After the president's opening remarks, Pétain read out a three-page statement in a clear, firm voice.

He began by saying that he spoke to the people of France,

* MRP stood for 'Mouvement Républicain Populaire'. Le Canard enchaîné pretended that it stood for 'Machine à Ramasser les Pétainistes'.

† Popova's delegation of ten women was supposed to represent a cross-section of Soviet womanhood. It included a sculptress, a writer, a medical scientist, an actress, a professor, the director of the Lenin Library, a hero of the Soviet Union and a worker.

who were not represented by the court convened to try him; and that once he had made his statement, he would remain silent for the rest of the trial. Pétain argued that everything he had done was in France's best interests. If the court found him guilty, its members would be condemning an innocent man, and they would have to answer before the judgement of God and of the future. After the hearing, he said to his gaoler, 'I made a fine speech.'

His words made little difference to the jurors. For them, Pétain's guilt was plain. When the defence exercised its right of veto on the jury, one of the many Communists disqualified shouted that his exclusion 'will not save Pétain from getting his dozen bullets from a firing squad'. Several other members of the jury were heard to say that the death penalty was inevitable.

Pierre-Henri Teitgen, the Minister of Justice, had a clear idea of how the case against Pétain should be presented. France's defeat, Pétain's elevation to head of state and the Armistice were to be avoided altogether, and the prosecution would concentrate on Pétain's actions after the North African landings in November 1942. From that moment, when he had given the order to fire on the Allied forces and had not opposed the German invasion of the unoccupied zone, it could be proved that Pétain's claims of acting in France's best interests had collapsed. Teitgen had outlined this plan to Jefferson Caffery, the American ambassador, at a meeting they had on 27 June. Yet, to judge by events, Teitgen was overruled by de Gaulle, who was determined that Pétain's trial should prove that Vichy had been an illegal regime whose chief crime had been to dishonour France. De Gaulle, not for the first time on a matter too close to his heart, committed a major blunder.*

---

* Teitgen makes no mention in his memoirs of his meeting with the American ambassador, and protests vehemently, but unconvincingly, that de Gaulle exerted no influence in the handling of the Pétain case.

The chief prosecutor was Procureur Général André Mornet, the man responsible for Mata Hari's sentence of death before a court martial in this same building twenty-eight years before. Her trial had been a miscarriage of justice, both brutal and incompetent. The conduct of the Pétain trial was to prove less brutal but even more incompetent. Given de Gaulle's probable interference in the case, this was not all Mornet's fault; but soon the prosecution was irretrievably bogged down in the events of 1940.

'They are putting the armistice on trial,' wrote Charpentier scathingly. 'The prosecution seems to think that the Marshal lost the war in order to overthrow the Republic . . . Never does it tackle head-on Vichy's real crime, the appalling ambiguity which, cloaked in the unequalled prestige of the head of state, led so many of the French into treason.'

The trial consisted of long and largely irrelevant speeches, which the president of the court Mongibeaux – who, like most of the judiciary, had sworn an oath of allegiance to Pétain – made little effort to bring back to the point. The politicians, who were the first to be called, were more interested in defending their own reputations than condemning Pétain. Only the socialist leader, Léon Blum, was impressive, his moral authority increased by his imprisonment in Germany. Pétain, said Blum, told the people of France that the humiliating armistice 'was not a dishonourable act, but an act in accordance with the interests of the country'. And because the Marshal, being who he was, spoke in the name of honour and glory, people believed him. 'His atrocious moral confidence trick, yes, that I think is treason.'

The politicians were followed by diplomats and generals, but few who came to the witness stand had anything specific to say. In several cases, the defence – especially the youngest and brightest member of the team, Maître Jacques Isorni – managed to indicate that the prosecution's witnesses were just as compromised as the old man in the dock; if not as traitors, then as fools.

As witness after witness droned on, Pétain sat in silence and the public seethed with impatience. It was not politicians and officials they wanted to see, but the victims of Vichy – particularly the *déportés*. The first *déporté* to appear was, however, far from typical. Georges Loustaunau-Lacau, skeletal and on crutches after his time in Mauthausen, was a former aide-de-camp to Marshal Pétain and had remained loyal. Loustaunau-Lacau, the founder of the 'Noah's Ark' intelligence network with Marie-Madeleine Fourcade, was a rarity in the Resistance: he was ferociously anti-Communist. Glowering at the court, he condemned the trial and its witnesses. 'I owe nothing to Marshal Pétain but that does not stop me from feeling sickened by the spectacle of those who, in this room, try to pass all their errors on to an old man.'

It was not until Pastor Boegner, president of the Protestant Federation of France, was summoned that one of the most important facts emerged: Pétain had been informed of the atrocities and injustices that were committed by the Vichy regime. Boegner had from the start protested against the racial laws and the deportations, and he continued to do so. He had brought to the Marshal's attention the fact that France was deporting German Jews who had sought refuge in France in the 1930s, and on 22 August 1942 he had written to the Marshal telling him of the deportation of Jewish children from the station of Venissieux, near Lyons. Boegner testified that Pétain had always expressed horror and indignation; but he had never lifted a finger to stop the crimes.

Not all the witnesses were for the prosecution. A great many generals were called who were for the most part loyal to their old leader. To the embarrassment of the American Embassy, Maître Isorni read out a letter from Admiral Leahy, Roosevelt's ambassador to Vichy, who wrote that in his opinion Pétain had always had the best interests of France at heart. Yet foreign observers were unimpressed at the general conduct of the trial. Almost anybody, including jurors, seemed to have the right to make remarks, even insults, without any reproach from the president of the court, and purely hearsay comments were accepted as evidence. Caffery reported in a signal to the Secretary of State in Washington, that Americans with legal training who had followed the trial were of the opinion that the great bulk of evidence so far submitted would have been thrown out by an American court.

The high point was the appearance of Pierre Laval on Friday, 3 August, in the second week of the trial. The spectators were agog at the sight of Pétain and Laval together again. The two men had each described the other as a 'dungheap'. Laval's entrance, however, was not impressive. He came in, uncharacteristically ill at ease, hugging a brown attaché case against his chest, and seemed confused about where he was supposed to sit. He still carried his grey felt Homburg, and wore his other trademark, a white gangster-like tie. Yet it was the change in his physical appearance that struck people most. 'The fat of his face is now gone,' wrote Janet Flanner, in court for the *New Yorker*. 'His oily, Moorish hair is now dry and gray and his mustache is the color of tobacco juice. His crooked, stained teeth make a dark cavernous background for his large lips...[His] rumpled gray-and-white-striped suit was so large for his frame that it looked borrowed.'

Although Laval seemed cowed and nervous at first, the sound of his own voice brought back his self-assurance. He spoke brilliantly, but everything he said was addressed to the public and the journalists. The gist of his message was indignation that he should be cast as the black side of the Vichy coin. He reminded the court of Pétain's statement five days after the Normandy landings: 'Monsieur Laval and I walk hand in hand. Between him and me there is perfect agreement both in thought and act.' Yet Laval did not answer a single question directly.

His presence roused Pétain from his long silence. The old man described his shock when, on 22 June 1942, he heard Laval announcing on the radio that 'I hope for the victory of Germany, because without it, Communism will spread throughout Europe.' Laval countered by saying he had shown the draft of the speech to Pétain. By that stage, nobody knew who to believe.

The jury sentenced Pétain to death, although not with the overwhelming majority that people expected. The incompetence of the prosecution, and Jacques Isorni's performance, had sown many doubts among those who had possessed none before. The jury also put in a request that the sentence be commuted to life imprisonment. Maître Isorni claims that this was to prevent de Gaulle from taking the credit for sparing the old man, who was to remain in prison on the Île d'Yeu until his death in 1951.

The trial failed to penetrate the enigma of Marshal Pétain. Did he really believe that he had outfoxed Hitler with a 'double game'? That he had served the Allied cause, as he pretended, even when giving the order to counter-attack the American landings in North Africa, or when writing to Hitler after the Anglo-Canadian raid on Dieppe to congratulate him for sweeping clean the soil of France? Did he believe all this or had he managed to convince himself of what he needed to believe?

Marshal Pétain recorded in a letter to Laval of 6 August 1944 – two months to the day after the Allied landings in Normandy – his horror at the accounts he had been hearing 'for several months' of the crimes of the Milice, including rape, murder and theft. He went on to express his dismay at the 'deplorable effect produced' by the Milice handing 'to the Gestapo their own compatriots and working closely with it'.

Joseph Darnand, the head of the Milice, replied to Pétain's reprimand in a telling fashion: 'For four years, I received your compliments and your congratulations and you encouraged me. And today, because the Americans are at the gates of Paris, you start to say that I am going to be a blot on the history of France. One might have made up one's mind a little earlier.' Darnand at his own trial was equally forthright. 'I am not one of those who are going to tell you I played a double game. As for me, I went ahead. I went all the way.'

Pétain's main method of evading responsibility for his regime's actions was to portray himself as a prisoner of the Germans. 'Each day, with a dagger at my throat, I struggled against the enemy's demands,' he protested at his trial. But if he was, as he claimed, a prisoner of the Germans, then why at the end of May 1944, in his speech at Nancy, was he still asking the French people to continue to follow him? 'Trust me. I have a certain amount of experience and I have pointed out the right direction.' There was no disavowal of his regime, over which he later claimed to have had no control. There was no hint of regret at what had been done by Vichy in his name.

On 2 May, shortly after Pétain had passed through Switzerland, Pierre Laval had managed to escape from the ghastly chaos of Germany's final collapse in a Junkers 88 trimotor aircraft. To avoid arrest, he had flown over France and landed at Barcelona. General Franco's government, not wanting to provoke the Allies in any way, refused to offer the former Prime Minister of Vichy political asylum, but at the same time did not want to hand him directly over to the French.

Finally, after almost three months of tortuous negotiations via the United States ambassador in Madrid, Laval was flown to the American zone of Austria in the same Junkers 88 – this time with the Nazi markings painted out. On arrival in Linz he was taken into custody by the US army, and on 31 July, eight days after the opening of Pétain's trial, he was handed over to the French military authorities. The following day he was flown to Paris, and transferred to Fresnes prison.

Throughout Pétain's trial, his defence had stressed that it was Laval, not the Marshal, who was responsible for the crimes of Vichy. Laval's appearance as witness had done little to mitigate that impression, despite his exaggerated respect for Pétain and his insistence that he had never taken any major decision without the Marshal's approval.

When Laval arrived in Fresnes, Benoist-Méchin caught sight of him from his cell. He too was struck by how much weight the short and solid Auvergnat had lost since the last time they had met. Laval, although suffering from cancer, continued to smoke five packets of cigarettes a day. He was amused to receive a request for his butts from the '*gamins*' in the cell on the floor above. They were hoisted up one by one tied to a string.

A handful of devoted followers, most notably his wife and daughter Josée, continued to believe every word he uttered. Comte René de Chambrun, his son-in-law, has made it his life's work to clear Laval's name. When asked what he most admired about his father-in-law, Chambrun replied that 'he was incapable of uttering a falsehood, even a white lie'.

Laval slept little and smoked constantly – his nervousness increased by the fact that he was denied access to the documents he had so carefully saved and annotated in Germany. He had to put together his defence from memory, and from a few copies of the *Journal Officiel*.

He was also denied access to any potential witnesses; and the inquiry into his case, which should have consisted of twenty-five separate 'interrogations', was suddenly closed after the fifth. This was because the provisional government wanted Laval's trial, which would dominate the press, out of the way before the referendum on 21 October.

The trial began on Friday 5 October, and was a cross between an *auto-da-fé* and a tribunal during the Paris Terror. Once again the court-room was full to bursting and all eyes were on Laval. He came in clutching his attaché case, on which was written: PIERRE LAVAL PRÉSIDENT DU CONSEIL. He appeared alone, without his lawyers. A statement from them was read out by the president, Mongibeaux, saying that their absence was a protest at the abruptly curtailed inquiry into Laval's case.

'The examination procedure has not been hurried,' Mornet, the chief prosecutor, replied. 'It started five years ago, the day that Pierre Laval, with Pétain, seized power.' At this point, both Laval's fists came crashing down on to the table. His face contorted with fury, he shouted, 'You were all under government orders, even you, Monsieur le Procureur Général! Condemn me straight away, that will make things clear.'

Things went from bad to worse, with those supposed to be conducting the trial completely on the sidelines. Laval never answered their questions directly. The basis of his defence was that he had played a double game, to deceive Germany and protect France. He claimed that his notorious statement – 'I wish for a German victory' – was intended to lull the Germans into a false sense of security. This line excused almost anything: his support for Hitler's New European Order and the Legion of French Volunteers sent to the Russian front in German uniform. Even the dispatch of Jews to concentration camps, and Frenchmen to Germany on forced labour, could thus be explained away as a stratagem to save many more from a similar fate. He also managed to give the impression that the reason his trial was so rushed was that he knew the truth, and those in high positions were afraid that he might reveal it.

The jury, however, were unashamedly out for his blood. They resisted his arguments, hurled insults and threatened him with 'a dozen bullets in his hide' – a phrase much in use during the *épuration*. At times the trial degenerated into a ferocious slanging-match between the jurors and the accused. And these were the parliamentarians, not those picked from the Resistance.

The *bâtonnier* Charpentier saw Laval as a wounded bull in an ignoble arena. 'Like Andalusian urchins who leap into the bullring, members of the jury insulted the accused and intervened in the proceedings.' 'The Laval trial is a scandal beyond description,' wrote Pastor Boegner in his diary. Charpentier went further. The whole exercise had become counterproductive. 'In this way, a man universally hated, whose conviction, after proper proceedings, would never have raised a murmur, has been turned into a victim.'

There was no appeal beyond this court, where decisions were final. Laval realized he stood no chance of saving himself and on the third day refused to appear, remaining in his cell from then on. He wrote to Teitgen, the Minister of Justice, complaining eloquently and bitterly of his treatment. Teitgen advised Laval's lawyers to urge their client back into the court-room or he would surely be condemned.

Laval did not take Teitgen's advice. He thought that absence from his own trial would become an insurmountable obstruction to its continuation, and persuaded his lawyers – who had long been under his spell – to agree with him. Wrapped in a cloud of self-delusion as thick as the cigarette smoke in his cell, he worked feverishly on a new defence for a new trial. On 9 October he heard to his stupefaction that the court had condemned him to death.

Four days later, Pastor Boegner went to the rue Saint-Dominique to ask for a commutation of Laval's death sentence, since his trial had been such a travesty of justice. 'If Laval is executed after what has happened,' he said to de Gaulle, 'will it really be an execution?' Boegner watched his reaction carefully. Not a muscle moved on the General's face. Laval's lawyers had a similar experience. Their client could already have been dead. François Mauriac also wrote to Teitgen begging for a re-trial, but received no reply.

Most executions took place at the fort of Montrouge, but Laval was shot at Fresnes. The official witnesses, including the Procurator-General, the presiding judge and Charles Luizet, the Prefect of Police, arrived at the prison soon after half past eight and went to the condemned cell on the ground floor. Laval, scorning his persecutors at the last moment, swallowed cyanide, which he must have kept concealed in his clothes. Almost immediately he went into convulsions. The official party panicked, not knowing what to do. The senior prison doctor called for a stomach pump. Céline observed later (in his other persona, as Dr Destouches) that the cyanide had almost certainly been spoiled by moisture. Others thought that Laval had failed to shake the phial.

It took over two hours to revive Laval sufficiently for execution. Half-carried, without his shoes, he was taken out and strapped to a chair. Laval apparently tried to rise to his feet as the firing squad took aim. Benoist-Méchin claimed that the soldiers were drunk with rum, given to steady their nerves during the wait. As the ragged volley was heard inside the prison, the inmates went into a rage, hammering on their cell doors with shoes and yelling '*Bandits! Salauds! Assassins!*'

The government tried to keep the grisliest parts of Laval's story from the people, but the news spread rapidly. France was split between those who felt that he deserved his fate, however it had been administered, and those sickened by the shameful episodes in court and afterwards. The question even provoked arguments within families. 'The only time I ever struck my husband,' said Liliane de Rothschild (her husband Élie had recently returned from his prison camp in Germany), 'was when he said that Laval had been badly treated.'

Early in November 1945 a sale was held at the Hotel Drouot to dispose of the jewellery and furs confiscated from profiteers and collaborators. The prices obtained were far higher than expected in such impoverished times. A yellow diamond ring went for 4 million francs ($80,000 at the time). The audience was an extraordinary mixture of poor people come to see a bizarre form of justice carried out and 'black-market queens' in their new dresses by Lucien Lelong.

This event said much about the mood of the time. Nobody was satisfied, except for those who had profited and escaped the consequences of their actions. The *épuration* was both too harsh and too weak. The failure to pursue some of the greatest criminals, particularly those responsible for the deportation of Jews, compounded by an attempt to rewrite history and close the lid on the past, created greater trouble in years to come. Over a quarter of a century later, a new generation began to probe the shameful secrets of the Vichy years.

15
Hunger for the New

After the Occupation, the urge to express ideas was quite over-whelming for a cerebral society. Galtier-Boissière was amused by the instant outpouring of prose by the French writers who had refused to write for the collaborationist press. An astonishing number of newspapers and literary magazines appeared, feeding the hunger for ideas. The greatest problem was the shortage of paper: *Le Monde* had to be reduced to tabloid size, and became known as the '*Demi-Monde*'. Paper supplies permitting, *Les Lettres Françaises* was selling over 100,000 copies by the end of 1944.

The main complaint about this deluge of printed matter, however, was the similarity of political approach. Even the review *Esprit*, published by Emmanuel Mounier, propagated a form of Christian Socialism which sought to bridge the chasm between Catholicism and Communism. Like many who shared the ideals of the Resistance, Mounier now believed that revolution was a vital renewal of the organism; this even led him into accepting the brutal transformation of Soviet-occupied Europe as natural in the circumstances.

The Liberation produced a heady mood for the young. 'To be twenty or twenty-five in September 1944,' wrote Simone de Beauvoir, 'seemed a great stroke of luck: all roads opened up. Journalists, writers, budding film-makers, discussed, planned, made decisions with passion, as if their future depended only on themselves . . . I was old. I was thirty-six.'

'Oh wonders!' wrote Emmanuel Le Roy Ladurie, of his first sight of the Boulevard Saint-Michel after the war. 'I was struck by the extraordinary concentration of young people, the highest in France to the square kilometre, in a nation which appeared to be a country of old people.'

Parisian youth had not been docile during the Occupation. Their response to the Pétainist slogan of 'Work, Nation, Family' had taken the form of 'resistance, black market, surprise-party'. Many had acted as messengers, or deliverers of tracts and underground newspapers. Others dealt on the edges of the black market: being forbidden, such activities acquired their own mystique of revolt. And 'surprise-parties' represented their revolt against a regime which they saw as boy-scouting in jackboots.

Some of them were *zazous* – a shamelessly unheroic and anarchic movement of disdain for Vichy, the Germans and all military values everywhere. *Zazous*, with their long greasy hair, have sometimes been described as the first beatniks, but the boys' fashion for long jackets with high collars and the girls' for very short skirts made them look more like teddy boys in the 1950s; while the anti-virile ethos of the boys had more in common with the hippies of the 1960s. To avoid military service, *zazous* used to crush three aspirins into a cigarette which they smoked an hour before their army medical examination. But *zazous* also ran a risk every time they appeared in public. If a gang of fascist youths from the Parti Populaire Français spotted a *zazou*, they would beat him up, or if a girl, torment her mercilessly.

Most *zazous* were children of the wealthy middle class. They organized their 'surprise-parties' – also known as 'pot-lucks', since American terms were all the rage – in the apartments of parents temporarily absent, with friends and gate-crashers bringing food and drink. These parties were essentially a response to Vichy's ban on jazz and dancing, so if you owned some Duke Ellington or Glenn Miller records the word spread. Because of the curfew, the parties often went on all night. After the Liberation, the real *zazou* fashion died out, but the word remained a term of abuse, employed by the puritan left and the right.

The Liberation changed everything for the young, or the 'J3s' as they were often called, after the name of the ration category for fifteen- to twenty-one-year-olds. There was no more curfew, so they savoured the freedom of the streets at night, even if that meant freezing on street corners outside jazz clubs in Saint-Germain-des-Prés. Staying up all night retained the thrill of the illicit. A lack of food produced a continual light-headed, sometimes vertiginous sensation. They ignored the last métro at eleven – many did not even have the fare – so they slept in doorways and walked home at dawn. The luckiest had roller-skates, on which they crossed half of Paris.

Clothes – best of all genuine American clothes – could be bought for almost nothing in the flea-market of Saint-Ouen, where they found on sale clothes sent by the Jewish community in New York to help fellow Jews. So by giving each other crew-cuts imitated from the GIs, and dressing themselves up in second-hand check shirts with trousers cut so short they came half-way down the shin, with vilely striped socks and tennis shoes, the ex-*zazous* created a new style.

Students seemed to live off nervous energy and ideas. The greatest hunger was for reading material, yet there was so little time and so much to read – Aragon, Camus, Sartre and Beauvoir as well as Apollinaire, Lautréamont, Gide, and now all the American novels which proliferated in translation, such as Hemingway, Steinbeck, Damon Runyan, Thornton Wilder and Thomas Wolfe. Everything formerly banned must be seen – whether the plays of García Lorca or the films of Buñuel. Philosophy student or not, you needed to be able to discuss Hegel's master–slave paradigm, the collected works of Karl Marx, and existentialism's less than apostolic succession from Søren Kierkegaard and the phenomenologist Edmund Husserl, via Martin Heidegger, then Jean-Paul Sartre and Maurice Merleau-Ponty.

Emmanuel Le Roy Ladurie's professor of philosophy, Beaufret, had an immense prestige among students: he had actually met Heidegger. Young Communist students, swollen with the importance of their historical mission, were far from impressed. In the eyes of the party, Heidegger was a Nazi and existentialism was decadent.

Lycées as well as university faculties in Paris were very politicized, a situation which had grown far worse during the Occupation when right-wing students had been recruited by the Milice to spy on their classmates. Now, the Communists attempted to exert a political and intellectual hegemony. Their first target was Catholic students, but by manipulating issues, anyone even on the left who did not demonstrate a strong commitment to *progressisme* as defined by the Communist Party was 'objectively' a fascist. Emmanuel Le Roy Ladurie made an appalling gaffe when he confessed in front of a Communist that he had been impressed by Oswald Spengler's *Decline of the West*. Every area of art came in for a relentless Marxist–Leninist critique. To admit that you enjoyed Alain-Fournier's *Le Grand Meaulnes* demonstrated a pathetic and *dépassé* sentimentality as well as reactionary tendencies.

Antoine de Saint-Exupéry had written of 1940 in *Pilote de guerre*, '*La défaite divise*'. The Liberation managed at first to unite the majority of the country under the banner of *progressisme*, as the opinion polls demonstrated in the massive support for the nationalization of banks and heavy industry. Simone de Beauvoir wrote of 'Paris in the year zero'. And indeed for Communists and their fellow-travellers there was a sense of marching with history. Another sign of the times, as Galtier-Boissière pointed out, was *Vogue* – of all magazines – publishing a poem by Éluard and a portrait of Marcel Cachin, the veteran Communist.

The death of the great poet Paul Valéry at the age of seventy-four seemed to underline the end of an era. Valéry, who had delivered the address of welcome to Pétain when he was elected to the Académie Française, died on 20 July 1945 – three days before the Marshal's trial. He was given a state funeral: the coffin was carried through the streets of Paris, accompanied by a guard marching to muffled drums. The coffin was placed just below the Trocadéro on a golden catafalque, lit by torches. Duff Cooper, who thoroughly approved of the French Republic's respect for men of letters, reflected ruefully on the difference in his own country. 'We have only to imagine how would be greeted the suggestion that the Brigade of Guards should march past the coffin of T. S. Eliot.'

The reappearance of the satirical paper *Le Canard enchaîné* brought some much-needed humour to the French press. It had been absent since 11 June 1940. After Vichy the appetite for irreverence was huge, and the *Canard* had no scruples concerning good taste. Its cartoon on the announcement of Hitler's death was to show the Führer in heaven pinning a Star of David on God. On the other hand, the publication had its own code of values. It refused to attack collaborators during the frenzy of the *épuration*. De Gaulle could not have been more wrong when he listed it as one of the magazines taken over by the Communists at the Liberation.

Those on the right, who saw existentialism as another form of Marxism, were also mistaken. The Kremlin defined existentialism as a 'reactionary bourgeois philosophy'. This was because existentialism was fundamentally anti-collectivist, declaring that man as an individual – not society or history – was responsible for defining his own life.

Sartre cannot be accused of following fashions. Having remained wary of Stalinism after the Liberation, when praise of the Soviet Union was obligatory in progressive circles, he began to support it in the early 1950s, when French writers outside the Communist Party had started to see it for what it was. His *Being and Nothingness* was first published by Gallimard in 1943.

A. J. Ayer, a sceptic, thought that apart from a few good psychological insights, the book was 'a pretentious metaphysical thesis'. He concluded that 'Existentialism, on this evidence, was principally an exercise in misusing the verb "to be".'

If Sartre had been just a philosopher, then few people outside a small intellectual circle would have heard of him. But by dramatizing his ideas and themes through novels and plays, and above all by his creation of doomed anti-heroes – Antoine Roquentin in *Nausea* and Matthieu in *The Roads to Freedom* – Sartre touched a deep, pessimistic chord in youth to a degree unimagined since Goethe's *Werther* led to a rush of suicides among the poetic souls of Europe. Albert Camus's renown also stemmed largely from his anti-hero Mersault in *The Outsider*, and existentialism is now remembered more as a literary movement than as a lasting body of philosophy.

This group, which dominated the artistic life of Paris after the war, had begun to assemble in the winter before the Liberation. Sartre first met Albert Camus in 1943, when Camus dropped in on a rehearsal of Sartre's play *The Flies*. Simone de Beauvoir then met him with Sartre at the Café de Flore and found that he had 'a charm based on a happy mixture of nonchalance and ardour'.

This gradually expanding group of friends lived around Saint-Germain-des-Prés, moving from one cheap hotel to another. They congregated, more by chance than by arrangement, in their habitual cafés, usually the Flore, where Sartre and Beauvoir wrote for six hours a day, but occasionally the Deux Magots. The Brasserie Lipp opposite was out of favour for a time, its Alsatian specialities having attracted too many German officers. Sometimes they joined Picasso and Dora Maar at Le Catalan in the rue des Grands Augustins, which was almost an extension of Picasso's studio.

Those who gathered around Sartre became loosely known as *la famille Sartre*, in the same way that young writers and actors who gathered round Jacques Prévert were known as *la bande*

Prévert. Prévert was famous as a script-writer; between 1936 and 1946, he worked on a series of scripts for the film-maker Marcel Carné – among which were *Les Visiteurs du soir* and *Les Enfants du Paradis.* But he never had much success with his poetry until 1945, when Gallimard published *Paroles.* Prévert's limpid, irreverent, light-hearted verses hit post-war Paris like a breath of fresh air. They were set to music and sung in the street, and within a few years Gallimard had sold over 100,000 copies. Paul Boubal, the *patron* of the Flore, felt that Prévert and his friends had sown the seeds of the Saint-Germain phenomenon (at least in his own café); but Simone de Beauvoir rather disapproved of *la bande Prévert,* because they were politically uncommitted.

While waiting for the Liberation, Simone de Beauvoir gave badly cooked little dinners in her 'toothpaste-pink' hotel room, with at least half the guests sitting on the edge of the bed. Sartre talked of founding a magazine with Beauvoir, Camus and Merleau-Ponty, and this took shape in the autumn of 1945 when the first issue of *Les Temps modernes* was published.

Despite the bleakness of his philosophy, Sartre could be very engaging. One who knew him well at that time described him as 'overflowing with charm, I have seldom known anyone as amusing, as sympathetic and as generous'. He was always the first to support a good cause, and help struggling artists. He organized a benefit evening for the artist Antonin Artaud, as well as giving him money. Very often, not wanting to hurt the pride of those he helped, he arranged for funds to be given in a roundabout way: financial help for the novelist Violette Leduc was always channelled through Gallimard, and paid as 'royalties' on her own work.

Simone de Beauvoir's relationship with Sartre was far more emotionally taxing than she ever dared admit. Sartre had nicknamed her 'Castor', the French for beaver. (Others referred to her as Notre Dame de Sartre, or La Grande Sartreuse.) At moments she could still look beautiful, but her seriousness and

suppressed anxiety about Sartre had started to mould her face
into that of an old maid. He had always dominated her, making
her put up with his compulsive philandering – what she termed
'*désordres amoureux*'. She remarked to a friend that 'Sartre had a
rather diabolical side to him: he conquered young girls by
explaining their souls to them.'

In spite of the parties and the drinking, most members of *la
famille Sartre* seemed to be finishing books to be published after
the Liberation. The upstairs room of the Café de Flore often
looked like a class-room, particularly in the winter of 1943–4: at
one table, Sartre was at work on *Roads to Freedom*, Beauvoir was
writing *All Men are Mortal*, Mouloudji was writing *Enrico*, and
Jacques-Laurent Bost *Le Dernier des métiers*. They read each
other's manuscripts, and usually gave them the attention that
work from a friend deserved.

Merleau-Ponty, however, wanted Sartre to read his manuscript as a philosopher, not as a friend. He left it with hardly a
word, and Sartre, who was as usual very busy, glanced over it in
a cursory way and made congratulatory noises. This was not
good enough for Merleau-Ponty. Sartre recalls the incident: 'He
discovered my bolthole, and confronted me there. I suddenly
found him standing in front of me, smiling, the manuscript held
out. "I agree with what you say," I babbled. "I'm very glad,"
he said without moving. "You should still read it," he added
patiently. I read, and I learned, and I ended fascinated by what
I was reading.'

Raymond Queneau, poet, novelist and philologist, was – with
Merleau-Ponty – one of the most distinguished members of
Sartre's circle. Queneau, who was a senior editor at Gallimard,
led a scholarly life oppressed by the most profound despair; yet
this never seemed to affect his conviviality, his infectious laughter, his passion for jazz and his fascination with logic and
mathematics.

Michel and Zette Leiris were also part of the group. Michel
Leiris was a novelist and ethnologist, while Zette managed

the gallery of her brother-in-law, Daniel-Henry Kahnweiler, Picasso's dealer, who lived with them secretly during the Occupation. Their apartment, which had often concealed other Jews and members of the Resistance, was on the Quai des Grands Augustins, overlooking the Seine. Paintings by Picasso, Miró and Juan Gris hung on its walls above good French bourgeois furniture. They had many friends among the artists of the Left Bank, including André Masson, Giacometti and Picasso, whose studio was literally round the corner; and it was in their apartment that Picasso's play *Desire Caught by the Tail* was first performed in a reading on 19 March 1944, over three years after it was written.

Camus was the presenter, with a large stick to thump the floor to indicate changes of scenery, which he described. The play was evocative of 'avant-garde works from the 1920s', as the list of characters shows. Michel Leiris had the main part – le Gros Pied. Other readers included Jean-Paul Sartre as le Bout-Rond, Raymond Queneau as l'Oignon, Jacques-Laurent Bost as le Silence, Zanie de Campan as la Tarte, Dora Maar as l'Angoisse Maigre and Simone de Beauvoir as la Cousine. Picasso and his friends put it on for their own amusement, but '*la fine fleur de l'intelligentsia Parisienne*' was breathless in anticipation of a major event. By seven o'clock the Leiris' salon was packed.

Picasso's little comedy, almost an exercise in nostalgia, served only to underline the obvious. Surrealism as a movement was as good as over before the war, having virtually exhausted its potential to subvert received thought, and foundered on the political split when Aragon, Éluard and others felt that only Communism had the answer. One day in the Flore, Sartre asked Queneau, a former Surrealist, what he thought was left from the movement. 'The impression of having had a youth,' came the reply.

In May 1944, shortly before the Liberation, Sartre and Simone de Beauvoir were sitting in the Flore when they heard a voice. '*C'est vous, Sartre?*' They were confronted by a tough, shaven-headed character with a broken nose. This was Jean Genet, described by his biographer as 'the Proust of marginal Paris'. Genet may have had a 'distrustful, almost aggressive look' as a result of the toughness of a life in reformatories, on the street as a male prostitute and in prison, but 'his eyes knew how to smile, and his mouth could express the astonishment of childhood'.

In the autumn of 1945, Simone de Beauvoir in a cinema queue on the Champs-Élysées met 'a tall, blonde, elegant woman, with an ugly face bursting with life'. She assumed she was a woman of fashion but in fact this was the unpublished novelist, Violette Leduc, who was living off her wits and strength as a 'suitcase-bearer', bringing back to Paris hefty cases full of butter and meat from Normandy, which she sold to black-market restaurants.

A few days later, Violette Leduc came to Simone de Beauvoir in the Café de Flore bringing the manuscript of her novel, *L'Asphyxie*. On being advised to change the ending, she disappeared and did exactly as she was told. Beauvoir was so impressed with the final result that she passed it to Camus, who was then on the editorial committee at Gallimard, and he accepted it immediately for publication. The only drawback was that Violette Leduc became completely infatuated with Beauvoir, who found that she had to lay down very strict rules if their friendship was to continue.

Violette Leduc struck up a close *entente* with Jean Genet, and these two outsiders provided a great deal of voyeuristic interest to Sartre and his friends. The one person with whom Leduc clashed temperamentally was Nathalie Sarraute, the novelist who had hidden Samuel Beckett during the Occupation. Leduc tried to get on with Sarraute, but their almost chemical incompatibility was made worse by jealousy: Sarraute was indubitably Sartre's protégée, while Leduc's position with Castor was far less secure.

The autumn of 1945 saw the great existentialist boom,

although Sartre and Beauvoir were irritated that the label was automatically attached to anything they wrote. In September Beauvoir's novel of the Resistance, *The Blood of Others*, enjoyed both a critical and commercial success. Over the course of the next couple of months came two volumes of Sartre's *Roads to Freedom* and the first number of *Les Temps modernes*. Sartre's lecture, '*L'Existentialisme est-il un humanisme?*', on 29 October 1945 was packed out; hundreds could not get into the hall, and women fainted in the crush.

Les Temps modernes wielded a tremendous influence. The title was partly inspired by Charlie Chaplin's film *Modern Times*, but the name was principally intended to stand for an era of intellectual change. Its editorial committee alone was enough to guarantee attention, for it included Sartre, Beauvoir and Camus, Merleau-Ponty as philosophy editor, and Michel Leiris and Raymond Queneau for poetry and literature, as well as Raymond Aron and Jean Paulhan, the grammarian, who was the only one with any experience of running a literary review. Malraux was invited to join but refused, partly, one suspects, because he was abandoning the radicalism of his youth. Considering Beauvoir's dislike of him – 'he takes himself for Goethe and Dostoyevsky at the same time' – it was just as well that he stayed out.

Gaston Gallimard agreed to back the publication and to give it office space: three of its editors – Paulhan, Camus and Queneau – were on Gallimard's own editorial committee, to say nothing of the others who were his authors. The first problem was to secure a paper ration. Beauvoir and Leiris went to see Jacques Soustelle, de Gaulle's Minister of Information, but he was reluctant because Raymond Aron, who had then turned against the General, was on their committee. In fact, Aron was to leave not long afterwards because of an ideological dispute.

Simone de Beauvoir saw *Les Temps modernes* as the showpiece of what she called the 'Sartrian ideal'. Almost immediately, however, she found herself swamped by manuscripts and besieged by earnestly ambitious young writers. It seemed as if half the young men on the left bank had been working on equally gloomy, pseudo-existentialist novels of the Resistance, because that was what was expected of them.

The theatre in France during the last two years of the Occupation had certainly proved itself alive, even if many leading members of the profession found themselves under clouds of varying sizes at the Liberation.

Parisian audiences had been educated to the avant-garde in the 1920s, and in the years before the war the playwrights Anouilh, Giraudoux, Salacrou and Cocteau had already prepared the ground for what is seen as the post-Liberation theatre.

Sartre's first play, *The Flies*, was performed in 1943. So too was Giraudoux's *Sodome et Gomorrhe*, although it was produced without France's greatest actor-manager, Louis Jouvet, who had taken his company into a nomadic exile in South America. One of the great successes had been Jean-Louis Barrault's production of Paul Claudel's *The Satin Shoe*, but Sartre and Beauvoir felt unable to judge the play objectively, so sickened were they by Claudel's '*Ode au maréchal*'. Early in 1944 Jean Anouilh's *Antigone* appeared, then shortly before the invasion of Normandy Sartre's *Huis Clos* was put on at the Vieux-Colombier. This play about hell, which Brasillach went to see before going into hiding, was the most influential. The notion that 'Hell is other people' passed into international currency.

More plays from the existentialist group followed over the next two years. In 1945 Albert Camus's *Caligula* received great acclaim, while Simone de Beauvoir's *Useless Mouths* was regarded as too mechanical. Then Sartre returned in the following year with *Men Without Shadows* and *The Respectful Prostitute* at the Théâtre Antoine, where his most politically important play, *Dirty Hands*, would follow. But while Sartre headed back towards realism with issues and moral dilemmas, the 'Theatre of the Absurd' of Arthur Adamov, Eugène Ionesco and Samuel Beckett, all influenced by Pirandello, was about to wander off in a very different direction.

Without doubt, the greatest success of the immediate post-war theatre was Jean Giraudoux's *The Madwoman of Chaillot* at the Théâtre de l'Athénée. Written during the Occupation, shortly before Giraudoux's death early in 1944, it was produced by Louis Jouvet at the end of the following year. Even if the story today may seem a curious piece of radical chic fantasy (an inspired madwoman, in a sort of modern court of miracles, manages to trick the exploiters of Paris by playing upon their greed and to imprison them in the city's sewers), Jouvet's direction, Christian Bérard's sets and the acting were superb. When the play opened in December 1945, and for a long time to come, the little theatre was packed with both the *beau monde* and Bohemia.

The world of painting and sculpture was also undergoing a period of intellectual and political ferment. When the Salon d'Automne opened on 6 October 1944, it was called the 'Salon de la Libération'. All painters deemed collaborationist were banned, including Derain, Van Dongen, Segonzac, Despiau, Belmondo and Vlaminck.

In an unprecedented mark of respect to a foreign painter, a special section entitled 'Hommage à Picasso' showed seventy-four paintings and five sculptures. On the morning of 5 October, the day before the opening of the exhibition, the front page of *L'Humanité* was not as usual devoted to the advances of the Red Army. Instead, across five columns, its headline declared:

PICASSO
THE GREATEST OF ALL LIVING ARTISTS
has joined the Party of the French Resistance

Picasso's rise to political consciousness caused a good deal of mirth and cynicism in non-Communist ranks. Many considered the decision to join the Communist Party a sort of insurance policy to safeguard a fortune, reputedly worth 600 million francs. Cocteau wrote in his diary that it was Picasso's 'first anti-revolutionary gesture'.

When the Salon opened, traditionalists and friends of the excluded painters held a demonstration inside. 'Take them down! Take them down!' they yelled in front of Picasso's paintings. Picasso is said to have been furious. Young right-wingers even went round Paris altering the chalked Communist slogans of '*Pétain au poteau*' ('Pétain for the firing squad') to '*Picasso au poteau*'. The strength of feeling did not abate – everyone was a committed *picassiste* or *anti-picassiste*. A year later at the ballet of the Théâtre des Champs-Élysées, a large part of the audience hissed the curtain which he had designed.

Picasso's commitment to the cause acted as a powerful recruiting campaign for the party. He even wrote in *L'Humanité*: 'Joining the Communist Party is the logical progression of my whole life, of my whole work . . . How could I have hesitated? The fear of becoming engaged in the struggle? But I feel much more free, much more fulfilled.'

Picasso's stand certainly inspired his more-resistant-than-thou colleagues. When a Resistance group asked painters for a work each to be sold for charity, Derain and Segonzac, both accused of collaboration, provided canvases. But Picasso, hearing that their work would be included, refused to give a painting; he offered 200,000 francs instead. Immediately, other artists threatened to boycott the exhibition if the two canvases by Derain and Segonzac were not withdrawn. The organizers felt forced to give way, but because the works of Derain and Segonzac were far more valuable than those of the protesters they sold them through dealers, without a word of apology to the two artists.

The dictatorship of the progressive intelligentsia after the war was a phenomenon which had a number of reasons, but few excuses. Ever since the *encyclopédistes* of the mid eighteenth century had encouraged the idea that thinkers would lead the masses to salvation, revolutionary and anti-clerical ideas generated their own form of spiritual arrogance. Jacobinism not only glorified political upheaval, endowing violence with romantic qualities, it saw Revolution as an entity with a life of its own: a terrible monster to be worshipped.

The exaltation of theory over bourgeois morality gained strength during the Resistance. Communist ruthlessness together with the party's vaunted professionalism attracted many of those ashamed of France's collapse in 1940 and the collaboration of Vichy. Never again should the right wing which had betrayed the country be allowed to regain control. Never again should Europe permit the horrors of Nazi rule. Only one country was strong enough and determined enough to oppose the return of fascism, and that was the Soviet Union.

Communists vigorously claimed that they were materialists, yet the wilful blindness towards the reality of life in the Soviet Union could only exist as a form of unquestioning religious belief. The spiritual aspect of Communism had been brought home to the British ambassador when a young priest came to see him in Algiers during the early summer of 1944. 'This emaciated young priest,' wrote Duff Cooper, in a report for Churchill's successor, Clement Attlee, 'with the fire of religious fanaticism burning in his eyes, assured me that having witnessed the Communists dying with the Catholics he could not but believe that the Communists too would go to heaven because, he said, they had died as martyrs to their faith.'

The eager subservience of intellectuals and their desire to be led is vividly illustrated in a letter from the French Communist deputy in the National Assembly, Alain Signor, to Stepanov of the international section in the Kremlin. It describes a meeting of the Central Committee. 'I must tell you that never before have I experienced such a feeling of the power of our party,' he wrote. 'Jacques [Duclos] was superb . . . André [Marty] strengthened Jacques' line of argument which even on its own had been very convincing. And finally Maurice [Thorez] showed by his contribution what a truly great guide he is for our party, a wise strategist and at the same time a true statesman ... We must work hard. We must do much to catch up with you. But we will catch up and join you.'

After the Liberation, some of the lighter-hearted Communist intellectuals joked in private about the clichés that filled almost every article and tract – 'sacred duty ... the directing role of the Party ... the glorious Soviet Union with Comrade Stalin at its head'. But any irreverent attitudes tolerated during the Resistance were soon suppressed by party cadres. There was a key question in the interview on joining the party: 'What did you think of the 1939 pact between the Soviet Union and Germany?' There was only one correct reply: 'I put my trust in the party.' Anyone who said that they had denounced it was immediately suspect. It was never a question of being right or wrong, it was a question of submission to discipline.

The real act of self-abasement before the party's authority was the need for all members to write their '*bios*', which were detailed autobiographical notes including every peccadillo in their lives. This written confession demonstrated the individual's trust in the party, but the real purpose was to give the party an effective hold over each member.

Introduction to a cell, with its sense of comradeship, was increased by the most emotional initiation of all – attendance at a mass rally. For many intellectuals, this was their first communion with the proletariat. Another opportunity was the open-air Fête de l'Humanité over a weekend in early September at Vincennes. The entertainment was all very proper. Bespectacled students from the Latin Quarter could wander around, savouring the smell of crushed grass, listening to accordions, and eating, drinking and mingling with the inhabitants of the '*ceinture rouge*' – the working-class suburbs such as Aubervilliers, Bagneux, Gennevilliers, Ivry, Montreuil, Saint-Denis and Vitry. The party never ceased to eulogize its proletarian life-blood in the *ceinture rouge*, but few card-carrying intellectuals ever visited those districts. They were more interested in discussing literature and politics, and their greatest ambition was to mix with the intellectual stars of the party.

Louis Aragon and Elsa Triolet were a devoted couple. Many people who liked Aragon deeply distrusted Triolet; they suspected her of being a KGB spy. Nobody could have been more fiercely defensive of Elsa than Aragon. When he was invited without her to an official lunch at the Quai d'Orsay, he rang Jacques Dumaine, the *chef de protocol*, in a state of high indignation. Dumaine explained that to invite men without their wives was the usual practice at midday. 'Monsieur,' retorted Aragon, 'I would have you know that Elsa Triolet is neither man nor woman, but a great French writer; as for myself, I have my own standards and do not wish to condone the practices of this government which calls itself provisional.'

Aragon was perhaps particularly touchy on the subject of Elsa Triolet's standing as a writer during that second half of 1945, because many people had voiced their suspicions about the way she had won the Prix Goncourt on 2 July for her novel *Le Premier Accroc coûte deux cents francs*. They pointed out that with three members of the Académie Goncourt under a cloud, including Sacha Guitry, the only way to win back public support for France's most important literary prize was to vote for a book which would be solidly supported by the Communist Party. Critics pointed out that Dorgelès, the Goncourt chairman, had approached Aragon several months before the vote; and later Aragon had published an article of his in *Les Lettres Françaises*. It smelled strongly of a '*dédouanement*' deal.

Triolet and Aragon, '*le couple royal*' of Communist letters, received guests in the palatial premises which the National Committee of Writers had taken over by the Élysée Palace, and entertained the most favoured to tea in their apartment amid the *objets d'art* they had collected. The novelist Marguerite Duras, on the other hand, cultivated a far more informal atmosphere. Her apartment on the rue Saint-Benoît rapidly became a semi-permanent rendezvous for Communist intellectuals, more like a private club than a salon. Her friends included the poet Francis Ponge, Maurice Merleau-Ponty, Clara Malraux (who had separated from André during the war), the Spanish Communist writer Jorge Semprun, Jean-Toussaint Desanti and his wife Dominique, and André Ulmann, the editor of *Tribune des nations*. The writer Claude Roy compared it to a meeting-place of the Russian intelligentsia in the last century.

The post-Liberation ferment, after the stuffiness of Vichy, was as much a clash of generations as of politics. One sociologist contrasted 'the bourgeois theatre of our father's generation with its stories about the stock exchange and finance, its calculations of income and dowries' with the new theatre 'where everyone proclaims their contempt for wealth, the impotence of finance, the boredom of middle-class life. Anouilh's characters talk of "your filthy money".'

Saint-Germain-des-Prés was unlike anywhere else in post-war Europe. In London, Edmund Wilson found a sense of depression and anti-climax. Graham Greene told him that he even felt 'a nostalgia for the hum of a robot bomb'. But in Paris, the Liberation had given the intelligentsia a powerful symbol of hope, even though the country was bankrupt. Rather as the Grandmaison doctrine in 1914 had represented the passionate belief that French *élan* would overcome German artillery, for intellectuals after the Liberation it was an article of faith that ideas would triumph over 'filthy money'.

16
After the Deluge

Paris remained a city of striking social contrasts, despite the political and intellectual longing for egalitarianism. This time, however, there was a difference. Parisians were divided not only by traditional class structure. Within their own social circles, there were the *bien vus* credited with a *jolie Résistance*, and the *mal vus* who had encountered *quelques ennuis à la Libération* ('a few problems at the Liberation').

In September 1944, several days after his arrival, the British ambassador was invited to a lunch given in his honour by Charles de Polignac. Those with a good war record were in evidence. They included Comte Jean de Vogüé – 'Vaillant' in the Resistance – who was wearing his FFI armband, and the Duchesse d'Ayen, whose husband was a prisoner in Germany. She did not yet know that he had died in Belsen.

At the top of the pyramid, well-connected Resistance heroes and Gaullists had a simple choice. Either they cut themselves off in moral indignation from friends and relations who had been Pétainists, or they had to adopt a more forgiving attitude. If Nancy Mitford's fictional hero, Charles-Édouard de Valhubert, is to be believed, the most aggravating sin tended to be social rather than political. His family lawyer had been a collaborator: 'You just don't know what that means. Two hours of self-justification before one can get down to any business. There's no bore like a collaborator.'

Those under a cloud often argued that the conflict between good manners and patriotism under the Occupation had been most difficult. There had been no guide to etiquette in such circumstances. Should a woman reject a seat offered by a German in the métro? Should one have refused to receive civilized, non-Nazi Germans whom one had known from before the war? Should one have turned one's back on a German friend in a public place?

Much, of course, depended on the individual case, but the different accounts of how people had behaved varied widely. The most improbable men and women claimed to have been in the Resistance, while those who had behaved heroically said very little. 'One rule here,' wrote Susan Mary Patten, 'is that those who suffered prefer not to talk about it, and it is next to impossible to worm Resistance stories out of them.' Maître Max Fischer, who had played a prominent part in the Resistance in the Vaucluse, admitted that he felt uncomfortable talking about his time in the *maquis* with anyone but his *anciens compagnons*; in their company, one spoke of little else. Back in Paris after the Liberation, Fischer wanted to put the past behind him and get on with his career in the law. Yet he was obliged to wear his medals in court; and those of his older colleagues who had sworn the oath of allegiance to Pétain, thus certainly compromising their chances of a decoration, cast sour glances at this young *blanc bec* who had already earned the Légion d'Honneur and the Médaille de la Résistance.

Gaullists often found themselves in a curious position on encountering old friends who had supported Marshal Pétain: more often than not, the Pétainist turned abruptly away in a mixture of embarrassment and shame, or even ran off down the street. Many, on the other hand, remained unrepentant. Those whose sympathies lingered with the white cockade of the Bourbons and despised 'the slut Marianne' of the Republic showed once again that they had learned little and forgotten little. Comte Jean-Louis de Rougemont, who had served with great bravery in the Resistance, returned to his old regiment after the Liberation 'expecting to be treated as something of a hero', but the reception he received was worse than chilly. The wives of fellow officers avoided him 'like a leper', regarding him as no better than a Communist fellow-traveller.

Some never concealed their Pétainist sympathies, even from Allied diplomats. When Adrian Holman, the British minister, and his wife arrived to stay for a weekend in 1945 with an *ancien régime* family, they were told that a mass would be held for the imprisoned Marshal in their private chapel. The Holmans promptly left.

'One asked nothing in Paris in those days,' said one of Martha Gellhorn's characters. 'There was a terrible discretion between friends.' Certain subjects were scrupulously avoided, unless you knew somebody very well and were alone. Nobody mentioned head-shaving, especially not the cases which had occurred in fashionable areas. There was also a terrible hypocrisy. The sales staff in smart shops who had served Germans without a tremor now patriotically refused to serve the wife of a collaborator.

Moral judgements at that time were thoroughly capricious. Somebody who had been merely imprudent, and no more selfish than most, could be whispered about as if they had denounced friends to the Gestapo; while others who might well have been executed if taken by the Resistance suffered little more than social ostracism. Baron Guy de Rothschild described an incident at one party. 'A Free French officer suddenly recognized among the guests a man who was a notorious collaborator with the Gestapo. He was asked to leave, accompanied by his wife and by the icy silence of the other guests, who lined up in two long rows between which he had to pass in order to reach the door.'

In such uncharted waters, the British ambassador and his wife relied on their 'pilot-fish', Gaston Palewski, for advice as to who could be invited and who could not. But Palewski's own behaviour was not exactly disinterested. Not long after Johnny de

Faucigny-Lucinge had seen the Duchesse de Brissac arrested, he had encountered Palewski, the very man whose name he had used to threaten the *fifis* with so little effect. Faucigny-Lucinge urged Palewski to help her, but Palewski surprised him with a rather frivolous reaction: 'Oh! All that's not very important. She can kick her heels a bit.' Faucigny-Lucinge, presuming that there must be 'some skeleton in the cupboard between them', did not persist. Then he heard that the duchess had been released without charge.

Some four months after her arrest, however, she invited Faucigny-Lucinge for a weekend in the country. As their property was some way from Paris and travel was still almost impossible at that time, Faucigny-Lucinge felt obliged to raise the problem of transport. 'There is somebody,' she replied, 'who could easily give you a lift, and that's Gaston Palewski.'

Those who had spoken in favour of the Germans, rather than just consorted with them, found it almost impossible to re-enter society. The Marquis Melchior de Polignac, who had been openly in favour of a Franco-German alliance since before the war, was an obvious target for arrest. He was the president of Pommery and became known in Épernay as the 'Führer of Champagne'. Members of the FFI hauled him out of his sickbed at the Château de Crayères and he was locked up in Fresnes prison. When his trial finally came to court, Polignac was able to prove that, thanks to his contacts with the Germans, he had saved a number of people from arrest and deportation. Although freed, he was avoided afterwards by much of Parisian society, a punishment which was probably worse for him than a prison sentence.

Foreigners mixing in grand circles in Paris were bemused by the contrasts of luxury and dilapidation. The newly arrived American diplomat Bill Patten and his wife Susan Mary went to a sumptuous dinner, but 'the house smelled of the black market, of corruption, of the greatcoats of the generals of the German

Wehrmacht, who, we later learned, had been honoured guests during the Occupation'. The next evening could not have been more different. 'Oh, the wonderful elegant shabbiness of the Mouchys,' wrote Susan Mary. This dinner consisted only of 'a very thin watery soup' and a main course of canned peas. 'There was no apology about the food, no hardship stories about the war. The china was museum quality and the oldest girl, nineteen, was very pleased with her dress, which was made from some old curtains.'

The inconveniences and discomforts of daily life seemed endless. Telephones were not the only service out of order. Candles were constantly needed, since the electricity failed at least twice a night. For many, the winter cold was a more terrible memory than the shortages of food. Susan Mary Patten, staying with friends at a château on the Loire, was asked by their little daughter if it was true that in America people could sit in a drawing-room without an overcoat on. In the Louvre, a British officer, seeing a crowd packed close to a picture, marvelled at the French appetite for culture. But when he came closer he saw that they were all trying to stand close to a grille dispensing hot air. Visitors discovered the elderly Comtesse Greffulhe, an original of Proust's Duchesse de Guermantes, huddled over a stove in her salon wearing her fur coat, a feather boa and button boots of grey glacé leather.

In the rue du Faubourg Saint-Honoré, the window displays of leather goods were restricted to one pair of shoes in real leather, marked 'model' to emphasize that they were not for sale, and straw scattered around as a sort of window dressing. In cafés, there was only fake coffee or *gazeux*, a sickly carbonated drink with a chemical taste. The *pâtisseries* were empty and in the windows of teashops like Rumpelmayer's there were cardboard cakes and dummy boxes of chocolates, again with a little sign saying 'model'.

All this came as a great anti-climax to Comrade Popova, the leader of the delegation of Soviet women, when they arrived from Moscow in June 1945. 'We were told that we would see some beautiful shops in France. But all the shops are either empty or shut. There is nothing to buy. The population as a whole walks on wooden-soled shoes . . . Nobody wears stockings. They wear very short dresses, not because it's the fashion but because there's no material. Yet on the hats one can see whole vegetable gardens and swallows' nests.'

In spite of the widespread decay and hardship, there were still many who remained far from poor, despite their protestations. A woman trying to sell the very best satin sheets at £400 a pair 'has more orders than she can put through,' wrote an astonished Diana Cooper to a friend in England, 'and all the orders are from the *French* – none from the US or UK and not from nouveau-riche black marketeers – just "nos vieilles clientes" – so you can see there's pots of money around'.

The *gratin*, or very uppermost crust in France, was more complex than it appeared from the outside. The Duc de Mouchy – a distinguished member of the Noailles family – claimed that he did not qualify as true *gratin* because he had an American grandmother. He painted a truly depressing picture of his peers: 'They crouch in their apartments discussing marriage settlements and degrees of consanguinity, they do not travel, their silver is dirty and their bronzes unshined, and their servants hate them for their meanness.'

Political views in such a milieu were perfect for a caricaturist's pen. 'Today,' wrote Nancy Mitford to Evelyn Waugh, 'I heard an old count say to another old count about a third old count: "But my dear friend, *very* left wing, he's an Orleanist."' But there were exceptions, especially among the younger generation after the Occupation. Margot de Gramont became partially estranged from her family because they were unenthusiastic about her heroic role in the Resistance. This also led to her marrying one of the great figures in the Dordogne *maquis*, Baron Philippe de Gunzbourg, a Jew of Russian origin. And the son of the Duchesse de La Rochefoucauld later volunteered to be the doorman of a subterranean night-club in Saint-Germain-des-Prés.

In the country, the traditional way of life had been much less affected. On 3 November 1945, the feast of Saint-Hubert, the Duc de Brissac insisted on celebrating the start of the hunting season in the old style. High mass took place in the church of Celle, with hunt servants in full dress blowing the large circular silver horns, and hounds brought up in front of the altar. A reception followed at the château. A vin rosé was served to the tenants, who came up afterwards to thank their landlord for restoring the old customs. 'Monsieur le duc, at last we are reassured . . .' they said.

French society after the Liberation, although firmly set in most of its ways, was much more welcoming to foreigners than before, particularly Americans and British. The Duc de Mouchy, however, warned Susan Mary Patten that she should not believe that his countrymen had suddenly changed. 'The French,' she wrote, passing on his explanation, 'having been thrown in on themselves for four years during the German occupation, were bored, bored, bored and eager for new faces.'

Foreigners, newcomers, and those returning after the Occupation were a welcome distraction from the cares of everyday life, and they themselves were equally eager to see their Parisian friends again. Daisy Fellowes, seeking to banish the embarrassment caused by her two elder daughters, resumed her entertaining. There was 'not a frill out of place', recorded one guest, 'gleaming, rich – no bibelots missing, carpets, cushions on the chairs and all the candles lighted on the stairs'. Daisy Fellowes also organized smaller parties. Claus von Bülow, who described himself in those days as no more than 'a Scandinavian student in wooden shoes', felt like 'a rabbit with a rattlesnake' when he turned up for dinner and discovered that they were *en tête-à-tête*.

The person who most wanted to be received, above all in

official circles, was the Duke of Windsor. The British ambassador wrote to Sir Alan Lascelles, King George VI's private secretary, supporting the idea that the Windsors should live in the United States. 'He can do no good in this country. Neither of them have ever liked the French or will ever begin to understand them; and here he can only find a place in that little cosmopolitan world, the existence of which in Paris will always continue, and which can never do anything but harm. The best French people, as you know, avoid it.'

Duff Cooper thought it rather sad that the Duke should attempt 'to entertain official personages as though he himself were exercising some official function'. The Duchess was the first to sense that Duff Cooper no longer took the ex-king seriously, and that the policy of Buckingham Palace and the Foreign Office was to keep him out of public life. 'Wally drew me aside,' wrote Duff's military attaché after one dinner, 'and said that she thought the Ambassador had treated H.R.H. disgracefully. France was the only country where he had not been presented to the Head of State or invited to an official reception. Lord Halifax [the British ambassador in Washington] had at once taken him to meet President Truman.'

Brigadier Daly harboured a certain sympathy for her view. During a round of golf, Daly had mentioned that the franc was liable to be devalued. The Duke had been most indignant that nobody had let him know before. 'I told him that I would keep him informed,' Daly wrote in his diary. 'After all he is still a Field Marshal and Admiral of the Fleet. People are apt to forget this.'

People were indeed apt to forget it, partly because nine years of exile had changed him so much. Lascelles, who had seen the Duke during a short visit to England, was particularly struck by the difference. 'The famous charm had vanished' and yet so had 'the old dictatorial attitude – "I want it so, therefore it must be so."'

Perhaps one of the most unintentionally sad remarks the

Duke ever made was when he said to Gaston Palewski, 'You ought to marry, look at us.' Nancy Mitford, who had just come to Paris in pursuit of Gaston Palewski, thought this uproariously funny, or at least pretended to. Secretly, there was nothing she yearned for more than to become Madame Gaston Palewski; though this was impossible since she was still Mrs Peter Rodd, and Rodd would not give her a divorce.

Palewski was intelligent, funny, ambitious and very vain – though he was no beauty and had terrible skin. He was also a notorious womanizer. Nine times out of ten, he probably had his face slapped; but his extraordinary persistence seems to have been rewarded often enough to have made it worthwhile. The best rebuff he received was from a woman to whom he offered a lift home after a dinner party, in his official car: 'No thank you, Gaston, I am too tired. I'd rather walk.' Men found him excellent company, and a number of women adored him, in spite of his looks.

Palewski had never pretended to be in love with Nancy. He had been opposed to her moving to Paris, and tried to make her realize that her love was hopeless. He told her that de Gaulle's views on morals were markedly conventional, and a liaison with a married Englishwoman would harm his career irreparably. (This was no doubt true, especially with Yvonne de Gaulle's abhorrence of adultery.) But Nancy could never abandon hope while he remained unmarried. She referred to herself, with bright sadness, as La Palewska.

They continued to see each other regularly. Most of the time, Nancy accepted the very restricted part she played in his life; but occasionally her self-control would crack, and she would throw a scene which was almost immediately regretted. 'Oh Colonel, I'm so ashamed of myself,' she told him on the telephone after one such outburst. Gaston was sympathetic. He replied, 'the rights of passion have been proclaimed by the French Revolution'.

Palewski, however, insisted on scrupulous discretion, which

sometimes gave their meetings the air of a bedroom farce. 'I end up by being shut up in a cupboard or hiding on the *escalier de service* and being found there by the concierge – so undignified I nearly die of it – apart from the fact that the whole of the time is taken up with these antics and I only get about five restless minutes of his company!'

Occasionally Gaston Palewski came to lunch at her house in the rue Monsieur, or she would accompany him to a party. At Princesse Sixte de Bourbon-Parme's ball, he arrived with Nancy Mitford on his arm. According to Nancy in a letter to Evelyn Waugh, 'we hadn't been there two minutes before the Colonel said we couldn't stay on account of the great cohorts of collaborators by whom we were surrounded; and firmly dumped me home'. She was mortified, having longed to show off her new dress, but made no objection.

Waugh tried to disabuse her in his next letter. 'Does it not occur to you, poor innocent, that the continental Colonel went back to the aristocratic ball and that while you lay sleepless with your fountain pen, he was in the arms of some well-born gestapo moll?'

17
The Salons

Women who held salons were considered, perhaps unfairly, to be either social-climbers or lion-hunters, competing with each other for the most interesting arrival on the scene. Every salon had to have a good balance between a 'kernel of faithfuls' and fresh blood, whether of new discoveries or of foreigners passing through Paris. Its highest purpose was to provide the right atmosphere for conversation – relaxed, stimulating, and not too earnest. Politicians did not go to talk politics. When somebody buttonholed Gaston Palewski at a salon in 1945 and asked him what he thought of the atom bomb, he replied, 'Well, as somebody who is very fond of porcelain . . .'

Salons revived gradually after the Liberation, though some were gone for good. The death of Princesse Edmond de Polignac was a sad loss to the music-lovers of Paris. Her protégée and cousin by marriage, Marie-Blanche de Polignac, continued the tradition of musical evenings. The beloved only daughter of the *couturière* Jeanne Lanvin, she had first been married to René Jacquemaire, a grandson of Clemenceau; but she had left him for Comte Jean de Polignac, the love of her life.

Jeanne Lanvin had given her daughter an excellent musical education. She played the piano and the harp; but her greatest gift was her voice, discovered and trained by Nadia Boulanger – whose Ensemble Vocal she joined in 1935. Soon after her second marriage, Marie-Blanche began to give musical parties on Sunday evenings in her house on the rue Barbet-de-Jouy. She had a music-room on the top floor, bare except for an organ, two pianos and some sofas and chairs. Her style of entertaining was relaxed and informal: she wanted nothing more than to enjoy music with her friends. Habitués included the composers Henri Sauguet, and Georges Auric with his wife Nora, a portrait-painter whose hair had been snow-white since youth. Francis Poulenc, with 'his luxury peasant accent', dedi-cated twelve songs to her and two pieces for piano; the pianist Jacques Février was another frequent visitor, as were celebrated foreign conductors and pianists who were passing through – Horowitz, Leonard Bernstein and Artur Rubinstein. As well as the music-room, the Polignac house also boasted a gallery of Impressionists collected by Mme Lanvin, who was often seen sitting alone at her daughter's receptions; but guests were not encouraged to approach the old lady. She had no desire for company, wanting only to watch her daughter's success.

Another fashionable salon was that of Marie-Laure de Noailles. She had vitality, an inquiring mind, and as a connois-seur of art she could impress even Bernard Berenson. She and her husband, Charles de Noailles, had built up one of the major collections of French twentieth-century art, and they were happiest in the company of artists and writers. When they first married, Marie-Laure adored her husband – and it came as a profound shock when, one day at their house in Hyères, she found him in bed with his male gymnastics instructor. After that they continued to share a roof but led largely separate lives, though they never lost a certain affectionate complicity.

The Noailles were considered so avant-garde that many of their peers in the *gratin* disowned them. They were patrons of the film-maker Buñuel, and the fact that they had financed his film *L'Age d'or* caused such a scandal that Charles de Noailles was nearly excommunicated. An even heavier blow (in this world, if not the next) came when his eldest brother, the Duc de Mouchy, told him that he must resign from the Jockey Club.

Charles de Noailles had never expected such a backlash, and became something of a recluse. Marie-Laure, on the other hand, still enjoyed provoking disapproval from the stuffier Parisian grandees. She took part in the marches of the Popular Front in 1936, and became notorious as '*la vicomtesse rouge*'. At the Liberation, however, she was shunned by many people who believed she had been too friendly with the Germans – which was considered particularly shocking since she was half-Jewish. This reputation arose because in 1941 she had been involved in a traffic accident, the others in her motorcar being Georges Auric and a German officer. As the story spread, the German officer was cast as her lover. However, the diary of her great friend Lise Deharme testified to the fact that Marie-Laure knew many resistants as well, most notably Paul Éluard.

Her *ennuis* did not last for long, and soon the question of a German lover was forgotten. A real lover, the cellist Maurice Gendron, installed himself in her life. He was a good musician who ended his career as a professor at the Paris Conservatoire, but Marie-Laure's friends suspected him of using her. In Colette's phrase, 'he was not somebody who ruined himself with women'.

The Noailles' house was a large *hôtel particulier* in the Place des États-Unis, left to Marie-Laure by her Bischoffsheim parents. Charles gave intimate lunches for his friends in a dining-room downstairs, and was rarely seen in his wife's salon. This very modern room was the work of the designer Jean-Michel Frank. Frank had commissioned Alberto Giacometti to make vases, tables and lamps for his interiors; and the effect was one of expensive simplicity. The paintings in this salon included works by Picasso, a portrait of Marie-Laure by Bérard, and a very fine Rubens. There was also another, more formal salon, with magnificent French furniture and gold objects by Benvenuto Cellini.

The Noailles also owned three full-length Goyas as well as paintings by Watteau, Delacroix, Miró, Burne-Jones, Max Ernst and Dali. The house reflected the spirit of Marie-Laure, who wanted to be both avant-garde and the Vicomtesse de Noailles. She liked mixing old and new, and enjoyed the juxtaposition of a Picasso over a Riesner commode. 'Oh, the objects in that house,' wrote Nancy Mitford. 'I can't even eat or speak for goggling.'

Florence Gould, a Frenchwoman who had married the American Frank J. Gould, was another *salonnière* who enjoyed the company of writers, artists and intellectuals. The daughter of a French newspaper tycoon who lived in Los Angeles, Florence Gould was a handsome woman with large blue eyes. She gave lunches, which started late and went on a long time, in her apartment on the Avenue Malakoff. ('On déjeune à Malakoff,' people would say.) Among her regular visitors were Marcel Jouhandeau and his wife, the painter Marie Laurencin, Henri Michaux, Paul Léautaud, and Jean Paulhan, who introduced Florence to the painter Dubuffet.

Mrs Gould's salon was furnished with comfortable armchairs made in the twenties and a huge dark-blue sofa, with oriental carpets on the floor and junk-shop curios on the tables. During the war she had also entertained cultivated Germans, like the writer Ernst Junger. He found her curiously generous: she showed him a book out of which she had ripped three pages because a friend admired them, and to Junger she gave a scarab.

Soon after the Liberation, Marie Laurencin, Léautaud and the painter Jean Oberlé were lunching with Florence Gould. As they were eating, the butler entered, went over to their hostess and bent to murmur a few words in her ear. She rose, asked her guests to excuse her, and left the room. Lunch finished, coffee and liqueurs were served, but their hostess still did not return. It was nearly five in the afternoon when the butler announced: 'I think, ladies and gentlemen, that it would be better not to wait any longer. Madame has been arrested.'

Jean Paulhan later became virtually the *maître de maison* in the Gould household and invited his own friends. Jean Galtier-Boissière, who was one of them, recorded how their hostess –

'a marvellous red-head' – appeared at two o'clock in an evening dress and wearing sunglasses. He suddenly remembered having described in his journal the famous lunch party of three years before at which his hostess had been arrested by *fifis*. Fortified by wine, he reminded her. 'I have forgotten the grievance,' she replied, smiling, 'but I still remember the date.'

The Duchesse de La Rochefoucauld, born Edmée de Fels, was a neighbour of Marie-Laure de Noailles in the Place des États-Unis. This was about the only thing they had in common. For whereas women like Marie-Laure and Florence Gould were stimulated and intrigued by contemporary art and young artists and writers, the Duchesse de La Rochefoucauld preferred astronomy and the older generation. Her salon could not be described as exciting, unless one appreciated a mandarin approach to literature and a low-voiced nostalgia for Marshal Pétain. The great star of her salon had been Paul Valéry, and her other guests included a number of elderly and eminent Academicians.

A similarly well-bred and worthy atmosphere reigned in the salon of the duchess's sister-in-law, Marthe de Fels. Her parties were deemed to be slightly more amusing, even though the invitations she sent out may not have given that impression: they offered '*un peu de thé, un peu de conversation*'.

Nancy Mitford once described 'a French *gratin-académie* tea-party' of this sort. She found 'savants and writers grouped round old Madame de Pange – sister of two Broglie *académiciens* – the mustiest little crowd of desiccated manners-bound horrors'. Most of these old gentlemen showed little interest in the opposite sex; so when the good-looking Swiss ambassador Carl Burckhardt appeared, he was immediately 'surrounded like the merry widow with all the men in the room'.

Some salons were more artistic, some more intellectual, but none was more cosmopolitan than that of Marie-Louise Bousquet. She too had entertained Ernst Junger during the

Occupation, and he particularly admired her panelled library, with its beautiful leather-bound books. Marie-Louise suffered from arthritis and walked with a cane, but she gave an impression of great agility, her black eyes bright with mischief. She could welcome a friend with effusive flattery – 'My dear, I've never seen you look so lovely' – and then, in a loud stage whisper to whoever was standing by, 'or so stupid'. No wonder Junger wrote that he treated her 'with a certain circumspection, like a chemist dealing with unpredictable elements'. Prince Jean-Louis de Faucigny-Lucinge, who was an old friend, described her as a *gavroche*, an urchin. Her attractions were certainly not physical. 'Marie-Louise can never have been beautiful,' Lucinge continued, 'but she had verve.'

Before the war, her salon had consisted of up to a dozen distinguished men, mainly writers such as Valéry, and ambassadors, seated in chairs of varying degrees of comfort; while Marie-Louise, a cigarette never far from her mouth, moved among them, stimulating the company with affectionate insults and funny remarks. Her husband was very deaf, and the amplifying part of his cumbersome hearing aid was lodged in his hip pocket. When he had not heard a remark he would turn his right buttock as far as possible towards his interlocutor and say, '*Plaît-il?*' M. Bousquet did not survive long after the war; and with her income gravely reduced, Marie-Louise became the Paris correspondent of *Harper's Bazaar*. She revived her salon in her apartment in the Place du Palais-Bourbon, which occupied the floor above that of Boni de Castellane's brother, Biche, also living in straitened circumstances. Her salon changed, and not just from Wednesdays to Thursdays. The old ambassadorial and *académicien* clique was much diminished by age and death: as one of her younger visitors put it, 'one saw less of the Paul Valérys, and more of the Cecil Beatons'.

For any traveller with an interest in modern art, a visit to Gertrude Stein was high on the list of things to do in Paris. The apartment in the rue Christine was 'a strange combination of sloppy comfort and a modern art museum'. In her portrait by Picasso, she is wearing the sort of turban worn by English gentlemen in the eighteenth century, when they had taken off their wigs. Her portrait by Picabia made her look like an ancient Buddhist. The eighteenth-century chairs were upholstered in *petit point* of abstract design, but Gertrude Stein preferred sitting on the sofa, her feet firmly apart. Her sitting-room could hardly be called a salon, since Stein never made any effort to bring people together, let alone on a given day of the week. Her friends came when they felt like it; people who wanted to meet her made appointments; but after the Liberation, the people Gertrude Stein welcomed most were the GIs.

Cleve Gray was a young American who received a warm welcome: he was not only in uniform, he was also a painter. When he rang the doorbell, it was answered by Alice Toklas 'looking like a little mongoose, very sweet and intelligent'. Gertrude Stein came in 'looking like Gertrude Stein'. She began to ask him about the GIs: Were they lonely? Were they enjoying Paris?

Natalie Clifford Barney, one of the principal expatriate *salonnières* of the period between the wars, returned to Paris in 1946 – two months before the death of her old friend Gertrude Stein. They had both settled in Paris before the First World War. Miss Barney's 'day' was reinstated on Fridays, avoiding any clash with Marie-Louise's Thursdays.

Natalie Barney, known as *'l'impératrice des lesbiennes'*, may have been feminine in appearance, but she possessed a masculine voracity for the chase. Her most famous triumph had been the seduction of the great *belle-époque* beauty, Liane de Pougy. Between the wars, Natalie Barney had been a focal point for what Sylvia Beach called 'the ladies with high collars and monocles'. Her two great loves during this time were the Duchesse de Clermont-Tonnerre, who did not go in for equestrian accessories, and the painter, Romaine Brooks, who did. When she revived her days after the war, the salon was an undisguised remnant from another age: a shaded, semi-forgotten island in the existentialist heartland of Saint-Germain-des-Prés.

The house, hidden beyond the courtyard of 20 rue Jacob, stood in an overgrown garden with a little Napoleonic temple in Doric style, all of which Radclyffe Hall had described in great detail in her lyrically pessimistic novel, *The Well of Loneliness*. The salon itself was interesting rather than comfortable. The young Truman Capote described the room, with its ceiling cherubs and hassocks for sitting on, as 'a cross between a chapel and a bordello'. The hassocks appear to have been a safer choice than the chairs.

The food and drink at Natalie Barney's Fridays, however, were infinitely superior to the crackers, orangeade and martini invariably offered by Marie-Louise Bousquet. Miss Barney's Edwardian tradition of cucumber sandwiches and tea was enhanced with the alternatives of champagne and delicious little strawberry or raspberry tarts made by her long-suffering and devoted cook, Berthe.

The hostess used to greet her guests wearing a white Vionnet tea-gown. (When she went out, however, her clothes, her car and her chauffeur's livery were all grey.) An *ingénu* would be guided 'to meet somebody because they were so-and-so in Proust'. She was loyal to old friends from before the war – Alice Toklas, for example, became a permanent fixture following Gertrude Stein's death – but there was always new blood. The greatest stir of the post-war salon was caused by the arrival of Greta Garbo, produced in triumph by another veteran of the lesbian international, Mercedes de Acosta.

Natalie Barney was no mere lion-hunting hostess. Although far from well-read, she spoke beautiful eighteenth-century French and cultivated *bons mots* to some effect. 'In England nothing is designed for women,' she once remarked, 'not even the men.'

*

Two names appear again and again in the 'who was there' lists of this period: those of Jean Cocteau and Christian Bérard. They were both prolific as artists, in spite of apparently turning up at almost every soirée, opening night, *vernissage*, cocktail party and salon in Paris. Jean Cocteau, with his spiky nose and long, thin hands, was so well known and so unusual-looking that he seemed like a caricature of himself. His hands moved constantly as he talked, in brilliant monologues bursting with extraordinary ideas and images. Proust had compared him to a seahorse – a creature that seems as alien in the sea as it would on land; yet Cocteau was a man of strong emotions, and Denise Tual described him as having '*le goût de la tendresse*'. She also remembered his delight in discovering and fostering new talent.

His was an art without compartments: whether he was drawing, writing plays or poems, or making films. Despite the richness of his imagination and the prolific quantity of his work, he was an artistic butterfly – someone dismissed him as '*le grand couturier des lettres françaises*'. The Surrealists in particular hated him, for he revelled in the worldly success and adulation they affected to despise. He enjoyed the gregarious world of the Parisian theatre, and although homosexual and an opium addict, was always afraid of shocking his concierge. He was also tortured by self-doubt: Ernst Junger described him as living 'in a hell of his own making'.

The same could be said of his great friend Christian Bérard. Like Cocteau, Bérard was an artist of great talent, and an opium addict. His need to finance the habit meant that he had to deploy all his energies on commissions: fashion sketches, theatrical costumes and set designs, which provided a more or less steady supply of cash. He never managed to get off this treadmill and devote himself to painting.

Known to his friends as Bébé, he was fat, with beautiful pale eyes, long red hair, and a huge bushy beard invariably dusted with cigarette ash. Bettina Ballard wrote that 'his lips had the rich, moist, indecent pinkness that a beard so often lends to a mouth'. Bérard lived in the rue Casimir Delavigne near the Place de l'Odéon, with his lover, the choreographer Boris Kochno. His room was all black and red and he spent much of his morning in bed, wearing a dressing-gown scarred by cigarette burns. His breakfast consisted of bread, cheese and black coffee, followed by a pipe of opium. He was not fastidious – his clothes were always spattered with paint and food. At one lunch at the British Embassy, Cocteau leaned across towards Bérard and asked, 'Darling, where do you manage to find that black for your finger-nails?' 'I get it from London,' came Bérard's instant but hardly diplomatic reply.

Bérard neglected his commissions until the last possible moment, when *Vogue* magazine or a theatrical producer would ring up and say that his work was needed in two hours at the latest. Then Bérard would leap out of bed, and – as Marc Doelnitz witnessed – perform the feats of a magician. 'In four strokes of a brush dipped in Chinese ink, outlines took on substance. A touch of colour brought them to life. Saliva smeared with a finger gave the impression of volume. Already, he was moving to a second sketch while I fanned the first to dry it.'

Bettina Ballard saw him feverishly painting a set with a brush in each hand, a cigarette hanging out of his mouth and ash on his beard. Once the work was over, Bérard – swearing he would never touch another commission – repaired, often with Cocteau, to the Méditerranée restaurant: their special haunt, as the Catalan was Picasso's. Another place where they went for relaxation and stimulation was the Salon Vert of the British Embassy.

One of the secrets of Lady Diana Cooper's entertaining was that she could give the smallest gathering in the grandest surroundings all the intimacy and excitement of a midnight feast. Guests coming up the graceful sweep of stone staircase had to make their way through two empty, formal, chilly drawing-rooms before they reached the Salon Vert, hung in green silk damask and warmed by a crackling fire in the grate. Apart from Cocteau and Bérard, a visitor might find Georges and Nora Auric, Marie-Blanche de Polignac, Denise Bourdet, Francis Poulenc, Jacques Février, and the dearest friend of both Duff and Diana's, Louise de Vilmorin. This was the inner core of a group of friends whom Diana and Louise called '*la bande*', and its members often brought their friends. The hostess might be talking to one or more of them, or perhaps still in her bath – it did not matter. Guests helped themselves to drinks from a side-table, upon which stood bottles of Scotch whisky and London gin. The Paris contingent would be enlarged by people passing through: Cyril Connolly, Isaiah Berlin, Harold Nicolson, Noël Coward, Benjamin Britten, Cecil Beaton, Victor Rothschild, Virginia Cowles, Martha Gellhorn or Evelyn Waugh. Artists and writers also mingled at official receptions downstairs with statesmen and generals. Malcolm Muggeridge was surprised 'to find Picasso in this throng, looking like some strange wild ape who had strayed into a film-set where the ball on the eve of the Battle of Waterloo was being filmed'.

When people criticized the Coopers for entertaining 'collaborators', they were usually referring to Louise de Vilmorin, Countess Palffy. Louise was then in her mid-forties, with pale skin and thick, long hair held in place with tortoiseshell combs or an eighteenth-century bow of black silk. An operation in her youth had left her with a limp.

She had been loved by Antoine de Saint-Exupéry and Jean Cocteau, both of whom proposed to her, and her novels and poetry enjoyed a considerable success (to the great irritation of Lise Deharme, who hated her with passion). She had a genius for conversation, and a hunger for love and attention: to Diana she admitted 'a desperate fear of being forgotten'. People either loved or loathed her. Those who loved her, like Duff and Diana, thought her the wittiest and most enchanting woman they knew; but others detested her. Evelyn Waugh described her as a 'Hungarian countess who pretended to be a French poet. An egocentric maniac with the eyes of a witch.'

Louise herself set out the charges against her in a letter to Diana, many years later: 'In 1937 I had married Paul Palffy, I lived in Slovakia and Hungary during the war; I had seen and mixed with Austrians and Germans with the result that my name was inscribed on a black list which Duff himself showed me.' She was interrogated by a purge committee after the Liberation, but they found nothing specific against her.

Louise vividly remembered her first meeting with 'les Duffs', as they were known, at a dinner given by Marie-Blanche de Polignac in early October 1944. Having heard so much about them, she looked at them closely. Neither was tall, and Duff, who had retained his officer's moustache from the First World War, was no longer so handsome, with the paunch and slight jowls of late middle age. His natural expression was quiet and reserved, for although a man of strong likes and dislikes, he was shy until animated by conversation. Louise noticed the elegance of his hands and feet, the whiteness of his linen, the way he held himself upright, and 'the slight cast in his eye that lent his look a mysterious charm'.

Diana too was in her fifties, but she remained astonishingly beautiful. Age had not taken away her perfect pale complexion, nor what Cocteau called '*le coup de pistolet bleu pâle de son regard*'. That night, Louise recalled in a letter many years later, her looks were made even more dramatic by her clothes: 'You, Diana, wore a dark wide-brimmed hat. Your dress was long and black and moulded to your figure. The bodice was of spider's web lace on a flesh-coloured lining that gave the effect of nudity, an effect so startling that Stanislas de Castellane, the palest of men, blanched visibly. Bending over to me, he whispered, "Her maid has forgotten her slip. She is naked. Tell her so."'

Despite the company the evening fell rather flat, and Louise felt she had made little impact on 'les Duffs'; but Gaston Palewski encouraged her to invite them to dinner at Verrières, the Vilmorin house some fourteen miles outside Paris, which she shared with her brothers Roger and André de Vilmorin. Louise described the dinner: 'Not much to eat, enough to drink, just enough light shed by aged yellow electric-light bulbs and candles ... Good spirits, gaiety, sparkling conversation, success.' Duff told her about his book on King David, and Louise immediately offered to translate it.

'We had just reached the coffee,' wrote Duff in his diary, 'when I got a message to say that the Prime Minister wanted to speak to me most urgently between 10 and a quarter past ... I left at once, leaving Diana behind and sending the car back for her. Louise Palffy took me to the door. I found myself kissing her and falling in love.'

Duff's extra-marital excursions were too numerous and short-lived to cause Diana much pain, and they never altered the profound love that was the bedrock of their relationship. Yet so delighted was Diana with Louise that she positively welcomed this affair, and Louise became an almost permanent resident in the embassy.

When the affair ended, Louise was distraught; but she continued to be a frequent guest, both at the embassy and the Coopers' country house at Chantilly. This prompted the Duchess of Windsor, who had dubbed Louise de Vilmorin 'Madame l'Embrassadrice', to remark that surely the worst part of having an affair with Duff was the prospect of Diana coming to comfort you when it was over.

18
Communists in Government

On the afternoon of Monday, 7 May 1945 word spread across Paris that the war was over. Germany had surrendered. Everyone waited for the bells to ring out, but only the newspapers, rushed off the presses, confirmed the news.

After dinner, Jean Galtier-Boissière expected the streets to be full of people, but the only sign of celebration was the occasional jeep rushing past, driven by a GI and piled with young Frenchwomen frantically waving Allied flags. He went with some friends to the old Boeuf sur le Toit nightclub where Moyses, the *patron*, offered them a free bottle of wine – '*une bouteille de la Victoire*' – in celebration. The painter Jean Oberlé joined them and together they listened to the orchestra playing 'Tipperary' and 'Madelon', the words sung lustily by American, British and French officers.

Everyone was in good spirits, but at about three in the morning a curious incident took place. Oberlé refused to shake the hand of a man who came up to him. The man, red in the face with anger, demanded why. Oberlé replied that he would not shake the hand of anyone who had broadcast on the German-controlled Radio-Paris. The man blustered, claiming he had been a prisoner and that someone else had spoken under his name. People at neighbouring tables joined in the argument. Suddenly, a waiter stuck out an accusing finger and shouted: 'I've seen this man have dinner with German officers!' This produced an uproar. But then a long-haired character, looking like '*une sorte de zazou*', spoke up to defend the accused.

'Who are you?' several people demanded at once.

'I'm a detective-inspector!' he replied, drawing himself up proudly. This provoked a roar of laughter. Then René Lefèvre, one of Galtier-Boissière's friends, started an argument with the plain-clothes policeman, and knocked him down. When the policeman stood up, Lefèvre hauled him to the door and kicked him all the way down the street. The sky was already light above eastern Paris. It was the dawn of VE Day.

The long-awaited morning turned out sunny, yet the streets remained curiously empty until the afternoon. Around three, the Place de l'Étoile (where huge tricolors flew beneath the Arc de Triomphe), the Champs-Élysées and the Place de la Concorde began to fill with people. Almost every house and vehicle seemed to be decorated with flags. The jeeps full of soldiers and young women were brought to a halt by Parisian youth – the middle-aged and old mostly stayed at home. The afternoon was noisy, with klaxons hooting, Flying Fortresses crossing low overhead, artillery salutes, church bells and air-raid sirens sounding a final all-clear.

General de Gaulle broadcast to the nation, making much of the fact that France had been represented at the surrender ceremony and was one of the victors. Once it was over, the Place de la Concorde became even more closely packed. The crowds were so thick that white-helmeted US military police had to force a way through to let people in and out of the American Embassy. When a man in khaki uniform came out on to the balcony and gave the victory salute, the crowd, thinking it was Eisenhower, yelled its acclaim. It was, in fact, William Bullitt, the pre-war American ambassador to France.

As darkness fell, the most famous monuments in the centre of Paris – the Arc de Triomphe, the Place de la Concorde, the Madeleine and the Opéra – were illuminated for the first time since the beginning of the war, the Opéra in red, white and blue lights. The fountains were also reconnected and lit up.

The Paris police struggled to push back the crowds in the rue Royale to make way for a ceremonial appearance of the Garde Républicaine on horseback, as they came trotting down from the Madeleine; but their arrival was as chaotic as the scenes around them. Their full-dress uniform, the shining cuirasses and dragoon helmets with long horsehair plumes, was dramatically offset by the fact that almost every soldier had 'at least one girl riding behind him on the horse, clinging to his Napoleonic uniform and screaming'.

As evening advanced, a strong breeze arose and the flags flying from the tops of public buildings cracked in the wind. The crowds below continued to sing the Marseillaise, 'Madelon', the '*Chant du départ*' and the songs of the Resistance. Red Army officers, easily recognizable by their thick shoulder-boards, were congratulated; but when a White Russian friend of Simone de Beauvoir began to chat with a group of Soviet soldiers in their own language, they demanded severely what she was doing in Paris and why she was not in the Motherland.

Castor and a couple of friends went up to Montmartre to finish the evening at the Cabane Cubaine. Afterwards they were given a lift home in a jeep. They felt slightly flat. 'This victory had been far away from us; we had not been waiting for it, as we had the Liberation, in a feverish anguish of anticipation.' At midnight a fanfare of trumpeters from the Paris fire brigade sounded the ceasefire. Others also felt that, unlike the Liberation, there was an artificial side to the celebration, partly because they were 'too exhausted to applaud a finale for which we had waited too long', but also because General de Gaulle's emphasis on France's glorious role did not ring true. They did not feel like victors.

The only people likely to feel triumphant were the Communists, basking in the reflected glory of the Red Army and the conviction that the party would be in power in the near future.

In 1945, the French Communist Party was the most powerful

political organization in the country, controlling a number of front organizations – the National Front, the Union of French Women, the Union of French Republican Youth, a veterans' association and most of the largest unions within the CGT, the Confédération Général de Travail. But there were some striking weaknesses, especially in Paris and its suburbs, where membership had not even climbed back to the level of 1938. Benoît Frachon, the Communist head of the CGT trades-union movement, reported: 'the principal reason ... is due to a certain temporary disappointment among workers. The workers were counting on a fundamental revolution in France and on social liberation immediately after the Germans were chased out.' But what Frachon does not mention is that the loss of workers in the suburbs was greater than acknowledged. Their loss was partly camouflaged by the number of intellectuals joining the party in Paris.

Many workers had indeed become Communists during the Resistance in the belief that victory would lead to revolution. The astonishment and disgust of many could hardly be contained when Maurice Thorez, on his return to France, called for increased production and – from the most famous deserter of 1939 – the creation of a powerful French army.

None of this, of course, meant that the French Communist Party had become a bourgeois party, even if some of its leaders, especially Thorez, were lulled into a certain *embourgeoisement* by the trappings of power. But their policy, until they received different directions from Moscow, remained a dual-track one. On one side, the party consolidated its position within the system of parliamentary democracy in order to install as many of its members as possible in positions of influence. And with the party's vote rising to close to a third of the total, the possibility of reaching power through constitutional means was not to be ruled out. Meanwhile, on the other side, revolutionary morale was kept up by attacks on collaborators and 'the fascist fifth column of Vichy'.

The continuing obsession with the fifth column was partly inspired by the campaign to remove more of the opposition – it was also the classic Stalinist method of accounting for setbacks due to incompetence – but the belief in a fifth column of Vichyist saboteurs was quite genuine.

Despite growing tensions between the party and General de Gaulle, Communist ministers stayed in the government, and Thorez proved himself a highly useful ally. At Waziers on 21 July 1945, he shocked his audience by telling them that the hunt for collaborators must come to an end, and that there were far too many strikes. On 1 September, Duclos proclaimed that Thorez's speech at Waziers had raised coal production. 'It's thanks to the Communist Party that the population will have coal this winter.'

The government and its officials could hardly believe their luck at Thorez's responsible line, although they had no illusions about the party's simultaneous efforts at infiltration. A very senior official in the Ministry of the Interior, responsible for its intelligence network in the country – he claimed to have 5,000 agents throughout France keeping a close eye on Communist activities – reported to the American Embassy that the party was devoting its efforts to planting members wherever they could wield influence. They were having much less success than they had hoped in the armed forces, but were managing to take effective control of the CGT trades-union movement. On the other hand, 'Every week they continue to support us is time gained and strengthens our position.'

For a materialist party, totally cynical in matters of *realpolitik*, the Communists devoted an astonishing amount of effort – and ruthless politicking – to the cultivation of myths and heroic symbols. In January 1945 the party had launched a campaign to have their star writer of the pre-war years, Romain Rolland, buried in the Panthéon. They lobbied, too, to get party members into the Académie Française. But nowhere had they been quicker off the mark than to have streets and métro stations re-named after their Resistance heroes.

Following the Stalinist model, a personality cult was developed around Maurice Thorez. Thorez, whatever one may think of his politics, was a man of formidable talents. His enemies may have seen his muscular, rubbery face as a mask of deceit, but as a devout Stalinist he believed in the necessity of lies. A miner by birth and by trade, he overcame his lack of education by sheer force of will, developing a formidable concentration.

He was acclaimed by the French Communist Party as 'the son of the people', also the title of his official autobiography – almost making him sound like the Christ of the proletariat. Yet, to demonstrate his place in the Communist universe, this was the same man whose request in Moscow to Dimitrov for permission to be interviewed by a journalist was dismissed as curtly as if he had been a clerk asking for an extra holiday.

On his fiftieth birthday, schoolchildren came to sing: 'Our Maurice is fifty years old – happy, happy birthday – for Jeannette, for their children – for his mother!' Jeannette Vermeersch, his companion and the mother of his children, was portrayed as a model of proletarian courage. The poverty of her childhood was recounted as the Stalinist equivalent of a Bible story. She too cultivated the legend, and her fiery oratory was modelled on that of La Pasionaria, whom she greatly admired.

The other, perhaps unsurprising, paradox came with the Communist Party's commercial empire. The opportunities for expansion had been greatly increased at the Liberation, when buildings belonging to collaborationist organizations were expropriated. The party's daily newspaper *L'Humanité*, for example, took over the building in the rue d'Enghien which had belonged to the populist newspaper *Le Petit Parisien*.

The party owned a bank, the Banque du Nord; and a shipping line, France Navigation, which had been taken over during the Spanish Civil War, and was almost certainly bought with part of the gold reserves of the Spanish Republic, used to purchase Soviet military supplies.

The party's publishing empire was huge, both in Paris and in the provinces, where it had 12 daily newspapers and 47 weeklies. In addition the Communist-run coalition, the National Front, had 17 weeklies, all tightly controlled. Instructions for 'political orientation' were issued each day to all provincial newspapers controlled by their front organization.

The flagship of the party's property empire was 'le 44', the great brick headquarters in the rue Le Peletier. It was well defended with never fewer than half-a-dozen security guards, all picked members ready against a surprise attack by fifth columnists.

Party leaders also expected assassination attempts. Thorez was driven each day to 'le 44' in a heavily armoured limousine accompanied by bodyguards. The moment they arrived outside, the bodyguards and the security members from inside the building would form a human screen so that Thorez could hurry inside safely. At Thorez's house, a small château at Choisy, the bodyguards served at table then took their meals in the kitchen. One visitor described the place as '*tristement petit-bourgeois*'. It had a private cinema, because Communist leaders (with the exception of Laurent Casanova) did not dare venture out to public places. The house also had a very uneven art collection. All the works had been donated and dedicated to *le camarade Maurice* by painters who were party members.

In 1945 the French Communist Party, then at the height of its influence, decided to push forward its most ambitious strategy: taking over the Socialist Party through amalgamation. The theme of working-class unity held a tremendous appeal at that time for the majority, especially the young, who had no experience of Communist ruthlessness in the pursuit of power.

Jacques Duclos declared that only enemies of the people were opposed to the unity of the working class: Socialists who resisted it were 'scissionists'. But veterans, such as the Socialist leader Léon Blum, remembered only too well the Spanish Communist Party's attempts to swallow the Spanish Socialist Party in 1936, early in the Civil War. They also remembered the Communist takeover of the CGT trades-union federation in the name of working-class unity.

The American Embassy kept a watch on these developments. Captain David Rockefeller, the assistant military attaché, maintained close touch with members of the Renseignements Généraux, one of the Ministry of the Interior's police intelligence networks. These officers persuaded him that the best bulwark for the Socialists to resist the Communists was the recently reformed Union Démocratique Socialiste de la Résistance. Although left-wing, it had proved its staunchly anti-Communist position by expelling Pierre Villon, a party member. Rockefeller predicted that if the Socialists and their allies stood firm, the Communists would have little alternative but to pull out of the government and sabotage 'efforts to bring about economic recovery'.

Blum and his colleagues at the head of the Socialist Party felt uneasy. The Communists looked as though they would win either way. If a majority of Socialists agreed to unification, the Communists would be able, through unscrupulous use of their superior organization, to take over every important post and win control. On the other hand, if Blum and his supporters managed to win the vote against unification, the issue might well split the Socialist Party, as had happened in Spain nine years before. The Communists would then win over the Socialist left-wing and most of their young members. Their only hope was to play for time.

Communist attempts to establish a monopoly of working-class leadership was damaged from an unexpected direction. The centrepiece of their propaganda in 1945 was the heroism of the Red Army. But when the party strove to win over the recently returned prisoners-of-war and deportees, it discovered that many had returned to France horrified by the rape, looting and murder they had witnessed in the Soviet zone of occupied Germany. Their stories spread. Communist leaders in Paris were beside themselves with rage. 'No word against the Red Army must be permitted!' thundered André Marty at a mass meeting. Posters appeared attacking those 'cynical Hitlerian scoundrels' who had infiltrated themselves 'to spread anti-Soviet calumnies' against 'the soldiers of the glorious Red Army who have saved the civilized world'.

The Kremlin, on the other hand, demonstrated little concern. Stalin's lack of interest in France continued beyond the end of the war. After the red flag was raised over the ruins of Berlin, his main preoccupation was the establishment of a *cordon sanitaire* of satellite states controlled by the Red Army. Never again did he want to be vulnerable to a surprise attack from Germany.

One of the best indications of how loose the relationship between the Kremlin and the French Communist Party had become appears in the stenographic account of a meeting of the international section on 15 June 1945. Stepanov, the official dealing with the French Communist Party, felt that its leaders were losing their way. 'For the whole period of the Liberation,' he told Ponomarev and his committee, 'one can say that the Communist Party acted in a very intelligent and very clever way. The party did not allow itself to be isolated from the rest of the resistance movement and the other parties . . . [Yet] one gets the impression that the Communist Party, although it is acting correctly from a tactical point of view, has no strategic perspective and no strategic objectives.'

Ponomarev disagreed. Thorez was right to 'avoid premature actions and anything which risked provoking conflicts which will play into the hands of internal forces of reaction allied with external forces in the form of the English and Americans. The French Communist Party's situation therefore is much more complicated than that for each Communist Party where our Red Army is present and where we have been able to bring about democratic changes. The proximity of the Soviet Union plays a role which is not small, and other circumstances play their parts too, but the decisive fact is the presence of the Red Army.' Like Stalin, Ponomarev focused primarily on the *cordon sanitaire* imposed at gunpoint. But in 1947, Stepanov's analysis would turn out to be the more accurate, with the French Communist Party caught on the wrong tack.

19

The Abdication of Charles XI

The problems of France's leadership were summarized in graffiti on the walls of Paris: 'De Gaulle has his head in the clouds and his feet in the shit'. Duff Cooper put the situation rather more gently. 'De Gaulle is much blamed for internal difficulties which are not really his fault, whereas his follies in foreign affairs, his *politique de panache* etc. are rather popular.'

There was little to be cheerful about in the second half of 1945. At a time when France showed no signs of rising out of its material misery, some of General de Gaulle's comments sounded uncharacteristically fatuous. 'When I asked him about the recent municipal elections,' Jefferson Caffery reported to Washington on 15 June, 'he said that the people voted for this and that party, but all the people voted for de Gaulle. Then he went on to say what a remarkable reception he had received in Normandy; "as I receive everywhere I go", he added.'

Most people tended to blame de Gaulle's entourage, especially Gaston Palewski, for this state of affairs. Others felt this was unfair. According to Claude Bouchinet-Serreulles, de Gaulle was well aware of such criticisms, and used to say, 'When people are discontented, it's the fault of the entourage.' Léon Blum, who admired de Gaulle, defined the problem rather differently. De Gaulle, he said, was 'a hypersensitive loner, and his close circle must be afraid to tell him what they think'.

De Gaulle had also begun to lose the confidence of industrialists and the liberal professions, partly because of his anti-American obsession, but also because he refused to tackle the problem of the economy. In some exasperation Monick, the governor of the Bank of France, told one foreign diplomat that Belgium was handling its affairs far better than France. De Gaulle's following was narrowing towards committed loyalists from the war, the more reactionary elements in the army and, with an irony that was typical of the *guerre franco-française*, the natural supporters of Marshal Pétain, who saw de Gaulle as their bulwark against the Communists.

In May, anti-colonialist disturbances in Syria threatened France's position in the Levant. De Gaulle was certain that General Spears, until recently Britain's minister to the Lebanon and Syria, had inspired a plot to expel the French. Spears had certainly been provocative during the war, and other British officials in the region did little to calm the situation. Yet although the British would have liked to supplant France in the area before the war, London saw no future there in 1945. Afraid that France's attempts to reimpose her rule would inflame the whole Middle East, the British government issued an ultimatum that French troops in Syria must return to barracks.

De Gaulle, impotent in the face of British military power there, became convinced that the British were determined to undermine him in other ways. He even claimed that while 'England was preparing the decisive blow in the Levant', she was pushing 'Washington to pick a quarrel with Paris'.

Whether out of frustration at events in Syria or in an unrelated attempt to increase French territory at the peace conference, de Gaulle had moved French troops across the Italian border into the Val d'Aosta. Once again, he did not inform his Foreign Minister what he was doing. Bidault was furious and embarrassed by such a pointless adventure in the face of the Americans. On 6 June, President Truman sent a strong message demanding the withdrawal of all French troops and cut off military supplies. Diplomats in Paris, certain that de Gaulle was on a suicide course, started to refer to him as 'Charles le Temporaire'. A week later, de Gaulle was forced into a humiliating retreat.

The following day, he was due to confer the Cross of the Liberation on General Eisenhower, but at the last moment Eisenhower was told that he could not bring any British officers, because of the dispute over the Levant. Eisenhower said that as Supreme Allied Commander, he would be bringing Air Marshal Tedder and General Morgan, two of his deputies, and if this did not suit General de Gaulle, he would not come. De Gaulle had to back down.

Palewski, apparently on de Gaulle's behalf, passed a message via Louise de Vilmorin to Duff Cooper saying that they both regretted that 'owing to recent events their relations with the British Embassy could not be what they had been in the past', but they wished the ambassador to know that they still had nothing but the friendliest feelings towards him personally. Duff Cooper was not impressed. 'This seems to me – I must say – the most extraordinary procedure. I am surprised that de Gaulle lends himself to it.'

De Gaulle began to realize that his hopes for post-war France were frustrated from within as well as from without. When the Consultative Assembly debated the crisis in the Levant on 17 June, he was appalled to find that the bulk of the criticism was directed, not against the British, but against his own government and France's traditional policy in the region. On the evening of 26 June he told General Pierre de Bénouville, a hero of the Resistance, that he 'intended to retire from politics altogether'. Bénouville then repeated this to Louise de Vilmorin 'under the seal of secrecy' – but she relayed the news to her lover, the British ambassador.

De Gaulle had far more serious causes for concern than the Levant, or his disastrous foray in the Val d'Aosta. The food situation was so bad that the Minister of the Interior sent a secret telegram on 7 July 1945 to the Governor-General of

Algeria urgently demanding two shiploads of sheep to avert a crisis. Beans and lentils were shipped in from South America. The country had less than two weeks' supply of grain. And this was summer. The winter would be far worse.

France's economy was in a disastrous state, but de Gaulle paid little attention to financial matters. Whether or not he ever uttered the famous remark '*l'intendance suivra*' – 'the baggage train will follow' – is an academic question, but this was certainly his attitude. When his two ministers responsible for economic affairs, Pierre Mendès-France and René Pleven, were locked in disagreement in the winter of 1944, he had summoned them to his residence in the Bois de Boulogne on a Sunday afternoon to discuss their opposing points of view. Pleven did not want a strict fiscal policy because of the hardship it would cause in the short term. He put his case simply and plausibly in under half an hour. Mendès-France, a far cleverer man, argued passionately for over two hours that unless the French government had the courage to stop paying inflationary wage settlements, it would never rise out of its present state of destitution. The result of this meeting was that never again would de Gaulle allow anyone to talk to him about economics for three hours.

Mendès-France's plan was absolutely correct in fiscal terms, but the country and the government coalition could not have withstood the political effects of the misery it would have caused. France's financial salvation, like that of the rest of Europe, lay not within her own resources but in the generosity or self-interest of richer nations. Yet the primary objective of de Gaulle's next trip abroad was not to raise loans, but to persuade the Americans to let France have the left bank of the Rhine and her share of an internationalized Ruhr.

Bidault told Duff Cooper that 'with de Gaulle in his present frame of mind the less travelling the General did in foreign countries the better'. But de Gaulle's trip to the United States at least did not turn out a disaster.

On 21 August, after the trial of Marshal Pétain was out of the way, de Gaulle set off for Washington accompanied by Bidault, General Juin and Gaston Palewski. The future peace of Europe, he told President Truman, would be guaranteed by reducing Germany to a collection of minor states restricted to agriculture, while France was built up as the industrial giant of Europe. De Gaulle dismissed Truman's view that the problem in establishing peace was essentially economic. Truman listened politely. He even put up with de Gaulle's little lecture on 'why France saw the world in a less simplistic manner than did the United States'.

De Gaulle might have taken a slightly different line if he had been aware of a briefing document given to Truman before their meeting. This report, if it deserves the term, conveyed in a series of crude caricatures the attitude still prevalent in US government circles. It summarized France thus: 'A country which, from the highest in the government down to the poorest peasant, is sitting back waiting for something to happen; which is completely unaware of American sympathy and aid; in which the cost of living permits only the rich to really subsist; a country where the young, from the best to the lowest families, live and thrive on the black market; a country with such an inferiority complex that frank discussion is difficult if not impossible; a country convinced that the United States and Russia will have to fight it out in a war in the near future, and which is convinced that in the interim the Communists will control Europe.' This diatribe ran on for three pages. It recommended that de Gaulle should be 'sent back to France with a sufficiently striking and publicized diplomatic victory to ensure the continuance of his government' provided he agreed to certain commitments, and that 'a sizeable American armed force should be kept in France to protect our lines of communication and supply to our occupying force in Germany'.

'Conclusion: The French people in their present desperate and discouraged state resemble to a frightening degree the

German people twelve years ago. Another really bad winter and the Allies may find that they have substituted the double cross of Lorraine for the crooked cross of Munich. This would not necessarily be de Gaulle's personal desire – but events might force his hand. It behoves us to move fast and forcefully.'

President Truman was fortunately not burdened by Roosevelt's historic dislike of de Gaulle, and on the whole their meetings passed off well. But there was one element in this document with which Truman firmly agreed, and that was the protection of military lines of communication. A year later he was to show that he would be prepared to move troops into France to secure the rear of the American forces in Germany, without informing the French government until the very last moment.

The 'full and free' elections, for which Roosevelt had originally wanted to wait before recognizing de Gaulle, finally took place on Sunday, 21 October 1945. Combined with the elections for a Constituent Assembly was a referendum on the basis for a new Constitution. Only the Radicals wanted to retain the discredited Third Republic. The main question for a Fourth Republic was whether the Assembly was to be given supreme powers, as the Communists especially demanded, or restricted powers, as de Gaulle insisted.

As for the elections to the Assembly, predictions on the outcome were mixed. Many people expected the middle class to vote Socialist as the best way of keeping out the Communists. But the conservative vote went elsewhere: to the Mouvement Républicain Populaire, headed by Maurice Schumann. Although impeccably liberal and resistant, the Catholic MRP bore out the jibe that it was a 'Machine à Ramasser les Pétainistes', because after the collapse of Vichy, no credible right-wing party remained. This deficiency falsified the post-war political spectrum from the start.

The MRP did very well in traditionally conservative areas

such as Brittany, Normandy and Alsace, and gathered in the considerable quantity of Pétainists in Paris. These were the first general elections in which women had the right to vote, a fact which undoubtedly benefited the MRP for, as all the polls showed, women were generally more conservative and pious than men.

The final result gave the Communists 159 seats, the Socialists 146 and the MRP 152. The Communists and Socialists could have formed an absolute majority between them, but in August the Socialist Party conference had rejected the proposals for a merger. The Socialists wisely insisted that a tripartite coalition was the only solution for the country. They could even argue that this was the expression of the charter of the Conseil National de la Résistance, which had been filled with well-meaning generalities about unity and *progressisme*.

Although all passed off quite smoothly, de Gaulle was disenchanted by the return of the party system. He frankly disliked the mechanics of constitutional government, especially since the size of the support for the Communist Party − five million votes representing just over 26 per cent of the total − made it the largest in France. The Communists had more than tripled their vote since 1936. Not surprisingly, they expected an appropriate level of representation in the Council of Ministers.

The opening session of the Constituent Assembly took place on 6 November 1945, in the *hémicycle* of the Palais Bourbon. A week later the Assembly was to vote on whether to re-elect de Gaulle as head of government. It also happened to be the day that de Gaulle invited Winston Churchill to lunch. Churchill was passing through Paris on his way to the south of France, for a holiday after his defeat by Labour. The party consisted of the de Gaulles, Palewski and Captain Guy, Churchill and his daughter Mary, and Duff and Diana Cooper. 'I never liked or admired [de Gaulle] so much,' recorded Duff Cooper in his diary. 'He was smiling, courteous, almost charming, and on this day and almost at the hour when his whole future was at stake, not only was he perfectly calm but one might have thought he was a country gentleman living far away from Paris. There were no interruptions, no telephone calls or messages, no secretaries hurrying in and out, no sign that anything was happening although Winston insisted on staying till three thirty, talking about the past, and the Assembly was meeting at three.'

De Gaulle, as events turned out, had little to fear. He was voted head of government by a unanimous vote of the Assembly accompanied by a motion that '*Charles de Gaulle a bien mérité de la patrie*', a rare honour in French history. This was, at least in theory, the crowning moment of his wartime achievements: it made the ensuing plunge into crisis all the more dramatic.

Two days later de Gaulle received Thorez and rejected his demands for ministerial posts. He, de Gaulle, was forming the government, not the Communist Party. Thorez then wrote and published a reply, saying that de Gaulle had insulted '*le caractère national de notre parti et de sa politique*' and the memory of their '75,000' martyrs. (As Galtier-Boissière put it, out of the 29,000 French men and women executed during the Occupation, 75,000 had been Communist.)

The following day, 16 November, de Gaulle encouraged a rumour that he was about to resign. But this exercise in brinkmanship had not been thought through: he was painting himself into a corner. He broadcast a speech on 17 November, saying that he would not entrust the Ministry of the Interior to a Communist and give them control over security matters, nor would he trust them with foreign policy, nor with the armed forces. Senior officials were dismayed by this pointless provocation.

Two days later François Mauriac, in *Le Figaro*, emphasized that without de Gaulle at the head of government, France would fall under the influence either of the Anglo-Saxons or of the Soviet Union. That same day, 19 November, Gaullist groups demonstrated on the Boulevard Raspail, chanting: 'It's de Gaulle we need! Down with Thorez!' The Palais Bourbon was sealed off by a cordon of troops and police set up road-blocks in many parts of Paris. The Communist Party, on the other hand, as Luizet reported to the Minister of the Interior, had evidently ordered its members to be very discreet.

Behind the military cordon, the general drift of the debate in the National Assembly went against de Gaulle. Despite expressions of admiration for the General, the message was clear. He had to accept a more or less equal division of ministerial posts between the three major parties.

That night, a depressed Gaston Palewski dropped in at the British Embassy. Everything, he thought, would be over in two days. Duff Cooper asked whether it really would be so dangerous to let the Communists have the Ministry of War for six months. Palewski was certain that they would turn the army round and stage a *coup d'état*.

Talk of *coups d'état* became infectious. A rumour ran round the next morning that de Gaulle, not the Communists, was planning to seize power with the backing of the army. The Communists restricted themselves to a vigorous complaint at de Gaulle's refusal to make one of their members Minister of War. The party warned that de Gaulle should not 'consider us as second-rate Frenchmen'. It had nominated General Joinville, an officer promoted from the FFI, as its candidate. Joinville, a well-known Communist sympathizer, was anathema to the regular army.

At the rue Saint-Dominique it was a day of negotiation, as political leaders arrived in groups or singly in answer to the General's summons. Meanwhile, the deputies in the Palais Bourbon waited in a fever of impatience, rumour and speculation. Throughout the country there was deep disquiet. Many feared that de Gaulle had played his hand so badly that he would be forced to give in to all the Communist demands. The directorate of Renseignements Généraux provided updated situation reports on the mood of the people every few hours.

When de Gaulle himself finally emerged that evening to go home, he faced a barrage of questions as to whether a government would be formed the next day. Confining himself to one of his delphic evasions, he said: 'One has the right to hope that.'

Of all the politicians visiting the rue Saint-Dominique that day, the most uncommunicative were the two Communist leaders, Maurice Thorez and Jacques Duclos. The next morning, a police spy in Communist Party headquarters – identified in the reports of the Renseignements Généraux only by the code XP/23 – overheard Duclos on the way to a politburo meeting say to a colleague, 'Yesterday we were tricked. Today all we can do is try to get one ministry more than the Socialists.' The Communists were furious because the Radicals had not supported them as they had expected.

In the end a compromise was reached. The Communists did not get a 'decisive portfolio' – either the Ministry of the Interior, Foreign Affairs, or the Ministry of War – but Charles Tillon was made Minister for Armaments. Maurice Thorez was made vice-president of the Council of Ministers, a deputy premiership which was meaningless, and the Communists received three other portfolios: Industrial Production, National Economy and Labour. According to Bidault, the Communists then became very cooperative. But the drama left a breach between de Gaulle and the MRP, whom the General refused to forgive for having supported the Communist demand for one of the three key ministries.

The winter did not improve. There was a feeling in government circles of a slide in slow motion towards disaster. From 10 December, the electric current in Paris was cut off either in the morning or during the afternoon. It also often failed in the evening, leaving parties in darkness and lifts out of order.

André Malraux, whom de Gaulle had appointed his Minister of Information in the new Council of Ministers, prophesied at an embassy lunch party on 3 December 'that the Communists would attempt to obtain power by force within the next twelve months and that they would fail'.

De Gaulle was thinking along similar lines. A conversation he had with Jefferson Caffery on 6 December was significant, because it revealed the fundamentally flawed state of his thinking, which was to persist for a number of years.

'There are only two real forces in France today: the Communists and I. If the Communists win, France will be a Soviet Republic; if I win, France will stay independent.'

'Who *will* win?' Caffery asked.

'If I get my breaks at all, especially in the international field, I will win. If France falls, every country in Western Europe will fall too, and all the Continent will be Communist.'

Paradoxically, during this period of drift one of the most decisive developments in France's post-war history took place. It was brought about by Jean Monnet, the least pretentious of great men.

Monnet, who came from a prosperous family of Cognac producers, had deep roots in the countryside yet believed passionately in industrial modernization. This 'father of the European Community' was the most admired and influential planner of the century, yet he possessed no formal qualifications. He joined the arms-purchasing committee on the outbreak of war, then after the fall of France Churchill recruited him for similar work in the United States, where he became the chief author of Roosevelt's Victory Plan to produce an overwhelming output of military material.

Monnet won the trust of virtually everyone he met. In all the major Western countries, he made friends with the leading bankers, industrialists, administrators and diplomats through small private dinner parties where the principal theme of conversation was the post-war reconstruction of Europe.

Monnet, although untalented as a public speaker, possessed a rare gift of finding the most telling argument for each person.

'You talk of greatness,' he had said to de Gaulle towards the end of the war, 'but the French today are pygmies. There will only be greatness when the French assume the stature to justify it. For that, it is necessary to modernize, because the French aren't modern.'

He returned to the theme in the second half of 1945. France had to transform itself if the country was to command any respect in the modern world. De Gaulle told him to prepare detailed recommendations: he liked the idea of a strategy which aimed to make France rather than Germany the industrial giant of Europe. On 5 December, Monnet submitted a five-page memorandum to de Gaulle. It was approved by the Council of Ministers on 3 January 1946. The decree was countersigned by nine ministers, including four Communists. Monnet's brilliant drafting allowed almost everyone – from industrialist to Communist – to read his own politics into the plan and agree with its objectives.

The Commissariat Général du Plan was rapidly established, with the help of Gaston Palewski. To avoid ministerial jealousies and manoeuvring, Monnet worked directly under the Prime Minister. He kept his staff small and very un-ministerial in style. Eighteen modernization commissions were set up, but the key in Monnet's mind was steel production. The previous record for production had been in 1929. Monnet's objective was to reach the same level by 1950, then rapidly exceed it by 25 per cent. De Gaulle dreamed of achieving France's domination of European industry by using coal exacted from the Ruhr, but the Americans were firmly opposed to a new version of the reparations which had embittered Germany after the First World War.

The plan was over-ambitious with France's catastrophic lack of fuel, raw materials and spare parts; and a ruthless application of priorities – a guns-before-butter approach – was politically unthinkable when the overwhelming majority of the population lived in such misery. But Monnet's infrastructure would be in place and ready when, in 1947, the Marshall Plan offered the French the opportunity to rebuild their future.

Two days after Christmas, the franc was drastically devalued. The official rate, maintained since the Liberation at 50 to the United States dollar and 200 to the pound sterling, plummeted to 120 to the dollar and 480 to the pound. Jacques Dumaine noted with regret that in comparison with other currencies, France was now eighty-four times poorer than in 1914.

New Year's Day 1946 was a beautiful day of winter sun in Paris, but the cold, brittle light did not flatter the chief actors at General de Gaulle's reception for the diplomatic corps. Many people were suffering from influenza. De Gaulle 'was looking ill,' observed one onlooker, 'and Palewski was looking even worse'.

The two men had good reasons for looking exhausted – Palewski mainly from his attempts to calm de Gaulle. The night before, the Socialists began demanding a 20 per cent cut in the defence budget, just when the government was sending reinforcements to Indo-China as British troops withdrew.

De Gaulle was disgusted that the political parties had recommenced 'their games of yesteryear'. To confirm his worst suspicions, the Constitutional Commission in the Palais Bourbon was determined to make sure that the President of the Fourth Republic would be entirely dependent upon the National Assembly. De Gaulle 'felt bound up like Gulliver by the Lilliputians'.

Two days later, on 3 January, the General was forced to relax: the marriage of his daughter Elisabeth to Commandant Alain de Boissieu, formerly of Leclerc's 2e DB, took place that day. After the wedding the bride's parents left for a holiday at the villa of Yvonne de Gaulle's brother at Cap d'Antibes. There, de Gaulle read and walked in the pine groves which surrounded the villa. He could not stray far, for reporters had tracked them down and tried to photograph every appearance.

De Gaulle apparently said to his host and brother-in-law, Jacques Vendroux, that the reason for coming down was to make sure that if he did resign, the country would not think that the decision had been taken on the spur of the moment.

'On January 20th,' wrote Duff Cooper, 'the eve of the anniversary of Louis XVI's execution, General de Gaulle cut off his own head and passed into the shadow-land of politics.' The ambassador was in a doubly bad mood because he had discounted all the rumours of an imminent resignation, when asked directly by the Foreign Office whether they were true. He had refused to believe that de Gaulle could contemplate resignation just when France was negotiating a vital loan from the United States.

De Gaulle's announcement was, however, entirely in character. He summoned his ministers to the rue Saint-Dominique, and without waiting for Bidault, who was a few moments late, he announced: 'Gentlemen, I have decided to resign. Bonjour. Au revoir.' Bidault appeared in the door, and de Gaulle simply said to him, 'Good-bye, Bidault, the others will tell you why I have asked you to come here.'

De Gaulle's entourage reacted in a mixture of shock, bewilderment, sorrow and anger. Several voiced a determination to fight on. André Malraux, who went to lunch at the British Embassy two days after the resignation, 'was as usual very interesting and somewhat alarming,' wrote Duff Cooper. 'He is convinced that France is moving towards a dictatorship and I don't think he regrets it. The question will be whether it is to be a dictatorship of the Communists or of de Gaulle, and it will be settled by force. He says that the resignation of de Gaulle is not the end but the beginning of Gaullism, which will now become a great movement throughout France.'

At first, the Americans were alarmed by de Gaulle's abrupt departure; Caffery feared 'a political crisis of the first magnitude' with the Communists increasing their grip through a Socialist–Communist coalition. But then they realized that the Communists might not want to be associated with economic failure, when they did not have complete power. The population of France as a whole took the upheaval far more calmly than expected. Caffery reported that de Gaulle's disappearance 'caused hardly a ripple'. In Paris there was a rather world-weary shrug, while in the provinces the notion that 'the great man fell victim to base political intrigues' confirmed provincial suspicions about the iniquity of the capital. According to the reports of prefects to the Ministry of the Interior, people were far less perturbed than during the political crisis of November. The Communists, sensing the mood, 'demonstrated their satisfaction with discretion'. Marcel Cachin claimed that they had got rid of de Gaulle without frightening the masses.

De Gaulle's belongings were removed rapidly from the rue Saint-Dominique. All his personal archives were piled in a corner of a room which had been lent to him. The only dust-sheet which could be found was a huge Nazi flag, scarlet with a swastika in the middle, which had flown from the Hôtel Continental and had been presented to the General after the Liberation.

A week later, an ADC of de Gaulle's delivered a letter from the General to the British ambassador. The handwriting was shaky. Lady Diana Cooper asked how the General was. 'Far from well,' came the answer. 'He never sleeps.'

General de Gaulle retired to the hunting lodge at Marly. It was all that remained of Louis XIV's private domain; but de Gaulle, with a dramatic view of his own circumstances, compared it to Longwood, Napoleon's house on St Helena.

Some six weeks after the resignation, Hervé Alphand went out there to visit the self-exiled ruler. Snow covered the park and the surrounding woods. To Alphand's surprise, there were no armed guards. He pushed open a wooden gate, and only after he had rung the bell for ten minutes did de Gaulle's faithful aide-de-camp, Captain Guy, arrive to let him in.

De Gaulle, who was working in an eighteenth-century study,

rose to greet his visitor. Alphand found him far more relaxed than during the previous months. If he had any regrets, he certainly did not reveal them.

Alphand warned de Gaulle that the United States wanted to rebuild a new Germany out of the western zones as a bulwark against Russia. The Americans, especially Robert Murphy and General Lucius Clay, who headed their military government from Frankfurt, were putting heavy pressure on the French. 'You cannot imagine how hard they are pushing: they're black-mailing us with the threat of cutting off all provisions to our zone if we don't agree to follow them, and proclaiming all over the place that we don't understand the situation at all, that we are confusing 1946 and 1919, that tomorrow the enemy will not be the Germany that we want to keep down, but Soviet Russia against whom we must unite all forces, including those of a reborn Germany.'

This news triggered an explosion of all de Gaulle's resentment against the United States: 'The Americans have been wrong about us for years.' Only when the Russians marched into Paris would they see 'what a grave mistake they have made in wanting to restore Germany and not France'. But like all exiled rulers, de Gaulle could do no more than rage in private.

Malcolm Muggeridge, returning to Paris as a journalist after his wartime service with the Secret Intelligence Service, arranged to interview de Gaulle. He found there was little competition. Gaullist fortunes were at such a low point that all the foreign correspondents in Paris had written the General off as being of no further interest.

Muggeridge went to de Gaulle's office, and found him seated behind a desk that was far too small for him. The air was thick with his cigarette smoke, and he did not look well. 'His stomach already protruded noticeably, his complexion was muddy and his breath bad; yet, as always, I found in him a nobility, a true disinterestedness, even a sort of sublime absurdity ... Our conversation began with one of his tirades about the *pourriture* of

French politics, and ended with my asking him what he proposed to do now, to which he replied with a majestic: "*J'attends!*" '

Gaston Palewski moved to 1 rue Bonaparte. There, he later became the neighbour not only of Nancy Mitford, who – living at number 20 – was delighted by the proximity, but also of Jean-Paul Sartre, with whom he almost came to war eighteen months later when Sartre and Simone de Beauvoir did a radio programme attacking de Gaulle and his entourage.

With his charm and tact, Palewski had done all he could to persuade de Gaulle to be more flexible, but he had never seriously examined the potential flaws in the General's world view. André Dewavrin, still known by his code-name of 'Colonel Passy', seems to have been the only member of the old team from London who did.

'Passy,' reported the British military attaché to the Directorate of Military Intelligence in London, 'said that de Gaulle's foreign policy was wrong from the start because it was a paradox. He was temperamentally anti-Anglo-Saxon, which led him to believe that the future of France lay in close accord with Russia as France's only chance of survival as a great power, and yet on the other hand de Gaulle was violently anti-Communist and finally ended up by thinking that he could act as a bridge-builder between the Anglo-Saxons and the Soviets.' This assessment could hardly have been more accurate.

Part Three
Into the Cold War

20
The Shadow-Theatre – Plots and Counter-Plots

The institution which was most disturbed by de Gaulle's resignation was the officer corps. There was nobody left to defend the armed forces from cuts in the military budget, and many officers feared that General de Lattre de Tassigny might take advantage of the situation. The Allies too had heard rumours that Lattre viewed himself as de Gaulle's replacement.

Lattre was a controversial character. His viceregal style when commanding 1st Army from Lindau on Lake Constance, where his headquarters received some touches worthy of Versailles, led to the names of 'Le roi Jean' and 'Le général soleil'. His flamboyant manner, combined with a new affinity for left-wing writers – Aragon, Elsa Triolet, Claude Roy and Roger Vailland were all invited to visit him in Germany – prompted another nickname: 'Général le Théâtre de Marigny'.

For all his intolerance and impatience, Lattre was undoubtedly a great military leader. A brilliant mimic, he was excellent company, and his wife was universally admired and respected. He got things done quickly, sometimes with spectacular fits of anger. But the theatrical side of his character probably had something to do with his bisexual nature. A number of officers referred to him as *cette femme*. General du Vigier, when asked by the Canadian military attaché how he got on with Lattre, replied: 'Very well indeed. I know how to handle women.' Yet Pastor Boegner said, 'The severe judgements made of him do not stop him from being prodigiously interesting.'

The fears of conservative French officers and the Allies centred on Lattre's ambition and political promiscuity: he had moved from the extreme right before the war to being a suspected fellow-traveller after it. And his resentment at having been deprived of his command in Germany to be given the empty appointment of Inspector-General seemed to magnify the risk. At a dinner in Strasbourg in November 1945, he had complained angrily to the British ambassador that he was 'unemployed' and did not even have an office. 'I said, half in fun,' Duff Cooper wrote in his diary, 'that I heard he got on very well with the Communists these days. He didn't deny it, and said that with the Communists one at least knew where one was.' A high official in the Ministry of the Interior told the American Embassy that Lattre had officially joined the Radicals, whom the Communists were trying to take over. There was a rumour that Thorez had offered Lattre the Ministry of War, but that General Revers had warned him off. In December 1945, the Canadian military attaché told his British colleague that 'the Communist Party had paid Lattre's debts amounting to some 2 million francs. He said Lattre was wildly extravagant and had got into serious financial difficulties.' The rumours gathered pace after de Gaulle's departure. On 20 March Lattre called on the British ambassador to say that word was going round Paris that the embassy had in its possession a Communist Party membership card in his name. Duff Cooper assured him that no such rumour had emanated from the embassy and that he would contradict it.

Like many political affairs, this one was more heavily influenced by a clash of personalities than of ideologies. Generals Juin and Lattre had loathed each other since they were at the École de Guerre together, and Lattre wanted Juin's job as chief of the National Defence General Staff. The two rivals, on the other hand, did agree about fighting the proposed budget cuts to the army. Lattre told Brigadier Daly how proud he was at having 'kept all the solid furniture in the military house, despite having lost some carpets and good pictures'. During the same meeting, there was a telephone conversation with the commandant of Saint-Cyr military academy: 'How many pupils do you have at your school now?' Lattre demanded. '1,800 you say. Reduce them at once to 1,200. Ultimately I intend to have only 600 of the very best students, and they will be reduced gradually from now on. Get rid of 600 at once and explain to the boys that it's in their best interests that they should go now. You didn't quite hear me, you say. Well, get rid of your telephone officer for having such a bad telephone.'

General de Lattre proved that he was not in the Communist Party's pocket by vigorously opposing their demands for a popular militia led by a very small regular cadre. Yet the wild rumours about him confirmed SHAEF in its reluctance to trust the French with intelligence. The 'thirteenth card' – Ultra intelligence based on intercepts of German signals traffic – had been kept from them, even though they had been closely involved in the original attempts to crack the code with an Enigma machine.*

The spring of 1946 which followed de Gaulle's departure was a time of deep unease. The new Prime Minister, Félix Gouin, found life uncomfortable with the General's brooding presence at Colombey-les-deux-Églises. Gouin, a Socialist lawyer from Marseilles, had defended Léon Blum when Vichy put him on trial in 1942. After the Liberation, he had become President of the Assembly and his reputation for conciliation had meant that the Communist Party had not opposed his candidature as head of government. De Gaulle despised him as a complete nonentity, and referred to him as '*le petit père Gouin*'.

Over the next six months, Gouin's administration dismantled

---

*An agreement on sharing military intelligence was concluded in Paris on 3 July 1945 between General Bloch-Dassault (brother of the aircraft manufacturer Marcel Dassault) and Brigadier-General Betts of US military intelligence, but the United States handed over very little.

a number of the General's creations and proceeded with the socialist programme generated by the Liberation. The nationalization of the coal-mining industry was voted through in an hour and a half; the nationalization of the largest banks took a whole day. This was the era of *tripartisme*, the uneasy power-sharing of Communists, Socialists and the Christian Democrat MRP; and the first political objective of the left was the approval of a draft constitution for the future Fourth Republic.

The Socialists, partly influenced by their traditional and visceral anti-clericalism on the subject of education, aligned themselves with the Communists against the MRP. This was a dangerous development, especially when they were still trying to establish their independence from the Communists. As a result the referendum to be held on 5 May 1946 took on a far greater significance than the issue at stake, and its unexpected outcome strongly influenced the subsequent elections planned for 2 June. The country, and the Communists themselves, began to see this plebiscite as a vote of confidence in the French Communist Party.

The spring of 1946 saw an upsurge of activity on the right. As early as 4 February, General Billotte approached Duff Cooper, hoping that His Majesty's Government would back a 'new political movement, a kind of centre party mainly with a view to fighting socialism'. Billotte's use of the phrase 'centre party' rather strained the usual understanding of the term.

Representatives of new right-wing parties also hurried round to the American Embassy. 'I have the honour to report,' wrote Caffery, with a hint of acerbic relish, 'that the Embassy has been approached by various groups, all, according to the promoters involved, enamoured with the United States. However, in each case it has developed during the course of the conversation that what they specifically had in mind was a subvention in one shape or another from the State Department.'

In electoral terms, the new right-wing parties amounted to

very little. The largest was the Parti Républicain de la Liberté, an 'anti-Communist vehicle' to bring together elements from the pre-war right and supporters of Marshal Pétain. It had a following in Paris, but was very weak outside the city.

At this time when, in Caffery's words, the situation was becoming 'favourable to chaos and to men on horseback', royalist hopes swelled. The Comte de Paris believed that he could unify the nation. Posters appeared on the walls in Paris: '*Le Roi ... Pourquoi pas?*' – a curiously diffident message in an age of political passion.

Colonel Passy was strongly against the idea of Americans or British helping right-wing groups. At a dinner with Brigadier Daly, he rightly identified the Socialist Party as the best political force to resist the Communists. But on other matters he was less prescient. The chief danger to France at the time consisted of right-wing coup attempts which, however amateur and unlikely to succeed, risked playing straight into the hands of the Communists.

At the beginning of April 1946 Brigadier Daly was approached by Comte Guy de Maillé, apparently on behalf of a committee of five representing the major anti-Communist political movements.

The affair became more complicated with the involvement of Kenneth de Courcy, a fanatical British anti-Communist. De Courcy told Daly that he was working closely with 'C' (Sir Stewart Menzies, the head of the Secret Intelligence Service) but this was not true. His main associates appear to have been Pierre de Werne, Duc Pozzo di Borgo and the Archduke Otto von Habsburg. De Courcy had fairly close contacts with the Duke of Windsor but whether the ex-King himself was mixed up in de Courcy's Ruritanian plot is hard to tell.*

---

*Philip Ziegler, the Duke's biographer, feels that because he was known to be so indiscreet, not even a 'gang of amateurs would contemplate confiding in him'.

Seeking to involve the British authorities in his schemes, Kenneth de Courcy took Brigadier Daly to lunch at Pozzo di Borgo's magnificent town house at 51 rue de l'Université. Daly had no idea that Pozzo di Borgo had been a prominent member of the Cagoule and had been arrested in 1937 with its leader, Eugène Deloncle, for plotting against the Republic.

Otto von Habsburg argued that the Russians, aided by Communist uprisings in different countries, would overrun Western Europe, and that this would pose a serious threat to the British Empire. The Communists would aid Arab nationalism in North Africa and this would cut off the British route to the Empire east of Suez. Habsburg also produced a report on the Paris police, which claimed that 6,000 out of 20,000 were Communists. The Americans, he complained, were not yet alive to the menace. He and Pozzo believed that a left-wing *putsch* would be led by General de Lattre de Tassigny.

It soon became clear that their candidate for leader of France was Prince Napoleon, the thirty-two-year-old great-great-grandson of King Jerome. This recently retired young officer, six feet six inches tall, had served with such bravery in the French Foreign Legion that de Gaulle had immediately granted him residence in France. Napoleon's go-between and adviser, the Vicomte de Ramolino, had approached the British ambassador the year before to assess the possibility of a marriage with Princess Elizabeth or Princess Margaret Rose. When Duff Cooper explained that this was out of the question, Ramolino suggested the Prime Minister's youngest daughter, Mary Churchill. Her father was greatly entertained by the idea.

Daly soon realized the danger of involvement when de Courcy revealed that he planned to finance the French right through some Paris assets of the Anglo-Persian Oil Company. The military attaché thought this 'all highly dangerous as far as we are concerned'.

On 8 May, Daly resolved to sever contact with de Courcy: he passed the message via Ninette de Valois, who was on a visit to recruit dancers for her ballet. But his decision came too late in one respect. Somebody had circulated some faked photographic evidence purporting to show that Daly had passed 300 million francs to the right-wing Parti Républicain de la Liberté. John Bruce-Lockhart, the SIS chief of station, thought that it might be a Soviet ploy to counter accusations that Moscow was financing the French Communist Party.

Daly, summoning his courage, confessed the problem to that veteran socialist, the British Foreign Secretary, then staying at the embassy. 'I have just been accused, Mr Bevin,' he announced, 'of financing the extreme Right here.'

'I thought all officers in your regiment were bankrupt,' Ernest Bevin replied, then roared with laughter. That night, a relieved military attaché wrote in his diary: 'I wonder if he knew what regiment I was in. In any case it was a good retort.'

The main danger of trivial events getting out of hand stemmed from the fact that in France everyone in military and official circles seemed to be spy-obsessed. It was a legacy of the Occupation and the Resistance. '*C'est la clandestinité qui mène l'affaire*,' a French intelligence chief acknowledged to a British colleague.

But the real problems being faced by British intelligence were in London. In 1944 Kim Philby, who later turned out to be one of the Soviet Union's star spies, had been put in charge of the new anti-Soviet department in SIS. When Muggeridge sent back to London a report, passed to him by a 'Colonel A' (presumably Colonel Arnault) on the extent of Communist infiltration in the French government, an instruction came back from Philby to disregard any material from this clearly unreliable source. Philby then sent Muggeridge a questionnaire on the measures being taken by the French against Soviet infiltration. Ironically Passy's organization, then under attack as an anti-Communist stronghold, thought it wiser not to cooperate. Even so, Passy considered most of the questions ridiculously simple – some of the answers, he said, could be found in the telephone directory. He and Soustelle suspected a British double-bluff.

Philby came to Paris at least twice. He came first in the winter of 1944–5 to visit Muggeridge, and stayed with him at the Avenue de Marigny. He paid another visit in May 1946. 'Philby, the Communist specialist of MI6 came to see me,' recorded Duff Cooper. 'He hadn't much to say that I didn't know already.' Yet Philby muddied the waters once more. Marie-Madeleine Fourcade, who had revived part of her 'Ark' intelligence network from the Resistance for use against the Communists, had kept in touch with the SIS representative in Paris. She had shown him transcripts of the most recent French Communist Party politburo meetings, and explained that she needed a substantial sum of money each month if this source was to continue. The SIS representative was convinced that the transcripts were genuine, and the senior director in London, Kenneth Cohen, who had supervised Marie-Madeleine's operations in the war, also believed in them. But the final decision lay with the head of the section dealing with International Communism – Kim Philby. He declared that the transcripts were forgeries, mainly on the grounds of what he claimed was unconvincing Marxist–Leninist phraseology. Since he was the expert, SIS chiefs in London were not prepared to override his opinion. Fortunately, Marie-Madeleine had concealed her source well, and Philby was never in a position to betray it.*

The Americans fared little better in the spring of 1946. The flood of rumours made it impossible to identify real threats. A report even circulated that the Russians were ready to invade

---

* Marie-Madeleine blew the agent several years later, when the first item on the agenda of the politburo meeting was to discuss the minutes of the latest meeting of the French National Defence Committee. She arranged for the publication of these minutes, which caused a national outcry, followed by the arrest of the Permanent Secretary of the Defence Committee.

France by parachute: D-Day would take place on 26 March. At the same moment, General Revers warned the British Military attaché that 'the Communists would create incidents on the Spanish frontier' to force a war with Franco and get the Russians to intervene. Revers, a fanatical anti-Communist, may also have been the source of a later rumour about international brigades training near the Pyrenees to fight in the Greek civil war. In fact, the danger in the area came from the opposite direction: extreme right-wing elements within the French army had been hoping to get the Spanish army to strike across the border at Communist *maquis* groups.

The American ambassador passed back such stories to Washington in a weary tone. 'The circulation of alarmist reports,' he wrote, 'is facilitated because the average Frenchman after the years of German occupation is prone to believe and to repeat as gospel almost any rumor no matter how fantastic it may seem. Indeed, since the Liberation stories have circulated with varying degrees of intensity that "a Communist coup is planned for next month"; often specific dates are mentioned.' American military intelligence staff in Paris, with the honourable exception of Charlie Gray, were far less sceptical.

There can be little doubt that American intelligence in Europe was hopelessly ill-informed. A briefing on 'Clement [*sic*] Fried – the principal agent of Stalin in France' warned that Fried was still very elusive. 'Prior to the war he seldom slept in the same domicile for more than a few nights and was not known to more than eight or ten members of the French Communist Party.' Fried had indeed been the French Communist Party's Comintern controller and Maurice Thorez's mentor, but there was a very good reason for his elusiveness in 1946: the Gestapo had shot him dead in Belgium three years before.

It is greatly to Jefferson Caffery's credit that he resolutely continued to discount the growing rumours of an impending Communist coup in the lead-up to the referendum of 5 May.

'While it is difficult to state with certainty the origin and purpose of such reports, they are being circulated in American military and other circles particularly by anti-Communist French elements.' All too often the very people circulating these reports 'subsequently approach us informally with a view to obtaining financial or other assistance for the coming elections'.

He further argued that 'an armed Communist uprising would not seem probable in the immediate future since the Communists would stand to lose much more than they might gain by such a gamble'. On the other hand, the Communists would certainly profit from an 'abortive attempt' by the 'lunatic fringe of the Right'. This would enable them to pose as 'the defenders of democracy against an attempt at dictatorship'.

Unfortunately, the War Department refused to heed the ambassador's warnings that all these rumours leading up to the referendum on 5 May should be ignored. It had received a report that the Communists planned to stage a *coup d'état* after fomenting trouble on Monday, 6 May, the day after the referendum.

In the early hours of Friday, 3 May, the War Department sent a top secret 'eyes only' signal to General MacNarney, Commanding General of US Forces European Theater, based in Frankfurt. This gave him formal authority 'to effect movement into France in case of serious disturbance there provided that such move in your opinion is essential to provide for security repeat security of US Forces or to secure supplies essential to them'. A reconnaissance by selected officers was permitted before the referendum of 5 May.

A signals officer in Washington, recognizing the telegram's potentially explosive nature, contacted the code room of the State Department, suggesting that the message should be cleared on their side. An urgent meeting was called by the European department's senior experts, John Hickerson and James Bonbright, who took the representatives from the War Department to see Dean Acheson, the Assistant Secretary of State. They reminded him that, whatever the right-wing rumour-mongers in France might be saying, a Communist coup was most unlikely.

Acheson and his colleagues expressed a very strong view that 'General MacNarney should not be given discretionary authority to move troops into France'. They pointed out that 'US troops moving into France to widely scattered places, in the event of civil trouble might well be misunderstood, give rise to incidents involving them, and, at the worst, might even cause the Communists to appeal to the Soviet Union and send for help on the grounds that the United States had intervened'. Not even Acheson and his subordinates in the State Department appeared to be aware of articles 3 and 4 in the Franco-Soviet pact signed by Bidault and Molotov in December 1944. That obliged either France or the Soviet Union, in the event of a threat, to take 'all necessary measures to eliminate any fresh menace coming from Germany'. The nationality of the menace had not been specified.

The State Department team drafted an alternative set of instructions which they took to a meeting of the Joint Chiefs of Staff at 1.30 p.m. The Joint Chiefs were only prepared to make minor modifications to the original instruction to General Mac-Narney. Neither side would compromise further, so that afternoon Admiral Leahy, the former ambassador to Marshal Pétain, took both drafts to the President for his decision. Truman, to Acheson's appalled disbelief, backed the War Department.

Acheson drafted a telegram to Caffery in Paris. He warned him of the situation, and told him that their attempts to stop the War Department instruction had failed – but then he cancelled the signal before it was sent. This is surprising since, to the State Department's dismay, MacNarney's authority to move troops into France remained in force: even after Monday, 6 May passed off without any disturbances. If Caffery ever heard of the War Department instruction, either from Acheson or anyone else, he certainly did not tell any of his colleagues.

The only satisfaction the State Department could extract

from this deeply disturbing episode was in a later communication debunking the cries of wolf in Germany which had led to such an extraordinary state of affairs. On 5 June, a top secret signal was sent to Robert Murphy, the President's representative in Germany: 'As you may already know the information planted . . . is entirely phony. The source belongs to an extreme Right Resistance group in France desiring to stir up trouble and obtain American arms and funds.'

21
Politics and Letters

In the lead-up to the referendum on 5 May 1946, all was fair in war and politics. Right-wing rumour-mongers claimed, without producing evidence, that the Kremlin was financing the French Communist Party. The Parti Républicain de la Liberté spread the word that the Communist leader, Maurice Thorez, was having an affair with Marie Bell of the Comédie-Française and sending her vast bouquets of orchids costing 50,000 francs. Galtier-Boissière was unconvinced. He did not see 'the nation's perfect baby, so carefully watched by the party, paying court while escorted by six bodyguards toting sub-machine guns'.

Cardinal Suhard called upon the faithful to 'vote and vote well' against a left-wing and anti-clerical Constitution. Suhard's message was repeated from pulpits in cathedrals and churches across France. The Archbishop of Bordeaux stated outright that Catholics must refuse to ratify the Constitution. This produced fears in the centre that intervention from the Church would play into Communist hands.

The most ingenious piece of black propaganda was mounted by the Communists just over two weeks before the elections. They arranged for one of their prominent union leaders to be arrested on the basis of charges originally laid against him by the Vichy government. The Ministry of the Interior had nothing to do with the arrest. According to a 'competent source', it was carried out by officers from the Communist-infiltrated Prefecture of Police.

The outcry in the party's press was predictable, claiming that Vichy reactionaries were still in control and that the Pétain regime was working from beyond the grave. The whole operation was a great success, to the frustration of Édouard Depreux, the Socialist Minister of the Interior whom the Communists loathed. Henaff, the union leader, was released amid triumphant demonstrations, while Depreux was left subtly tainted with Vichyism. But it would not be long before Depreux began to organize an effective revenge.

The Communists demanded a '*Oui*' in favour of the draft constitution, but they allowed, and then even encouraged, the May referendum to be turned into a 'plebiscite for or against Communism'. Some rich '*paniquards*' planned to leave France if they won. The American ambassador was scathing about the fatalistic assumption that 'the Cossacks would soon be arriving on the Place de la Concorde'.

De Gaulle was one of the very few to predict that the Communists would lose, whatever the opinion polls said. He told his secretary Claude Mauriac, the son of François, that the Communists had made a major mistake. Out of sheer over-confidence, they had allowed the tables to be turned at last. Until then, the left had managed to manipulate and define issues in terms of fascism and anti-fascism. Now, for the first time, the issue was Communism and anti-Communism. 'And that's a development of capital importance for the future,' said the General. He had the hugely satisfied air of a man who had put together a clever plan. 'I managed to tie a good-sized saucepan to their leg with the referendum,' he said. It was one of the very few electoral measures he had been able to achieve in the face of the Constituent Assembly.

In the week before the referendum, the walls of Paris were scrawled with '*Oui*' or '*Non*' in chalk, often crossed out by the other side. In the 16th *arrondissement* well-dressed little girls with buckets and brushes were seen scrubbing out the *Ouis*. In a less elegant part of the city, a green metal *vespasienne* urinal bore the more anarchic slogan:

Voter OUI, voter NON
Vous serez toujours les CONS!

No May Day in Paris was complete without the scent of lily-of-the-valley. Traders came into Paris that morning with great baskets of the flowers on their arms, tied into little bunches; and everyone wore sprigs of it in their buttonholes. After the May Day parade from the Place de la République to the Place de la Nation, there was a Communist Party rally at six o'clock in the Place de la Concorde. As Thorez addressed the great crowd in the evening sunlight, he was watched from above. Baron Élie de Rothschild and other friends had brought field-glasses for this purpose to a drinks party on the roof-garden of Donald Bloomingdale's penthouse at the Crillon hotel only a few yards away.

'I have little doubt that there will be a majority of Ouis,' wrote Duff Cooper in his diary on Sunday, 5 May, the day of the election. 'All my friends of the right say it will be the end of France, which of course is nonsense.'

The following morning, 6 May, the date on which American troops were ready to move into France, the narrow victory of the *Nons* was confirmed. After the Communists' great efforts, it was seen as a significant setback for them. 'De Gaulle was right,' Claude Mauriac wrote in his diary.

The American delegation to the Paris Peace Conference, then under way, did not hide its jubilation during a dinner at the Quai d'Orsay. Jacques Dumaine, although also relieved by the outcome, felt they were seeing things only in black and white. 'They imagine that France is divided into two camps of which one will overcome the other', and thus they deliberately ignored 'the heterogeneous free-for-all which is the essence of French politics'. But politics in France, as in most countries of the world, were doomed to be polarized by the Cold War.

Simone de Beauvoir had lunch that day with Merleau-Ponty at the Petit Saint-Benoît to discuss the referendum. But in the evening, the *famille Sartre* forgot politics and rallied round Jean Genet, who had just been through an author's worst nightmare: Gallimard had apparently lost his only manuscript of *Funeral Rites*. This resulted in a series of furious rows between Genet and Gaston Gallimard's son Claude.

The other news which people had to digest that day was of a scandal in intelligence circles. The previous evening, just before voting finished, Agence France-Presse announced that Colonel Passy had been arrested. The motives for making the announcement at such a moment are unclear. Félix Gouin's government, alarmed by the upset in the elections, may have leaked the news either as a belated attempt to alter the outcome or as a warning shot to de Gaulle, whose prestige would be enhanced by the results. The Passy scandal was a murky affair from which the government emerged with little credit.

On 4 May, Passy was summoned to the offices of the organization which he had originally built up in London, now called the SDECE.* 'We have discovered some irregularities,' the new chief told him. 'Where are the secret funds?' Although no formal charges were made, Passy was accused of embezzling intelligence service funds and was held incommunicado. His wife, not knowing what had happened to him, became frantic. One of the reasons for the sudden announcement of his arrest on the night of 5 May was the difficulty of keeping it a secret for much longer.

American intelligence, which may have been misled by representatives of the government, reported that the financial irregularities had been known about for some time. The real reason

---

*Gouin's government had not only set about reorganizing the intelligence service as the Service de Documentation Extérieur et de Contre-Espionage. It had also put an end to the Gaullist proconsuls from the Liberation, the Commissaires de la République.

for Passy's arrest, it said, was that he had been trying to sabotage Léon Blum's efforts to seek an urgently needed loan from the United States. The Socialists and their coalition partners were both outraged and alarmed.

There was never any question of Passy embezzling funds for personal use. The main charge of irregularities in London was ridiculous. The BCRA had been so afraid of Vichyist infiltration that very few written records were kept. What Passy had almost certainly been trying to do was to build up a fighting fund in Switzerland, so that if the Communists did take over in France the Gaullist resistance would never again have to go cap in hand to the British or the Americans.

Passy was locked up without any form of trial or access to lawyers. Conditions were very bad, and his gaolers drugged him. He fell seriously ill, lost twenty-three kilos, and his blood-pressure fell alarmingly. When his wife finally managed to have him removed to the Val-de-Grâce hospital, the doctor told him, 'You've been poisoned.' When he asked what the poison was, the doctor replied laconically, 'We'll know after the autopsy.'

During his imprisonment, Passy passed a message to the Americans claiming that Gouin's government was blackmailing him to hand over any written instructions from de Gaulle to do with the money. Such evidence would have enabled Gouin and his government to tarnish the General's reputation and destroy his political hopes. This Passy refused to do. One thing was certain. The government did not want a public trial. 'It appears that the more the affair is investigated,' Caffery reported to Washington, 'the more it becomes apparent that a number of important politicians belonging to different parties have either had their palms greased or have received money from secret funds.'

At the end of August, on an order from the Council of Ministers, Colonel Passy was stripped of his rank, the Legion of Honour and the Order of the Liberation, and suffered the confiscation of personal property to the value of the sum exported. (Most of his honours, including the Legion of Honour,

were later restored.) Passy, with justification, protested angrily
that the Council of Ministers was not a court of justice: if he was
to be tried, it should be in front of a properly constituted
tribunal. Even Teitgen, the Minister of Justice, was privately
uneasy about the way the affair had been handled.

The Passy scandal may have been the talk of Paris, but it seems
to have made little impact in Saint-Germain-des-Prés. Simone
de Beauvoir's life was busier than ever, as the record of her
afternoon on Friday, 10 May shows. After lunch at the Brasserie
Lipp, she went to the offices of *Les Temps modernes*, which Gaston
Gallimard had lent them. Vittorini of the Italian Communist
Party paid a visit. He was very put out to hear that Sartre and
Simone de Beauvoir were to be the guests of '*un éditeur réaction-
naire*' on their forthcoming visit to his country.

Gaston Gallimard arrived. Simone de Beauvoir went into his
office, but found André Malraux and Roger Martin du Gard
there too. Embarrassed at encountering a political enemy, she
found herself obliged to shake Malraux's hand. Then she had to
listen to Gallimard's explanation of Genet's lost manuscript
before she could escape. Back in her own office, she was buttonholed by an aspiring young novelist who had brought her his
typescript to read. He naïvely asked if Sartre would vote for him
on the jury of the Prix de la Pléiade. She then had a brief chat
with Michel Leiris, and took the novelist Nathalie Sarraute's
manuscript to Jean Paulhan. He showed her a little painting by
Wols – a painter whom Sartre greatly admired also – which he
had just bought. Finally, at seven o'clock she left the office and
went to meet Raymond Queneau at the bar of the Hôtel Pont-
Royal.

This day was easy in comparison to some, and no doubt Castor
rather welcomed the manic activity around her. It must have
helped her forget her fears at this time that Nathalie Sarraute
was trying to take her place as Sartre's intellectual companion.

*

On 12 May there was a ceremony at the Arc de Triomphe to commemorate the victory of the year before. Félix Gouin 'made a good speech,' Duff Cooper recorded, 'but he looks terribly insignificant on such occasions. His generous reference to de Gaulle was loudly cheered.' De Gaulle, however, had refused Gouin's invitation to attend. Instead he had gone to the Vendée to pay homage at Clemenceau's tomb on the same day, the day commemorating Joan of Arc.

A few days before, Claude Mauriac had asked the General if he would make a speech during this visit. 'I will perhaps say a few words, yes,' he had said, 'but we must not tell anyone.' This was disingenuous. Claude Guy, his ADC, was already organizing a reception for journalists.

The speech over Clemenceau's grave was to be the forerunner of several which, although ostensibly commemorating a particular event or anniversary, had a definite political purpose. De Gaulle had seen that his prestige was rising again, and was preparing the ground for the foundation of a full Gaullist political movement. André Malraux told Louise de Vilmorin that the General 'will be President of the Republic in September and that he, Malraux, will be Minister of the Interior'.

The crowd awaiting de Gaulle at Clemenceau's tomb was large. Claude Mauriac felt uneasy at the cries of '*De Gaulle au pouvoir!*' and was embarrassed by the event's faintly fascist aspect. The supposedly modest visit was well attended by the French and international press, who were briefed by one of de Gaulle's staff.

Little heed was paid to de Gaulle's Vendée speech at the Casque d'Or restaurant the following day, where Simone de Beauvoir and the sculptor Alberto Giacometti were lunching with friends. The main subject of conversation at their table was how André Breton – one of the very few Surrealists to have denounced Stalinism – would be received on his return to Paris from the United States.

*

There is no doubt that the Communists were chastened by the results of the May referendum. The setback had been doubly embarrassing for the party leadership, since Molotov was in Paris at the time for a meeting of Foreign Ministers.

In 1946, most Western intelligence agencies had very little information on Communist objectives. In Paris, a number of attempts were made to penetrate the inner circles of the French Communist Party. The only successful operation at that time seems to have been that of the former Resistance leader, Marie-Madeleine Fourcade. Although Kim Philby had rejected her material, it would appear that she had better luck in placing it with the Americans.

The first summary from US military intelligence covered a politburo meeting on 16 May, chaired by Marcel Cachin. They discussed Molotov's setback at the Big Four conference in Paris with dismay. James Byrnes, the American Secretary of State, and Ernest Bevin, the British Foreign Secretary, had surprised the Soviet delegation with their firmness.

Then Thorez, chastened by the failure of the referendum vote on 5 May, expressed his pessimism about the outcome of the 2 June elections. The French Communist Party might have to decide whether to go into opposition or stay in the government. He feared 'intensive anti-Communist activity in France'. He was furious with Blum for opposing the Communist plan to 'liquidate the French Socialist Party through fusion or other means'. If the chance of taking over the Socialists definitely disappeared, Thorez told the politburo, then they should 'seriously reflect before taking any violent action'. Soviet diplomacy needed peace and was not willing to take undue chances.

Another piece of intelligence passed on to the Americans said that Molotov was 'deeply chagrined' by the outcome of the referendum and had strongly warned the leadership of the French Communist Party against attacking Léon Blum and the Socialists. Such actions could only force them into an alliance with other parties of the centre-left and 'push them closer to the

British Labour Government. This in turn might result in a Franco-British pact which would form the basis of a Western bloc.'

At a further politburo meeting on 20 May, the arguments about seizing power intensified. Laurent Casanova said that armed action must be considered in the near future. If the Communists failed at the forthcoming elections, the new government would purge every part of the administration. This would be 'the worst catastrophe that could befall the Communist Party in France'. If they were obliged to attempt an armed uprising, he warned that they could not count on any support from Moscow for 'at least thirty days'. On balance, he felt that 'it would be a grave error to withdraw from government and pass to opposition'.

These reports certainly sound plausible on the basis of other evidence, particularly contemporary documents of the international section in the Kremlin. The French Communist Party was not receiving detailed instructions at that time.

For the elections at the beginning of June, the Communists adopted a low-key approach, relying more on whispering campaigns in cafés and queues than on strident propaganda. This did not, however, stop the French Communist Party from claiming that 340,000 tons of Russian grain had left Black Sea ports *en route* to France, with a balance of 160,000 tons to come. The United States Embassy was furious: no mention had been made of the 7 million tons of supplies delivered by the Americans since March 1945.

When the results were announced on 3 June, the Communists found that they had not done nearly as badly as they had feared. It was the turn of the Socialists to be disappointed, mainly as a result of their unwise policy over the referendum. They lost most of those non-Socialists who had voted for them to keep the Communists out. These tactical voters switched their support to the Christian Democrat MRP, which, to the Communists' irritation, now replaced them as the *premier parti de France*.

The Communists at first strongly opposed the idea of serving in a government led by Georges Bidault, and attempted to resurrect another Gouin administration, but the Socialists preferred to leave the responsibility of dealing with a virtually bankrupt economy to others. The Communists, finding that their refusal to serve with Bidault would bring *tripartisme* to an end, rapidly compromised, and de Gaulle's oft-humiliated Foreign Minister finally achieved his ambition of becoming head of government.

The most important development following the elections was General de Gaulle's return to the political stage. De Gaulle's prestige had greatly increased in the last two months of uncertainty; and the news that he had refused Gouin's invitation to celebrate the anniversary of his own 18 June appeal from London, coupled with his plan to speak at Bayeux two days earlier, caused great interest.

The speech at Bayeux, the American ambassador reported, 'struck a more responsive chord throughout the country than its reception by the phlegmatic Norman audience indicated'. The meeting took place in heavy rain, with General de Gaulle bareheaded and in a uniform without decorations. He warned the French against their unfortunate inclination to divide into parties; but the event gave a strong impression of a military movement with the uniformed presence in de Gaulle's entourage of Admiral Thierry d'Argenlieu, General Juin and General Koenig, as well as Malraux, Palewski and Soustelle.

The speech was important. De Gaulle put forward his idea of what the constitution of the French Republic should be. It was, in many ways, the blueprint for the Fifth Republic, which he finally established after his return to power in 1958.

De Gaulle remained suspect in the eyes of many potential followers, particularly those who had supported Marshal Pétain, because he had made deals with the Communist devil during the war and had gone to Moscow to sign a pact with Stalin. These suspicions were soothed a year later, when the General took up an openly anti-Communist position. From that point de Gaulle, despite his dislike of two super-power blocs, helped to force French politics into the frame of the Cold War.

22

The Diplomatic Battleground

For the second time in thirty years, Paris found itself hosting a modern Congress of Vienna. First came the meeting of Foreign Ministers of the Big Four in May 1946, to be followed by the sixteen-nation Peace Conference which continued in bursts from August until mid-October.

The Quai d'Orsay and the embassies were very busy. Jacques Dumaine, the *chef de protocol*, was continually going out to Le Bourget or Orly to meet distinguished visitors. He summed up the diplomatic contest at that time in terms of a poker game. 'We do not know if Stalin is playing poker with good cards and unlimited funds; but we can only realize that his American opponents are standing and that the British cannot double their stakes.' His wife was about to have a baby and he worried about what life held in store for their child with a future 'full of foreboding'.

On 24 April, Dumaine was at Orly to greet James Byrnes, the Secretary of State, with the American delegation, which included Senator Tom Connally and Senator Vandenberg. 'After twenty-four hours on the aeroplane they still managed to look their normal, cheerful, well-shaven selves, while their wives appeared as fresh as ever with their orchids.' That afternoon, Dumaine had to wait at Le Bourget for Molotov, who arrived 'looking neat and scrubbed like a country doctor. His expression is hesitant and relatively gentle, but his actions are distrustful and forbidding.'

Ernest Bevin arrived the following morning and the first meeting of the Four took place late that afternoon in the Palais du Luxembourg, now almost entirely repaired.

The conference opened far more smoothly than most people had expected, but after a week or so became bogged down in the usual fashion. Some issues were more interesting, such as what to do with the former Italian colonies, including Libya and Cyrenaica. Bevin wanted to give them complete independence, but the French were alarmed at the effect that this might have on their own North African colonies. Molotov then retreated from an agreement he had made on Italy the previous September, and Byrnes became very angry. As it was the 1 May public holiday, Bevin, acting as chairman, insisted on a break. 'The next item,' he announced, 'is a half-holiday which will be passed unanimously.'

The break did little to unblock the accumulating log-jam of differences. 'Agreement was reached on one subject,' the British ambassador recorded testily the next day, 'the future of the Pelagosa and Pianosa islands, which contain one lighthouse and no inhabitants.' Duff Cooper was in a bad mood because his new love, Gloria Rubio, had just had to fly to New York at short notice. It was also almost impossible to remain awake after heavy official lunches. Bevin, who had noticed Duff Cooper drop off to sleep, said, 'Tell Duff I'll call him if anything happens', then added to those around him, 'He's the most sensible man in the room. It's all a waste of time.'

The round of official entertaining became almost as numbing as the meetings themselves, though like the conference it had begun well. Félix Gouin gave a successful lunch in honour of the three delegations. 'Thorez was dimpling prettily,' noted Dumaine, 'and kept taking Molotov's arm and patting his shoulder with great good humour, although such familiarity would have been unthinkable in Moscow three years ago.' Duff Cooper, who sat next to Thorez, noted afterwards that he could not help liking him.

The British Embassy gave a lunch party for the two white-haired senators, the Texan Tom Connally, who wore a string tie, and the immensely powerful Arthur Vandenberg. James Byrnes hosted a drinks party at the American Embassy, where the sandwiches were voted excellent; but Ernest Bevin made the mistake of giving a buffet lunch at the Hôtel George V, a practice which the French abhorred.

'Ernie is aggressively real,' wrote Diana Cooper to a friend, 'the size of three Buddhas hardly hewn at all – not a vestige of good manners – cigarette hanging on pendulous lip – he laughs uproariously and is nicely naïve and quite uninhibited.' Jacques Dumaine, at a dinner held for Bevin at the British Embassy, observed him with a slightly bemused eye. 'Whisky improved his temper and caused him to tell endless stories about drunkards and churchmen. He unbent so far as to sing some old songs accompanied on the piano by Ashley Clarke [the minister at the embassy], while Mrs Bevin kept clucking: "Sing us some more, Ernest." Lady Diana beamed on the scene with a fond eye. The salon of Pauline Borghese was filled with the comic atmosphere of a cosy cordiality more usually to be found round a pot of tea or a coal fire.'

The real nightmare of such conferences were the huge banquets, such as the one given for the delegates at the Sorbonne. The *place-à-table* always seemed to ensure that large numbers of people had neighbours with whom they shared no common language. Madame Bidault had to talk to Molotov through an interpreter sitting behind them. 'I had Mme Duhamel on my left,' wrote Duff Cooper, 'who is always very nice and pleasant to talk to. She had Guroff, the Russian ambassador in London, the other side of her, who knows a little English but no French and with whom she couldn't exchange a word ... Mrs Bevin, opposite me, was between Dr Roussy, president of the Sorbonne, and Thorez, neither of whom could say a word that she could understand.'

As well as the official round there was also a semi-official round, prompted partly by the large number of newspaper proprietors and editors attracted to Paris. Some wielded enormous influence, often without the knowledge to use it well. Henry Luce, founder of *Time* magazine, was a shy man, ill at ease and sentimental. 'Luce is a queer duck,' wrote David Bruce on a subsequent occasion. 'He gives the impression that he soaks up what one is saying without becoming mentally wetted by it. His youthful missionary background and his later enormous influence and affluence, combined with other factors, have complicated his personality. He appears driven by ambition and fanaticism to extremes of judgement.' Henry Luce came round to the British Embassy where he met Louise de Vilmorin and promptly fell 'madly in love with her'. Duff Cooper was very amused, but he had more sympathy for Henry Luce than for Luce's wife Clare. Caffery had brought her over to the British Embassy after dinner in the first winter after the Liberation. 'She is as pretty as ever,' he wrote then, 'and as self-satisfied, as tiresome, and as foolish.' He had much more time for Mrs Ogden Reid, wife of the proprietor of the *New York Herald Tribune* and the real controller of the newspaper. 'Mrs O.R. is a very sensible and well-balanced woman. She is what America has best to offer at the present time – and that is very good. Her husband is a drunken jackass and brays like one.'

The coming and going did not slacken, even during the conference recess. Admiral Lord Louis Mountbatten arrived in Paris to receive the Grande Croix de la Légion d'Honneur. Diana Cooper described their guests at the embassy: 'Dicky [Mountbatten], portly, fine-looking still, though not glamorous: Edwina shrivelled like the Mummy Rameses – with huge scarab blue eyes and a little real hair showing under her St John hat.' General Juin made the presentation at the Invalides, and that night at the embassy a big dinner took place at which 'Edwina looked like Gandhi dressed in a sari' and Suzy Solidor sang afterwards. Next day, Mountbatten gave a speech at the Hôtel de Ville in French. 'This made a deep impression on the audience,' wrote Duff Cooper. 'That any Englishman should be able to speak French is surprising, but that an Admiral should do it very well is stupefying.'

At the conference table, self-fulfilling suspicions were developing rapidly on both sides. Whenever the Americans stood up to Stalin over breaches of the Yalta agreement, he feared their confidence was based on a secret plan to use the atom bomb. He ignored the massive demobilization of their forces across the world.

At the same time, the Americans underestimated Stalin's paranoia, and therefore misjudged his obsession with establishing a protective *cordon sanitaire* round the Soviet Union. They assumed that his moves towards controlling those countries of Central Europe and the Balkans occupied by the Red Army was motivated entirely by ideological imperialism. His refusal on 1 March to withdraw troops from northern Iran, within striking distance of the oilfields, was defensive in the context of his paranoid mentality.

Five days after the 1 March deadline, Churchill made his 'iron curtain' speech at Fulton, Missouri. The reaction of the American press and public was unfavourable at the time. Truman refused to be drawn into the ensuing debate, though he and senior officials in the United States government were already starting to think along similar lines. They had been strongly influenced by George Kennan, the Kremlinologist at their Moscow embassy. He had sent a long telegram analysing the Soviet threat, which was a prelude to the policy of containment which he elaborated the following year.

In Paris the Turkish ambassador, a shrewd observer, said that the Russian failure to evacuate Persia as agreed 'was an irretrievable mistake because it resulted in the Americans developing a foreign policy'. It may not have actually developed the policy, but it certainly concentrated minds upon it. This would lead to the so-called Truman Doctrine in the spring of 1947, when America took over responsibility for the defence of Greece and Turkey on the collapse of British power in the region.

There are much stronger grounds for tracing the development of the Cold War to Germany which, even in its ruined and occupied state, remained the focus of Stalin's nightmares. George Kennan acknowledged that Russia's fears were understandable, in view of her terrible history of invasion by Mongol, Pole, Swede, and French, as well as the two waves of German occupation within the last thirty years.

Duff Cooper, who sympathized with the French fear of Germany – which was inevitably similar to that of the Soviet Union – was alarmed to hear in late May that the British Chiefs of Staff wanted 'a strong Germany to fight Russia'. Two years before, when still in Algiers, he had submitted a plan for a European bloc based on Britain, France, Belgium, the Netherlands and Luxemburg. He had vigorously pushed the idea; but Anthony Eden, terrified of upsetting Stalin, had opposed it. Cooper argued that at the end of the war the Russians would not be afraid of a Western European bloc. What terrified Stalin was the idea of a Western bloc dominated by the Americans and linked to a reconstructed Germany.

The French had started to harbour well-grounded suspicions that American and British service chiefs wanted to build up Germany. These hardened in June 1946, following articles by Walter Lippman and a speech by Ernest Bevin. The French were very uneasy about developments in Germany. Renseignements Généraux had recently reported *'une certaine nervosité'* between Anglo-Saxons and Russians in Berlin.

The Soviet Union kept an even closer watch on developments in the three western zones of Germany. Ponomarev's department was given a special responsibility for this. One striking point emerges from Ponomarev's paper to Molotov and Malenkov on the subject: the French Communist Party was of interest at this time only because it might influence events in Germany. The Kremlin complained that despite having eight posts in the government, the French Communist Party 'has not taken any steps to change the policy of the French occupation authorities' which 'protect fascist and reactionary elements'. Clearly the Kremlin failed to appreciate the fact that the French Communists had little control over the French army.

The conference of Foreign Ministers resumed in mid-June, with James Byrnes in residence at the Meurice and Ernest Bevin at the George V. Almost immediately, the conference was thrown into panic by reports from Washington that the Red Army was going to take over Trieste and then advance westwards across northern Italy towards southern France. Even Bevin felt inclined to believe the story because Molotov had been in such a strange mood that day. This flutter of nerves coincided with de Gaulle's speech at Bayeux.

Despite this dramatic start, Molotov's perpetual stalling slowed proceedings until Bevin and Byrnes developed a guillotine tactic to bring things to a conclusion. Byrnes was to be chairman and he would insist either upon the immediate settlement of each outstanding subject or else its relegation to the peace conference. Despite the scepticism of many, the plan cooked up by Byrnes and Bevin to accelerate business worked, and invitations were issued to the sixteen nations who were to convene for the full conference in August.

During that diplomatic summer, the centre of Paris had started to lose the look of wartime privation. The bicycle-powered *vélotaxis* were a conveyance of the past. Five thousand proper taxis were now available in Paris. Before, only people with a government pass or a doctor's certificate could use one. Now they were available to anybody who could afford the hefty fare. In the Tuileries gardens, children enjoyed rides on donkeys, or in little carts pulled by goats with jingling harness. Baby-carriages had also reappeared, having taken a considerable battering during the Occupation, when they were used for the transport of everything from logs and coal to turnips.

The great hit of the season was the musical *Auprès de ma blonde*, with Yvonne Printemps and her husband, Pierre Fresnay. It was a sophisticated comedy of family manners – with lavish costumes by Lanvin – working backwards in time from the 1930s to the *belle époque* of the 1890s.

As August approached, the centre of Paris became almost empty with the departure of 750,000 Parisians on summer holiday – a further sign of the gradual return to normality. The influx of foreigners was not entirely due to the conference. The Golden Arrow train service, from Victoria Station in London to the Gare du Nord, had been resumed in April; and an air terminal had been opened at the Invalides, heralding a new era of travel.

The great assembly of diplomats and journalists from around the world provided trade for more than hotels and restaurants and nightclubs. Nancy Mitford wrote to one of her sisters that 'I'm told the *maquereaux* [pimps] stop the Peace Conference people practically as they leave the Luxembourg and offer them *l'Amour Atomique*. Aren't they heaven?'

The round of entertainment recommenced. On 9 August Bogomolov gave a party for Molotov with 'more class distinction than ever'. The top thirty guests were ushered into 'a *cul-de-sac* room shut tightly against all others' with Molotov and the Americans and British 'cracking jokes over the vodka' like the members of 'an exclusive gentlemen's club', until Vyshinsky spoilt the impression by getting extremely drunk.

The following day Cy Sulzberger organized a lunch in honour of Senator Tom Connally in a private room at LaRue's. He asked Mrs Connally for suggestions about possible menus. It appeared that there was only one: dry Martinis, steak, French fries. Sulzberger also invited Raymond Offroy from the Quai d'Orsay. '"Old Tawm" cheered up a bit with the cocktails,' Sulzberger wrote later, 'but still seemed somewhat sulky, although looking most impressive with his black string tie and white mane of hair.' When 'a real steak' arrived, 'he warmed perceptibly. After a few munches he turned to me solemnly and asked: "Cy, where's Westphalia?"

'"Why, in Germany, Senator."

'"They signed a treaty there, didn't they?" (Offroy was watching, fascinated, awaiting a clue to American policy and wisdom.)

'"Yes, sir, the Treaty of Westphalia. It ended the Thirty Years War in 1648."

'"Yup," said Tawm. "That's where Napoleon was whipped." Offroy gulped.'

The other great senator, Arthur Vandenberg, managed to have a similar effect on another senior official of the Quai d'Orsay. 'Senator Vandenberg beside me,' wrote Jacques Dumaine after a lunch given by the Conseil Municipal de Paris, 'could not take his eyes off the beaming face of Maurice Thorez and kept repeating: "How can such a healthy-looking man be a Communist!"'

Hervé Alphand's brilliant mimicry of Byrnes, Bevin and Molotov reduced dinner parties, such as the Duchess of Windsor's, to helpless laughter. This proved a slightly double-edged talent. Duff Cooper, who was a friend of Alphand's, wrote in his diary: 'It is odd how Alphand inspires dislike and distrust in Englishmen. I think it is because being a highly skilled civil servant and *inspecteur de finances* he looks and behaves like an actor. No English civil servant could ever be persuaded to take Noël Coward seriously.'

The Peace Conference, for all its tedium, had surprising devotees. All through the 'Turkish bath weather' Momo Marriott, one of the daughters of Otto Kahn, went every day to follow the proceedings as if it were a fascinating murder trial. But few trials lasted as long. The five peace treaties were not finally signed until 10 February 1947, with Italy, Romania, Hungary, Bulgaria and Finland. The process took the whole day, so Duff Cooper read Graham Greene's *A Gun for Sale* during the intervals. The final ceremony took place in the Salon de l'Horloge of the Quai d'Orsay, on the table where the wounded Robespierre had been laid before he was guillotined.

For all the outward signs of a return to normality in the summer, a general sense of unease returned in the autumn of 1946. Yet spy-mania and the fear of Communism produced a number of comic moments. The Windsors, wrote Nancy Mitford to Evelyn Waugh, were telling everyone that 'France is on the verge of Communism and they must put their jewels in a safe place.' Also that October, word spread that Bogomolov, the Soviet ambassador, was not only showing great admiration for Princesse Ghislaine de Polignac, but was having an affair with her. The princess was very amused by the rumour, particularly when Eric Duncannon rushed round to ask her to spy on Bogomolov for the British.

The appointment of the pro-Communist General Petit as Deputy Military Governor of Paris caused alarm in sensitive circles. General Revers, not an entirely reliable source because of his extreme anti-Communism, claimed that Thorez had arranged it.

In London, the War Office and the Foreign Office consistently opposed staff talks with the French throughout this period, to Duff Cooper's exasperation. Suspicions about the French inability to maintain effective security went back to the disastrous Dakar expedition in 1940, and had been greatly compounded by exaggerated fears of Communist infiltration through FFI officers.

In the autumn of 1946, the Foreign Office wanted to have wireless transmitters concealed in consulates around France 'in case of trouble', whether a *coup d'état* or an invasion by the Red Army. The ambassador vigorously opposed this suggestion put forward by William Hayter, then chairman of the Joint Intelligence Committee. He felt that the measure would only succeed in upsetting the French.

The nascent Cold War had also begun to affect literary life. Arthur Koestler, who was living in Wales at this time, came to Paris on 1 October 1946 to attend the rehearsals of his play *Twilight Bar*, produced as *Bar du Soleil* by Jean Vilar at the Théâtre de Clichy.

One day very soon after his arrival, he visited the Hotel Pont-Royal and went over to Sartre in the downstairs bar to introduce himself. '*Bonjour, je suis Koestler.*' *La famille Sartre* found him full of life and interested in everything – Sartre, especially, became fond of Koestler – but his competitive bumptiousness, encouraged by his great success with *Darkness at Noon* which had sold nearly 250,000 copies in France, rather irked them.* Simone de Beauvoir soon had another reason to be irritated when, after one of the many nights on which she had drunk too much, she woke up in Koestler's bed.

She and Sartre had another unpredictable evening with Koestler some time later. On 31 October Koestler and his beautiful companion, Mamaine Paget, whom he married not long afterwards, took them out to dinner at an Arab bistro with Albert and Francine Camus. Sartre had to give a UNESCO lecture the next day, so hoped for an early bed. But after dinner they went on to 'a little *dancing* with blue and pink neon lights and men with hats on dancing with girls with very short skirts'. Mamaine described 'the engaging spectacle' of Koestler 'lugging Castor (who has I think hardly ever danced in her life) round the floor' while Sartre, with a similar lack of experience, 'lugged Mme Camus'.

* One could hardly blame Koestler for being pleased at such figures, especially since he had heard that 'the French Communist Party had orders to buy up every single copy of *Le Zéro et l'infini* immediately', so in this way he was being 'enriched indefinitely from Communist Party funds'.

Koestler insisted that they all go on to the Schéhérazade night-club, a White Russian establishment which German officers had loved during the Occupation. The combination of Russian tzi-gane music, almost total darkness, vodka, champagne and zak-ouski combined to make his guests forget the next day's commitments.

Koestler seemed to find the Schéhérazade an appropriate spot for launching into an anti-Soviet tirade. The more they argued, the more they drank. Soon only Camus and Mamaine Paget were comparatively sober; the rest were very drunk, especially Sartre. At four in the morning, Koestler persuaded them to go on to a bistro in Les Halles, where they had *soupe à l'oignon*, oysters and white wine. Sartre became even more drunk. He kept pouring pepper and salt into paper napkins, then 'folding them up small and stuffing them in his pocket'.

At eight o'clock in the morning, half-blinded by the sunlight, Simone de Beauvoir and Sartre found themselves in a pitiful state, weeping dilute vodka, on one of the bridges over the Seine. They wondered out loud whether to throw themselves in. Yet despite only two hours' sleep, Sartre managed to write and deliver his lecture.

Koestler was feeling under threat at the time. He had become a major hate figure for Stalinists, and like all lapsed party members he was vilified even more than a committed fascist. He returned to Wales almost immediately after the night at the Schéhérazade. Not long afterwards, *Les Temps modernes* pub-lished Maurice Merleau-Ponty's attack on Koestler under the title '*Le Yogi et le Prolétaire*'. In this piece Merleau-Ponty, profes-sor of philosophy at the École Normale Supérieure, set out to excuse the 1936 Moscow show trials on the grounds that the Soviet Union, isolated and threatened, could only save its revolu-tion at the cost of a monolithic firmness; 'objectively', in the Marxist–Leninist sense of the term, opposition was treason. 'He subordinated morality to history, much more resolutely than any existentialist yet,' wrote Simone de Beauvoir in a revealing passage. 'We took this leap with him – without yet letting go – conscious that moralizing was the last defence of bourgeois idealism.'

Camus was outraged by the article, and by the decision of the editorial committee to publish it. An argument broke out at a party given by the writer and jazz-player Boris Vian and his wife Michelle. Camus arrived late, towards eleven o'clock in the evening. He had just returned from a journey to the South of France. He immediately attacked Merleau-Ponty for his article, accusing him of justifying the Moscow show trials. Merleau-Ponty defended himself, and Sartre supported him. Camus was appalled and left, slamming the door. Sartre hurried after him and caught up with him in the street. He tried to persuade Camus to return to the party, but Camus refused.

This marked the beginning of the rift in Camus's relationship with Sartre, which finally exploded in a celebrated exchange of correspondence in *Les Temps modernes* a few years later. His friendship with Simone de Beauvoir, on the other hand, had never been particularly warm. She had long suspected Camus's political ambivalence, ever since November 1945 during the ministerial crisis. Camus had defended de Gaulle's position. Camus, unlike Koestler at this time, was no Gaullist, but in Beauvoir's eyes he had revealed his true anti-Communist colours.

Sartre and Castor also began to fall out with Raymond Aron in the autumn of 1946. Sartre's play about the Resistance, *Men without Shadows*, opened at around the same time as Jean-Louis Barrault was producing *Les Nuits de la colère*, Salacrou's play on the same subject (about which Sartre allegedly remarked that the author knew his *collabos* better than his *résistants*). On the first night of *Men without Shadows*, the torture scenes – though off-stage – became too much for Raymond Aron's wife, who was not well. Aron took her home. Simone de Beauvoir, even more than Sartre, refused to accept his wife's illness as a valid excuse for leaving.

Whatever Beauvoir's stand on such issues, one must not forget that Sartre was still regarded with deep distrust, even enmity, by the Communists. On encountering Sartre at a literary lunch soon afterwards, Ilya Ehrenburg strongly criticized him for depicting members of the Resistance as 'cowards and schemers'. Sartre retorted that Ehrenburg clearly had not read the play in its entirety. His previous plays had also been attacked on similar grounds. In *The Respectful Prostitute*, for example, he had failed to present the black victim as 'a true fighter'. And his next major play, *Dirty Hands*, was to bring down upon him virtually every insult in the (admittedly rather limited) dictionary of Stalinist obloquy.

Over the next few years, with the onset of the Cold War, Sartre began to shift his position on politics and artistic expression. 'The Communists are right,' he later wrote in a compromise formula which was strikingly short on philosophical rigour. 'I was not wrong. For people who are crushed and exhausted, hope is always necessary. They had all too many occasions to despair. But one should also strive to work without illusions.'

23

The Fashionable World

During the Occupation, even Communists had regarded Parisian fashion as a weapon of Resistance. Lise Deharme, the Surrealist hostess, wrote in *Les Lettres Françaises*: 'Yes, true Parisiennes were supremely elegant during the four years; they had the elegance of racehorses. With a tear in the eye but a smile on the lips, beautiful, perfectly made-up, discreet and insolent, they exasperated the Germans. The beauty of their hair, of their complexion ... their slimness as opposed to the fat ugliness of those overgrown trouts packaged in grey [the German servicewomen], yes, that provoked them. These Parisiennes were part of the Resistance.'

Haute couture had emerged from the war in much the same shape as the elegant Parisian women: slimmed to the point of emaciation, but still defiantly maintaining the standards of French taste and craftsmanship. Yet if the Germans had had their way, the French fashion industry would not have survived at all. In August 1940, they warned Lucien Lelong, head of the Chambre Syndicale de la Couture, that all the great French designers, plus the skilled workers of their *ateliers*, would be transferred to Berlin. With their knowledge and expertise, Berlin and Vienna would become the centres of fashion in the New Europe, while Paris dwindled into insignificance.

'You can impose what you will by force,' wrote Lelong in response, 'but Paris's *haute couture* is not transferable, either *en bloc* or bit by bit. It exists in Paris or it does not exist at all.' This was not merely spirited talk. The industry employed some 13,000 skilled artisans. The fabrics and trimmings they worked with were the product of highly specialized workshops that had developed in France over generations: it would be impossible to transfer an industry so widely spread and so deeply rooted. The Germans were forced to agree, but they were still determined to break the power of Paris fashion. The industry was forbidden to export its goods. Each major fashion house could produce only 40 models in each collection instead of 150, and was subjected to the severest rationing of cloth. Many folded during the Occupation, but the industry did not die because there was still a demand for its work. It is often supposed that the principal customers for luxury clothes were the occupiers themselves; yet the ration cards known as *cartes couture*, issued to buyers, proved otherwise. The Germans took only 200 per year out of a total which dwindled from 20,000 *cartes couture* in 1941 to 13,000 in 1944.

At the Liberation, Lelong called for a *comité interprofessionnel d'épuration* for the couture industry. The committee looked into fifty-five cases of collaboration, most of which had to do with textile handling rather than the running of the great couture houses. It was a remarkably mild *épuration*, for one simple reason. Rich women all over the world, particularly in the Americas, were willing to pay a fortune for fine clothes; and France was desperately short of foreign currency.

French *haute couture*, however, was no longer in the commanding position it had enjoyed before the war, when fashion was dictated from Paris. American designers in particular had found their own style and expanded their markets in the four years they had been cut off from France, and they had been encouraged by the belief that Paris *haute couture* was dead. After the Liberation, something had to be done to show the world that the vitality of French fashion was as strong as ever, and that it was ready for business.

In the autumn of 1944 an idea arose which was to re-launch

the French fashion industry in a most spectacular way. The spark, curiously enough, came from Entr'Aide Française – an umbrella organization for French war charities. Its president, Raoul Dautry, suggested that the couture industries put on a fund-raising exhibition.

Robert Ricci, the son of the designer Nina Ricci, and head of the Chambre Syndicale, recognized the idea as a wonderful opportunity. The exhibition could display the first post-war Paris collection (spring and summer, 1945) in miniature, modelled on dolls. French dressmakers had always used exquisitely dressed dolls to show the courts of Europe the latest styles from Paris; but the dolls for this very special collection must be entirely new and unexpected. The design for the new dolls was entrusted to Eliane Bonabel, barely twenty but already known for her illustrations in Céline's *Voyage au bout de la nuit*. They were made entirely of wire, looking more like modern sculptures than toys, and the Catalan sculptor Joan Rebull was commissioned to make plaster heads for the figures, which he insisted should remain free of make-up.

Christian Bérard was appointed artistic director of the exhibition, and he gathered together a remarkable group of artists to paint backdrops for the models. Among the painters, sculptors and set-designers involved were Bérard's lover Boris Kochno, Jean Cocteau, Grau-Sala, Georges Geffroy, the young André Beaurepaire, and Jean Saint-Martin, who specialized in wire sculptures and had made the dolls from Eliane Bonabel's design. All gave their services free.

The image that was to unify the whole exhibition came from Ricci: 'I finally had the idea of a little theatre in which each of the artists would construct a set and we would put on the stage dolls dressed by the couturiers.'

Each couture house had to produce between one and five models. Christian Dior is thought to have been responsible for two of the miniature dresses presented by Lucien Lelong, for whom he worked as designer. With their nipped-in waists and full skirts, they stand apart from much of post-war fashion, which had not yet shaken off the war years.

The couture houses set to work with a will. Throughout that winter, in freezing studios, seamstresses, shoemakers, milliners and glovers warmed their fingers every few minutes over candle flames and plied their craft in miniature, and such was the rivalry between the couture houses that no trouble was too great. Patou had one fabric specially woven so that it would fold properly on the model. The striped fabric on a Carven dress called '*Sucre d'orge*' was cut up and re-sewn to make the stripes sufficiently small.

The exhibition opened on 27 March 1945 at the Pavillon de Marsan of the Louvre, and was accorded such importance that the Garde Républicaine, *en grande tenue*, formed a guard of honour on the opening night. Over 100,000 people came to see the exhibition over the following weeks. Most of them had had no new clothes since 1939, and *haute couture* was way beyond their means. Yet the numb, grey years of the Occupation had made them thirsty for colour and luxury, and the effect of these beautifully dressed wire dolls in their fantastic settings was magical. Some of the sets were surrealist, but most were firmly Parisian. The centrepiece was Christian Bérard's theatre, the stage and boxes of which were thronged with dolls dressed in the most elaborate evening gowns, sparkling with jewels by Cartier and Van Cleef & Arpels. Underneath the satin and chiffon, some of the dolls had even been given silk underwear.

To go with its fashions, 'Paris always has to have a current beauty who is the rage,' wrote Bettina Ballard of *Vogue*. Gloria Rubio arrived in Paris in the summer of 1945, and was immediately 'the rage'. She was Mexican, and was dressed by Balenciaga: a designer known for a certain dramatic elegance that bordered on the vampish. For the next year she was very much on the social scene, and had the added attraction of being between husbands. She was in the last stages of divorce from her

German husband, Count von Fürstenberg, and was engaged to the Egyptian Prince Fakri. (She later married the English million-aire Loel Guinness.)

Gloria Rubio did not come to dinner at the British Embassy until March 1946. She was good at chess, and brilliant at bridge; while her *femme fatale* beauty, her money and her foreign husbands all added up to what Diana Cooper called 'a child's idea of an international spy'. Duff admired her, though he was wary of getting into what he called 'any more complications', and apprehensive about the return of Louise de Vilmorin, temporarily away from Paris: 'Gloria knows Loulou and is a friend of Etty [née Wurmbrand-Stuppach] whom [Paul] Palffy divorced to marry Loulou. Etty then married Tommy Esterhazy who also divorced her in order to marry Loulou and now Loulou won't marry him.'

Louise returned a week later, and Duff threw discretion to the winds by taking her to a party given by Gloria. 'I was rather nervous. There was much jealousy in the air. Everyone was looking at everyone with suspicion. Like a ball in Balzac ... Gloria with husband and lover, the Egyptian princess very décolletée and beautiful – Gloria almost too demonstrative to me.'

The importance of being fashionable came as a shock to Susan Mary Patten when she planned one of the first charity balls in post-war Paris in the summer of 1946. Dark and pretty, Susan Mary was intelligent, entertaining and very well-read. She and her husband Bill Patten had a great many friends, both Parisians and among the diplomatic community.

The ball was to be in aid of the orphans of war-torn Lorraine. She booked the Pré Catalan, a restaurant in the Bois de Boul-ogne, hired an orchestra and sent out tickets for a masked ball, thinking that people would willingly buy them for such a good cause. One of her French friends told her she was mad: 'No one is going to come to anything in this city for a good cause unless it's fashionable, and you aren't fashionable.' Aghast, Susan Mary begged Diana Cooper for help. Diana said she would talk about it everywhere, and they would visit the dressmakers. 'Reboux, Schiaparelli, Lanvin, Balenciaga were our first stops,' wrote Susan Mary. 'At each one Diana asked, "Could I please see the models for the masks for the ball at the Pré Catalan? I'm terribly sorry to be so late; you must be running out of materials already."' No couturier dared admit he had never heard of it, and 'the bluff paid off. Two weeks later we were oversold and a nice little black market in tickets had started.'

Gambling had always been one of France's most lucrative tourist attractions, whether on the sea at Cannes, Biarritz or Deauville, or at the inland spa towns, where the casino was compensation for the austerities of a health cure.

All gambling clubs had been closed during the war, both in the occupied and unoccupied zones; and after the Liberation casinos in France were refused materials for repair, as priority had to be given to housing. Ironically, one of the first to apply for a return of its gaming licence was the casino at Vichy. Its application was based on the grounds that a certain number of its former staff, prisoners of war and deportees, were in 'urgent need'.

Most casinos did not open until the spring of 1946, and then only after mayors, members of the National Assembly or prefects had written to the Minister of the Interior begging for his intervention to save towns whose only natural resource was tourism. The time was ripe, for the devaluation of the franc in December 1945 had acted as a powerful incentive for foreigners to come and spend money in France. Couture had never been so reasonable, and what they saved on clothes they would spend at the tables. The country's desperate need for foreign exchange was the best argument against Communist attacks claiming that ministers were in the pockets of casino-owners.

The most enthusiastic, and the most silent, supporters of the revival of gambling were the big black-marketeers. Casinos offered the easiest way to launder large amounts of money. Before French casinos reopened, these men and women would travel to Monte Carlo with a suitcase full of grubby notes, and return with a pristine cheque from the Société des Bains de Mer and an unbreakable story that their fortune came from a lucky streak at the tables.

The casino at Deauville, which had been taken over by the United States Army, only just managed to get itself reopened for the 1946 season. Duff Cooper flew from London to Deauville for the weekend of 26 July, with Loel Guinness and General Bob Laycock. They were met by the embassy Rolls and driven to the Hotel Normandie, where they found Seymour Berry with Kick, Lady Hartington, and Gloria Rubio, who had come up from Paris. After dinner at Ciro's they went to the casino. Duff left the gaming tables long before Gloria – 'she plays very high,' he noted. On Friday she won 250,000 francs. On Saturday she lost 300,000 francs. Duff left for Paris before lunch on Sunday to prepare for a visit by Clement Attlee. He later heard that Gloria had won again – over a million francs.

In the years following the Liberation, racing was more controversial than gambling, since it attracted the rich French in a very public display of money and fashion, while casinos catered more to foreigners. The racing correspondent of one newspaper denounced as scandalous the fact that racegoers – or *turfistes* as they were called in the popular press – were running up restaurant bills of 10,000 to 12,000 francs for lunch. He also declared that 'the paddock is overrun by the cream of the collaboration'. Guy de Rothschild recorded in his memoirs that 'the owner of an important racing stable had his face publicly slapped at Longchamp by a man who was, moreover, not entirely irreproachable himself. A few years after the war, the same owner had the luck to win the Arc de Triomphe two years running; fearing the hostile reaction of the crowd, he didn't even dare to leave his box.'

*

The first presidential inauguration of the Fourth Republic took place on 16 January 1947. Nobody wanted to be President more than Vincent Auriol, the Socialist from the south-west who joked about his Languedoc accent. Auriol had been so nervous about the outcome of the election by the Assembly that he had hardly stopped touching wood.

It was freezing on the day of the inauguration, but the sun was out. That night the Élysée Palace was illuminated, and the floodlit tricolor above it was flown for the first time in seven years. On 11 February President Auriol gave the first large reception held since the war. The palace was brightly lit, some thought too brightly; the women wore very formal dresses, but the men were in dinner-jackets rather than tail-coats. The most crowded room was the dining-room.

Auriol was a *bon vivant* Socialist who nevertheless took such pleasure from the trappings and the traditions associated with the office that the Communist minister François Billoux dubbed him *'l'intoxiqué de l'Élysée'*. He had a strong sense of the dignity of his new position. At the first meeting of the Council of Ministers, Jules Moch, an old companion-in-arms from the Socialist Party, turned to him and addressed him by the familiar *tu*.

'Allow me,' replied the President of the Republic, drawing himself up in his chair, 'to make the observation to Monsieur le Ministre des Travaux Publics that . . .'

The new President was also passionately fond of shooting and trout-fishing, and whenever ambassadors arrived to present their credentials the talk soon turned in that direction. He was determined to improve the presidential shoot at Rambouillet, which for him was one of the most enjoyable perks of his position.

The guns, up to ten in number, would meet at the Château de Rambouillet in the middle of the morning for hot chocolate or coffee before the first stand. Each guest was provided with two loaders, who had the additional task of counting and marking every bird shot by their gun. The guest of honour was given the centre peg on each drive, and was thus expected to account for the highest proportion of the bag.

The shooting went on until the early afternoon. The guns would then gather at the end of the lawn where the bag was meticulously laid out. President Auriol presented each gun with a card showing the number he had shot, not the total bag. Bad shots awaited this moment with a sensation akin to that of a dunce at school.

The President then led them all into the house for a magnificent lunch, but the pleasure of the day was soon spoiled: the conversation inevitably turned to the political situation, and everyone was plunged in gloom. By the time they rose from the luncheon table at about five o'clock, night had fallen.

February marked the start of the spring collections. It was always an exciting time, and the shows at the different *maisons de couture* were announced in the press in far larger letters than any opera or exhibition. And 1947 saw the emergence of a new designer, Christian Dior – who was to change the direction of fashion overnight.

Bettina Ballard described Dior as a 'pink-cheeked man with an air of baby plumpness still about him, and an almost desperate shyness augmented by a receding chin'. On 12 February 1947, the day he was due to present his first collection, he arrived early at 30 Avenue Montaigne: a beautiful *hôtel particulier* with an ornamental doorway, which framed an awning on which his name was written in discreet black lettering.

The house was in a frenzy of activity. Workmen were still tacking down the carpet, and people ran around with armfuls of fresh flowers for the reception rooms. Behind the scenes, the mannequins tried to calm their nerves by concentrating on their make-up. The main salon and the little one beyond were crammed with gold chairs. On each chair was a name card, every one of which represented hours of minute adjustment so that every fashion editor and important guest should feel that they had not only been correctly placed, but were sitting next to people of equal rank with whom they were on good terms.

No attempt had been made to drum up publicity; but Dior had powerful friends, such as Comte Étienne de Beaumont, Marie-Louise Bousquet, Christian Bérard, and Michel de Brunhoff of *Vogue*. All had recognized Dior, from his work at Lelong, as a designer of prodigious talent. This had stirred up a great deal of excitement and curiosity about Dior's new fashion house. The crush was so great that some people even attempted to get in through the top of the house with ladders.

At half past ten, with the salons full to overflowing, all was ready. Having greeted his guests, Dior escaped to the sanctuary of his office to endure his agony of nerves as far from the catwalk as possible. The very first model to step out was so agitated that she stumbled; and once off-stage she dissolved into mascara-blackened tears and was incapable of making another entry. But as each new dress appeared, it was greeted with gasps of admiration and applause. Members of Dior's staff kept bursting into his office to report each new success; but he could not quite believe what had happened until he emerged from his office, to be given a thunderous standing ovation. Among the most enthusiastic was Carmel Snow of *Harper's Bazaar*. 'Your dresses have such a *new look*!' she exclaimed – and so the name was born.

The clothes looked simple, but they were extremely complex in construction. The most famous dress of his first collection was '*Bar*': a white shantung jacket, nipped in at the waist and exaggerating the curve of the hips, above a wide black pleated skirt. Dior's favourite dress in the collection, however, was called '*Chérie*': beneath a tight bodice and tiny waist, the skirt consisted of yard after yard of white faille. A rumour went round that Dior's backer, Marcel Boussac, actively encouraged Dior's extravagant use of cloth to boost his textile sales. Dior always hotly denied it, and pointed out that Boussac dealt mainly in cotton – a material for which he had very little use.

The impact of the show was astonishing, and reached far

beyond the world of fashion. One old regular of the Jockey Club, M. de Lasteyrie, remarked that he had never heard a couturier's name mentioned on the premises in the forty years he had been a member – but now '*on ne parle que de Dior*'.

Balmain, like Dior, had spent the early part of the war in the unoccupied zone, in his native Aix-les-Bains, where he had met Gertrude Stein and Alice B. Toklas. After they had returned to Paris, Balmain and Dior worked side by side, designing all the clothes that the house of Lucien Lelong produced, for Lelong himself never pretended to be a designer. Dior wrote: 'Neither Balmain nor I will ever forget that Lelong taught us our profession, in spite of all the restrictions of wartime and the constant fear of sudden closure.'

In 1945, Pierre Balmain left Lelong to found his own *maison de couture*. His first collection was pronounced fresh and imaginative. Although not particularly avant-garde, the opening show was graced by the presence of his friends from Aix: 'Gertrude Stein with her familiar cropped head, and Alice B. Toklas with her dark mustache, sitting in the seats of honour watching the pretty striped numbers go by, noting them meticulously on their cards with the same intensity of interest as they had noted the Matisses or Picassos that had passed through their lives.'

Susan Mary Patten went to Dior's first collection, and as one of the *vendeuses* had become a friend of hers, 'I was allowed into the fitting-rooms afterwards to try on some models. This was more dangerous than entering a den of female lions before feeding time, as the richest ladies in Europe were screaming for the models, shrill cries of "WHERE is '*Miss New York*'?" I had it and someone has stolen it right from under my eyes!'

Daisy Fellowes, on the other hand, did not have to fight with the crowd in the Avenue Montaigne – the clothes which everyone desired so desperately came to her at the Ritz. 'She is living in the most magnificent apartment on the first floor,' wrote Duff

Cooper, 'and there *vendeuses* from Dior were showing her dresses and drinking her champagne. It was an exhibition of great wealth.'

The conspicuous extravagance of Dior's clothes was offensive to those for whom the war had meant five years of misery. 'People shout *ordures* at you from vans,' wrote Nancy Mitford to Eddy Sackville-West, 'because for some reason it creates class feeling in a way no sables could.' Just how offensive was proved by a photographic session organized in March 1947, which was designed to display Dior's clothes in typically Parisian surroundings. Among the obvious settings such as the Eiffel Tower and the Champs-Élysées, someone thought of a street market in Montmartre.

The clothes were dispatched to Montmartre in great wooden packing-cases on board a *camionette*. The models changed into them in the back room of a bar. But when, proud and graceful, the first one walked out into the rue Lepic market, the effect was electric. The street sank into an uneasy silence; and then, with a shriek of outrage, a woman stall-holder hurled herself on the nearest model, shouting insults. Another woman joined her, and together they beat the girl, tore her hair, and tried to pull the clothes off her. The other models beat a hasty retreat into the bar, and in a very short time clothes and models were heading back to the safety of the Avenue Montaigne.

Even in the conservative confines of the 7th *arrondissement*, Dior clothes provoked some hard stares. Nancy Mitford was wearing her Dior suit when 'a strange woman said would I excuse her asking but does it come from Dior? This was in the bistro I go to – and of course everybody knows about Dior's prices. So I made up a sort of speech about how I saved up the whole war for a new coat etc! But I know mine will soon be the same fate of *l'élégante de la rue Lepique* [sic]. Between the Communists and the *ménagères* one's life is one long risk.'

But despite the disapproval of the great and the good, and the outrage of the poor, there was no turning back: the New Look was in such demand that it represented 75 per cent of the total export sales from France's fashion industry for 1947. It was also relentlessly copied. 'The London New Look made me die laughing,' wrote Nancy Mitford. 'Literal chintz crinolines. Apparently Dior went over: and when he reflected on the fact that he was responsible for launching it, he was ready to kill himself.'

24
A Tale of Two Cities

The Communist view of Paris was not just of a city of stark contrasts, but of two different cities juxtaposed. 'There is the Paris of banks, of boards of directors, of ministries, of American films, of insolent GIs, of American cars from the embassy of which the government is an annex; the Paris of nauseating luxury, of town houses inhabited by elderly dowagers who are lost in the labyrinth of their rooms.' Then there was 'the other Paris . . . at the same time much older and much younger' – the working-class Paris of 'Belleville, La Chapelle, la rue Mouffetard, Charonne, Ménilmontant . . .'

Political rhetoric aside, the stark division of Paris between *beaux quartiers* and *quartiers pauvres* came largely from Baron Haussmann's drastic re-shaping of the city under the Second Empire. The populous slums in the centre were razed after their inhabitants had been evicted by force, and a golden boom of unrestricted property speculation began along his strategic boulevards laid out for the field of fire they offered against revolutionary mobs. Haussmann's dictum that 'architecture is nothing else than administration' made town-planning akin to a military campaign, waged on behalf of a brashly triumphant bourgeoisie. There can be no doubt, as the sociologist J. F. Gravier wrote in 1946, that Haussmann's cleansing of the lower orders from central Paris 'strongly reinforced class consciousness'.

The shift in population created new slums around the

northern, eastern and southern perimeter of Paris. This became
known in the 1930s as the *'ceinture rouge'*, even though it never
encircled the city. The uprooted poor and successive waves of
migrants to the capital were forced to live in cheaply built
tenements and houses, which soon began to crumble. At the end
of the war over a sixth of all buildings in Paris were in a
seriously dilapidated state, and this proportion rose to well over
a quarter in working-class districts. The central problem was
that rents were so over-controlled and so low – in 1945 rent took
up only 4 per cent of the family budget as opposed to nearly 19
per cent in 1908 – that landlords never spent any money on
repairs, let alone improvements to their property. Nearly a
quarter of the houses and apartments depended on a tap in the
courtyard or on the landing, and nearly half had no inside
lavatory. The lack of hygiene extended to cooking, which was
dangerous in the cramped conditions. The Prefect of the Seine,
in a report to the Municipal Council, spoke of 'slums which ruin
the health and morals of our working people'.

Some 450,000 people, roughly a tenth of the population of
Paris and its suburbs, were defined with bureaucratic euphemism
as *'les plus défavorisés'*. Worst of all were *'les îlots insalubres'*, the
slum pockets in sunless, narrow streets, with squalid little apartments where a total of 186,594 people lived in 4,290 buildings,
often with four or five people to a room. Up to 30 per cent of
such inhabitants succumbed to tuberculosis, a record as bad as
that of 1918. In one slum, the death rate reached 43 per cent.
The Prefect, however, appeared to be most concerned with the
moral aspect of parents and children sharing beds. 'We are
faced with a major crisis of disastrous social implications . . .
Family life exists in an atmosphere of disintegration, where the
degree of promiscuity is appalling.'

In the waves of immigration before the war, the ancient and
beautiful town of Saint-Denis on the northern boundary of Paris
was swamped. 'One cannot,' wrote Gravier, 'forgive the archi-
tects, the developers, and the property companies who built the

cheap rented accommodation in Saint-Denis, for having changed a lively city full of history into a sordid concentration camp for immigrants.'

A large proportion of the migrants to Paris came from Brittany and the Auvergne. Although devout Catholics, they had far fewer children once they reached the city than the average in the communities from which they had sprung. In a country obsessed with increasing its birth rate after the slaughter of the First World War, Paris was therefore seen as a vampire, depopulating the countryside by attracting its young, then reducing their fertility at a stroke. One writer argued that the loss in births from internal migration to Paris between 1921 and 1936 came to the equivalent of the total French casualties during the Second World War. The main causes for this abrupt demographic change were brutally simple: the physical restrictions of tiny tenement apartments and the cost of food. All too many young wives had to resort to back-street abortionists.

In eastern Paris, the districts of Belleville and Ménilmontant lay mainly between the Parc des Buttes Chaumont, the Porte des Lilas, and the cemetery of Père Lachaise, burdened with the memory of the massacre of Communards in 1871. Alleys, steep little cobbled streets, and houses with grey shutters and peeling grey stucco bore testimony to a very different sort of history from that of the spacious and grandiose centre of the city.

After the thick slush of winter, the only colour in spring came from the blossom of a few stunted and polluted lilacs or optimistic shoots from ruthlessly pollarded plane trees. The begrimed romanesque façade of Notre-Dame-de-la-Croix in the Place de Ménilmontant appeared to belong to an industrial city of the north, not to Paris. Few buildings matched in height and the chaotic roofscape was completely unlike the Haussmann-imposed discipline of central Paris. There were not many shops: the odd under-provisioned grocer optimistically entitled '*Alimentation Générale*', the dingy little establishments run by migrants from the

Auvergne selling wine, firewood and coal, and bare cafés with little more than a zinc counter for those in cloth caps and blue overalls who needed a *petit vin blanc* to start the day. Housewives still did almost all their shopping in the street markets, like the one on the rue de Ménilmontant.

As well as the Jewish leather-workers and cobblers and garment workshops in Belleville, the area was filled with artisans of every description: watchmakers, woodcarvers, caners, cabinet-makers, monumental masons for the gravestones in Père Lachaise, all working in tiny ill-lit premises, in most cases no more than a cubbyhole with a workbench, pigeonholes and a single bulb on a flex above.

From the water-towers overlooking the cemetery of Belleville round to the abattoirs of La Villette, to the marshalling yards and railway workshops of La Chapelle, eastern and northern Paris were areas of great working-class solidarity, however fragmented their population.

In the 18th *arrondissement*, which included the central workshops of the French railways, young Communists hero-worshipped their elder brothers who had taken part in the Resistance: the centre for the activities of the resistants had been the basketball club.

On Sunday mornings, the men of the Gager family put on their Sunday suits and went off to sell Communist Party newspapers. Hersz Gager, the father, sold *L'Humanité*, and the elder son Georges sold *L'Avant-garde*. Each had his own pitch in the rue de l'Olive next to the market.

Activities for Communist youth were taken as seriously as the Church's activities for young Catholics. There were outings to politically approved plays, the cultural programme of l'Association France–URSS which usually involved watching films about the heroism of the Red Army, and camping for boys and girls in a very puritan atmosphere. The only relaxation came when young Communists in the 18th *arrondissement* used to organize a dance known as *la Goguette*, the name coming from Saturday-night parties on the banks of the Marne before the First World War. They danced *le swing* and loved *le be-bop*. The Communist Party decided not to maintain its anti-jazz line too strictly – it needed to recruit the young.

Hersz Gager's weekly cell meeting took place in the rue Jean Robert, and started after supper. He always shaved carefully before setting out. (Cell meetings in factories took place after work, but most workers preferred to avoid a cell linked to their job, because if the boss found out you would be the first to be fired.)

The Communist year had its feast-days and days of political observance. Supposedly the happiest, like an ancient spring rite, was the *fête des remises de cartes*. This was a family event, with cakes and wine, and singing and dancing to an accordion. The cell secretary would make a speech, and then present the party membership cards with jocular remarks, such as 'Perhaps this year you'll manage to sell a few more copies of *l'Huma!*' Other major festivals included May Day, the mass pilgrimage up to the Mur des Fédérés at Père Lachaise, where the Communards had been shot, and the Fête de l'Humanité. Even protest marches were a social event, however serious their purpose.

At the opposite end of Paris from the artisan workshops of Belleville lay the vast, disciplined Renault complex at Boulogne-Billancourt. Sirens regulated the day. Each morning, the crowd of capped workers assembled at the tall entrance gates, and when they opened, the men ambled forward under the eyes of the security guards. Then the gates closed again. A young intellectual who joined the work-force to share the experience compared it in an article in *Les Temps modernes* to entering a prison each day.

Food remained the greatest cause for concern in poor districts of Paris. Their inhabitants, whether industrial workers or state employees, were the most vulnerable in all of France. The country, as a SHAEF report put it, suffered from 'a chronic shortage of food made worse by an imbalance in consumption'. With average incomes still 20 per cent lower than before the war, the urban poor and those on weekly salaries were receiving 30 per cent less of the share of national income.

Nine months after the Liberation, SHAEF reported that 'the food position in France continues to be grave. Urban France has never approached the ration of 2,000 calories per head.' The ration target for the 'non-farm population' in the summer of 1945 was 350 grams of bread a day, 100 grams of meat a week and 500 grams of fats a month. In April the population of Paris averaged only 1,337 calories a day, but this overall figure hid terrible imbalances between the *beaux quartiers* and working-class districts where many, especially the old, virtually starved to death. The effect of malnutrition on the young should not be underestimated either. The average height of children was to fall dramatically.

Subsequent improvements during 1945 were short-lived. The announcement that bread rationing, which had been relaxed, was to be reintroduced on 1 January 1946 had provoked turmoil in the last few weeks of de Gaulle's administration. Groups which had nothing in common politically, from the newly formed Comité de Défense de la Petite et Moyenne Boulangerie to the Communist-dominated Union des Femmes Françaises, protested vociferously. And just before New Year, people stormed bakeries in a surge of panic buying. Customers at the back of the queue attacked those coming out with several loaves, even though they too had planned to buy as many as they were allowed.

Those with peasant relatives not too far from Paris stood a much better chance of obtaining provisions. The less fortunate needed all their wits to survive. As during the Occupation, you had to resort to '*le Système D*' – the D standing for *débrouiller*, getting yourself out of trouble by any means necessary. This encompassed everything from raising rabbits and hens to dealing on the black market, selling items stolen from work, and, above all, avoiding the cash economy. Almost everyone exchanged goods and services. Prostitutes, garage mechanics, plumbers and artisans rarely received payment in cash. Even factory-workers were often given produce from the factory in lieu of wages. It was not surprising that the government had such trouble in collecting taxes.

Penury afflicted those on fixed incomes as well as industrial workers. Outside the Ritz, the wife of an American diplomat who threw away a half-smoked cigarette was deeply embarrassed to see a well-dressed old man pounce upon it. There was even a trade in cigarette butts, sold in tens. Those on low salaries defended themselves as best they could. Conductors on over-crowded trains required a tip if they were to find you a seat, a practice which provoked members of the middle class to complain that this was extortion.

Certain shopkeepers, especially butchers, were notorious for increasing their profits by holding back supplies and offering them to richer customers. 'If you want some entrecôte, Madame, there is some – *au prix fort*.' At Barbizon, outside Paris, half a dozen of the best properties were bought up by butchers. One butcher, visiting a house for sale, offered three and a half million francs in used notes on condition that the owners were out by the next day. In January 1946, the Minister of Supply ordered the Prefect of Police to arrest four leading members of the Syndicat de la Boucherie, but this was little more than a gesture.

The greatest scandal of all, at a time when the wine ration was only three litres per adult per month, concerned the disappearance of large quantities of wine imported by the Ministry of Supply from Algeria. As usual, the law-abiding saw little wine, while everyone else profited – from those who registered at several wine shops to multiply their ration, or kept a dead relative on the books ('The dead generally take their drink dry,' remarked the secretary-general of the Confédération des Agriculteurs), right up to the major wholesalers who are alleged to have made huge profits selling the produce abroad. The Minister of

Supply, Yves Farge, sacked all forty members of the directorate dealing with wine, but their faults probably stemmed more from inexperience than deliberate wrongdoing. The *épuration administrative* had removed many competent officials; their places had been often taken by candidates with a good Resistance record but little aptitude for the job.

The affair grew fast, implicating more and more prominent names from the Socialist Party until even the former Prime Minister, Félix Gouin, was dragged into it. The only people who really benefited from the great Wine Scandal of 1946 were the press, who had a field day.*

Almost everyone caught with black-market produce claimed that he was the father of a large family and was just trying to feed his starving little ones. Many no doubt spoke the truth, but at least half the population seemed to be pilfering or dealing in one form or another. A gang of schoolboys at the Lycée Condorcet – their chief was thirteen and a half years old – was found to be buying chewing-gum in bulk from the Americans and selling it at huge profits. The group's treasurer was caught with 10,000 francs on him.

Nobody stuck scrupulously to their own trade when they could get hold of something else to re-sell '*au prix fort*'. Galtier-Boissière's barber offered him American chocolate for 800 francs. A couple of days later, his wife Charlotte told him that she had at last managed to get hold of some fish.

'Where was that?'

'At the butcher I go to.'

Those with good connections in the catering trade always managed to survive. During the Occupation, for example, Roland Petit's ballet troupe, whose star was Zizi Jeanmaire, were fed

---

*Félix Gouin sued Farge for the allegations in his book *Le Pain de la corruption*, but lost the case in March 1948, a setback which finished off any lingering political ambitions.

free at the restaurant in Les Halles owned by Petit's father, who was immensely proud of his son's success. Diplomats, senior officers and officials with cars and a petrol allowance found a farmer as their regular supplier, and drove out at weekends to buy supplies of eggs and butter and perhaps a ham. They did not even bother to hide their purchases; for cars, especially official vehicles, were seldom stopped.

Diplomats certainly did not undergo any hardships. 'I'm suffering today from a baby hangover,' wrote one guest after a party at the Turkish Embassy. 'The Turk did us proud – the board over-groaned. I would have been ashamed *"en pleine révolution"*, for that is how these days are referred to here – to show such langoustes, such pink foie gras – oysters in such quantities – only wings and breasts of chicken floating in a Turkish cream of nuts.'

A few people were shamelessly flippant about the situation. Noël Coward described in his diary a dinner for the Duke and Duchess of Windsor: 'I gave them a delicious dinner: consommé, marrow on toast, grilled langouste, tournedos with sauce béarnaise, and chocolate soufflé. Poor starving France.' Some found such attitudes hard to forgive. Yves Montand, singing in Le Club des Cinq, was so angered when a customer just below the stage ordered a whole lobster, picked at it, then ground out his cigar in the half-eaten carcass, that he punched him.

Resentment was fuelled because there were three sets of rules, one for the poor, one for the rich and another for the Americans and British. Smart Parisians with places in the country were able to supplement the tiny meat ration by bringing back game to the city. Since few deer had been culled after the surrender of firearms under the Occupation, large supplies of venison were available provided you could lay hands on ammunition. Every shot had to count, since the ration was twenty cartridges a year. A woman in Paris was overjoyed to discover two boxes of pre-war cartridges under a pile of books in her attic. She was able to convert these, via a complicated barter with a friend who was a first-class shot, into 'two pheasants, a kilo of butter and a roast of veal'.

The British and Americans were even more privileged in the winter of 1946, with the black-market rate reaching 250 francs to the dollar and 1,000 to the pound sterling. This was at a time when a housekeeper-cum-cook could be found for 2,500 francs a month. A number of diplomats and journalists made honourable attempts to have nothing to do with the black market. The daughter of Cy and Marina Sulzberger was not even allowed to play with the children of parents who resorted to it. Bill Patten forbade any use of the black market in his household. He explained to their cook, Madame Vallet, how to toast K ration biscuits. As soon as he had left, she went straight to Susan Mary and informed her flatly that they must use the black market, but Monsieur need not know about it.

The pressure to succumb was overwhelming when almost everybody else accepted that under *le Système D* rules were there to be broken. When Susan Mary Patten went to an employment agency to hire a maid, the *patronne* immediately said with a gleam in her eye, '*Naturellement Madame aura les provisions de l'armée américaine.*' The significance of US army rations had been obvious from the beginning, even though they came in inconvenient quantities once every six weeks – huge cans of processed vegetables, fruit juice, bacon, powdered egg, and army powdered milk known as Klim. There was little choice, but for the French it was like treasure at a time when one grapefruit cost the equivalent of four days' pay for a skilled worker. Susan Mary Patten's housekeeper 'caressed the cans, almost crying'.

In the autumn of 1946, prostitutes had an even greater need to resort to *le Système D*. To the horror of men and most of the medical profession, brothels became illegal.

Paris brothels were sometimes known as *maisons d'illusions*, the sort of euphemism which foreigners had come to expect of the city. The more technical definitions were *maisons de tolérance*, where the prostitutes lived, ate and worked; and *maisons de rendez-vous*, where 'the women come to work as prostitutes usually during the afternoon'.

The police vice squad – the Service des Mœurs – was responsible for enforcing the many regulations. Windows and shutters were to be kept closed; on the ground and first floors, the shutters had to be solid wood, not louvred; each inmate had to be registered with the police and in possession of an up-to-date medical card, or *carnet sanitaire*; and inspections had to be carried out twice a week by a designated doctor.

On 13 April 1946 the new law outlawing brothels was passed, to take effect on 6 October. One of the principal motives behind this measure had nothing to do with morals or with health. Marthe Ricard, a councillor of the Ville de Paris and one of the MRP candidates elected to the Constituent Assembly, had in fact introduced the bill ordering the expropriation of brothels and their conversion for use by impecunious students. There was a desperate shortage of accommodation for students in Paris, but this only complicated the debate over the advantages and disadvantages of registered brothels.

The main battle seems to have focused on the medical question. If official brothels were suppressed, then the 7,000 registered prostitutes would simply swell the number of 'clandestines' out on the streets, and disease would spread rapidly. But most of those who supported the measure did so because they found the old system – under which '*les pouvoirs publics organisaient la prostitution*' – morally reprehensible and open to police abuse.

For many traditionalists, the legislation was tantamount to an attack on French culture. Pierre Mac Orlan said, 'It's the foundation of a thousand-year-old civilization which is collapsing.'

Galtier-Boissière was another with a nostalgia for the gossip and banter of brothel life. His favourite *maisons de tolérance* were in the rue Sainte-Apolline and the rue Blondel, and included

Aux Belles Poules (one of the ones on the list provided for American troops) and Aux Belles Japonaises. He used to take the painter Jean Oberlé and Claude Blanchard, his great friends and colleagues on the *Crapouillot* magazine, with him. They were much less enchanted than their bear-leader, who was fascinated by Paris's underworld – *le Milieu* – and used these sorties to gather colour and dialogue for a novel. 'In most of these brothels,' wrote Oberlé, 'the inmates struck me as ghastly in appearance, violently made-up, and their gaudy silk shifts camouflaged what were in most cases sad bodies.'

Oberlé and Blanchard were much happier accompanying Galtier-Boissière to the rougher *bals musettes* – to the As de Cœur in the rue des Vertus, to La Java in the Faubourg du Temple and to the Petit Balcon in the rue de Lappe. The three men would find a table and order one of the staple drinks – a *diabolo-menthe* or a glass of acidic white wine. After the end of each dance, while the musicians rested for a moment, the *patron* would shout out: '*Passons la monnaie!*' and go round to collect the coins, dropping them in a bag round his waist. Once he had made the collection, he would call up to the three musicians in their balcony – accordionist, banjo-player and harpist: '*Allez, roulez!*' And off the couples would go in another waltz or a java. Prostitutes taking a break from their pitch on the street would push past the tables to dance a few circuits of the well-waxed parquet floor purely for pleasure, not to find custom.

Any illusion in the summer of 1946 that France had come through the worst was shattered a few months later, during a winter often described as the worst of the century. For many, the memory of the cold far outlasted memories of hunger. The disastrous shortages of heating fuel – some areas received only a third or a quarter of their allocation – left schools as well as offices unheated. Children had such bad chilblains that they could not write, and secretaries in the Quai d'Orsay could only type wearing mittens. Nancy Mitford was unable to work at home. She wrote to Gaston Palewski – the telephones were not functioning – begging three or four logs because her hands were so cold she could hardly hold a pen. 'Every breath is like a sword,' she wrote to one of her sisters.

In the need to cut electricity consumption, all illuminated signs were forbidden, shop windows left unlit and street lights turned off arbitrarily. In fact so little warning was given of power cuts that, in hospitals, surgeons in mid-operation frequently found themselves abandoned in darkness.

Once again connections helped, even when unintended. Susan Mary Patten was deeply embarrassed when an American general, having noticed a chilblain on one of her fingers during a dinner at the Windsors' overheated house, sent round the next morning a work-party of German prisoners-of-war to unload a truck of coal for her.

The vicious circle continued. Blizzards halted coal production and trains bringing fuel. Pipes froze, burst, poured forth and refroze in huge icicles. 'I never saw anything like the burst pipes in this town,' wrote Nancy Mitford to her sister Diana, 'every house a waterfall.'

Each morning dozens of small children, well wrapped-up except for their knees blue above thick socks, set off to buy milk, clutching metal billycans. The threat of tuberculosis meant that the milk was boiled in a huge metal vat set up in the *laiterie*, and the shopkeeper poured the steaming milk ration into the can with a ladle which held exactly one litre.

Rationing in times of great shortages will always create a black market, and there are all too many examples of its counterproductive effects in France. One of the most shocking could be found in Brittany fishing ports, where trawler-owners could make more money from selling their allocation of fuel on the black market than by sending their boats to sea.

On the other hand, a failure to maintain rationing would

have triggered dangerous unrest and brought down any government which attempted to follow such a course. The inequalities
were far more terrible in France than they were in Britain,
where the rationing system as a whole was more thoroughly and
effectively applied. It could be argued, however, that the effi-
ciency of the system contributed greatly to Britain's slow economic recovery afterwards.

The French economy, with its unofficial slide towards the free
market which caused such misery, found itself in a much better
position to take off in 1949 once foreign aid arrived in sufficient
quantity to kick-start commercial activity. 'It's a triumph for
private enterprise,' wrote Diana Cooper, 'although in the long
run they may succumb from immorality.'

25
Fighting Back against the Communists

'It looks as though the Communists are having everything their own way everywhere,' wrote the British ambassador in 1946. 'They have the great advantage of knowing what they want.' This belief was widespread, but not entirely true. French Communist leaders were still receiving remarkably few instructions from Moscow, and they had been lulled into a false sense of security by their comparative successes within the democratic system.

Communist strength on paper appeared almost overwhelming. Benoît Frachon, during his secret conversations with Suslov in Moscow in June, claimed over five and a half million members in the Communist-controlled trades-union movement. Even if this figure was inflated, his assertion that 'through the CGT, the French Communist Party influences the working class' was largely true.

The French Communists, however, did their best to hide their control of the CGT, as a senior member of the party acknowledged in a letter to the Kremlin. 'After the CGT Congress we ended up with a committee of seven communists and six reformers. This was conditioned by our situation: we must not hand ammunition to our reactionary enemies allowing them to describe the CGT as Communist.'

In his report to Suslov, Frachon did not paint a very optimistic picture. It is of course possible that this was a defensive measure after Ponomarev's demand that the party intervene in the running of the French zone of Germany. Communist influence within the army was 'very weak', Frachon told him. The army was 'full of Vichyists', which explained 'the reactionary policy of the French military administration in Germany and Austria'. He then added that whatever the influences within the army, 'I do not believe that the reactionary forces are planning to use the army against us in a *coup d'état*.'

De Gaulle's increasingly palpable presence in the political wings began to alarm both the left and the centre. After the speech at Bayeux in June 1946, the General permitted René Capitant to found the Union Gaulliste. It was a way of testing the waters without risking his own dignity. This prototype virtually collapsed under its own sudden success, attracting half a million members and twenty-two members of the Constituent Assembly by September. The Communists renewed their accusations that '*le général factieux*' wished to return as a dictator. The Christian Democrats of the MRP also began to worry that the Gaullists might poach their supporters.

Bidault, the MRP's first Prime Minister, hoped to make an alliance with de Gaulle; but the General had not forgiven his party's weakness during the ministerial crisis of November 1945.

De Gaulle concentrated his ire upon the proposed new Constitution, which he denounced in a scathing communiqué through Agence France-Presse on 20 December. Nine days later the draft was voted through the Assembly. Refusing to give in, de Gaulle spoke a few hours later at Épinal, urging French voters to reject it. '*Franchement non!*' he exclaimed. 'Such a compromise does not appear to us to be a framework worthy of the Republic.' Compromise, in de Gaulle's canon, was still a mortal sin.

Ironically, de Gaulle was making the same mistake as the Communists had made in May: he was turning the referendum on the Constitution into a vote for or against himself. When polling booths closed on 13 October, there were three million more abstentions than in May, but the draft Constitution for the

Fourth Republic was approved. The General was undeterred. Only 35 per cent of those eligible to vote had supported it, so he decided to plan his own mass movement.

Bidault's government resigned after more legislative elections on 10 November in which the Communists once again won the greatest number of seats. Their share of the total vote had increased to 29 per cent. Maurice Thorez, as leader of '*le premier parti de France*', demanded to be Prime Minister.

The Socialist Party faced a most uncomfortable dilemma, made worse by Thorez's studied moderation as he lobbied for support with dignity and charm. One of their leaders is said to have burst out in sobs: 'I'd prefer to slash my wrists than vote for Thorez!' But Gouin argued that they had no option, otherwise they would lose all credibility: the workers would not understand their supporting Bidault, a Christian Democrat, then refusing to support a Communist. Yet he was certain that, even with their support, Thorez would never receive the absolute majority necessary. Vincent Auriol, a wise and experienced Socialist of the old school, agreed with Gouin.

They were proved right when the vote took place on 4 December. Thorez had made his bid and lost. Jacques Duclos, defending Thorez's candidature in the National Assembly a few days later, made an uncharacteristic blunder when he lauded him as 'a man who has stood the test of battle'. The non-Communist benches erupted with laughter at this description of France's most famous deserter. The Communist deputies could only sit there, stony-faced and furious. After Thorez, it was Bidault's turn, but he received even fewer votes.

A week later, Blum having resigned, President Auriol selected Paul Ramadier to form an administration – having first made a show of asking Félix Gouin, as an expression of confidence after the wine scandal. Ramadier, with his goatee beard and fussy professorial air, provided an easy target for caricaturists. He was known as a man of compromise, and for being painstakingly slow to reach a decision; but he was untainted by ambition, and scrupulously honest in a profession not renowned for its probity. He had accepted the post of Minister of Supply in de Gaulle's government, knowing that it would make him unpopular. He was also a hard worker, often at his desk soon after four in the morning. When he began to telephone his ministers a little later, he was surprised to find them still in bed.

The American Embassy, however, was deeply disturbed when the new Prime Minister nominated the Communist François Billoux as Minister of National Defence. The fact that Ramadier managed to restrict Billoux's position to a largely symbolic role by strengthening the three service ministries was overlooked by most of his critics on the right.

Caffery had become much more alarmist in the course of the last nine months. In March, after a wave of strikes which included the newspaper unions and the Paris police, he warned the Secretary of State that while the Communists were not strong enough to 'align France with the Soviets against the West', the country could be denied to the Western powers. 'Communist armed action combined with paralysing strikes, sabotage and other subversive activities would certainly prepare the way for Soviet intervention on a scale larger even than was the case in the Spanish Civil War.' Not all Americans saw the strikes in such dramatic terms. 'The French enjoyed having the police on strike,' wrote Susan Mary Patten to a friend, 'and had a lot of fun driving up one-way streets the wrong way. The cook says good riddance. The police were just a band of assassins anyway.'

The Communists, from the other side of the fence, were equally suspicious of developments. The Franco-British pact which they opposed so resolutely came into effect on 4 March as the Treaty of Dunkirk, a place chosen by Bidault to symbolize the darkest moment of the war. For Socialists such as Blum and Depreux, it signified a counter-balance to the Franco-Soviet pact signed by de Gaulle. Afterwards Duff Cooper, who had worked long and hard for this expression of friendship between the two countries, felt able to write in his diary: '*Nunc dimittis*'. He had achieved his principal aim in his last job.

Six days later the Foreign Ministers of the Big Four – General Marshall, Bidault, Bevin and Molotov – met in Moscow. Only Marshall and Bevin knew that post-war relations were about to take a decisive turn. For Bidault, the Moscow conference represented a Soviet betrayal. He felt he had behaved most correctly with Molotov, but the Soviet Foreign Minister, having encouraged his hopes that the Saar would be given to France, refused to support her claim in a volte-face which humiliated Bidault personally. He did not forget this. Molotov was equally unforgiving. He regarded the Treaty of Dunkirk as a move aimed directly against the Soviet Union.

General George C. Marshall, one of the most honest and selfless of all American public servants, had become Secretary of State on 21 January 1947. He was not a 'hawk', but he was more resolute than James Byrnes and a thorough pragmatist. He expected 'brutal candour' from his staff, and assured them that he had no feelings 'except those which I reserve for Mrs Marshall'.

At the end of February, the State Department was warned by the British ambassador in Washington that the collapse of Britain's economy meant that no further support could be provided to Greece, then in the midst of civil war, or to Turkey, still threatened by Soviet probing on its north-eastern frontier. President Truman summoned a conference with Congressional leaders in the White House on the morning of Wednesday, 26 February. As a mark of how far things had changed, the most passionate advocate of American intervention to thwart the Soviet threat came from Marshall's deputy, Dean Acheson – the same man who had been appalled by the plan to move troops into France the previous May. 'When we were convened to open the subject,' Acheson wrote dramatically, 'I knew we were met at Armageddon.'

'Soviet pressure on the Straits [the Dardanelles],' he told the Congressmen, 'on Iran and on northern Greece had brought the Balkans to the point where a highly possible Soviet breakthrough might open three continents to Soviet penetration. Like apples in a barrel infected by one rotten one, the corruption of Greece would infect Iran and all to the east. It would also carry infection to Africa through Asia Minor and Egypt, and to Europe through Italy and France, already threatened by the strongest domestic Communist parties in Western Europe.' After Acheson had finished speaking, 'a long silence followed'. Then Senator Vandenberg said solemnly, 'Mr President, if you will say that to the Congress and the country, I will support you and I believe that most of its members will do the same.'

Predictions of conflict beween the United States and the Soviet Union were developing into a self-fulfilling prophecy on both sides. Few in Washington doubted that 'a major turning point in American history was taking place'. On 12 March President Truman addressed the House of Representatives. 'I believe that it must be the policy of the United States to support free peoples who are resisting attempted subjugation by armed minorities or by outside pressure. I believe that we must assist free peoples to work out their own destinies in their own way ...' This statement soon became known as the Truman Doctrine.

In France, a 'new resistance' to Communist infiltration had become apparent before Truman's speech. Ministers were beginning to reverse the tide in several ministries as well as in the Paris police.

The Socialist Minister of the Interior, Édouard Depreux, a great admirer of Léon Blum, exploited every opportunity to reduce Communist influence in the administration. He had removed the Communist prefect of the Haut-Vienne from office in July 1946, having arranged financial compensation. His greatest preoccupation, however, remained the Paris police, which the Communists had infiltrated during and after the Liberation. Depreux blamed Charles Luizet, the Prefect of Police appointed by de Gaulle in August 1944, for not having done enough to counter the process. His chance came when a scandal blew up involving that notorious double-dealer Joanovici,* who had been bribing police officers by playing poker with them and losing most generously. Joanovici, who had testified against his former comrades in the Bony–Lafont gang, had been as happy to make money with the Communists as with the Nazis. The minister promptly gave orders for the arrest of two leading Communists in the police who had links with him, a risky course, with the lack of evidence at the time. The Communist press exploded in anger, but Depreux kept his nerve.

His other move was to replace Luizet by Roger Léonard, a strong anti-Communist reputed to be a 'very effective administrator'. During the Occupation, Léonard had been a Vichy official, but was fortunate to have been sacked by his superiors early enough to escape the attentions of a purge committee at the time of the Liberation. Just to be sure, the American Embassy reported, he had even pretended to be a fellow-traveller 'for reasons of temporary political opportunism'.

Forcing back the inroads of Communist infiltration was just one side of Depreux's strategy. What he and his colleagues feared most was an attempted coup from the right, which would allow the Communists to cast themselves as the saviours of Republican liberty. Depreux knew that, above all, he must not allow himself to be portrayed as purely anti-Communist. He therefore made conspicuous moves against right-wing plotters,

---

*Joanovici was a Bessarabian Jew who had come to France in 1925, where he built up a successful scrap-metal business. During Depreux's investigations, Joanovici was arrested, but then released. He fled to the American zone of Germany in 1947. He was finally put on trial in 1949, condemned to five years in prison and fined 600,000 francs.

including such cynical manoeuvres as the arrest of a group of priests and nuns who had been sheltering collaborators.

Depreux and his colleagues had good reason to be worried about a plot from the right playing into the hands of the Communists. In May 1947, the American Embassy was informed that two colonels from the US army in Germany had been offering to arm rightist groups. This shadowy affair was hushed up. Depreux, however, made another plot public, a conspiracy known as the '*Plan Bleu*', because the document was on blue paper.

The police had been amassing evidence for several months, but Depreux waited for the right moment before making anything public. The opportunity came in June 1947, shortly after the Communists left Ramadier's government. Depreux's timing of the announcement that a plot against the Republic had been thwarted was aimed at elements within his own party; the left wing of the Socialist Party wanted to attack the anti-Communist stance of their ministers.

The details of the plot itself were too sketchy to be really convincing. It apparently involved General Guillaudot, the Inspector-General of the Gendarmerie Nationale, and several veteran anti-Communists including Loustaunau-Lacau, the only member of the Resistance to have testified on behalf of Marshal Pétain. General de Larminat was also suspended from his duties on grounds of suspected collusion. The uprising against the government was supposed to start in Brittany, where small groups would seize arms depots and American stores to equip rebel formations. 'At the same time four tactical groups, one of them armoured, would have advanced on Paris.'

Caffery feared that Depreux had overplayed his hand. His dramatic version of the plot had allowed the Communists to exploit the 'plot to [a] maximum, smearing all present and potential anti-Communist elements – General de Larminat, General Koenig, General de Gaulle and even widening the attack to include the MRP, "party of the Cassocks and the reactionary West".'

Depreux's next move, ten days later, was to deprive the Compagnie Républicaine de Sécurité, the riot police, of its light machine-guns and mortars. The CRS had a strong Communist presence, through party members from the Resistance who had joined from the FFI. The French Communist Party immediately denounced this measure as an attempt to leave the Republic defenceless against would-be military dictators.

François Mitterrand, the new minister for Anciens Combattants et Victimes de la Guerre, also impressed many by the stamina and effectiveness of his efforts to reduce Communist control within his jurisdiction. This had grown up during Laurent Casanova's time in the ministry.

In the Ministry of War, the Communists' chief enemy, General Revers, managed to resist all the calls for his removal from the post of Chief of Staff of the French army. Revers, while punctiliously polite to the new Minister of National Defence, swiftly removed Communists or fellow-travellers from sensitive appointments. He also purged the Gendarmerie Nationale, which came under the Ministry's control. Of the 2,000 army officers, mainly from the FFI, who were regarded as Communists or fellow-travellers, many had already been sidelined through such devices as the so-called 'Opération de Tarbes'. This simply involved posting officers of left-wing sympathies to outposts like Tarbes in the Pyrenees, where they languished in non-existent jobs with no access to confidential information.

March 1947 was an eventful month in Paris as well as in Washington. On the very day that Truman addressed Congress, the French Communist Party found itself in a difficult position on the issue of Indo-China, where fighting had broken out the previous December between French forces and Ho Chi Minh's followers led by General Giap. Moscow's instructions on the subject were explicit. Communist deputies had to support the

Viet-Minh and oppose the policy established by Admiral Thierry d'Argenlieu.

On 18 March, the Assembly stood in silence in memory of the French servicemen killed in Indo-China. François Billoux, the Communist Minister of National Defence, remained seated. This immediately became an issue of patriotism.

The more the Communists were isolated, the more they drew in upon themselves. Communist speeches in the National Assembly took up the most time not so much because of their content, but because their deputies, forming a claque, would applaud their leaders' speeches at every pause. One cynic remarked that their hands were hard not from manual labour, but from clapping.

A number of factors encouraged General de Gaulle to return to the political arena in the spring of 1947. One of the most immediate was Ramadier's appointment of Billoux as Minister of National Defence. De Gaulle's sense of destiny – he once said that each day he spent several minutes wondering how his actions would be seen by history – told him that the people of France would recall him to power very soon.

To the relief of his supporters, de Gaulle began to spend more and more time in Paris. They dreaded the three-hour drive out to Colombey-les-deux-Églises. The atmosphere of the house, La Boisserie, was as lugubrious as its setting. There the chain-smoking General worked on his memoirs, surrounded by wartime memorabilia, his collection of swords, and signed photographs of former world leaders, while 'Madame de Gaulle clicked away with her knitting needles as the rain battered against the windows'.

In Paris, de Gaulle established his headquarters at La Pérouse, the hotel near the Arc de Triomphe which his wartime secret service had used as its first headquarters at the Liberation. On Sunday, 30 March 1947, he made a speech at Bruneval in Normandy, the site of a commando raid during the war. As an

11. Scandalized women in the rue Lepic tear the New Look from a Dior model, spring 1947.

12. The street-market in the rue de Menilmontant.

13. Opening the Communist-backed exhibition *Art et Résistance* – Elsa Triolet, Louis Aragon, General Petit, Picasso, Charles Tillon, Laurent Casanova.

14. Fighting in the coalfields.

15. The dramatist Jacques Audiberti outside the Théâtre de la Huchette.

16. Dancers in the basement of the Vieux-Colombier.

17. Juliette Gréco, Anne-Marie Cazalis and Marc Doelnitz reading of their sudden fame outside the Café de Flore.

18. The Marshall Plan reaches Paris. David Bruce signing, watched by Jacques Dumaine, with Robert Schuman and Jefferson Caffrey in the background.

19. Picasso's portrait of Stalin, which caused such outrage within the Communist Party.

official commemoration, the meeting attracted the presence of the British and Canadian ambassadors as well as detachments from their countries' armed forces. Yet the idea for this event had come from Colonel Rémy, as a way of assembling former members of the Resistance under de Gaulle's new banner. Ramadier was exasperated, but any attempt by the government to restrict the 'Liberator' – as the Gaullists called their leader – looked churlish. The Communists meanwhile claimed his audiences were composed of 'ladies in mink coats and old colonels smelling of mothballs'.

De Gaulle finally decided to go ahead with the plan for creating a mass movement, the Rassemblement du Peuple Français. '*On va refaire la France Libre*' was a popular cry among his wartime associates, '*les hommes de Londres*'. But their tendency to refer to the new movement by its initials, the RPF, displeased the General. That sounded like yet another of the political parties he loathed so much. He insisted on calling it '*le Rassemblement*'.

The creation of the RPF was announced to the people of France at Strasbourg on 7 April. Soustelle set up the first group in the capital of Alsace that evening. A week later, the movement was officially registered. The Strasbourg celebrations were again linked to a semi-official event which drew the American ambassador, Jefferson Caffery, from Paris. He and de Gaulle inspected a guard of honour together, which confirmed Communist suspicions. But both French and Russian Communists were wrong to assume that Caffery's attendance signalled that the American government was planning to back de Gaulle. In normal circumstances Caffery always punctiliously refused to meet de Gaulle, making an exception only for occasions such as this.

A propaganda struggle had meanwhile broken out at a wonderfully trivial level. When Nancy Mitford had wanted to dedicate her unexpectedly successful novel *The Pursuit of Love* to her adored 'Colonel', he had been flattered and told her to put his full name in the dedication, not just his initials. He regretted this bitterly when the Communists realized that Nancy Mitford was the sister of Unity Mitford. In February, a Communist publication produced an inaccurate article under the equally inaccurate headline, 'Sister of Hitler's mistress dedicates daring book to M. Palewski'. It was followed by several other pieces. Palewski, fearing the General's wrath, persuaded Nancy to go abroad until the fuss died down. She obediently departed into temporary exile, and wrote to him from Madrid in the middle of April, 'Like the Archangel Gabriel, you chase me away from heavenly Paris.' But to turn the tables on the Communists, she said she would dedicate her next book to Jacques Duclos – 'Let him laugh that one off.'

By the end of April the Socialist Prime Minister, Paul Ramadier, had come to think that it might be possible after all to govern without the Communists. The end of *tripartisme* was accelerated by the contradiction of Communist deputies voting against the government in which their own leaders were ministers. Ramadier, with studied courtesy, insisted on the principle of collective responsibility within a government.

On 25 April, an unofficial strike at the Renault factories spread with great speed, taking the Communists by surprise. They accused Trotskyists of fomenting trouble, but the strike became so popular that Communist leaders had to shift their position if they were to retain any credibility among the workers. The party's politburo denounced the government's refusal to raise wages. Thorez, the Vice-President of the government, did not worry about such a flagrant paradox. He refused to believe that Ramadier contemplated an administration without Communist ministers.

He was not alone in this attitude. Gaullists were certain that the Socialists would find it impossible to continue. This led them to the optimistic notion that the resulting crisis could be solved only by their leader sweeping back to power. Left-wing Socialists, meanwhile, never imagined that such a momentous step could be taken without their agreement.

Bidault, on his return from Moscow, did not hide his feelings about Molotov and Stalin in front of his Communist colleagues in the Council of Ministers. Thorez promptly voiced his support for Stalin and rejected the government communiqué. On the eve of the 1 May demonstration, Ramadier summoned General Revers. He asked him to put the army on a discreet state of alert and to prepare military transport in case a general strike took place. Armoured vehicles from the 2e DB were brought in from Rambouillet and concealed in the École de Guerre.

The decisive day came on Sunday, 4 May. The Communists had formally withdrawn support from the government's policy of freezing wages, so Ramadier had called a vote of confidence in the National Assembly. Supported by the Christian Democrat MRP, he won by a strong margin – 360 votes to 186. Soon after nine o'clock that evening, Communist ministers were summoned to a meeting of the Council of Ministers at the prime ministerial residence, the Hôtel Matignon. Ramadier was polite, but inflexible. Thorez refused to resign, so Ramadier read out the section of the Constitution which gave him the right to withdraw portfolios. Thorez and his four colleagues left the room. The remaining ministers sat there, astonished at how easy it had been.

This realignment was not limited to France. In Belgium, Communist ministers had left the government in March; while in Italy, they had been forced out in April. Western Europe was clearly entering a new stage.

Paul Ramadier had a less exacting duty to perform six days later – the presentation of the Médaille Militaire to Winston Churchill. The Médaille Militaire is France's highest military decoration, and can be presented only by a man who already holds it. Ramadier was an impeccable choice, having won the decoration as a sergeant during the defence of Verdun.

Churchill, dressed in the uniform of his old regiment, the 4th Hussars, was met at the entrance to the great courtyard of the Invalides by a small guard of soldiers with fixed bayonets. He was then marched forward to where Ramadier awaited him with a whole battalion, drawn up in review order. Churchill wept with emotion during Ramadier's speech.

That evening, President Auriol organized a dinner in Churchill's honour at the Élysée Palace. 'Churchill,' wrote Jacques Dumaine in his diary, 'his tail-coat plastered with decorations and a cigar sprouting from the middle of his smile, strolled down the Faubourg Saint-Honoré on his way to the banquet. This was a sight which brought everyone to their windows, and cheering broke out as he passed.' The old statesman was thrilled by the apocryphal story that any holder of the Médaille Militaire, if incapacitated by drink, had the right to be driven home without charge by the police.

The next day, Churchill received a rousing welcome from the crowds at the march-past at Vincennes celebrating the second anniversary of Germany's defeat. Afterwards, Duff Cooper took him off to lunch at the Château de Saint-Firmin at Chantilly. There, he met Odette Pol Roger, one of General Wallace's three daughters who were so famed for their beauty that they were known as the Wallace Collection. Madame Pol Roger became Churchill's last flame.

Ramadier's government had also offered a Médaille Militaire to General de Gaulle, but he had refused it brusquely. He also refused Auriol's invitation to the dinner in Churchill's honour. Although he could not admit it, Ramadier's effective stand against the Communists had exasperated him. He refused to change his tune, however. 'Make no mistake,' he said to Claude Mauriac, 'we are right into a Weimar Republic.'

De Gaulle's pact with Stalin three years before had blackened him in the eyes of many potential followers on the right. But at Rennes on 27 July he openly attacked the 'separatists'. He described the French Communist Party as 'a group of men whose leaders place the service of a foreign state above every-thing else. I say this all the more forcefully because I myself have tried, up to the limits of the lawful and possible, to attract them to the service of France.'

While de Gaulle compared Ramadier's administration to Weimar, the Communists compared RPF mass meetings to the Nuremberg rally. Nancy Mitford went to the Vélodrome d'Hiver on 2 July to see her adored 'Colonel' speak to a huge crowd. Palewski was a far greater success than anyone expected. Claude Mauriac wrote that 'he was suddenly transfigured'. Malraux followed. His speech began in its habitual way, difficult to understand, but then 'finding its rhythm little by little, as a torrent finds its bed. And then emerged a great prophetic voice which electrified the whole audience, the voice of a sage, of a poet, of a religious leader.'

26

The Self-Fulfilling Prophecy

On Saturday 7 June 1947, the American Secretary of State, General Marshall, made a speech at Harvard on receiving an honorary degree. Never has a short reply of thanks at a university had such significance. Marshall, without fully warning his officials, had decided that this was the moment to make the most important foreign policy statement of the post-war era.

The terrible winter of 1946 had revealed Europe's inability to raise itself out of penury. Economic collapse was imminent, with political disaster almost certainly close behind. Marshall declared that the United States must make a huge effort to combat 'hunger, poverty, desperation and chaos'. But the initiative 'must come from Europe', because 'it would be neither fitting nor efficacious for this Government to undertake to draw up unilaterally a program designed to place Europe on its feet economically'.

The message behind General Marshall's speech at Harvard had a wide parenthood, including Eisenhower, Jean Monnet and Dean Acheson; but the formulation, which brilliantly avoided all the mines in such a dangerous field, was entirely his. Most important of all, he carefully made a point of extending the project to all of Europe, including countries occupied by the Red Army.

Marshall's brief address electrified the governments of Europe, once they grasped its significance. It offered their only hope.

Russia, laid waste by the German invasion, was in no state to help. France had no currency reserves left and a balance of payments deficit of 10 billion francs. Since September 1944 it had received close to $2 billion in credits for coal, food and raw materials, but this had done no more than enable the country to survive. The Marshall Plan offered the chance to rebuild. 'Examples of such solidarity are very rare in history,' wrote Hervé Alphand. But behind the scenes the State Department insisted that 'the United States must run this show'.

Ernest Bevin, the British Foreign Secretary, was reputedly the first to leap at the opportunity. After a weekend of discussion and deliberation, he sent a Most Immediate and Top Secret telegram to Duff Cooper in the middle of the night instructing him to discuss the matter with Bidault in the morning. A week later Bevin himself flew over to Paris, with a large contingent of advisers from various ministries. The city was still gripped by an endless succession of strikes. After dinner at the British Embassy with Ramadier, Bidault, Massigli, Chauvel, Alphand, Marjolin and Monnet, the discussions continued. 'There was almost entire agreement on the line that we should take,' Duff Cooper wrote the next morning. 'The important thing is the approach to the Russians. They must be invited to participate and at the same time they must be given no opportunity to cause delay. This will not be easy.'

On 27 June, a conference between Bidault, Bevin and Molotov to discuss the Marshall Plan opened at the Quai d'Orsay. The air was oppressive from the heatwave which had reduced Paris to torpor, and the atmosphere was further weighed down by Molotov's suspicions. He was certain that some sort of trap had been laid for him by Bidault and Bevin at their private meeting ten days before. Soviet confidence had not been helped by an ill-judged statement for the press which had been released by the Quai d'Orsay before the Russians were told what was happening.

Bevin, despite the heat, was in excellent spirits. Molotov, as expected, used blocking tactics from the start. Bidault described his intention as '*flagrante et obstinée*'. (Molotov did not say '*Niet*' but 'No K', thinking that this was the antonym for OK.)

A great storm on the night of Saturday, 28 June broke the heat, but the atmosphere was even heavier on Monday morning. Ignoring the aims of the proposal, Molotov read a prepared statement based on a telegram which had obviously just arrived from the Kremlin, demanding that the United States government should say in advance how much it was prepared to give and whether Congress would agree.

That evening Jefferson Caffery came round to the British Embassy to compare reactions. Bevin, on Duff Cooper's urging, 'impressed upon him the importance of helping France at this juncture'. But Caffery's reply was unequivocal: if the Communists got back into the government, France wouldn't get a dollar from America. It was, as Duff Cooper put it, 'an interesting evening'.

Bevin's mind was also made up. Bidault's attempts to bridge the chasm between them and the Soviet Union were a waste of time. They would brook no further obstruction from Molotov. By the next morning, he had decided to 'go straight ahead with the French and to issue invitations to all the nations of Europe to join in'. That afternoon Duff Cooper flew to London to brief the Prime Minister, Clement Attlee. Attlee agreed with everything that Bevin was doing and asked for advice on the next step. Cooper replied that the circumstances did not require a meeting of the Cabinet, but a firm statement of support would no doubt be appreciated by the Foreign Secretary.

The conference ended abruptly on 3 July. Alphand wrote in his diary the next day, 'seeing Molotov descend the steps of the Quai d'Orsay, I said to myself that we were entering a new era which could last for a long time and even take a dangerous turn'.

No time was wasted. Twenty-two countries in Europe were invited to a conference just over a week later to formulate a European plan for presentation to the United States government.

If any government from behind the iron curtain expressed interest, that interest soon declined after pressure from Moscow. Nobody was surprised. The important point was to maintain a momentum of cooperation. 'All is going well so far,' noted the British ambassador on 7 July, 'and the Ramadier government survives.'

On 11 July, Foreign Ministers began to assemble for the conference, which took place in the dining-room of the Quai d'Orsay. The table was so long that it was impossible to hear what was said at the far end, but despite the acoustic problems Molotov's absence meant that everything was 'unanimously agreed'. Meetings often lasted less than two hours, instead of whole days. This did not necessarily mean that everyone behaved in an exemplary fashion. According to Isaiah Berlin, who had joined the British delegation on the orders of Lord Franks, the European attitude towards the American offer was that of 'lofty and demanding beggars approaching an apprehensive million-aire'. There was also a tendency to revert to national stereotype. At one point the Italian delegate exclaimed dramatically, 'If we do not get this, there will be blood on the streets of Rome!' The Swedish delegate, Dag Hammarskjöld, replied, 'Maybe you . . . er . . . exaggerate a little?'

The good weather had put Paris in a joyful mood, though the drought promised ill for the farmers and food supplies that winter. On the eve of Bastille Day, 14 July, people were dancing in the streets as Duff and Diana Cooper returned at around midnight with Pierre Balmain from a dinner at Verrières given by Louise de Vilmorin and her brothers. 'Near the Porte d'Italie our car was surrounded by a dancing crowd of young people who made a circle round us and some of them came and kissed us through the window. They were all so gay, friendly and charming. It was a warm evening and we were very happy.'

The Marshall Plan conference concluded on 15 July to every-one's satisfaction, but two causes for friction had surfaced. The

British government's attempt to maintain the limit on Jewish emigration to Palestine – this was the time of the *Exodus* affair – had brought it into conflict with the French, who had allowed the refugees to embark in southern France, despite an agreement to the contrary.

Bidault and his officials in the Quai d'Orsay were far more disturbed to hear that the Americans were planning to come to some private agreement with the British over Germany. Bevin tried to explain the state of affairs, but with little success. On returning to the embassy, he and Duff Cooper asked Caffery, and Averell Harriman who happened to be in Paris, to come round. The Americans were told that Bevin had been forced to admit that talks about Germany had been taking place, even though General Lucius Clay had 'strongly objected to any communication being made to the French on the subject'.

The next morning, 17 July, Bevin went to say goodbye to his French counterpart. 'Bidault seemed sad and tired,' wrote the British ambassador, 'but he didn't know the worst.' Only late that morning did Duff Cooper himself hear that 'an Anglo-American agreement has been concluded for the raising of the German level of industry, the handing over of management to the Germans and other things'. This, he knew, would be 'a terrible blow to the French'.

When the news was broken that afternoon to Chauvel, Alphand and Maurice Couve de Murville at the Quai d'Orsay, 'it was very badly received'. De Gaulle's fears expressed on that winter afternoon at Marly to Hervé Alphand had materialized within eighteen months. Germany, not France, was to be revived as the motor for European recovery. The next step was not hard to guess: Germany would become the centrepiece of America's counter-Soviet strategy. The Clay–Robertson agreement, as it was called after the names of the American and British military governors in Germany, provoked the headline in *L'Humanité*: 'French Mothers Must Start Trembling Again'.

*

The beautiful summer of 1947, although disastrous for agriculture, encouraged every form of hedonism in Paris. 'The season here has become giddy,' wrote Nancy Mitford, 'people are doing all sorts of things they will regret later. Someone we all know at a party the other night took off his collar and tie and revealed on *his* bronzed neck a collar of rubies, three rows, with a ruby and emerald tassel hanging down *his* back. His protector who was present remarked drily: "X is a very good chap, but we can't expect him to live on his charm for ever" (X having said, on showing the rubies, "not bad for a working girl").'

The summer also brought a fresh influx of visitors. One of them was Señora Eva Duarte de Peron, who had come on an official visit – the perfect opportunity to take Dior's New Look back to Argentina. As a matter of courtesy, the French government awarded her a minor decoration: what used to be called a 'dinner medal'. Hervé Alphand made the presentation at the Quai d'Orsay; but when Evita Peron took off her thin summer coat, she revealed a dress cut so low that Alphand simply could not decide where to pin it. Finally he opted for a point between bosom and waist.

Another visitor to Paris that summer was the film-maker Alexander Korda, who agreed to buy the film rights of Duff Cooper's book on King David for a million francs: the timing was ironic, with the author so recently embroiled in the *Exodus* crisis. After going through the draft of the Marshall Plan report with its author, Isaiah Berlin, the ambassador went out to dinner with Korda, Rita Hayworth and Cary Grant at Véfour's to celebrate the deal. 'Rita Hayworth is very pretty,' he wrote in his diary, 'but I don't like dyed yellow hair and she has beautiful hands but the nails were too long and dirty. Odd that a film star should take so little trouble.'

The most striking play of 1947 was, without doubt, Jean Genet's *Les Bonnes*. His idea of writing a play about two maids who plotted to murder their mistress dated back to the autumn of 1943. Genet denied that it was based on the notorious case of the Papin sisters before the war, and although there were superficial parallels with reality, the plot was entirely his own.

Bérard and Kochno first talked to Louis Jouvet, the great actor who was also the director of the Théâtre de l'Athénée, about Genet's play when they were all down in the Midi. Jouvet refused to consider the idea until after he returned to Paris; on his return, however, he found himself assailed by other fervent believers in the play including Cocteau and Marie-Blanche de Polignac. Cocteau handed over the manuscript 'as though it were a treasure'.

During its run from the spring, it provoked a fury among audiences and reviewers. Genet even punched the critic of *Le Figaro* for what he wrote. Sartre and other friends supported him loyally, so loyally indeed that they managed to swing the jury of the Prix de la Pléïade to give Genet the prize that year, even though he was not strictly eligible.

The *famille Sartre* was less well disposed towards André Breton, who, since his return to France, had started with Marcel Duchamp to organize a second international exhibition of Surrealism in Paris at the new Galerie Maeght. He planned to build a staircase with each step modelled as the cover of a book whose titles were linked to the Tarot pack. There would be a '*salle de superstitions*' and another room beyond with a dozen octagonal cells, each dedicated to a sign of the zodiac and containing a voodoo altar. The last room would be a kitchen serving 'a surrealist meal, above all distinguished by a new taste'.

Breton and his Surrealist friends completed the preparatory work for the exhibition during the first week of July. When Madame Maeght, the owner of the gallery, saw what they had done, she screamed: 'We're ruined!' But the exhibition attracted huge crowds, and, instead, the Galerie Maeght was made. Soon the Maeghts were exhibiting Braque, Miró and Chagall; and, most important of all, they obtained a monopoly on Giacometti's work by paying for all his casting.*

The exhibition included works by Max Ernst, Miró and Tanguy, but Breton was forced to conclude that the Surrealist movement as a whole showed little sign of life, except perhaps in Romania and Czechoslovakia. He took comfort, however, from the controversy which the exhibition had provoked over three months. 'It's wonderful,' he said, 'to be so reviled at our age.'

Since the Communist ministers left Ramadier's government in May, a dangerous air of unreality had affected the party leadership. Thorez and his colleagues continued to speak and act as though their removal from government was simply a temporary setback. They had been partially seduced by the trappings and self-importance of ministerial rank, but an equally important influence was a gut instinct that *tripartisme* must be resumed: only by working from within could the party come to power. But the real problem lay elsewhere. The lack of firm direction from Moscow had allowed them to lapse into a false sense of security. Even Thorez and Duclos, with all their experience of the Kremlin's capricious logic, had half-forgotten what Stalin's absolute priority – the Soviet Union before everything – could do to subordinate foreign parties. They were soon to be brutally awakened.

In September 1947 nine European Communist parties received invitations from Warsaw to send delegations to a secret meeting. The real organizer of this conference was Andrei Zhdanov, who had ruthlessly directed the defence of Leningrad against the Germans. On 22 September the delegations arrived at a large hunting-lodge at Sklarska Poreba in south-west Poland.

---

*Aimé and Marguerite Maeght had made their first lucrative deals in the art world by bartering food for paintings during the Occupation (Marguerite's parents were in the grocery business). In this way, they were able to acquire a number of works by Bonnard and Matisse.

Only two of them, the French and the Italians, came from outside the Soviet bloc. They included neither Thorez, nor the Italian Communist leader Palmiro Togliatti. Jacques Duclos, who was accompanied by Étienne Fajon, arrived in affable, even self-satisfied form. As a veteran of international Communist conferences, he seems to have been confident that he would acquit himself satisfactorily.

Zhdanov put this secret meeting in its international context, from the dissolution of the Comintern in May 1943. He made no mention of the Comintern's successor organization, the International Section of the Soviet Central Committee Secretariat. Clearly it was more convenient, in view of the abrupt change of party line about to be revealed, to pretend that there had been virtually no further contact between Moscow and its satellite parties. Zhdanov nevertheless argued that 'such a separation between parties is bad and harmful and, basically, is not natural'. In other words the *laisser-aller* of the immediate post-war period had come to an end.

It is astonishing that Jacques Duclos, a veteran of the Comintern, did not perceive the full implications of Zhdanov's speech. When called upon to speak, his account of the French Communist Party's activities since the Liberation was complacent in the extreme. Zhdanov left the ritual humiliation of the French Communist Party to the Yugoslav delegation, of Edvard Kardelj and Milovan Djilas. Duclos was horrified at the depth of the trap into which he had fallen. His only chance was to grovel without hesitation.

The point of the conference was already clear. Zhdanov, on Stalin's orders, was setting up a neo-Comintern, to be called the Cominform, to mobilize foreign Communist parties to defend the Soviet Union against a reconstituted Germany and the economic backing to an American hegemony in Europe – the 'Plan Truman–Marshall'. 'France has sacrificed half of its autonomy,' claimed Zhdanov, 'because the credits offered it by the United States in March 1947 were conditional upon the elimination of the Communists from the government.'* France and England were therefore 'the victims of American blackmail'.

Zhdanov quoted their leader. 'Comrade Stalin has said: "In short, the policy of the Soviet Union to the German problem boils down to the demilitarization and the democratization of Germany. These are the most important conditions for installing a lasting and solid peace." This policy of the Soviet Union towards Germany meets the frenetic resistance of the imperialist circles in the United States and England. America has broken with Roosevelt's old course and is switching to a new policy – to a policy of preparing new military adventures.'

Duclos returned to Paris shaken and angry. Soon after his arrival, a meeting of the French politburo was called to discuss the débâcle. Duclos summed up the conclusions: 'Zhdanov said that whether Communists were in government or in opposition was a problem of no interest, and we had been far too preoccupied with it. The only objective is to destroy the capitalist economy and systematically to unify the living forces of the nation. In future the Kremlin will be completely indifferent to whether or not Communists are in or out of government, but all parties must fight against economic aid from the United States. He also insisted on the need to destabilize the government.'

Thorez must have had to suppress a grim smile when remembering Stalin's personal instruction not to rock de Gaulle's boat, and the subsequent approval of their policy from Ponomarev. But he, like Duclos, was too old a hand to complain. There was no time to be wasted. The whole of the French party had to be turned round. Even if they won in the next elections, they could

---

* Even though Caffery revealed to Bevin and Duff Cooper that France would almost certainly not receive economic aid if Communists were allowed to become ministers again, there is absolutely no evidence to support the assertion that Ramadier was blackmailed by the US government into expelling them from his administration.

not even contemplate entering government because it would 'look too much like a compromise'.

The Cominform was to be based in Belgrade 'to avoid problems', such as the 'calumny' that the Kremlin controlled foreign Communist parties and the 'lie' that the new organization was simply the old Comintern under fresh colours. This plan did not last long – Tito was pronounced a heretic the following year – but the basic arrangements, especially the newly tightened control over foreign Communist parties, were unaffected. 'Information on attack groups, training schools for cadres and arms depots will be collated there [in Belgrade]. Paris and Rome can put forward their proposals but they must follow the decisions taken by the Cominform in Belgrade. Duclos underlined the importance of this, because Moscow will completely control the activity of the French Communist Party.'

To comply with the order to prepare for clandestine activity, if not guerrilla war, Auguste Lecoeur received orders from Thorez to make all necessary arrangements. Lock-up garages were acquired, as well as vehicles which could not be traced to any member of the party. Secret printing presses and radio transmitters were obtained or reconditioned. Groups with expert engravers were told to start preparing sets of identity papers, passports and ration books. Weapons hidden since the autumn of 1944 were dug up and oiled.

Most people remained untouched, ignorant of such dangers, but some hint tainted the atmosphere. Koestler and Mamaine Paget returned to Paris at the end of September, just when the Cominform was meeting in Poland. On the evening of 1 October 1947 they met André Malraux and his wife Madeleine in the bar of the Plaza-Athénée, which according to Mamaine was 'full of glamorous demi-mondaines in extravagant clothes'. Malraux, after much indecision, decided to take them to the Auberge d'Armailhès. There they ate caviar and blinis and *soufflé sibérien*, and drank vodka. Malraux became rather drunk. He told them 'that in using his reputation as a man of the Left to help the reactionaries he was taking a big gamble, in which he believed he would succeed; but if he didn't (i.e. if de Gaulle, once in power, did not act as Malraux thought he should) he would feel he had betrayed the working class and there would be nothing left for him but to *se faire sauter la cervelle*. When K. said "What about the General's entourage?" Malraux replied "*L'entourage du Général, c'est moi*." We thought this rather silly, but were later told that Malraux is in fact the only man who dares to give de Gaulle advice, who sees his speeches before he makes them, etc.'

Exactly a week later, Albert Camus and his wife Francine gave a picnic dinner for Koestler and Mamaine. Everyone brought food and drink. Koestler, with his compulsive generosity which could seem ostentatious, brought a cold roast chicken, a lobster and champagne for the others, and shrimps and clams for himself and Mamaine. They were accompanied by Mamaine's twin sister Celia and the American journalist. Harold Kaplan. The other guests were Sartre and Simone de Beauvoir.

Koestler, who had seen little of Sartre since the attack on his book in *Les Temps modernes* the previous autumn, could not resist another skirmish. When Harold Kaplan left, Sartre attacked the American as 'anti-semitic and anti-negro and anti-liberty'. Koestler was so furious 'that he let fly at Sartre and said who are you to talk about liberty, when for years you've run a magazine which was *communisant*, and thus condoned the deportation of millions of people from the Baltic states?' Still according to Mamaine Paget, 'Sartre was a bit taken aback by this, and as the atmosphere had anyway become intolerable we left.'

Koestler wrote a letter of apology to Sartre the next morning. He 'received in return a long letter in his small, neat hand, which was both endearing and characteristic'. Yet as events soon showed, Sartre's friendships, partly as a result of Simone de Beauvoir's influence, could not transcend politics.

Koestler's dislike for Simone de Beauvoir became intense: 'At times she reminded me of the *tricoteuses*.' On his return to Wales, he decided to write an article on Parisian intellectuals 'in which Le Petit Vieux Ivan Pavelitch, leader of the Existenchiks, and Simona Castorovna and other friends play their parts'.

Yet Sartre himself still stood out against the Communists. In the July issue of *Les Temps modernes* he had written: 'Stalinist policy is incompatible with an honest approach to the literary profession.' The Communist attacks on him even encouraged Ramadier's government to offer the editorial board of *Les Temps modernes* a weekly programme on the radio. But a scathing satire on the Gaullists after the RPF enjoyed a sensational victory in October at the municipal elections caused a bitter row. Some suggested that Sartre should be imprisoned, but de Gaulle, who had a French respect for ideas, replied, '*On n'embastille pas Voltaire.*' The most angry of all the General's entourage was André Malraux: he was determined to take revenge.

De Gaulle did not hide his disdain for Ramadier's coalition of Socialists and Christian Democrats, which became known as the Third Force because it stood between Gaullism on the right and Communism on the left. He rather hoped for a general strike, which he was certain would cause the collapse needed to persuade the country to call him back to power. His '*égocentrisme vertigineux*', as Claude Mauriac described it, seemed to be reinforced by the success his Rassemblement was enjoying. His speech at an RPF rally at Vincennes on 5 October, an attack on Soviet dictatorship, was reported back to Washington as 'a spectacular success' – an opinion widely shared.

Other RPF meetings were less decorous, especially when held in working-class areas. Gaston Palewski had 'a wonderful new tease for the Communists,' Nancy Mitford wrote to her sister, Diana Mosley. 'He makes the chief agitator come on to the platform and then says now I only want to ask one question – *si les blindés russes envahissaient la France* [if Russian tanks were to invade France] would you fight to defend *le territoire*? So the poor *type* doesn't know what to reply and it always ends up in a free fight!' On 17 October, when a Socialist yelled at Thorez that he was a deserter, the burly ex-miner punched him hard in the face and then left his bodyguards to continue the thrashing.

The greatest triumph for the RPF came with the results of the municipal elections on Sunday, 19 October. Rassemblement candidates won 38 per cent of the vote against the Communist Party's 30 per cent. The Socialists achieved only 19 per cent. Such a result, compounded by an even greater swing to Gaullist candidates in the second round, lifted conservative hearts.

A few days later, at lunch at the Escargot, Duff Cooper and Louise de Vilmorin heard the latest news of the Rassemblement from Malraux, who told them that the Gaullists were 'very pleased with the story that when the results of last Sunday's elections were coming out on the radio [the General] switched it off and played patience'.

Whatever the Gaullist successes, the real struggle was developing between the Communist Party and the CGT on one side and the government on the other. The Communist objective was to destroy the French economy before the Marshall Plan could be made to work.

Britain, which still had the commitments of a world power, reached the point of bankruptcy in October; and Europe as a whole faced ruin that winter after the drought and disastrous harvest. The question for many, ever since Vyshinsky had accused the Americans and the British of preparing to fight, was not whether the Marshall Plan would have a chance to work, but whether the Third World War would break out first. Madame de Gaulle timidly broke into a lunch-time discussion to suggest that there might be an enemy parachute drop round Colombey-les-deux-Églises in the first few hours of hostilities.

Almost all gatherings in Paris that autumn had a nervous edge. 'People talk only of the imminence of war!' wrote Roger Martin du Gard to André Gide, who had just been awarded the

Nobel Prize. 'People don't doubt that it will happen, they only discuss how soon it will start. It is hard to react against this atmosphere of inevitable catastrophe!' Officials and ambassadors at parties found themselves buttonholed by frightened women and men who asked how many days it would take the Russians to reach the Channel ports or the Pyrenees.

Cold War fever had affected both sides of the Atlantic. It was depressing, wrote Duff Cooper to the British Foreign Secretary, but not surprising, that even Bidault should be catching it, 'when supposedly responsible people, such as the American Senator Bridges, shout down the dinner table at the American Embassy – "Say, Monsieur Bidault, we want to know what you're going to do when we drop our first atomic egg on Moscow."'

The Republic at Bay

The unrest which France had experienced in the summer of 1947 appeared minor by the autumn. On 28 October a pitched battle took place in the streets round the Salle Wagram near the Place de l'Étoile. Anti-Communists organized a meeting in the hall – used until quite recently by GIs for Tuesday dances – to denounce Stalin's crimes. Some 10,000 Communist counter-demonstrators advanced to attack. But large forces of police, gendarmerie and CRS riot squads managed to maintain their cordon round the area. The heavy fighting left one killed and 300 injured, including Communist municipal councillors and mayors. The police were almost as tough in their treatment of press photographers and newsreel teams.

That day had also seen a stormy session in the Assembly. Jacques Duclos had accused the government of being Pétainist valets of the United States. 'It was a remarkable parliamentary performance,' wrote one observer. 'He succeeded in goading everybody else to fury while remaining perfectly calm himself.'

Two weeks later, Marseilles erupted in riots. The Communists, exploiting a rise in tram fares, led an all-out attack on the new Gaullist mayor, Maître Carlini, the winner in the municipal elections. The law courts were sacked by a mob intent on releasing prisoners arrested in earlier demonstrations. The crowds then converged on the Hôtel de Ville, which they took by storm, and proceeded to beat up Carlini. Things were so bad that Gaston Defferre, the Socialist baron of the city, did not dare go out in a car without a sub-machine-gun on his lap.

On 17 November, the mining regions of the north and the Pas-de-Calais came out on strike without any warning. Within five days every coalfield in France had been closed down. The situation was equally volatile in Paris and its suburbs. Metalworkers, including those at Renault, came out on strike in the middle of November, demanding a 25 per cent pay increase. De Gaulle warned his entourage that the franc would collapse. There was only one consolation for the government. The purges of the Paris police seemed to have worked. Depreux felt confident enough to send them in to clear the Citroën works occupied by strikers.

De Gaulle became increasingly convinced that his return to power was at hand. Ramadier's government of Socialists and Christian Democrats seemed to be cracking up, so the General tried to treat the municipal election results as a referendum which had produced a vote of confidence in the Rassemblement. He demanded the dissolution of the Assembly and a general election. But this only strengthened the determination of the Socialists and the MRP to resist him.

Contradictory signals were coming out of the Gaullist camp. While one of the General's associates reassured the American Embassy that he was not anxious 'to pull the rug at this moment', he himself announced 'we haven't arrived at the Rubicon to go fishing'. Jacques Soustelle told a contact in the US Embassy on 3 November that de Gaulle did not want to come to power before the hard winter was over; and Gaston Palewski repeated the same message the following day. Ten days later, Colonel Passy was sighted at lunch with de Gaulle and Soustelle. There was also a belief, shared it would seem both by de Gaulle's entourage and by the Americans, that the Communists were trying to provoke a crisis 'that would bring de Gaulle to power before de Gaulle [was] ready'.

*

Paul Ramadier, worn down, continued in office only in answer to President Auriol's pleas. The results of the municipal elections had been a severe blow to his position and morale. In the second week of November he suffered from a heavy bout of flu just as he came under pressure from his MRP partners for a change of ministers to counter the Gaullists. Finally, on the afternoon of 19 November, he offered his resignation again, having heard that he did not have the full support of his own party. This time President Auriol had to accept it. The next morning (the day of Princess Elizabeth's wedding to Prince Philip of Greece in Westminster Abbey), France was without a government and paralysed by strikes.

Léon Blum, seventy-four years old and still frail from his imprisonment in Germany, appeared the only candidate who might muster sufficient support. On 21 October, in his speech to the National Assembly proposing his candidacy as head of government, he warned of the double danger facing the political system. When the votes were counted shortly before midnight, Blum was nine short of the minimum. Robert Schuman, the Minister of Finance, was told: 'It's your turn.' The following afternoon Schuman received his majority, with only the Communist Party and the semi-official Gaullist group of deputies opposing his candidature.

Schuman, an austere Catholic bachelor and a firm moderate, had a slightly crooked, rubbery-looking face, with a bald crown and large ears. Once, when a junior official failed to recognize him, he raised his hat and said that surely he recognized the cranium, it had been caricatured enough in the newspapers. Schuman came from Lorraine, which meant that during the First World War he had been obliged to serve in the Kaiser's army: a turn of fate which the Communists used shamelessly in their attacks on him. The other knife which they turned mercilessly was his very brief service in Pétain's first administration in July 1940. They did not mention the fact that Schuman was one of the first politicians arrested by the Germans.

The other key member of the government was Jules Moch, who took over as Minister of the Interior. Moch, with his round tortoiseshell glasses, pinched face and toothbrush moustache, looked like a provincial schoolmaster. He was a *polytechnicien*, pitiless with statistics and mathematical calculations. Yet his predecessor Édouard Depreux described him as 'a sensitive man, loyal and faithful to his friends', and, most significant for the times he was about to live through, he possessed 'a profound sense of the State'. The Communists found it hard to attack him: as a Jew, an anti-cleric and a Socialist, his loathing of Vichy had been unfeigned, and his son had been killed by the Gestapo.

Moch faced the hardest ministerial task since the Liberation. The autumn coal strike, with stocks still depleted from the previous terrible winter, made the government extremely vulnerable. The miners from the north of France were in combative mood when colonial troops were ordered in to protect the pits from sabotage, but the *'gueules noires'*, as the miners called themselves, received an unexpected boost. Spahis from the garrison at Senlis stacked their rifles on the platform at Lens station and refused to take them up, despite threats from officers. The Ministry of the Interior quickly sent in CRS riot police to seize their weapons and force the Spahis into a train which returned them to barracks.

At the Bully coalfield, some thirty German prisoners-of-war in their field-grey overcoats joined the attack on the CRS. A number of carbines were seized from them, and three CRS were taken prisoner by the miners. They were apparently so frightened that they told their captors all they knew. A Resistance veteran was disgusted. 'Do you realize that we had friends who died under torture having not said a word?' The miners released them, but held on to their identity cards so that they could be pursued if they broke their promise to say nothing to their superiors.

The idea of Spahis and Germans helping the miners aroused

great hopes of international solidarity. The Communist Party press encouraged its followers to see this struggle as the last push needed to overthrow a tottering regime.

As the strike hardened, and miners' families were left without money for food, the party organized the evacuation of their children to Communist households elsewhere. Miners who defied the strike call and continued to work were called 'canaries' because they were yellow. Their wives were often ambushed outside shops by the wives of strikers.

When Moch took over as Minister of the Interior on 24 November, he suffered from a shortage of riot police to deal with the outbreaks of violence. He also found that he had inherited an over-centralized system, never designed to cope with simultaneous emergencies right across the country. The situation was desperate, but this very fact forced the government to be courageous.

The Ministry of the Interior was in a state of pandemonium. Moch had to be in constant contact with up to ninety prefects of *départements*. Many prefects, afraid of getting no reinforcements from the Ministry of the Interior, turned to the general commanding their military district and, without informing Paris, asked him for troops. Others who had been instructed to send help to one of their besieged colleagues either questioned their orders or delayed implementing them in case their own area erupted. During the last week of November and the first week of December, the ministry received an average of 900 telegrams a day. In one twenty-four-hour period, Moch subsequently informed the prefects, the number rose to 2,302. Since most of these signals were in code, the cypher clerks were submerged.

Moch was so short of men that at one point he found himself sending bodies of riot police of fifty or fewer from one part of the country to another and back again. The station at Brive, for example, was finally relieved by fifty men from a CRS company based in Agen and 100 men allocated to the Massif Central.

Even more alarming, Moch found that, in spite of his predecessor's purges, several CRS units still contained so many Communists from the FTP that they were completely unreliable, and had to be disbanded.

'The strikes were called,' Moch wrote in a debriefing paper for the prefects, 'because the economic situation gave the working class real grievances.* The Communist Party showed great cleverness in exploiting these legitimate grievances to set in motion an overall movement which had a definite political and international character, and one of whose main objectives was that of discouraging American aid to Europe.'

The US Embassy became extremely perturbed at the determination of the Communist union leaders. The way that the strikers broke machinery in factories, to make sure that scab labour could not be brought in, indicated a determination to sabotage the economy before the Marshall Plan could take effect. James Bonbright, Douglas MacArthur Jnr and Ridgway Knight begged Caffery to help finance Force Ouvrière, a non-Communist breakaway from the CGT; but Caffery refused to contemplate such intervention in France's internal affairs. In fact, funding was found elsewhere, and passed through the American trades-union movement.

The atmosphere of violence grew more oppressive. Henri Noguères, editor of the Socialist Party newspaper *Le Populaire*, received a warning from Moch that the Communists might attempt a commando raid on the newspaper. Knowing that the police were too short-staffed in Paris to offer permanent protection, Moch sent round two containers of weapons from the Ministry of the Interior so that the staff of the paper could defend the building themselves. Leading figures in de Gaulle's Rassemblement also felt in danger from surprise attack. 'The

---

* Wages had risen by 17 per cent while prices had increased on average by 51 per cent.

Colonel [Palewski] sleeps with a great gun by his bed,' wrote Nancy Mitford to her mother, 'far more frightening than anything, as you can imagine he has no idea about guns!'

By a curious stroke of fate, a prominent figure associated with de Gaulle was killed in an accident a few days later. On 28 November, a dark foggy day on which snow fell in Paris, news arrived in the evening that General Leclerc, the city's liberator three years before, had died in an air crash aged only forty-four. A rumour rapidly circulated that somebody had put sugar in the petrol. Some compared his death to that of General Sikorski. 'The whole population of Paris,' wrote Nancy Mitford, in a sweeping generalization, 'is certain it was sabotage and it's done the Communists a lot of harm.' She was, no doubt, repeating the Colonel's firm belief.

Palewski, whose brother-in-law was also killed in the crash, had dined with Leclerc a week before his death. He claimed that Leclerc had said that evening, 'We are all in danger now.' Rumours, almost certainly beginning in the wilder fringes of the Rassemblement, spread that Leclerc had even urged de Gaulle to seize power. The fact that *L'Humanité* devoted only a couple of lines to the announcement of Leclerc's death confirmed Gaullist suspicions that the Communists had been responsible.

At the same time as Leclerc's death, public order operations took on an increasingly military aspect. The Ministry of the Interior was in constant contact with the Ministry of War, exchanging information and discussing options. French troops in the north were strengthened to prevent Belgian Communists from slipping across the border to sabotage the mines and prevent them from reopening. But even the army did not have enough men for the tasks allotted. Altogether 102,000 reservists from the classes of 1946 and 1947 had been recalled from the middle of November. In addition, the French army had reformed the Senegalese troops guarding German prisoners-of-war into a further nine battalions ready for deployment. But even these reinforcements were not considered sufficient: the government announced on 30 November that it was recalling another 80,000 reservists from the class of 1943.

In Paris, there had been comparatively few disorders. A minor insurrection took place in the 18th *arrondissement* when an officer of the Fire Brigade led 300 young Communists in an attempt to capture the telephone exchange. Before the assault the Communists, many of them sons of railway workers, smashed all the police telephones in the area. Those who escaped arrest were forcefully reprimanded by their superiors in the party for having acted without orders. The Prefect of Police, Roger Léonard, could hardly believe his luck that the Communists did not try more such adventures. He had only 150 policemen left in reserve to cover the whole city.

The capital was particularly vulnerable to strike action. For those coming into the centre of Paris to work by métro or suburban rail, life became almost intolerable. 'The train is jammed and often obliged to stop, either by sabotage or by the women and children of the strikers lying down on the tracks.' Strikes in the public services included the mail, refuse collection and power supplies. Cooking became impossible, electricity was cut without warning as it had been the previous winter, and water pressure dropped so low that the top floors of buildings failed to get even a trickle from the tap.

The real threat lay outside Paris. Moch felt forced to elaborate a contingency plan which would concentrate all his forces on Paris and the routes from the capital to Le Havre, Belgium, Lyons and Marseilles. The rest of the country outside these Y-shaped corridors would be effectively abandoned until sufficient troops could be brought back from Germany.

On 29 November, the day after General Leclerc's air crash, the Palais Bourbon – cordoned off by troops and police – became the scene of the most violent exchanges ever seen in the National Assembly. The Schuman government presented a

of measures to defend the Republic, including an anti-
ge bill. During these days Robert Schuman impressed
he with his air of calm. Jules Moch was equally resolute.
ew that he had less than a week to bring the country
control. If public order collapsed, then de Gaulle might
a move which could trigger the Communists into civil
But de Gaulle preferred to stand back while his two
es, the Communists and the government, fought it out.

the *hémicycle* of the National Assembly the Communists
insults at Robert Schuman and his government. Schuman's
in the German army in the First World War was thrown

ere's the boche!' cried Duclos.

here were you a soldier in 1914, Prime Minister?' shouted
Charles Tillon, one of the Black Sea mutineers of 1920.

'Prussian! German!' screamed Alain Signor, the author of the
cringing letter to Stepanov in the Kremlin.

The barrage of insults swelled and slackened in the course of
the marathon sessions. Deputies of other parties flung back their
own jibes, reminding the Communists of Stalin's alliance with
Hitler. Every resentment and suspicion from the Occupation
surged to the surface.

Sunday, 30 November, the second day of the session, was very
cold and foggy. The streets of Paris were empty. 'All seems quiet
today,' wrote the British ambassador in his diary. 'It isn't
revolution weather.' Marie-Blanche de Polignac refused to
cancel her traditional Sunday-night musical salon.

Monday was another day of fog. No aeroplanes could land or
take off, so, with the train strike, no diplomatic bags could get
through. Roger Martin du Gard, demoralized by cold meals
and the lack of water and heating, found the atmosphere of the
city 'sinister': he could not wait to escape to Nice as soon as the
trains began to run again. Nancy Mitford, who swung like
many between alarm and disdain for alarmists, expressed her
exasperation at the way the British press were reporting the

French troubles with a streak of *schadenfreude*. 'I told the *Times* man,' she wrote to her sister Diana, 'he really must point out that blood is not actually pouring down the gutters.' The electricity failed again, and Artur Rubinstein's concert that night took place by candlelight.

On the third day of the marathon session in the National Assembly a Communist deputy, Raoul Calas, took over the tribune to speak. He appealed to the army not to obey the murderers of the people, a clear case of incitement to mutiny. Édouard Herriot, the president of the National Assembly, announced that it was his duty to maintain respect for the law. A resolution for Calas's exclusion was then passed in spite of Communist protests. The session was suspended amid pandemonium.

Calas still refused to leave the tribune. His fellow Communists crowded round to protect him and offer support. The stalemate continued through the night. Shortly before six in the morning Colonel Marquant of the Garde Républicaine arrived with a written order from Herriot to expel Calas. But each time Marquant began to advance on the tribune, the Communist deputies burst into the Marseillaise. On hearing the national anthem, the Colonel had to spring to attention and salute. As soon as they stopped singing, he tried to move forward once more, but again the Marseillaise broke out, and he had to return to the salute. Finally, Colonel Marquant reached the tribune and gently took hold of Calas's arm. '*Je cède à la force*,' said the deputy.

The session which had started on 29 November did not end until 3 December. During its course, the balance of power tipped decisively in favour of the government. Already there were signs of the strike cracking, with non-Communists returning to work despite the violence threatened and used against them. Then, in the early morning of 3 December, a small group of Communist miners in the north destroyed their own cause. Hearing that a train full of riot police was on its way, and acting on their own initiative, they sabotaged the Lille–Paris line near Arras by dislodging twenty-five metres of track. Instead of a troop train, however, they derailed the Paris–Tourcoing express. Sixteen people were killed in the crash and thirty were seriously injured. News of the disaster reached Paris in the morning. By the afternoon, there was no traffic in the Champs-Élysées and the city appeared in a state of siege, with armed police at every intersection in the centre.

On hearing the news in the National Assembly, Communist deputies expressed no regret for the victims. They accused the government of having carried out the sabotage, and compared the incident to the Nazis setting fire to the Reichstag and blaming the Communists. Such tactics did them little good. Newsreel cameras had been rushed to the site of the crash. Their slow pans across the wreckage created stark black-and-white images of carriages split open, revealing battered corpses inside. One commentator, in a voice vibrant with anger, talked of an 'abominable attack' carried out by 'anonymous criminals'. These newsreels, shown in cinemas all over the country, had a powerful effect. The derailing of the express immeasurably strengthened the hand of the government.

On the day after the session ended in the Assembly, Maurice Thorez went north to talk to the miners of Hénin-Liétard and rally their spirits. He made no mention of the derailment. While he was absent, a grenade – a German grenade – exploded in the garden of his residence at Choisy-le-Roi. It was most probably an attempt to divert attention from the victims of the train crash.

Perhaps the most decisive effect of the rail disaster was the split it produced among strikers over the question of violent methods. The postmen who had just returned to work were given police protection. Other workers still out on strike came under increasing pressure from their wives to resume work before Christmas. Distrust of the Communist Party's intentions spread even more rapidly after the crash. These suspicions proved well-founded. Not long before his death in 1993, Auguste Lecoeur admitted calmly in interviews with the film-maker Mosco that sabotaging the French economy and splitting France politically was simply part of 'the struggle against American imperialism'.

A growing number of workers resented being used by the Communists for political ends and demanded secret ballots on whether or not to continue the strike. At first the Communists resisted this by intimidation, but by the second week of December the pressure had become too great. 'Under these circumstances,' wrote Moch in his debriefing document to the prefects, 'the Communist directors of the CGT no longer had any choice but to begin strategic withdrawals or suffer a total defeat. If they had delayed another forty-eight hours in giving the back-to-work order they would have lost complete control of the CGT membership. The end of the strike must therefore be considered as a Communist withdrawal, implying a serious check but not a definite defeat.'

General Leclerc's funeral service was planned for 8 December in Notre-Dame. The event had taken on strong political overtones in the circumstances. 'All Leclerc's boys are pouring into town,' Nancy Mitford wrote to her sister. 'It is like mobilization – there will be 2,000 of them in Notre-Dame'.

President Auriol and most of the diplomatic corps attended. 'The ceremony was fine and impressive,' wrote Duff Cooper in his diary, 'but the twelve other unhappy coffins detracted from the grandeur of the central figure without gaining any themselves. One regretted their presence yet felt doubly sorry for them on that account. A man's funeral is his last appearance and he ought to have the stage to himself.' The British ambassador then led the diplomatic corps on foot from Notre-Dame to the Invalides through two heavy showers. Leclerc's loss would be felt most in the direction of French policy in Indo-China. He was one of the few realists left in a senior position. His strong advice that the French should negotiate independence with Ho Chi Minh had embittered relations with his superior, Admiral d'Argenlieu. Politicians in Paris, even in the Socialist Party, felt obliged to support d'Argenlieu: they had not grasped how much the world had changed.

The last strike collapsed on the morning of 10 December. The headline in *L'Humanité* – 'This morning, 1,500,000 combatants returned to work as a group' – represented a desperate attempt to paint defeat as victory of a sort. Huge mounds of refuse still lay in the streets of Paris.

That night Duff and Diana Cooper gave their farewell ball at the British Embassy, and it turned out to be the 'gala occasion it could not have been the week before'. Nancy Mitford wrote to her mother that the embassy had received 600 acceptances, 'in spite of the fact that no letters have been delivered for a week'.

Churchill flew over from London on the morning of the party. He arrived to a beautiful day. News of his presence caused huge crowds to gather outside the embassy in the rue du Faubourg Saint-Honoré chanting their demands for his appearance. He went out to address them in his inimitable version of the French language, and received an exuberant ovation – 'a thing he always enjoys', his host noted with amused affection.

The party began at half past ten. Virtually all the *corps diplomatique* came. The 'conspicuous exceptions' were the Russian, Polish and Yugoslav ambassadors. Churchill, beaming, in white tie and full decorations, entered the salon where his parents, Lord Randolph Churchill and Jenny Jerome, had been married. On his arm was the beautiful Odette Pol Roger in a spectacular red satin dress.

Guests wandered in admiration through the high-ceilinged and gilded reception rooms. Like Churchill, all the men were in white tie with full decorations, the ribbons and sashes vivid against the black tail-coats and starched waistcoats. Diana Cooper had invited several designer friends – Dior, Balmain,

Rochas and Molyneux – and they looked at their own and other creations with a critical eye.

Susan Mary Patten wore a dress by Schiaparelli – 'heavy ivory grosgrain, with an enormous bustle, very *Lady Windermere's Fan*'. Christian Dior bowed to her and said, 'That is one of the greatest dresses I have ever seen, and I wish it were mine.'

The Gaullists there that night, such as Gaston Palewski and Pierre de Bénouville, were puffed up by John Foster Dulles's statement the day before that General de Gaulle was 'the coming man in France'. Dulles had even made a point of ignoring Bidault at the London conference. Jefferson Caffery was one of many who were exasperated at this clumsy intervention in French politics. Support for de Gaulle would have been more to the point in 1944; in December 1947 it simply came as an insult to Schuman and Moch, whose determination and stamina during the previous two and a half weeks had won the respect even of Malraux and Palewski.

Susan Mary Patten was deeply embarrassed when the playwright Henri Bernstein came up and said, almost within Robert Schuman's hearing, 'Well, thank God you Americans have at last declared yourselves for de Gaulle. Bravo for Mr Dulles.'

Perhaps provoked by Dulles's praise of de Gaulle, Jules Moch made sure that the Americans appreciated the efforts made to defend Republican order; but his main objective was to put pressure on the Americans to hasten their financial aid to France before unrest erupted again. With Caffery, he was, of course, preaching to the converted. The ambassador's reports to Washington extolled Moch's 'courageous and energetic measures which have tended to bolster the government's and his own prestige'. But he also believed firmly that without the announcement of the Marshall Plan, the Schuman government would never have been able to inspire sufficient determination among its officials and political colleagues to resist the Communist onslaught.

The Minister of the Interior did not rest on his laurels during the remaining months of that winter. He bombarded the prefects with briefing papers and plans for improving the countrywide security apparatus. Political Orientation Instruction No. 1 of 26 December 1947 set out the background to the recent strikes. In it Moch warned that the majority of the population still faced real hardship, and that the Communists would make the most of it. The civil authorities must therefore expect renewed disorders next year, probably between mid-February and mid-March, because that would be the period of greatest scarcity of foodstuffs and coal. (In fact the next serious wave of unrest did not come until June.)

Moch hurried forward his predecessor's programme of eliminating Communists from the Paris police and the CRS riot police. Such was the success of this procedure that the balance was entirely reversed. By the summer of 1948, it was estimated that 19,000 out of 23,000 policemen in the capital were anti-Communist. The Ministry of the Interior meanwhile altered the distribution of CRS riot police around the country so that more were deployed close to the main danger areas – the coalfields of the north and the larger industrial centres of the east. Moch also asked the Ministry of War to form new squads of Gardes Républicaines from the gendarmerie. In critical regions, the army was to allocate infantry battalions as permanent reserves for security duties.

The idea of commanders of military regions exercising control was anathema to Moch. He said that he wished to avoid 'the psychological and political disadvantages which often accompany a declaration of martial law', but he also did not trust anybody else, certainly not the Ministry of War, to control civil unrest. Neither he nor Robert Schuman lost sight of the fact that only a real improvement in the standard of living would reduce the power of the Communists, and that depended on the Marshall Plan.

28

The Great Boom of Saint-Germain-des-Prés

The bars, bistros and cafés of Paris had long acted as intellectual incubators, but never so much as in Saint-Germain after the war. An extraordinary array of talent had come together in two square kilometres of Paris at a time when the cross-fertilization of ideas had never seemed more exciting and important, when every art appeared on the point of a new departure. This could not have happened without places in which people could meet, talk, argue and write, from morning until late at night.

The ideas were new, but the café setting was reassuringly familiar. Whether the floor was of wood or tiled, whether the triangular ashtrays on the little tables advertised Byrrh or Dubonnet, whether the posters for the latest plays and exhibitions were tacked to the door or pegged to the yellowing net curtains, the smell was always the same. It was warm and sociable, established over the years from imperfectly washed bodies, Caporal tobacco smoke and cheap wine. Entering a familiar café was like a homecoming.

Café life in Saint-Germain observed certain conventions. Sartre observed that 'people would come in and find they knew everybody; each person knew the smallest details about the private life of their neighbour; but one did not bother to say *bonjour*, although one would immediately if one met any of them elsewhere'.

Before the effects of his fame became too distracting, Sartre used to work at the Café Flore for three hours in the morning and three hours in the afternoon. The morning session began with him bustling through the door, his pockets stuffed with books and papers. He threaded his way through to his favourite corner table, settled down, lit his pipe, downed a couple of cognacs while spreading out his papers, and started to write.

The proprietor of the Flore, Paul Boubal, at first had no idea of his customer's identity. He often came with a dark-haired woman, who also wrote – in the same corner of the café, but at a different table. They left at twelve, but came back after lunch and worked in the room on the first floor till closing-time.

One day there was a telephone call for a Monsieur Sartre. Boubal had a personal friend called Sartre, and told the caller he was not in the café. The caller insisted that he must be, so Boubal called out the name – and up stood the little man with the pipe and pebble glasses. 'From that moment he became my friend, and we often had a chat in the morning; later, the telephone calls increased to such an extent that I decided it was necessary to put in another line specially for him.'

The *famille Sartre* and the *bande Prévert* used to patronize both the Flore and the Deux Magots. The great period of the Deux Magots had been between the wars, when – according to Vercors – the café was so filled with celebrated artists, politicians and men of letters that it was almost impossible to find a place; particularly since young disciples would bring up chairs and sit two or three deep round the tiny tables, listening attentively to the conversation of the great figures. Yet by the late thirties the Flore had also gathered an impressive group of regulars which included not only the *bande Prévert*, but also André Breton, Picasso and Giacometti. Towards the end of the afternoon, people often drifted to the Deux Magots, where they could enjoy the last of the sunlight.

Communists, if they were not in Marguerite Duras's apartment in the rue Saint-Benoît, favoured the Bonaparte, on the north side of the Place Saint-Germain, while musicians tended to gravitate towards the Royal Saint-Germain, opposite the Deux Magots on the south side of the Boulevard. In the evening other places came into their own: the Rhumerie Martiniquaise, the Bar Vert, and the bar of the Hôtel Montana.

The central point of this café life was the square between the Deux Magots and the ancient, much-rebuilt abbey of Saint-Germain-des-Prés. The frontiers of the *quartier* were clearly defined: on the east, the Boulevard Saint-Michel; on the west, the rue des Saints-Pères; on the north, the *quais* along the Seine; on the south, the rue de Vaugirard. The narrow streets were still cobbled then, gently dipping between tall houses that leaned this way and that. Roofs, stucco, bricks, cobbles, shutters and paintwork provided every shade of grey from zinc to soot. Occasionally, when the large door of a *porte cochère* was open, one might catch sight of a courtyard with a few shrubs and potted geraniums; otherwise the only green was that of the leaves of the plane trees on the broad boulevards.

As it was considered bourgeois to have an apartment, young intellectuals lived in dilapidated hotels which came to symbolize the rootless and unmaterialistic life of an existentialist. The Louisiane in the rue de Seine, the Montana and the Crystal in the rue Saint-Benoît, the Pont-Royal in the rue Montalambert, the Madison in the Place Jacques Copeau: all were cheap, offering little more than a bed and basin. The concierge – usually the proprietress – who sat glowering behind the desk was a figure to be feared and placated, especially when one was behind with the rent. Juliette Gréco was so terrified of the landlady of the Louisiane that she scarcely dared ask for her key or her mail. Yet these little hotels had the atmosphere of a university hall of residence, happy and familial.

Since cooking in the rooms was strictly forbidden in most establishments, the bistros were important in the life of Saint-Germain: the Cheramy, the Catalan, the Petit Saint-Benoît, Les Assassins, l'Esculape. Everyone knew everyone; if not well, then enough to exchange a '*Bonjour, ça va?*' in the street, or swap quotations from Raymond Queneau's *Exercices de style*. This little masterpiece was both a brilliant demonstration of the versatility of language, and one of his funniest and most accessible works.

Despite the cold and lack of money, the tiny theatres of Saint-Germain, like the Théâtre de la Poche, the Vieux-Colombier, the Huchette and the Noctambules, all flourished. This was the *anti-théâtre, le théâtre de l'absurde, le théâtre révolutionnaire, le théâtre des idées* – 'more ideas than theatre,' grumbled the critic Jean-Jacques Gautier. One of the most original and inventive playwrights of the post-war theatre was Jacques Audiberti. His plays were noted for the fertility of his language, which managed to be both musical and rooted in the everyday.

These little productions worked as cooperatives: the actors were also scene-shifters and costume-makers, they swept out the theatre and painted the scenery. The odd-job man round the corner could sometimes be persuaded to knock up a flimsy set, or rig up another spotlight. As for the audience, they were people who lived the same bohemian lives as the actors. They somehow found a few francs to applaud a friend, or see the latest production that everyone was talking about.

The youth of Saint-Germain lived off coffee, sandwiches, cigarettes, cheap wine and small loans from friends. The men were recognizable by their American-style plaid shirts, crew-cuts and gymshoes. Tartan featured prominently in the mid-forties; and in the cold winters that followed the Liberation, the *canadienne* – a felt jacket designed for lumberjacks – had the dual advantage of being warm and looking proletarian. Girls no longer had their hair built up above the forehead; fringes were in fashion, and the rest was left long and droopy. High-necked, tight-fitting tops and sweaters, short black skirts and ballet-shoes completed the costume. After 1946, black became increasingly fashionable for both sexes.

The face and voice which came to epitomize the youth of the

late 1940s were those of an inexperienced actress called Juliette
Gréco. Her father was a *commissaire de police* from Montpellier,
and her mother had almost lost her life in Ravensbrück
concentration camp. Juliette had come to Saint-Germain in
1943. For a time she was a member of the Communist youth
organization and sold its newspaper, but then she became sickened by it. In four years her acting career had not advanced,
but later she was to become notorious as the figurehead of
corrupt Parisian youth; yet she always retained an innocent,
unworldly quality which was part of her appeal. Christian
Bérard designed for her a pair of tartan slacks, trimmed with
mink around the ankles. Gréco asked what mink was.

Her introduction to the *famille Sartre* came through Maurice
Merleau-Ponty, a quiet man of great charm whom Boris Vian
described as 'the only one of the philosophers who asked women
to dance'. Gréco was amused by the way the waiters in his
favourite haunt were used to receiving his silver cigarette-lighter
until he could pay the bill. One night, at the Bal Nègre in the
rue Blomet, he introduced her to Sartre and Simone de Beauvoir.
Sartre she found very accessible. 'He was a great one for jokes
and talked easily to the young', and answered any question you
put to him. Simone de Beauvoir, on the other hand, had
'*un aspect plus difficile*'. Also sitting at Sartre's and Beauvoir's
table was a red-haired girl in black velvet called Anne-Marie
Cazalis.

Cazalis was a poet. She was also tough and ambitious, and
reminded Boris Vian of a goat 'in her laugh, her malicious
expression, a little obstinate but always diabolic'. Simone de
Beauvoir distrusted her deeply, and said that 'she pushed gossip
to indecent extremes'. Gréco, whom Cazalis took under her
wing, described her as 'full of inventive ideas, full of fantastic
imagination, but machiavellian'. Soon the two young women
were sharing a room in the Hotel Louisiane, and they became
known as 'the muses of Saint-Germain-des-Prés'. Gréco said of
their life in those days, '*C'était une période nocturne mais lumineuse.*'

The best live jazz in Paris was played by Claude Luter's band, known as Les Lorientais, at a club of the same name in the cellar of the Hotel des Carmes. They had begun by playing at illicit 'surprise-parties' during the Occupation, and moved to the Hotel des Carmes in June 1946 as little more than amateur enthusiasts, playing only between five and seven in the evening.

Even after they became famous, Luter and his band still played for parties given by friends, such as the one to celebrate Simone de Beauvoir's return from America in February 1947. This was what Michel Leiris and Sartre liked to call a 'fiesta'. Boris Vian organized the bar, which served infernal alcoholic mixtures. Giacometti fell asleep, perhaps as a result, and when the organizers cleared up afterwards somebody found a glass eye in the piano.

Vian was perhaps the most talented of the young *Germano-pratins*. Trained as an engineer, he was also writer, novelist, poet, car enthusiast and jazz trumpeter, whose work – both musical and literary – was admired by Sartre, Prévert and Queneau. The years 1946 and 1947 were ones of tremendous activity for him. As well as playing the trumpet in Claude Abadie's jazz band, he had a regular column in *Jazz Hot*, where he wrote not only about music but about ignorance, injustice, racism and the horror of war. Vian was not an intellectual (he pretended that Heidegger was a new brand of Austrian tractor), but Sartre immediately recognized him as an '*écrivain engagé*,' and for a brief time he also wrote a column for *Les Temps modernes* called '*Chronique du Menteur*'. Their friendship soured when Sartre began what was to be a long affair with Vian's wife Michelle – although by then the Vian marriage was almost over.

J'irai cracher sur vos tombes, Vian's third and most scandalous novel, was published in November 1946. It appeared under the pseudonym of Vernon Sullivan, supposedly a young American writer whose book Vian had merely translated. Written in fifteen days, it is a hard, angry, iconoclastic book about a black man's erotic revenge on the white race – complete with murder and explicit sex scenes. The press was outraged, the book became a bestseller, and Vian kept his anonymity for as long as he could; but in April 1947, the campaign against the book became serious. A man murdered his mistress in a scene copied from *J'irai cracher sur vos tombes*; not only that, but he left the book open at the relevant page, with the murder scene underlined, before turning the gun on himself. Vian was eventually forced to admit authorship. He was fined 100,000 francs, and the book was banned.

Late at night in Saint-Germain-des-Prés, there was nowhere to go but the cafés. Gréco and Cazalis would hang out with their friends in the Bar Vert in the rue Jacob until about one in the morning, when it closed. Then little groups would huddle outside, stamping their feet and having one last cigarette before they walked away.

There was only one place which stayed open later than the Bar Vert: a little café in the rue Dauphine called the Tabou. The Tabou served coffee and croissants well into the small hours and in 1946 gradually became a haven for insomniacs and *noctambules*, including Cazalis, Sartre, Camus, Merleau-Ponty, and the film-maker Alexandre Astruc.

Bernard Lucas of the Bar Vert persuaded the owners of the Tabou to lease him their cellar. It was a tunnel of a room, some fifteen metres by eight, with bare brick walls curving into a low vaulted ceiling. Lucas installed a bar, an ill-tuned piano, a gramophone and a few tables and chairs. The cellar was named Le Tabou, like the café above; and the work of making it popular and minding the bar was given to Gréco, Cazalis and Marc Doelnitz, a restless, red-haired young actor and insatiable party-goer, whose well-connected family enabled him to be equally at home on the right bank of the Seine as on the left.

Lucas had chosen well: within every group of people there is always a small nucleus of members who somehow embody its spirit. Doelnitz, Gréco and Cazalis were at the centre of Saint-

Germain life, and they knew it. The Tabou opened on 17 April 1947. Within a few nights it was generating tremendous excitement, with spontaneous jam-sessions and wild dancing. Boris Vian sometimes played the trumpet. By now people knew that he was the author of *J'irai cracher sur vos tombes*, which gave the Tabou an even more subversive cachet. Filled with sweaty, exhilarated couples and thick with smoke, the Tabou was soon the only place to be after midnight in Saint-Germain. 'To be part of the very fabric of *Germano-pratin* life gave one a very satisfying sense of superiority,' wrote Doelnitz.

Barely a month after its opening, an article appeared, instigated by Cazalis, which brought the Tabou and its *habitués* to the shocked attention of the whole of Paris. This illustrated feature appeared on 3 May 1947 in *Samedi-Soir*, with the headline: 'THIS IS HOW THE TROGLODYTES OF SAINT-GERMAIN LIVE'. The main photograph showed a tousled young man (Roger Vadim) holding a lighted candle, and a young woman in trousers, whose dark hair was full of cobwebs (Juliette Gréco). They were described as 'two poor existentialists'. These young 'existentialists', wrote the journalist Robert Jacques, live in cellars by night and cheat their landladies by day. 'They are drinking, dancing and loving their lives away in cellars until the atom bomb – which they all perversely long for – drops on Paris.'

Without actually saying so, *Samedi-Soir* had no difficulty in implying that, along with their energetic dancing, black clothes and indigent life-style, the existentialists were indulging in unbridled sex. Yet the life of most young *Germano-pratins* was surprisingly chaste. An incorrigible womanizer like Sartre certainly seemed to think so. He described jitterbugging as 'a violent form of exercise, both light-hearted and healthy, which does them the greatest physical good and leaves them far too tired for lascivious thoughts'. Yet perhaps Sartre was trying to play down the whole Saint-Germain phenomenon, for which the press seemed to hold him responsible. He was blamed for contributing to juvenile crime, and encouraging suicides. Attacks on Sartre became so vitriolic that *Combat* ran an article with the ironic headline: 'Should Sartre be burned at the stake?'

What Sartre and his circle did object to was the article's use of the word 'existentialist'. From having represented a body of philosophical ideas, the term 'existentialist' suddenly became a generic for jazz-soaked be-boppers. This was partly due to Sartre's young friends, who when asked to describe themselves by *Samedi-Soir*, replied that they were 'existentialist'.

The immediate effect of the article in *Samedi-Soir* was to turn the Tabou and its exotic denizens into a tourist attraction. The Tabou became even more frenetic, the gramophone was replaced by a band, and the curious and the fashionable squeezed down the narrow stairs to see the 'existentialists'. The tourists went home deliciously shocked after one particular evening when girls in bikinis competed for the title of 'Miss Tabou'.

The French Communist Party saw the effect of existentialism as the greatest threat to its own influence on the youth of France. Maurice Thorez had denounced existentialist writing as 'the expression of a rotting bourgeoisie', and any outsider who thought that the young pseudo-existentialist rebels of Saint-Germain-des-Prés were Communist would have made a true Stalinist laugh bitterly. The rigidly puritan Communists felt that young people should be watching *Battleship Potemkin*, not enjoying corrupt American imports. Reports in Moscow reveal genuine dismay and anger that Parisian youth should be enthralled by so many aspects of American life. Two Soviet journalists who claimed to have visited the Tabou wrote afterwards in the *Literary Gazette*: 'These poverty-stricken young people live in squalor and ask you to pay for their drinks. It is a youth revelling in the most vulgar sexuality.'

The Tabou's meteoric rise was matched by the speed of its fall. Complaints to the authorities about the noise and disturbance grew: the club was obliged to close at midnight and soon it was attracting more tourists than *Germano-pratins*. The great period of the Tabou had lasted less than a year, but its effect spread. Imitation Tabou clubs sprang up in different parts of France, from Toulouse in the south-west to Charleville in the Ardennes.

Other clubs soon appeared in Paris to take the Tabou's place. Marc Doelnitz was commissioned to decorate and launch the Vieux-Colombier in the cellar of the Théâtre du Vieux-Colombier. And in June 1948, the Club Saint-Germain opened. Boris Vian joined Marc Doelnitz in making the Club Saint-Germain the newest attraction. All the great jazzmen passing through Paris – including Duke Ellington, Charlie Parker and Miles Davis – came as Vian's guests.

By the summer of 1948, the tourist invasion of Saint-Germain was well and truly under way. The curious came to the Café Flore and asked to see the table of Monsieur Sartre (who had long since fled to the bar of the Pont-Royal). Janet Flanner described the place as 'a drugstore for pretty upstate girls in unbecoming blue denim pants and their Middle Western dates, most of whom are growing hasty Beaux-Arts beards'.

That autumn, left bank and right bank met in a new venture – the ballet *La Rencontre* which began playing to packed houses at the Théâtre des Champs-Élysées. This told the story of Oedipus and the Sphinx: choreography by Lichine, music by Henri Sauguet, and programme notes by Sartre. The ballet was set in a huge shadowy circus, and was one of the last sets completed by Bérard before his death early the next year. The Sphinx, on a high platform under a trapeze, was played by the seventeen-year-old Leslie Caron, wearing a black body-stocking: the performance launched her career.

Another modern adaptation of Greek tragedy was attempted in a film by Alexandre Astruc, called *Ulysse, ou les mauvaises rencontres*. It was filmed in the Vieux-Colombier theatre, in the cold, foggy months of 1948, and the list of participants is a tribute to a time when successful people were prepared to take part in an adventure, simply because it appealed to them as curious or amusing. Jean Cocteau played Homer, Simone Signoret was Penelope to Marc Doelnitz's Ulysses, and Juliette Gréco was Circe. Jean Genet was to have been the Cyclops, but he pulled out and Astruc was obliged to take the role himself. There were no rehearsals and 'Astruc was the only one who understood what was going on'.

Gréco had not yet sung professionally, and still thought of herself as an actress. Yet Anne-Marie Cazalis was convinced that she should sing, and said so to Sartre as they were walking back after dinner one night. Sartre laughed and said, 'If she wants to sing, then she should sing.' Gréco was walking in front of them. Irritated by this exchange, she said over her shoulder that she had no intention of becoming a singer. Sartre asked why not, to which Gréco replied, 'I don't know how to sing, and also I don't like the songs that one hears on the radio.' – 'Well, if you don't like them, what sort do you like?' She mentioned the names of Agnès Capri and Yves Montand. Sartre had the last word. 'Come round to me at nine tomorrow morning.'

The next morning when Gréco arrived at the rue Bonaparte, Sartre had looked out a pile of poetry books for her. Among the poems she chose were *C'est bien connu* by Queneau, and *L'Éternel féminin* by Jules Laforgue. Sartre also gave her a song he had written for *Huis clos*. He told her to visit the composer Joseph Kosma, who lived in the rue de l'Université. Kosma wrote the music for the Queneau poem (renamed *Si tu t'imagines*), for *L'Éternel féminin*, and for Sartre's poem *La rue des blancs manteaux*. These were to be among the songs for which Juliette Gréco is still remembered – along with her rendering of Prévert's *Les Feuilles mortes*, also set to music by Kosma.

At about the same time, Marc Doelnitz had been asked to resuscitate the most famous Parisian cabaret from between the wars – Le Boeuf sur le Toît. The Occupation, the rise of Saint-Germain and the death of its creator, Louis Moyses, had left it almost defunct.

Doelnitz hired a dancer, a singer and a trombone-player; but what he needed was a star. There were no funds to hire Edith Piaf, Yves Montand or Charles Trenet, so Doelnitz decided to risk all on creating one: Juliette Gréco. Gréco had many recommendations apart from a good voice. She had so often featured in the popular press that people stopped her in the street and asked for her autograph, and – perhaps what Doelnitz relied on most – she had an unconscious magnetism.

The irony is that when Gréco found success as a singer, it was not in Saint-Germain-des-Prés but on the right bank in the rue du Colisée, off the Champs-Élysées. She had only a few days' rehearsal and her first-night nerves were immeasurably intensified by the fact that *le tout Saint-Germain* had crossed the river to applaud her début. The next night was the real test, because the audience was exclusively *rive droite*. Juliette Gréco had made no concessions to the conventional idea of how a female entertainer should dress: she wore black trousers, her bare feet slipped into golden sandals. The ladies of the audience in their little feathered hats were affronted: 'Is it done to show oneself in public dressed like that?' Yet even they were seduced, and walked out into the night humming '*Si tu t'imagines*'.

To some, Gréco's move to the right bank seemed like a defection. She did not in fact stay there long. Within a few weeks she was in the South of France with Claude Luter's band. By the end of 1949 the great days of Saint-Germain-des-Prés were over; nevertheless, the party had been memorable. 'In Paris, perhaps one needs a war to launch a *quartier*,' remarked Jacques Prévert.

29

The Curious Triangle

The year 1948 was the most dramatically dangerous of the Cold
War. Today, after the sudden collapse of Soviet power, it is
increasingly hard to imagine the fear people felt of a new world
war and another occupation, this time by the Red Army. Events
had accelerated in such a way that, for many, the Marxist–
Leninist claim of historical inevitability began to appear
invincible.

Nancy Mitford might have laughed at the Windsors in 1946
for advising people to put their jewels in a safe place and get out
of France, but in March 1948 she wrote to Evelyn Waugh in a
very different mood. She was convinced that the Russians would
invade at any moment. 'Unable to be angry with them, I am
quite simply frightened. I wake up in the night sometimes in a
cold sweat. Thank goodness for having no children, I can take a
pill and say goodbye.'

After the collapse of the strikes the French Communist Party
prepared to go underground again. Auguste Lecoeur, the miners'
young leader who had directed Communist security with such
effective ruthlessness during the Resistance, had not wasted time
since receiving his instructions after the Cominform meeting at
Sklarska Poreba in Poland.

Communist dockers in major ports, such as Le Havre, were
delegated to block work on ships bringing military supplies to
the US forces in Europe. Intelligence was the key to clandestine

warfare on both sides, so networks of informers were re-formed, many from the wartime groups. Party members in the postal workers' unions organized the interception of mail to important figures. The most useful moles were unidentified party members in the security services, especially the Renseignements Généraux, and junior officials in the Ministry of the Interior.

The Prague coup on 20 February acted as the clearest signal in the West that the Cold War had really started. The diplomat Hervé Alphand saw the Communist takeover in Czechoslovakia as similar to that of Hitler in March 1939, only rather less crude. The democrats in the Czech government played what was probably an impossible hand very badly. They tendered their resignations in protest at the action of the Communist Minister of the Interior; they assumed that this would force President Beneš to dismiss him along with the Communist premier, Klement Gottwald. But the Communists, under Soviet direction, simply seized the opportunity. A Communist mass rally threatened civil war, and Benes gave in, allowing Gottwald to form a new government composed of Communists and fellow-travellers. Jan Masaryk, the non-Communist Foreign Minister, fell from a window of the Czernin Palace to his death shortly afterwards. Although this tragedy was probably suicide from despair and the intolerable pressure put on him by the Communists, many people in Paris were struck by the coincidence that Jean-Louis Barrault's production of Kafka's *The Trial* was playing at the Théâtre de Marigny.

On 23 February, three days after the Prague coup, the London conference on the future of Germany assembled. Hervé Alphand and Couve de Murville took the Golden Arrow boat train from Paris. The Siberian weather – a cutting wind and flurries of snow – seemed symbolic of the times. Their relief at reaching Claridge's dwindled on finding that coal was as short in Britain as it was in France.

The Prague coup had one positive effect for Western Europe. It had shocked Washington and saved the implementation of the Marshall Plan from any further prevarication: Congress approved the bill with uncharacteristic rapidity. The coup also concentrated the minds of European governments. On 17 March the Brussels Treaty was signed between France, Britain, Belgium, the Netherlands and Luxemburg. Truman announced his full support to Congress that very day. A year later this developed into the Atlantic Pact, the basis of the North Atlantic Treaty Organization. Most European leaders now accepted that, for their own survival, 'they had to engage the United States in Europe'.

In France, the Communists faced a problem of strategy. They did not know whether to concentrate their attacks on the government or on de Gaulle. They followed the Kremlin's instructions and depicted the government as a second Vichy with the Americans as the new occupying power, yet a gut instinct made them fear de Gaulle more. Jacques Duclos called for 'the dissolution of de Gaulle's illegal and fascist paramilitary organization aimed at the establishment of a dictatorship'.

Large groups of Communists turned up to disrupt meetings of the RPF. After Raymond Aron was shouted down by students, Malraux organized a much bigger meeting, but this time with a large contingent of the Rassemblement's *service d'ordre* of volunteer security guards to demonstrate 'that we had the strength to impose respect, and to hold our meetings when and wherever we wanted'.

De Gaulle behaved as though the Rassemblement was the only force which could prevent the Communists from seizing power. He still could not acknowledge the role that Schuman and Moch had played in holding the pass against them in November. The United States Embassy, however, continued to be impressed by the government's firmness. Caffery reported that Schuman and Moch 'have given very careful thought, in the event of a new Communist offensive, to outlawing the Communist Party and arresting all of its leaders who can be apprehended'.

Alarmist rumours continued to circulate in April, with stories of arms parachuted into the Lyons area: some thought for Communists, others thought for the right, others suspected Zionist agents. But the Americans were now confident that France would not collapse. Marshall Aid should start to have an effect within the next year.

The Gaullists offered prefects their 'shock troops' for any action against Communists. The prefects, however, knew that they would be in trouble from the Minister of the Interior if they accepted. The government even asked Jefferson Caffery not to have any meetings with de Gaulle. The ambassador sympathized and, after consultation with Washington, passed a message via General de Bénouville. General de Gaulle was warned that any attempt by him to unseat the Schuman government would be seen 'as proof of placing personal ambition before the vital interest of his country'.

The message was received and digested. Ridgway Knight, Caffery's political adviser, had a private meeting with Colonel Passy, who assured him that de Gaulle would take power illegally only in the event of a Soviet invasion, or of the failure of the government of the day to resist a Soviet ultimatum.

Passy also tried to assure Knight that the hotheads in the RPF were leaving the movement to join paramilitary groups on the far right. Knight, however, was much better informed than Passy realized. Although there was a basis of truth in the claim that some of these elements had started to drift away, Knight knew the White Russian chief of staff of the Gaullist *service d'ordre* in Paris, Colonel Tchenkeli, who had told him about all the extreme right-wing groups the Gaullists could call upon.

De Gaulle's speeches became increasingly concerned with foreign policy, and in the spring of 1948 that meant Germany. His address on 7 March to a Rassemblement gathering at Compiègne had demanded once again that Germany should be split into separate states. The Reich must not be recreated. But within two weeks, events in Germany began to overtake him.

On 19 March, forty-eight hours after France, Great Britain, the Netherlands, Belgium and Luxemburg had signed the Treaty of Brussels, Marshal Sokolovski, the Soviet commander in Germany, walked out of the Allied Control Commission in Berlin. The gesture signalled the end of wartime cooperation.

Robert Schuman, meanwhile, was uneasy at the speed with which his Foreign Minister was coming round to American and British views on Germany. Bidault had been encouraged by Churchill the previous October to accept the inevitability of reconciliation.

Within the French government, Georges Bidault was indeed the driving force for change, even if a number of his colleagues saw him more as a wagon hitched to an Anglo-American express. The London Accords on Germany were ratified in the National Assembly by a majority of only fourteen votes after the debate on 16 June. The most implacable opposition came from the Communists on one side and from de Gaulle and his followers on the other. De Gaulle, in a radio broadcast on 10 June, claimed that the London Accords involved 'the formation of a Reich at Frankfurt' and that nothing could 'prevent the growth of a totalitarian state in these circumstances'.

Many senior officials were certain that de Gaulle's view would prevail in the end. The Schuman government was clearly about to fall, and the head of the European Department at the Quai d'Orsay predicted that, within a month or two, the General would be in power.

One part of the prediction was correct. Bidault's signature in London led to the downfall of the Schuman government, an event which took place on 19 July. But even the ensuing political crisis did not bring de Gaulle to power. One administration after another staggered to its feet, then collapsed again. France was to be left without a stable government until 11 September. Robert Schuman was appalled at the bickering – the worst offenders were in the Socialist Party – when Europe was on the brink of war.

In Berlin, the introduction of a new currency – the Deutschmark – in the American and British sectors on 23 June had been answered immediately with a blockade of the city by the Red Army. Marshal Sokolovski announced that Allied military government had ceased to exist. General Lucius D. Clay, the autocratic and exci. American commander, known as 'the Kaiser' to the State Department, wanted to fight through the Soviet zone to Berlin to reopen the city's land corridors. Fortunately Truman rejected his pleas, and decided on an airlift instead. On 29 June, the US air force and the RAF began their air-bridge into Tempelhof airport, with a cargo plane landing on average every eight minutes.

Rumours of war intensified again. American diplomats and officers who had been in Berlin talked of 'Custer's last stand' during visits to Paris. Bogomolov, the Russian ambassador, did not disguise the menace. 'You're following a very bad policy,' he said to a journalist. 'You'll repent of it before long, before the end of the year.'

France was returning to a state of turmoil reminiscent of the previous autumn. On 25 June, the day after the blockade of Berlin started, fighting broke out in Clermont-Ferrand. The Communists, according to Moch, tried to drive government forces out of the town. No fewer than 140 policemen were wounded, a number of them with acid burns.

In August, French forces became involved in the air-bridge by constructing a new airport at Tegel in their zone of Berlin. The Communist Party launched a poster campaign and a wave of demonstrations with such slogans as 'Down with the anti-Soviet War', 'The French people will never fight the Soviet Union'. Dockers in the Communist stronghold of Le Havre, following Lecoeur's instructions, refused to unload military supplies for the US army. The renewal of political strife at home and events in Berlin provoked even greater fears and a flight of capital.

That summer, leaders of the Rassemblement were even more conscious of a threat to them than the previous November. General de Bénouville had an unexpected and anonymous visitor one night. It turned out to be Colonel Deglian, a Communist leader whom he had known in the Resistance. 'Don't ask why I've come to see you,' said Deglian. 'But are you able to defend yourself?'

The Communists at this time went beyond minor acts of sabotage to disrupt Rassemblement meetings. Groups of militants attacked whenever the opportunity presented itself. The Gaullist *service d'ordre* did not hesitate to respond. After Communist attacks round Nancy and Metz, members of the Rassemblement were proud to have sent 'some forty Communists to hospital'.

One of Malraux's aides told an American Embassy official that the RPF had decided 'to schedule meetings for other regions of France where Communists might attempt serious obstructions'. Caffery reported to Washington that the Communists appeared to be trying to bait the Gaullists into a false move.

De Gaulle's whistle-stop tour of south-eastern France in September was the Rassemblement's answer to the Communist challenge. After a well-ordered start on the Côte d'Azur, the Rassemblement's organization fell apart disastrously in Grenoble. On the evening of 17 September de Gaulle reached the outskirts of Grenoble where, in a brief ceremony, he placed a wreath on the war memorial. Next morning, as he drove into the town, his entourage found that nails had been scattered all over the road. When they entered Grenoble, a large and noisy Communist demonstration greeted them. Virtually no Rassemblement escort was in place, and few police were to be seen. Soon de Gaulle's car came under attack as missiles of every sort were hurled from windows. The mayor of Grenoble, a member of the RPF, was hit at de Gaulle's side.

That afternoon, de Gaulle made his speech as planned. But

afterwards, as he was leaving the town, the RPF marshals were attacked by Communists with such violence that they sought refuge in a gymnasium. The police are said to have stood back while the Communists attempted to set the gymnasium on fire. A group of RPF stewards arrived to help the besieged group and opened fire, as did some of the Gaullists inside the building. Several people were wounded in the firing and one Communist was killed.

There was no apparent link between incidents such as those in Grenoble and the state of international tension over Germany. Yet in Moscow, Foy Kohler, one of the State Department's most highly regarded Kremlinologists, had been watching events in France with growing suspicion.

Kohler knew that Stalin's fear of Germany was entirely visceral. His declaration in 1943 at the Teheran conference that it would be necessary to execute between 50,000 and 100,000 senior German officers was not merely a turn of phrase to impress his audience. And the Soviet leadership's paranoia, caused by the Americans' haste to change the Statute of Occupation, was entirely in character. Stalin had been traumatized by the German invasion of Russia mainly because he had so disastrously underestimated the threat of invasion.

It is worth transcribing Kohler's telegram in full.

To: Secretary of State　　No: 2325, October 14, 5 p.m.

As seen from Moscow, current Communist-directed disturbances in France seem likely to be deliberately calculated to hasten the advent to power of de Gaulle, with primary objective of thus bringing about the destruction of the London decisions and disrupting the dangerous (to Kremlin) unity of Western Powers. Soviet leaders clearly demonstrated during the Moscow talks that restoration of western Germany is their main present concern and at same time learned there was no chance of preventing such restoration by negotiation, even at the price of concessions with respect to Berlin. In view his clearly-expressed views, de Gaulle would apparently be second-best only to a Communist government in France in bringing about these Soviet objectives and French Communists who suffer at his hands are clearly 'expendable'.

In Moscow, two days before the events in Grenoble, Georges Soria of the French Communist Party had told Kamenov that 'in the present situation, the tasks of the French Communist Party are very complicated and difficult. At one meeting Thorez warned that a tenacious struggle will take place and that this conflict could even be armed.' The statement can, of course, be read in different ways. But the general content, and the complicated and difficult tasks unspecified by Thorez, are compatible with the Kohler analysis.

The French Communist Party may have been the 'eldest son of the Stalinist church', but Stalin was hardly the man to shrink from playing Abraham. He knew that if the Gaullists had come to power – a prospect which seemed more likely at the time than it does in hindsight – they would have suppressed the Communist Party. Their plans for the rounding-up of Communists were an open secret. Colonel Rémy later confirmed to Ridgway Knight that 'the arrest of 500 Communists would decapitate and paralyze the movement, and the RPF knew exactly where these 500 men were'. Colonel Passy told American diplomats that the General should start by shooting several hundred people, but 'unhappily he hasn't got the stomach for it'.

The Kohler hypothesis, if true, prompts a number of thoughts. Stalin had almost certainly misjudged de Gaulle. However much de Gaulle loathed the deal on Germany or despised politicians, he would have considered seizing power illegally only if the government had looked like caving in to the Communists or to a Soviet ultimatum. Civil unrest, even with attacks on the Rassemblement, was not enough.

*

The political crisis in Paris, which had lasted most of the summer with one politician after another failing to form a government, only came to an end on 11 September. Dr Henri Queuille of the Radicals, a country doctor famous for his lack of panache, finally succeeded. Queuille immediately reinstated Moch as Minister of the Interior.

The Communist Party's efforts that autumn were directed once again through the CGT, and once again genuine grievances were exploited for political ends. Moch and other members of the government desperately wanted to reduce food prices, but the economic situation did not yet permit it. On 17 October, the franc had to be devalued by 17 per cent.

From 8 October, railway strikes spread. Other industries followed. The Communist Party was, however, wary about throwing its weight behind the strike at Renault, having had its hands burned there the year before. Paris was less affected by strikes than the previous year; most of the city's population continued to work as usual. For Samuel Beckett, it was probably his most fertile period. He started to write *Waiting for Godot* on 9 October 1948, as an escape from his unsuccessful novels. He finished it less than four months later, on 29 January 1949.

Once more, the main centres of unrest were the coalmining districts in the north of France. On 20 October the region was placed under a state of siege. Hundreds were arrested, including the Communist deputy René Camphin. Miners occupied the shafts and winding gear, having barricaded the entrances to the pits. They claimed that they were maintaining the mines, but after the sabotage of machinery the previous year Moch refused to take their word for it. Troops and armoured vehicles were brought back from the army in Germany to break down the barricades.

The war of attrition, which spread to the heavy industry of Lorraine and elsewhere, continued into November. The new British ambassador reported to London, 'France is the present front line in the Cold War.' Moch was as resolute as the year before: only unconditional surrender would be accepted. 'The government has decided to maintain order with the greatest energy and re-establish the authority of the state,' the Minister of the Interior reminded one of his colleagues. The new Prime Minister, Henri Queuille, formally instructed Jules Moch to forbid all prefects and inspectors-general 'any sort of negotiation with the unions' without his authority.

Moch received enough reports to convince him that he was dealing with a foreign-controlled operation directed against the Republic. He was determined to track down the source of Communist Party funds used to prolong the strikes. In a message marked '*Très Secret*' to the Secretary of State for Finance, he asked him to investigate all 'import licences without payment'. He was convinced that the Soviet Union was exporting goods via roundabout routes, which French Communist commercial fronts then sold off, never having paid for them.

Predictions of civil war and the return of de Gaulle produced a strong sense of *déjà vu*. Raymond Aron, at a curiously mixed dinner party – it included Bevin's deputy, Hector MacNeill (who had brought his protégé Guy Burgess with him to Paris), Loelia, Duchess of Westminster, and Esmond and Ann Rother-mere – predicted 'six months of strikes and misery, then the return of de Gaulle'. Gaullists, both by belief and self-interest, tended to talk up the degree of disorder.

Although the General's personal popularity was waning, the elections of 7 November proved a surprise success for the Rassem-blement. General Leclerc's widow, Madame de Hautecloque, 'accepted a place on an RPF ticket because she was assured that she would not be elected and was much astonished to find herself in office'. Yet the Rassemblement was doomed to decline, because the autumn of 1948 marked the last frenzy of civil war paranoia. Despite all de Gaulle's predictions, the Fourth Republic had not crumbled.

Meanwhile the Communists no longer stood a chance of achieving power by constitutional means. After the Prague coup and the threats over Berlin, the majority of France's population, whether they liked the idea or not, knew that their only place now was within the Western camp. Right into the 1960s, however, France remained the KGB's 'main target' in 'its policy of working for an internal split in NATO'. The man given the responsibility for forcing France to leave NATO was none other than Boris Ponomarev.

30
The Treason of the Intellectuals

Within the mainly left-wing circles of French intellectual life, a David and Goliath conflict between a handful of libertarians on one side and a pro-Stalinist majority on the other was starting to make itself felt. Only when the Cold War began to develop its own Manichaean logic did the French Communist Party find itself on the defensive.

Thorez's remarks after the Prague coup, tantamount to an admission that Communists would support the Red Army in the event of war, put them back into an ideological ghetto comparable to their position in 1939 after the Nazi–Soviet pact. Most of the admiration for the Soviet Union which had existed in France in 1944 and 1945 turned into distrust, even fear, by the end of the decade. The group in French society which most conspicuously failed to follow this change was the *progressiste* intelligentsia, their resolve strengthened by anti-American rhetoric. If the Communist Party could no longer present itself as the standard-bearer of French patriotism, it could still portray itself as the defender of French culture against a transatlantic invasion.

Shortly after Communist ministers had left government, Thorez called for the establishment of a *Front littéraire*. The party, with political power slipping from its grasp, wanted to secure the commanding heights of art and thought. This determination redoubled after it lost so many working-class members as a result of the disastrous strikes in 1947 and 1948. Laurent Casanova, the cultural commissar, called on writers to formulate new values. A commission of intellectuals met weekly under his direction. They included Annie Besse (now the historian Annie Kriegel) and Victor Leduc, the son of a Russian revolutionary. Leduc, an academic and a fanatic, became a member of the *section idéologique* – the Communist Party's equivalent of the Holy Office.

Intellectuals were managed through an appeal to idealism and moral blackmail. To let the Party down in the slightest way was portrayed as a betrayal of the hopes of 'all progressive mankind'. Often little pressure was needed, because most Communist intellectuals longed to be accepted by the working class, and only *engagement* in its international movement could absolve them of bourgeois guilt.

After his return from the United States, André Breton observed that: 'The ignoble word of "*engagement*", which has become current since the war, exudes a servility horrifying for poetry and art.' *Engagement* meant eradicating the truth at the whim of the party. Paul Éluard confessed to suppressing a poem he had written about the bombing of Hiroshima after Aragon told him that it did not follow the party line.

The party policy of mingling intellectuals and workers was more symbolic than real. Annie Besse, who was in charge of the *Quartier Latin* – an area where intellectual and working-class life overlapped round the Place de la Contrescarpe and the rue Mouffetard – managed to achieve a mixture in the cells. They may have sold *L'Humanité* alongside each other in the Sunday morning market of La Mouffe, but the result was bound to remain contrived.

Cell meetings took place for Emmanuel Le Roy Ladurie every week or fortnight in a bistro or café on the rue Gay-Lussac. Over glasses of cheap beer, they would 'talk for hours at a stretch about party dialectics'. In the Latin Quarter, the

Communist Party could tolerate the odd eccentric, even Michel Foucault, the most unpredictable of members, who was 'already absorbed in his research into madness'.

Paul Éluard, who took a genuine interest in working-class life around him in the 18th *arrondissement*, had few illusions about the possibility of intelligentsia and proletariat mingling unselfconsciously. In 1945 Éluard had returned to live on the rue Marx Dormoy, close to his old haunts. His interest in the political life of the *quartier* was genuine. He encouraged the sons of party workers to follow further education, and even wrote marching songs for the local Communist youth. Éluard, unlike some party stars, was naturally modest. Jean Gager, who accompanied him to a meeting of railway workers, remembered that he never said a word throughout the proceedings, because he felt that he had nothing useful to contribute. But as they left, Éluard had turned to him: 'Are you sure that they did not change their vocabulary in my presence?'

'Yes, it's true,' Gager had to acknowledge. Their language had been much more formal than usual.

The submission of intellectuals to dogma may have seemed stultifying to an outsider, but the party was clever. It knew how to flatter young writers. Maurice Thorez took Pierre Daix aside after a meeting to congratulate him on his novel *La Dernière Forteresse*. For a young Communist, this was the greatest moment of his life. Thorez's companion, Jeanette Vermeersch, then featured Daix on the cover of the party's magazine for women, *Femmes françaises*.

The party also knew how to flatter fellow-travellers, and manipulate sceptics who could still be useful. Georges Soria, one of its senior journalists, explained at his meeting in the Kremlin in September 1948 that Julien Benda, the author of *La Trahison des clercs*, was judged useful because 'even though he was against Marxism and Communism, he supported the party's present policies in France'. Soria went on to explain that they had set up various magazines, '*Pensée* in particular, precisely to attract fellow-travellers such as Benda'.

The first great post-war test of Communist loyalty arrived in the spring of 1948. Almost overnight, Marshal Tito, the hero and role-model of Communist members of the French Resistance, was declared to be a traitor. The accusations against Tito even extended to 'hiding White Russian officers who tortured and killed the mothers and fathers of Bolsheviks during the Revolution'.

The French party leadership had a very clear idea of the situation, and was only too keen to follow Moscow's orders. Yet some party members, including Louis Teuléry, the former member of Tillon's ministerial cabinet, did not conceal their feelings that Tito had been wronged. They paid for their views with summary expulsion. Teuléry was privately warned by a friend, 'they're going to accuse you of being a Trotskyist'. After he was ejected, his comrades, a number of them old friends from the Resistance, refused to speak to him – or their wives to his wife – for over thirty years.

Several hundred members of the French Communist Party were expelled. The novelist Marguerite Duras also left at this time. Daix swallowed the brutal change in the party line because men he respected, such as Charles Tillon, had accepted it without a murmur. 'You've got to know how to grit your teeth,' Casanova had told him.

The prostration of some intellectuals before the party could provide moments which were beyond satire. Just after the war, Jacqueline Ventadour (later the wife of the painter Jean Hélion) was married to Sinbad Vail, Peggy Guggenheim's son, who founded the literary magazine *Points*. She was then a Communist and a member of the same cell as Victor Leduc, the philosophy professor in the *section idéologique*. Leduc was married to Jeanne Modigliani, the daughter of the painter and a close friend of both Jacqueline and Sinbad. The austere and fanatical Leduc had renounced all wealth, so Jeanne, desperate to leave their squalid little apartment, needed a deposit to move to a slightly better one, and borrowed the money secretly from Sinbad. But when Leduc discovered that she had borrowed from an American capitalist, he became hysterical with fear that the party might find out. Sinbad and Jacqueline had to swear never to say anything to anybody, and Leduc went round begging money from party comrades to pay them back.

At the time of Tito's break with Stalin, Sinbad and Jacqueline went to dinner with Victor and Jeanne. Several leading French Communist intellectuals were there, as well as the Hungarian cultural attaché, the writer Zoltán Szabó. The conversation inevitably locked on to the subject of Tito, arch-criminal and traitor. Someone, forgetting that Sinbad Vail was not a party member, asked him what he thought. Sinbad, exasperated by the grotesque conversation, said that he still considered Tito a great man. A shocked and frightened silence fell. Eventually, it was broken by a low, rumbling laugh from the Hungarian: he had never seen anything so funny as the terrified faces of these French intellectuals.

Sartre at this time was involved in the only formal political venture of his life. In the autumn of 1947, he joined the Rassemblement Démocratique Révolutionnaire, a party founded by Georges Altman and David Rousset to create a movement independent of the United States or the Soviet Union.

The Kremlin already had its eye on the 'Trotskyist and *provocateur*' Rousset. The French Communist Party underlined the danger of Sartre's contribution. 'There are two ideological dangers in France,' Georges Soria told Kamenov, his interlocutor in the Kremlin. 'The first is the militant fascism of Malraux with his false heroism – the ideology of Gaullism – and the second is the philosophy of decadence expounded by Sartre which now acts openly against Communism by talking of a "Third Force".

Both have their followers and an influence, especially among the young.'

It was Andrei Zhdanov who masterminded the attacks on Sartre and his 'bourgeois reactionary philosophy'. The most vicious campaign was triggered by Sartre's play *Dirty Hands*, which opened in April 1948. The play depicts brutal power politics within the Communist Party of a Balkan country during the war as the Red Army advances upon it. Sartre argues from both sides of the fence with clever dialogue, and although his characters lack psychological depth, they are at least intellectual rather than political pawns. His seemingly improbable choice of Jean Cocteau to take over as director proved a good decision. The production and the acting were powerful.

Anybody in touch with reality would have known that the Communists would be infuriated by this chilling portrait of party life; yet Sartre, as David Rousset observed, 'lived in a bubble'. French Communists were even more furious, because Hoederer, the Communist leader assassinated on orders from within the party, had been following a similar line to that of Maurice Thorez during the war. Ilya Ehrenberg told Sartre that he had nothing but contempt for him. Sartre might shrug this off, but he seems to have been genuinely dismayed when the play was used as anti-Communist propaganda. The Kremlin had *Dirty Hands* suppressed in Finland on the grounds that propaganda hostile to the Soviet Union was against the provisions of their peace treaty. But within five years, Sartre's own position had changed to such an extent that he would consent to productions of the play only with the agreement of the local Communist Party, which of course meant suppressing it entirely.

Stalinist hatred for Sartre burst forth in an astonishing piece of stage-management in August 1948, during the Congress of Intellectuals for World Peace at Wroclaw (formerly Breslau) in Soviet-occupied Poland.

Some 500 participants were invited from forty-five countries to this typical Communist-front event, organized by Andrei Zhdanov two months after the Soviet blockade of Berlin commenced. The congress's main objective was to protest at the American and British plan to rebuild Germany, claiming that it was a plot to make it a base once more for aggression against the popular democracies and the Soviet Union. The choice of Poland as the venue was deliberate.

The French delegation included the painters Pablo Picasso and Fernand Léger, and the writers Vercors, Roger Vailland, Jean Kanapa, Pierre Daix and Paul Éluard, still mourning the death of his wife, Nusch. Laurent Casanova was their organizer and chaperone. The British delegation was more mixed, with the historian A.J.P. Taylor, the scientist J.B.S. Haldane, the 'Red Dean' of Canterbury, Dr Hewlett-Johnson, and the young George Weidenfeld. The Russian delegation included Alexander Fadeyev, president of the Union of Soviet Writers, the ubiquitous Ilya Ehrenberg, and Mikhail Sholokhov, the author of *And Quiet Flows the Don*. Jorge Amado came from Brazil and George Lukacs from Hungary. The joint presidents were Julian Huxley, the Director-General of UNESCO, who was neutral, and Irène Joliot-Curie, who was a Communist.

On arrival, the delegates were greeted by lavish yet unenjoyable entertainment amid the ruins. The Poles received Picasso like royalty and put him in the bedroom which Hitler had used during the war. Once the congress started, Picasso made his first political address, calling for the release of his friend Pablo Neruda who was imprisoned in Chile. His speech did not last long, and its simplicity had a powerful effect. He was followed to the rostrum by Alexander Fadeyev; the contrast could not have been greater.

Zhdanov had instructed the speaker carefully. Fadeyev, whose most recent novel, *The Young Guard*, had been severely criticized for not having exalted the role of the party, was desperate to clear his name. He demanded open war against the decadence of Western literature and art. Picasso was not mentioned by name, but the thrust of the attack was clear. Only painters of socialist realism could be accepted as aligned with the working class. But when Fadeyev described Sartre as a 'jackal with a pen', delegates from the West instinctively snatched off their headphones in disbelief. Ignoring the effect in the hall, Fadeyev simply went on reading his text.

Despite the watchful eye of Laurent Casanova, several members of the French delegation – Picasso, Léger and Vercors – did not hide their disgust. For Vercors it was a major blow to his faith. He would turn against the party before the end of the following year and prove a formidable critic of the show trials in Eastern Europe. Julian Huxley, after a brief exchange of notes with his co-president, Irène Joliot-Curie, left the hall and took the next flight home.

That evening in the bar of the Monopol Hotel, Picasso became drunk, exasperated by arguments with Russian socialist-realist painters. Journalists kept asking him what he thought of the congress, but he refused to answer.

On the last day of the congress, delegates were shocked by news of the unexpected death of Zhdanov. For Fadeyev especially, it was a devastating blow. The journalist Dominique Desanti saw Fadeyev's hands shake after he received the news. He must have assumed that his controller had been liquidated on Stalin's orders – the circumstances of Zhdanov's death are still uncertain – and feared that he would follow him. Fadeyev, who had sold his soul to the system, committed suicide after Khrushchev's revelation of Stalin's crimes at the Twentieth Party Congress. His self-destruction was a harshly appropriate ending to a tale of those times.

After the congress, Picasso, Éluard and Daix were taken by the Polish Communist Party on a visit to Auschwitz and then to Warsaw, where they stood, Picasso in tears, on the crushed rubble of what had been the ghetto. Nazi atrocities still formed one of the strongest themes in Stalinist propaganda – only the

Soviet Union, it was claimed, could prevent the recurrence of such crimes.

The French Communist Party, however, found itself pushed into ever more indefensible positions as the era of Eastern European show trials began. Every negative was turned into a positive. The bigger the lie, the greater the leap of faith, and the more desperately would loyal party members defend it. Their rationale was based on one of the most shameless manipulations of logic ever known. Comrade Stalin and Communist parties everywhere were fighting for the good of the people. They were therefore incapable of torturing a loyal Communist to force him to confess to appalling crimes.

The greatest challenge to the reputation of the Soviet Union came early in 1949 with the Kravchenko court case in Paris, an event which was followed with obsessive interest all round the world.

Viktor Kravchenko, a Russian engineer who had defected from a Soviet trade mission in the United States in 1944, published his memoirs, *I Chose Freedom*. The book became one of the great bestsellers of the post-war period and was translated into twenty-two languages. It was the first widely published account by a Russian eye-witness of Stalin's forced collectivizations, the persecution of the kulaks and the famine in the Ukraine; it also gave a clear idea of the Soviet labour camps twenty-five years before Alexander Solzhenitsyn's *Gulag Archipelago*.

The book's appearance in France in 1947 caused a sensation. It sold 400,000 copies and received the Prix Sainte-Beuve, yet such was the power of the Communist Party in the publishing world that none of the major houses had dared touch it.

The party denounced all the book's allegations, especially the idea that there were labour camps in the Soviet Union. *Les Lettres Françaises* led the attack on 13 November 1947 with an article signed 'Sim Thomas', supposedly a former officer of the

American OSS. This piece claimed that American intelligence agents had written the book, not Kravchenko, who was dismissed as an alcoholic and compulsive liar. There were other insulting articles by the Communist writer André Wurmser. On hearing of these attacks Kravchenko, who had temporarily settled in the United States, launched a libel case against 'Sim Thomas', André Wurmser, *Les Lettres Françaises* and its director, Claude Morgan, a former right-winger who had turned Communist.

When the trial opened on 24 January 1949, the Palais de Justice was overrun by newsreel crews, journalists and press photographers. A company of the Garde Républicaine had to be brought in to restore order. The scope and significance of the battle taking place in the overcrowded court-room quickly became clear. However much the defence tried to turn the case into a trial of Kravchenko's character, it remained what Kravchenko had intended it to be: a tribunal by proxy of the Soviet Union and Stalinism. Both sides brought in their witnesses, entirely at the plaintiff's expense. Although the American authorities provided no financial aid, they helped Kravchenko assemble Ukrainians from displaced persons' camps in Germany who could testify to conditions during the 1930s.

The *Lettres Françaises* defence team turned to the Soviet Union for witnesses. The NKVD rounded up individuals who could be persuaded to blacken Kravchenko's character and veracity. The most vulnerable of all was Kravchenko's first wife, because her father, a former officer in the White army, was still in a prison camp.

Before the Soviet witnesses appeared, the defence tried to play the card of French patriotism against a defector and thus a deserter in wartime. When Kravchenko's counsel countered with the question of Thorez's desertion in 1939, and Wurmser's lawyer Maître Nordmann demanded '*un peu de respect pour ce grand homme politique français*', there was an outburst of derisive laughter in court.

Because the vast majority of the public present openly

supported Kravchenko, the Communist press claimed that the benches were packed with women from the *beaux quartiers* in fur coats. It is true that this trial had become such a sensation in Paris that American bars were offering an 'I-Chose-Freedom' cocktail, a mixture of whisky and vodka, as a publicity gimmick. Many people did come to the trial to see Communist noses rubbed in the dirt – André Gide would hardly have been human if he had not relished the prospect after what *Les Lettres Françaises* had said about him. But many others came who were not prejudiced against the defendants, such as Sartre and Simone de Beauvoir.

Nordmann brought in the most prominent fellow-travellers available to express their disdain for Kravchenko – Pierre Cot, the aviation minister in the Popular Front government of 1936, Louis Martin-Chauffier, the president of the National Committee of Writers, Emmanuel d'Astier de la Vigerie, Dr Hewlett-Johnson and General Petit – as well as Communist writers – Pierre Courtade, Vercors and Wurmser's brother-in-law, Jean Cassou – the former Communist minister, Ferdinand Grenier (who gave his profession as bakery worker) and the ubiquitous Nobel laureate Frédéric Joliot-Curie who, during his testimony, proceeded to defend the Moscow show trials of the 1930s. The one witness the defence never produced was 'Sim Thomas', the alleged American author of the original article. He did not exist. The author had in fact been André Ulmann, editor of the Soviet-backed *Tribune des nations*.

On 7 February, Kravchenko's former wife, Zinaïda Gorlova, made her appearance for the defence. The court-room became tense with anticipation. 'She's a prepossessing blonde,' wrote an eye-witness, 'thirty-six years old, with what used to be called "advantages" which are tightly restrained in a corset. She wears a black dress. Her face is pale, with a closed expression.' Gorlova had been flown into Paris with a woman guard, presumably from the NKVD, who escorted her everywhere from an apartment rented by the Soviet Embassy in the Boulevard Suchet. In a voice which sounded monotonous from over-rehearsal, she recounted that Kravchenko had beaten her, broken china and forced her to have an abortion. He was a liar, a womanizer and a drunkard.

Kravchenko's lawyer, Maître Georges Izard, had little difficulty in making the poor woman squirm. She refused to admit that her father was either a former White Guard or in a prison camp. She claimed that he was dead. She had never seen the scenes of famine in the Ukraine which Kravchenko had claimed to witness with her. The effort was so great for her that she had to ask for a chair so that she could sit down. Nordmann, for the defence, tried to stop Kravchenko speaking to his former wife. The president of the court told him to be quiet. A furious row broke out between them, and in the uproar Gorlova continued to repeat mechanically the insults against her former husband. 'Always the same recording!' Kravchenko yelled, as the president of the court brought the session to a hurried close.

The proceedings were often chaotic. One exchange led to Kravchenko throwing himself at Wurmser, before being dragged back by a gendarme. Many of his remarks were not only clever and funny; they cut to the bone, to the delight of his supporters on the public benches. Claude Morgan, on another occasion, burst out: 'They're not the public, they're *cagoulards*!' André Wurmser, too, could not contain his unfeigned outrage that a man he considered a traitor should be allowed a public hearing.

Over the next few days, Gorlova's appearance changed. She had become listless, her face looked yellow, her hair was unkempt, she had lost weight. Kravchenko felt sorry for her, knowing that her failure to make an impression boded ill for her and her family. 'She did not come to France voluntarily,' he cried to the court. He promised to look after her in the West for the rest of her life: 'But she must say why she came here!' The court-room was electrified. Gorlova collapsed, vainly searching for a handkerchief in her handbag. Her female guard sat frozen beside her. Before the court reassembled, Gorlova was taken to

Orly where a Soviet military aircraft was waiting to fly her back to the Soviet Union.

It was then Kravchenko's turn to call his witnesses. Almost all came from camps for displaced persons in Germany, but his most effective witness had arrived from Stockholm. This was Margarete Buber-Neumann, the widow of a pre-war leader of the German Communist Party, Heinz Neumann. On Hitler's rise to power the couple had sought refuge in Russia, but were sent to Soviet labour camps, accused of political deviationism.

In 1940, after the Molotov–Ribbentrop pact, the Soviet Union handed them and some German Jews over to the Nazis. Margarete Buber-Neumann survived five years in Ravensbrück, and managed to escape just before the Red Army arrived. According to Galtier-Boissière, who was watching closely, Claude Morgan and André Wurmser looked down at the ground during her description of the Soviet labour camps. Her account was clear and unflinching in every detail, and revealed an astonishing courage and stamina. Only the most fanatical Stalinist could have disbelieved her. That other Communist renegade, Arthur Koestler, exulted at the effect of her contribution. Buber-Neumann went to stay with him and Mamaine Paget for a couple of days.

The verdict in Kravchenko's favour was announced on 4 April, the same day as the signature of the North Atlantic Alliance. Almost as if to prove his point, the press in Russia claimed the opposite: that Kravchenko's case had collapsed before the truth of the Soviet position. Yet news of the Communist defeat in Paris still reached Solzhenitsyn in the prison camp of Kuibyshev, bringing a glimmer of hope.

The trial, coming after the Communist Party's reverses in 1947 and 1948, began to convince France that the Soviet Union was not a workers' paradise. The debates in the court-room launched a wave of cynicism, and people were no longer frightened of criticizing the Communists openly. On the last day of the month the anti-Stalinist left held a conference at the

Sorbonne on war and dictatorship, an event unthinkable two years before.

On 20 April, just over two weeks after the end of the trial, the Soviet Union tried a new tactic. The French Communist Party launched the Mouvement de la Paix at a meeting at the Salle Pleyel, presided over by Professor Joliot-Curie. Picasso's dove, the emblem of the movement, was prominently displayed. A mass meeting followed on the same day, and soon propaganda posters with the dove covered walls across the city. It was not long before an anti-Communist group, Paix et Liberté, began to produce counter-propaganda. The dove of peace was portrayed as a Russian bomber – '*La colombe qui fait boum!*' – in a poster campaign designed to challenge the Communists' virtual monopoly of the walls of Paris.

At the time of the Kravchenko trial, Koestler and Mamaine moved into a house called Verte Rive on the Seine at Fontaine-bleau. Just as they were moving a fresh row exploded, only this time Koestler took Sartre and Beauvoir's side against André Malraux. Malraux had been outraged by a recent attack on him in *Les Temps modernes*, and Gaston Gallimard had suddenly withdrawn his support for the publication. Sartre and Beauvoir discovered that Malraux had apparently threatened to expose Gallimard's record during the Occupation if he continued to support *Les Temps modernes*.

Mamaine Paget recalled the evening of 1 March 1949, when Koestler 'bearded' Malraux. 'At first when K. asked him about this, Malraux made evasive replies, but finally he more or less admitted that it was true ... K. feels that his great faith in and friendship with Malraux is at an end – it really was a stinking thing to do ... in fact, simply blackmail.'

The last joint outing of the three couples – Koestler, Sartre, Camus – had a certain air of *déjà vu*, although this time they did not go to the Schéhérazade, but to the Troika, another smart nightclub run by White Russians.

A few days later, Sartre, Camus and Simone de Beauvoir discussed the evening. Camus asked: 'Do you think we can honestly go on drinking like that and work?' When Sartre and Beauvoir next encountered Koestler outside the Hotel du Pont-Royal and he suggested that they should all meet up again, Sartre took out his diary as a matter of habit, then stopped himself. 'We've nothing more to say to each other.'

'Surely we're not going to mess everything up for purely political reasons!' Koestler protested.

'When one has such different opinions,' Sartre replied, 'one can't even see a film together.'

Koestler, who did not duck his share of the blame for the ending of their friendship, encountered Sartre again in June 1950 at the Gare de l'Est. They were both taking the overnight train to Germany. Koestler and Mamaine, now his wife, were off to Berlin for the Congress of Cultural Freedom, while Sartre was leaving for a conference in Frankfurt. Without the disapproving presence of Simone de Beauvoir, they shared their picnic supper with Sartre, along with two anti-Communist Poles and a police bodyguard assigned to Koestler by the Sûreté after he had received death threats from the Communists.

Sartre, although looking very ill − according to Mamaine, he was virtually living off a form of amphetamine called Corydrane − made a great effort, and they had an amusing time together. But Koestler and Mamaine felt sorry for him. 'On that evening in the sleeping-car,' Koestler wrote at the end of his life, 'Sartre complained that they hardly went out in the evening because there were so few people left with whom they agreed about politics.'

The year 1949 saw a wave of doubt among many Communist intellectuals. Both Vercors and Jean Cassou, Wurmser's brother-in-law, resigned from the party, and were attacked by *L'Humanité* on 16 December as 'traitors'. For *Les Lettres Françaises*, however, which was trying to appeal against the verdict in the

Kravchenko case, this decision by two of their witnesses was embarrassing.

Sartre's rift with Camus had also widened. After Camus returned to France from South America, his play *Les Justes* appeared in December 1949 at the Théâtre Hébertot, where his *Caligula* had proved such a great success in 1945. *Les Justes*, which dealt with revolutionary violence in Tsarist Russia, marked a further step away from his *communisant* contemporaries. Some saw the play as a veiled attack on the Resistance, but Camus's target was clear: the idea that revolutionary violence could be justified by the vague promise of a better future. The next step away from Sartre was his essay, *The Rebel*, which came out two years later. It constituted a direct attack on intellectuals who allowed political considerations to corrupt their artistic integrity.

Sartre did not believe that a writer could ever stand aside politically. In his case, political commitment was already subordinating art. He was patronizing about Camus's scruples and refusal to swim with the progressive tide of history. 'I only see one solution for you,' he concluded, 'the Galapagos Islands.'

The final break did not come until 1952. Sartre saw Camus in the bar of the Hotel Pont-Royal and warned him to expect a savage review of *The Rebel* by Francis Jeanson in *Les Temps modernes*. The editorial committee had refused to censor what had been written.

Camus replied to the article on 30 June. Ignoring Jeanson, he addressed his letter to Sartre – as '*Monsieur le Directeur*'. In particular, he attacked 'the intellectual method and attitude' of the piece. His arguments may have lacked philosophical rigour, but he posed enough well-directed questions to render his opponents very uncomfortable. 'One does not decide the truth of a thought according to whether it is right-wing or left-wing.' He pointed out the fundamental contradiction of Existentialists justifying a system which was totally opposed to the idea of the responsibility of the individual.

'Such a polemic,' commented Raymond Aron, 'would hardly be understood outside France and Saint-Germain-des-Prés.' There, more than anywhere else, progressive intellectuals continued to turn a blind eye to Stalinist methods. Some acknowledged them, but justified them. Others, like Simone de Beauvoir, acknowledged them and dismissed them as irrelevant. She argued that if you made an issue of them you must be a supporter of American capitalism. She accepted that, though she disliked Kravchenko, the trial had undoubtedly proved that labour camps existed in the Soviet Union. Yet she revealed herself in a passage describing the American writer, Richard Wright. 'With his eyes shining from misguided fanaticism, he was breathlessly recounting stories of clandestine arrests, betrayal and liquidation – no doubt true – but one did not understand either the point or the scope of what he was saying.'

This new *trahison des clercs* was firmly in the Jacobin tradition: an intellectual terrorism justifying physical terror. Stalin's regime might be pitiless, his apologists argued, but all revolutions had a terrible majesty. What mattered was that the Soviet Union's stated philosophy was on the side of human justice. Against this, the United States offered no ideological or social programme except economic freedom, which simply meant the freedom to exploit others.

Those who were not sealed inside bubbles of morally vacuous theory might have fallen for the wartime appeal of a party of martyrs. But they could not blind themselves to the suspicion that the terrifying sacrifices which had fuelled the Soviet system had been wasted and were still being wasted. No Utopia could be built on a mass graveyard.

Part Four
The New Normality

31
Americans in Paris

American Paris of the Montparnasse era had ceased to exist after the Wall Street crash of 1929, yet a certain pale renaissance occurred after February 1948, when the franc was devalued against the dollar. France once again became affordable for writers and anyone else with artistic pretensions. But the most conspicuous American presence in Paris at the end of the decade consisted of diplomats, soldiers and Marshall Plan executives.

For those cashing cheques at Morgan's Bank in the Place Vendôme at the beginning of February, it was 'like Christmas morning, strangers beaming at each other'. A hundred dollars obtained over thirty thousand francs. For those who cared about clothes, a Dior dress was within their grasp.

Downstairs, Morgan's Bank was an eminently respectable setting for American ladies in their gloves, waisted suits and close-fitting little hats. They could not see the painted ceilings and frescoes upstairs in the masculine preserve of management. These erotic sprawls from the *belle époque* included one of a naked woman on a river-bank putting a smouldering cigar to her mouth in a most suggestive manner.

Paris had again become a focus for rich expatriates and semi-nomadic socialites. Some adapted better to their surroundings than others. Laura Corrigan had again arrived at the Ritz, where her only demonstrably national practice was to give

Thanksgiving lunches with 'lobster and young turkey with all the trimmings American style'.

Elsa Maxwell, on the other hand, 'burst upon Paris like a stink-bomb,' wrote Lady Diana Cooper to a friend. 'She lunched today and really embarrassed me before [General] Béthouart and Minou [de Montgomerie, his wife] and Cocteau and Lulu [de Vilmorin], with her appalling French and revolting appearance.' Prince Jean-Louis de Faucigny-Lucinge acknowledged that Elsa Maxwell's '*anti-charme*' gave her a certain originality. 'She shamelessly mixed people and places in a cocktail-shaker which she jiggled about violently.' At fancy-dress parties she used to dress up in grotesque costumes as a sailor, or Napoleon III, or Sancho Panza.

The most famous of these rich itinerants was Barbara Hutton, whom Truman Capote dubbed the 'dime-store maharani' after staying with her in Tangier. He observed that 'Miss Hutton never travelled; she merely crossed frontiers, carting forty trunks and her insular *ambiente* with her.' Miss Hutton's chief claim to fame in Paris had occurred in the tense summer of 1946. At that time of threatened *coups d'état*, she had featured in *Life* magazine being escorted from the Ritz by an astonishing number of policemen. Her crime, however, was not political: she had been evicted for wearing a pair of silk Bermuda shorts.

Arthur Miller, who reached Paris in the winter of 1947, formed a very different impression from those whose lives revolved around the Place Vendôme and the rue du Faubourg Saint-Honoré. He found a city which had been 'finished' by the war. 'The sun never seemed to rise over Paris, the winter sky like a lid of iron graying the skin of one's hands and making faces wan. A doomed and listless silence, few cars on the streets, occasional trucks running on wood-burning engines, old women on ancient bicycles.'

The Pont-Royal hotel on the rue du Bac, where Miller stayed, was gloomy but cheap. The concierge wore a tail-coat which was coming to pieces, and 'his chin always showed little nicks from having shaved with cold water'. Once a day this prematurely aged man rushed home across Paris to feed his rabbits, the only source of meat for his family, as for much of the population. The 'hungry-looking' young prostitute who sat in the lobby all night watched passers-by 'with a philosopher's superior curiosity'.

Miller went off in search of Jean-Paul Sartre, having heard that he could be found in the Montana bar: had he but asked, the frayed concierge and the philosophical prostitute could have told him that Sartre and his friends now met in the basement bar of the very hotel in which he was staying. Far more important to Miller's work, however, was an evening watching Louis Jouvet in Giraudoux's *Ondine*. The theatre was freezing, the audience wriggling their feet in their shoes and blowing on their hands. Jouvet himself was so ill that he sat throughout the play in an armchair, wrapped in sweater and muffler. Looking at the audience, Miller felt that 'there really was such a thing as a defeated people'; Jouvet, however, managed to connect with them 'in a personal way I had never experienced before, speaking to each of them individually in their beloved tongue. I was bored by the streams of talk and the inaction on-stage, but I could understand that it was the language that was saving their souls, hearing it together and being healed by it, the one unity left to them and thus their one hope. I was moved by the tenderness of the people towards him, I who came from a theatre of combat with audiences.'

Truman Capote also stayed in the Hotel Pont-Royal, in a tiny room on the top floor. 'Despite the waterfall hangovers and constantly cascading nausea,' he wrote, 'I was under the strange impression that I was having a damn good time, the kind of educational experience necessary to an artist.'

Simone de Beauvoir was frequently seen in the hotel, since the *famille Sartre* had moved to its 'leathery little basement bar' after fleeing the tourists in the Café de Flore. Capote sensed that he was a figure of fun in their eyes: according to one friend, he felt 'he was the victim of some intangible conspiracy of malediction'. Beauvoir had not liked Capote's *Other Voices, Other Rooms*, and had little respect for 'fairies'. She compared the tiny American, in his over-large white jersey and pale-blue velvet trousers, to a 'white mushroom'; and laughed with the barmen who pointed out that his first name was that of the President of the United States, while his surname was the French slang for condom.

Capote replied in kind with his description of the Sartre clan in the Pont-Royal bar. 'Wall-eyed, pipe-sucking, pasty-hued Sartre and his spinsterish moll, de Beauvoir, were usually propped in a corner like an abandoned pair of ventriloquist's dolls.'

Camus was the only one who was always kind to the young American. Capote, however, later claimed that one night Camus, the great womanizer, had suddenly succumbed to his attraction and gone to bed with him: a story impossible to deny, but unlikely.

One day, after a number of visits to Natalie Barney's salon, the 'empress of the lesbians' herself turned up at the Pont-Royal to collect him. Alice Toklas – 'Miss Stein's widow' – was seated in her car. They drove off, and stopped outside a shabby building. Miss Barney led them up several flights of stairs, which reeked of cat's urine.

They entered a studio, but the lights did not work. Natalie Barney cursed. '"Dog take it," she said, suddenly very prairie-American, and lighted a candelabrum.' With this source of light held high, she led Capote round the room to study the paintings. They were all canvases by her old lover, Romaine Brooks, including her best-known work, the dramatic study of Una, Lady Troubridge with Eton crop and monocle.

According to Capote, who no doubt improved the dialogue, Alice Toklas regarded the paintings closely. '"Romaine," said the widow, smoothing her fragile moustache, "Romaine had a certain technique. But she is *not* a great artist." Miss Barney disagreed. "Romaine," she announced in tones chilled as Alpine slopes, "is a bit limited. *But* Romaine is a very great artist."'

Natalie Barney also arranged for Capote to visit her old lover Colette, who received him from her bed '*à la* Louis Quatorze at his morning levée'. He described her 'slanted eyes, lucent as the eyes of a Weimaraner dog, rimmed with kohl; a spare and clever face powdered clown-pale; her lips, for all her considerable years, were a slippery, shiny, exciting show-girl red; and her hair was red, or reddish, a rosy bush, a kinky spray.' She asked him what he expected from life. He told her that he did not know what he expected, but he knew what he wanted, which was to be a grown-up person. 'Colette's painted eyelids lifted and lowered like the slowly beating wings of a great blue eagle. "But that," she said, "is the one thing none of us can ever be."'

One of the first writers to migrate to France after the Liberation, as opposed to those who arrived in uniform, was the black writer Richard Wright, author of *Black Boy* and *Native Son*. Thanks to the combined efforts of Gertrude Stein and Claude Lévi-Strauss, then French cultural attaché in Washington, he arrived in Paris with his wife Ellen (who was white) and their daughter Julia in May 1946.

The State Department had been very reluctant to give him a passport, but once in Paris – where he was an honoured guest – they could hardly ignore him. Nevertheless, Wright was seen as a distinct liability. At an official reception at the American Embassy given a few days after his arrival, he was told, 'For God's sake, don't let these foreigners turn you into a brick to hurl through our windows!'

Wright could not get over the welcome accorded to him by the French. He was made an honorary citizen of Paris, and his French publisher, Gallimard, threw a party in his honour at which the guests included Roger Martin du Gard, Michel Leiris, Maurice Merleau-Ponty, Jean Paulhan and Marcel

Duhamel. His move to Paris had been made to gain a better perspective on the core of his fiction: the racial problems of America. He acted as a consultant for *Présence Africaine* and Sartre's *Les Temps modernes*, and in 1948 he became active in Sartre and Rousset's Rassemblement Démocratique Révolutionnaire.

James Baldwin, another black writer living in Paris, was deeply indebted to Richard Wright, who did much to help him in the first stages of his career as a writer. Yet Baldwin's feelings towards Wright were complex, almost Oedipal, and they spilled out in an essay for *Zero* magazine called 'Everybody's Protest Novel'. Baldwin argued that the protest novel was flawed because its essential humanity was obscured by politics. Wright took this as a personal attack on *Native Son*, and was bitterly hurt. The relationship between the two writers never recovered, even though Wright continued to bail the impoverished Baldwin out of debt from time to time. Baldwin managed to survive only by scrounging off friends and hustling in gay bars, yet Paris helped him gain confidence. He was treated as an American writer, not a black, and like many foreign writers he found that in France writing was respected as a profession.

The largest contingent of left-bank Americans in the late 1940s were young soldiers who had become students under the GI Bill of Rights. Once the franc was devalued, their $20 a week provided just enough to live on. A number of them were in a belated state of rebellion against the stupider indignities of military discipline, and became attracted to radical politics. The French Communist Party, through its Maison de la Pensée Française, made special attempts to win over foreign students in Paris, especially Americans. The American Embassy was concerned by this development and kept an eye open, but there was little it could do, except pass the matter on to the FBI and CIA.

From the spring of 1948, Paris saw a very different American influx with some 3,000 new residents, all of them under the umbrella of the Economic Cooperation Administration: the executive arm of the Marshall Plan. When Paul Hoffman, the chairman of Studebaker who had been appointed to oversee the Marshall Plan, outlined his staff needs to the Senate Appropriation Committee, he said: 'We hope to hold our organization down to approximately 500 in the United States and approximately one thousand in the eighteen nations in which we must be represented abroad'; but the task proved far greater and more complex than envisaged. There was also no shortage of applicants. Some 32,000 young Americans, imbued with idealism and the longing to live in Paris, came forward eagerly.

Averell Harriman, the Secretary of Commerce, had been at the forefront of persuading the American people, and especially the business community, that their self-interest and moral duty lay in helping Europe. The accompanying message was that Europe needed to learn American ways. 'We have developed a system through which an American worker can produce many times more than a worker in any other country,' said Harriman to the Pacific Northwest Trade Association in Seattle. 'Less than half a million American miners produced last year 50 per cent more coal than did two million miners in Europe.' Yet the Marshall Plan proposal declared that it would be an 'unwarranted interference with the internal affairs of friendly nations' to demand that they adopt the American model of capitalism.

Harriman's main objective was, in fact, strategic: he did not want to see a ruined Europe fall prey to Communism. Business leaders made it very clear through their lobbying offensive on Congress that the generosity of the Marshall Plan – up to 17 billion dollars to Europe over five years – should not be a one-way affair. American industry had to be allowed to profit, whether through the guarantee of increased export markets or the chance to dump excess stocks. This would lend some substance to the instinctive suspicion of many in Europe, mostly on the left but also on the right, that the Marshall Plan was

America's economic version of the the Trojan Horse. (A public opinion poll in France showed that 47 per cent of the sample believed that the Marshall Plan was dictated by America's need to extend its markets.) On the other hand Jean Monnet, France's greatest planner, defended it strongly, since to have continued with a ruined economy and severe social unrest would have allowed far less independence in the medium and long term.

Once the huge package of measures was sold to Congress, President Truman appointed Averell Harriman as the Special Representative of the Economic Cooperation Administration. His swearing-in took place just after the *John H. Quick*, the first American cargo ship full of Marshall Plan grain, had steamed out of Galveston, Texas. Within a few months, 150 vessels a day were crossing the Atlantic in a logistical operation that dwarfed any comparable movement during the Second World War.

Averell Harriman had already proved himself at almost everything he touched. As a rugged, good-looking and rich young man, he had rowed for Yale, skied superbly and excelled as an eight-goal polo-player and member of the American team which defeated the Argentines in 1928. He had been a highly competent chairman of the Union Pacific Railroad before Roosevelt had persuaded him to serve his country, most famously as United States ambassador in Moscow during the war. Now, Harriman took over the Hôtel Talleyrand on the corner of the Place de la Concorde as his headquarters in his battle to thwart Communism in Europe.

The announcement of the Marshall Plan may have been greeted by beleaguered European politicians like the distant trumpets of an army coming to its relief. But once the first tranche of 4·9 billion dollars was on the table to be divided between nations, Harriman needed all his experience of international dealings, all his toughness and all his self-control. He faced skirmishing and blocking actions in almost every direction: the British, who felt that they deserved special treatment after their wartime sacrifice, were trying to protect the status of sterling as a reserve currency; General Lucius Clay, 'the Kaiser', demanded that Germany be treated no differently from France; the French wanted no interference in the use to which they put the aid; and bureaucracy in Washington wrangled over every detail.* During interminable meetings, Harriman kept his temper by drawing vigorous doodles – then pushed hard at the crucial moment. His skin was thick enough to ignore the barrage of Communist attacks against '*La 5e Colonne Américaine en France*'. Most important of all, his relations with Paul Hoffman in Washington were based on mutual trust, so no transatlantic dispute ever escalated into a civil war.

Harriman was fortunate in key members of staff. He managed to persuade Milton Katz, the Harvard law professor, and David Bruce, the lawyer and diplomat, to join him in Paris. He was also extremely lucky that France appointed Robert Marjolin, a brilliant financial civil servant, to be secretary-general of the Organization for European Economic Cooperation. Marjolin needed all his skills in dealing with the high-handed and eccentric Sir Edmund Hall-Patch, the British chairman of its executive committee.

The young American professionals arriving in Paris to staff the ECA were all eager to save Europe from famine and Communism and to have the time of their lives. 'The boys had all been through the war,' wrote a secretary at the United States Embassy, 'and felt cheated of a knowledge of life. Before they settled down to an executive desk, they wanted to savour a taste of something they might never have again.'

In the enthusiasm of these young men, even out-of-order elevators and erratic telephones seemed to possess a certain exotic charm. The envy of the French, however understandable,

* The French were the most successful in their endeavours. Jean Monnet persuaded David Bruce that the government should be allowed to divert Marshall Plan funds into industrial regeneration.

was the hardest thing they had to come to terms with. Hard currency gave Americans the choice of the best apartments, and pushed up prices for others; while they shipped over everything unobtainable in Europe, notably cars and shoes. 'How will you recognize me?' asked a young American, on the telephone to the French family who were to meet him at the railway station. 'By your shoes,' was the immediate reply.

The quality of American officials varied greatly. There were those who knew France well and spoke the language admirably, while others barely spoke French at all. Many could not pronounce the name of the French Prime Minister, Henri Queuille, and just referred to him as 'Kelly'. This became a joke, and even French-speakers at the embassy picked it up.

Some members of the Economic Cooperation Administration, responsible for direct contact with the French, were incapable of reading a set speech and understanding the questions put to them afterwards. On 3 December 1948, a senior member of its information service gave a lecture on the philosophy of the Marshall Plan. The arguments were so incompetently put over that virtually everything he said was easily ridiculed by a French philosophy professor who was a member of the Association France–URSS, and almost certainly a Communist. So embarrassing was this spectacle that the Minister of the Interior wrote to Robert Schuman, the Minister of Foreign Affairs, begging him to advise the American ambassador of 'the need to send out only talented speakers, who know our language properly and are able to reply without difficulty to questions which might be put to them'.

The Communist campaign was relentless. 'At times,' remembered a member of the ECA's public relations staff, 'we could not show a film on the Marshall Plan without getting a brick through the screen.'

David Bruce, the ECA chief of mission, had no problems with

the language after his experience of France before and during the war. He was delighted to be back in Paris, this time installed with his wife Evangeline in a beautiful apartment in the rue de Lille. After a few months, however, they decided they needed somewhere larger, and David Bruce promised to start looking.

One day Bruce returned hiding a smile. 'I think I've found somewhere to live,' he said.

'But where is it?'

'It's on the Avenue d'Iéna.' He was referring to the residence of the United States ambassador. He had just been asked if he would replace Jefferson Caffery.

Bruce returned to the United States for discussions at the State Department before taking up the post. On 10 May 1949, a strategy meeting on France was held with Dean Acheson, the Secretary of State since Marshall's retirement, Philip Jessup, George Kennan, Chip Bohlen and Bob Murphy. 'The presentation of the United States' viewpoint was thoroughly and exhaustively discussed,' Bruce recorded dryly in his diary. He was sceptical about any approach which smacked of American intervention.

On 14 May David Bruce landed at Le Bourget to an official reception, and was driven into Paris with a motorcycle escort. 'The Embassy flag fluttered bravely atop a fender,' he wrote in his diary, 'and I think the bystanders were somewhat baffled by the lone funereal old Cadillac car, surrounded by helmeted police, speeding with unknown occupants to an unknown destination.'

Their destination, 2 Avenue d'Iéna, was a house built by President Grévy in the 1880s and purchased by a previous American ambassador. 'It is a large, typically French, rich, bourgeois dwelling of the later nineteenth century, with a small but attractive garden. On the ground floor, it is well disposed for large receptions and dinners. Upstairs, the bedrooms are rather appalling, and it is not nearly as attractive or as well furnished as those in most good Paris homes. However, it is a joy to be here.' One of the joys turned out to be the chef, Robert. A 'simple Sunday night dinner' prepared by Robert consisted of onion soup, a timbale of lobster with thick wine sauce, followed by chicken and salad.

Bruce went over the mission's domestic arrangements thoroughly. There had been trouble with the Marine guards, now quartered in the Hotel Continental. Bruce wanted them in civilian dress. This was not a time to allow America to be characterized as a proconsular power, whatever the realities of its economic hegemony.

He had little time to read himself into the job. Within a fortnight of his arrival, foreign statesmen began to assemble for the Conference of Foreign Ministers. This was to be held in the Palais Rose on the Avenue Foch – 'Boni de Castellane's ostentatious monstrosity' – and followed the usual set pattern. The four delegations, headed by Dean Acheson, Vyshinsky, Robert Schuman and Ernest Bevin, were seated in an inward-facing square. Acheson's aide, Lucius Battle, described Vyshinsky as 'sinister, tight, gaunt, with the beadiest eyes I have ever seen'. Bruce was most impressed by Schuman: 'What a fine man he is, sympathetic, direct, intelligent.' Dean Acheson was rather fond of the ebullient Bevin. Years later, he told Lucius Battle that he infinitely preferred being called 'My boy' by Bevin than 'Dean dear' by Anthony Eden.

The proceedings at the Palais Rose were almost unbearably tedious. After Vyshinsky had talked for forty-five minutes in Russian, his speech had to be translated by a member of the Soviet delegation into English, and to make matters worse, this interpreter was utterly incompetent. At one point Lucius Battle turned to Chip Bohlen and asked, 'Haven't they got a better interpreter than this?' Bohlen, a fluent Russian-speaker himself, replied, 'Everyone in their delegation speaks better English! This is the water torture, designed to drive us all crazy!' The Americans soon installed their own interpreter, who translated while Vyshinsky spoke. 'The Russians went on with their English translation,' remembered Battle, 'but at least it gave us forty-five minutes to talk and plan, while the Russian interpreter droned on.'

Dean Acheson, 'after a steady four and a half hours at the Council', acknowledged that 'his ass was tired'. As light relief, the Bruces took him and Luke Battle to the Monseigneur, with its 'dozen violinists, a cellist, a pianist, a harpist and heaven knows what other players'. But although the choice of this White Russian establishment had never been intended as a political statement, it almost turned into one when Acheson became very exuberant on champagne and rose to his feet.

'I want to drink a toast to the Berlin airlift,' he announced.

'Luke, make him sit down!' ordered Bruce, afraid that matters might get out of hand. If a journalist was present and word got out, the Communist press would have a field-day.

'But how?' asked Battle, looking up at his towering boss.

'Pull him down by his pants.' Battle heaved as instructed, and the Secretary of State dropped back into his seat with surprise, but without a diplomatic incident.

Even if Bruce could play little effective part in the Conference of Foreign Ministers, he soon found that the power of the American ambassador in France was very great, almost embarrassingly so, now that the importance of economic aid was finally appreciated. In striking contrast to the aloofness which de Gaulle had shown his predecessor, French prime ministers came to consult him even over the composition of a new government. At the same time, Bruce did what he could to restrain Washington's compulsion to direct affairs. On Friday, 10 June, exactly a month after the strategy meeting on France, Bruce was against putting pressure on the French to grant Indo-China unrestricted independence. He felt it could only provoke them into a more obstinate frame of mind.

The reason for the ambassador's power was very simple. After a late lunch at the Travellers' the previous Monday, 6 June,

Bruce had returned to his office to work on a speech for the next day. The telephone rang. It was Maurice Petsche, Queuille's Minister of Finance, asking him to come round for an urgent meeting. Bruce agreed. The reason was not hard to guess. 'As usual,' he noted in his diary after seeing Petsche, 'there is a financial crisis, and the government wants to borrow 80 billion francs.'

Bruce admired Petsche for his courage in the face of ill-health – 'his ankles are swollen, his face is purple' – and for his refusal to give in to members of his own party who objected bitterly to his stand on taxes and agricultural prices. Petsche's character, shamelessly original for a politician, appealed to Bruce. When Petsche remarked that his Prime Minister, Queuille, was 'an adorable man', Bruce observed in his diary: 'that term would seem odd if one of our Cabinet officers were to apply it to a President'.

The Bruces were also amused by Petsche's contempt for the dietary advice of doctors. Evangeline Bruce remembers a lunch where Petsche, explaining that he was on a special regime, was served an ungarnished truffle the size of a small fist as his entrée. His health was so bad that his friends expected his death at almost any moment, but with an inexplicable resilience (curiously reminiscent of France's economy) his body somehow continued to function in defiance of all received wisdom.

Americans were struck by the way that food played such a ritualistic part in French political life. The day after Petsche asked for the American loan, President Auriol gave a magnificent lunch for Dean Acheson, John Foster Dulles, Chip Bohlen, Bob Murphy and David Bruce at the Élysée Palace. 'The chef is famous,' noted Bruce, 'and the lunch consisted of cold eggs Lucullus, suprême de sole Gallière, poulet grillé Béarnais, fonds d'artichauts Marigny and soufflé glacé Petit Duc.' He also approved of the wines: Château Carbonnieux 1936, Mouton Rothschild 1940 and Mumm Cordon Rouge 1937.

As if to balance an indulgence reminiscent of the *belle époque*, members of the American Embassy, with the rest of the diplomatic corps, assembled in Notre-Dame the next day for Cardinal Suhard's memorial mass: a ritual impregnated with the defiant spirit of *vieille France*. General de Gaulle's interdiction of nearly five years before – Suhard's punishment for according Pétain's Minister of Propaganda a mass after his assassination by the Resistance – was an unmentioned, looming memory.

Bruce, however, was soon preoccupied with the Coca-Cola War, which took a decisive turn just after the Bruces came back from a long weekend visit to Château Lafite with Élie and Liliane de Rothschild.

Two senior executives of the Coca-Cola Company, Farley and Makinsky, came to see the ambassador on his return. They told him that they were pushing ahead with their plans to sell Coca-Cola in France. The French government was continuing to resist because of protests from small wine-producers, urged on by the Communist Party's campaign against '*la Coca-colonisation de la France*'. So emotional had the whole issue become that many wine-producers really believed the claim that soft-drink imports would destroy their livelihoods.

To bar Coca-Cola from the French market was a flagrant violation of the Marshall Plan agreement on free trade. Yet David Bruce, while angered by the dishonest antics of the Communists and the protectionist lobby, was almost as exasperated with his own countrymen. 'It is a clear case of discrimination,' he wrote in his diary, 'and we have protested vigorously against it, although I think that the Company's advertising proposals are psychologically extremely stupid.' Coca-Cola apparently wanted to 'engage in their usual advertising displays, including among other features, a blazing sign on a 142-foot tower. They have relinquished, rather regretfully, the idea of using the Eiffel Tower.'

The Communist Party in France openly proclaimed that American culture was stifling the nation. Laurent Casanova announced that Henry Miller's pornography and American crime stories were attacking the soul of France. He would have sounded like an arch-conservative if the target of his hatred had not been the United States and its influence. Yet as one or two writers have pointed out, the Communists' xenophobic conspiracy theory owed much to a right-wing, anti-masonic tradition.

To complete this curious reflection of right-wing prejudices, the magazine *Action*, run by Communist writers such as Pierre Courtade and Roger Vailland, attacked 'the pederasts of the American intelligentsia in Saint-Germain-des-Prés'. In all seriousness it went on to recount: 'The other day a cavalry colonel in civilian clothes was the recipient of undisguised propositions, even though he was accompanied by his charming wife.' It was just what one would have expected from reactionary monarchist publication.

For some time, the sale of Coca-Cola was portrayed in the Communist press as not far short of drug-peddling to infants. 'Each evening, a Coca-Cola truck stops at the entrance to the Square des Innocents, in the 1st *arrondissement*, and the driver distributes bottles to unaccompanied children who drink it on the spot.'

The power of the American ambassador meant that Parisian eyes were now on the American Embassy, and no longer on the British. But much of the fascination was due to the sociable natures of David and Evangeline Bruce, who could hardly have been less like Jefferson and Gertrude Caffery. David Bruce, tall, silver-haired and patrician, with his slight Virginia drawl and dry humour, greatly appealed to the French. Jean Monnet described him as 'a deeply civilized man' with 'rare foresight and good faith' who 'does not think of his country in terms of domination'. Meanwhile, as one of the embassy staff wrote of his wife, 'everyone was struck by Evangeline Bruce's beauty'. Tall and slim, elegant and intelligent, with a low, amused voice, she was precisely the sort of woman whom Frenchmen admired most. Nearly fifty years on, veteran politicians of the period still sigh as they remember: '*Ah, la charmante Madame Bruce!*'

The scale of entertaining expected was considerable. No fewer than five thousand invitations were sent out for the Fourth of July party yet within hours of the first postal delivery, the embassy switchboard was jammed with calls from people asking why they had not been asked. The logistical preparations were on army corps scale. Bruce gave orders for the preparation of a punch. The recipe had a certain numerical simplicity: 2,000 bottles of white wine, 200 bottles of Cointreau and 200 bottles of Cognac. Rather optimistically, as it turned out, Bruce estimated that teetotallers would require 2,000 bottles of Coca-Cola as well as 'bathtubs of fruit juices'.

On 3 July, the kitchen staff worked throughout the night in a crescendo of activity, preparing 37,000 items of food, including 'hundreds of canoe-shaped horrors, supposedly edible, adorned with the American flag'. Eight thousand people turned up. A considerable proportion wanted to buttonhole the host and hostess, whether to thank them for the party, complain about the French or offer an opinion on the current political situation. Hundreds of hands had to be shaken and smiles returned.

After two hours, David and Evangeline Bruce were obliged to slip away to a French government reception, but this did not stop the party continuing until half past ten. The ambassador and his wife were fortunate to escape the alcoholic battlefield. 'Drunks were plentiful and visitors invaded the house.' Embassy staff even claimed that a couple of casualties had been found in the bushes next morning. The only complaint – especially from gate-crashers – was that so many people had been invited.

32

The Tourist Invasion

Once the war ended, the urge to travel as a civilian, not a soldier, became strong. In Britain, there was a longing to escape the austerity of war, socialism and bomb damage. Only a very few, however, were in a position to afford and arrange such a luxury. In the late summer of 1945 Winston Churchill, recovering from his defeat in the General Election, went to stay at the Hotel de Paris in Monte Carlo. He registered under the *nom de guerre* of Colonel Warden and followed '*une véritable cure de Pommery Rosé 1934*', to use the words of Monsieur Roger, the *chef sommelier*, who had to beg for more supplies.

Britain remained in the grip of rationing for much longer than France, and appeared no closer to pulling itself out of destitution. The *milord anglais* was now little more than the remnant of a distant past, conspicuous mainly by his rarity. In April 1946, once the mines were cleared from their part of the Côte d'Azur, the Duke and Duchess of Windsor returned to the villa La Cröe and reassembled a staff of twenty-two indoor and outdoor servants. That summer, the Earl and Countess of Dudley drove to the South of France with a packet of a million francs obtained in Paris from Loel Guinness, at the black market rate of 700 francs to the pound.

The chief obstacle, for those who were prepared to respect the law, was the £25 travel allowance imposed by the Labour government. More and more Britons began to flout it in their desperation to escape the greyness and austerity of Attlee's Britain; which, in comparison with France, seemed to have progressed little beyond Nissen huts, short-back-and-sides and suet pudding. The appeal of Paris fashions, boulevard cafés and sumptuous food became overwhelming.

From May 1948, American citizens had been allowed to bring home 400 dollars' worth of goods, but the real boom in tourism began in the summer of 1949. By then, travel arrangements were easier and Europe slightly better prepared. 'We are informed that 3 million tourists are upon us,' wrote Nancy Mitford to Evelyn Waugh in April 1949. 'The Ritz say they have no room until 10th October.'

'Americans in Europe,' Letitia Baldrige wrote home from her job in the United States Embassy, 'do create harm and ill-will often. I hate to think of the careless, complaining, spoiled people who flounce through these struggling countries making the Europeans feel even more embittered and inferiority-complexed.' The main objection amongst Europeans of the old school, however, seemed to be sartorial. 'You should have seen them in the Ritz here as I did this morning,' Nancy Mitford wrote to Waugh at the end of August, 'all dressed up in beach clothes.'

To greet the invasion of dollar-packing tourists, shops in the rue du Faubourg Saint-Honoré had arranged window displays on the theme of the Seven Deadly Sins. Fresh oranges and bananas symbolized 'greed', a point which may have been lost on tourists from a land of plenty, while at Lanvin 'envy' was represented by a headless mannequin in formal brocade and weighed down with jewellery. Cartier even laid in 'gold swizzle sticks at 11,000 francs and a semi-automated version at 21,000', appliances which horrified the French.

Everyone was drawn to Paris for a combination of reasons, whether shopping, sightseeing, the inspiration and excitement of the place, or simply curiosity. For those who had dreamed of the Montparnasse era, the voice of the nightclub singer Jacqueline François singing '*La Vie en Rose*' was enough to make them feel 'like a young Scott Fitzgerald character sopping up the romance of Paris'.

The city also symbolized sexual liberty, from the sequinned G-strings of the Folies-Bergères to the excitement of seeing the art student revellers from the Quat'zarts Ball. On the night of 5 July, they swarmed across Montparnasse 'dressed, or rather underdressed,' noted the American ambassador when his car was good-naturedly overrun, 'as Indians or Japanese warriors, with smears of paint, the only visible garments being loin cloths'.

But while the younger American longed for such liberty, his stuffier compatriots expressed shock and disapproval. French indiscipline – political, sexual, hygienic, and gastronomic – provided subjects for much moral condemnation In the summer of 1948, the first trickle of tourists criticized the seemingly endless political crisis as one Cabinet after another failed from July to September. And puritanism was outraged by the waste of *grande cuisine* at a time when France as a whole was supposed to be 'on welfare handouts'. Even the gastronomic extravagance of the French middle class struck many of them as immoral, and they did not keep their views to themselves. Often their censure was influenced by their own inability to cope with rich and unusual food. Laden with remedies for upset stomachs, they had a horror of squatting over a hole in the floor. Nor was their concern with hygiene helped by the water shortages in the summer drought of 1949.

The French were not the only ones taken aback by opinionated or self-absorbed tourists. In June 1949, a young American woman staying at the Ritz rang David Bruce at the United States Embassy to ask him 'to have her mattress changed as it was too lumpy'. Later Bruce was accosted at a party by a New York model who demanded to be introduced to some interesting French people because she wanted 'to increase her vocabulary'.

Bruce, however, was certainly not stand-offish from the swelling American community in Paris. He made an effort to go to every *soirée vernissage* of exhibitions by young American painters, however much he disliked their work. One exhibition which the Bruces attended with more enthusiasm than usual was that of Edward G. Robinson's wife at the André Weill gallery. She was selling her paintings for charity to help rebuild a French village. Over the next few weeks, while Robinson was filming on the Côte d'Azur, Gladys enjoyed herself in Paris. The Bruces saw her again for lunch at Maxim's, 'slightly over-cocktailed but very funny', before she staggered forth for a fitting with Marcel Rochas.

One feels slightly weak when contemplating the resistance to alcohol required in those days. American influence in Paris had introduced a 'cocktail hour' in hotels, a sort of limbering-up session, before going out to dinner and a show. But the cocktail hour was in fact two and a half hours long, from six to eight-thirty, a bibulous counterpart to the French period of *cinq à sept* reserved for adultery.

There were half a dozen favourite places, very different from the austere French establishments with their zinc counters and tiled floors. The Crillon bar, full of journalists and Marshall Planners, was reputed to offer the best Tom Collins in Paris. The Ritz barman, André Guillerin, was famous for his champagne cocktails. The passing trade from Hollywood tended to stay at the George V or the Prince de Galles, where the barman Albert remembered the taste and capacity of even the most infrequent customer. The Meurice and the Claridge had small, quiet bars for talking, while the bar of the Plaza Athénée offered the advantage of a quick snack before the theatre.

Those visitors who could afford it wanted to go to the most famous places. Albert, the *maître d'hôtel* at Maxim's, now back in his old job, bowed to the rustle of dollar bills, the currency of what the Communists called the 'new occupying power'. The Tour d'Argent was still famous for its pressed duck and the view of Notre-Dame by night. On warm summer evenings, middle-aged romantics were tempted by the Pavillon d'Arménonville in the Bois de Boulogne, where they could dine out by the lake with Chinese lanterns in the trees, and the ubiquitous violinists playing tzigane music. Or there was the Pré Catalan nearby, sited on the traditional duelling ground.

For most Anglo-Saxon visitors with limited French, the theatre tended to mean the Folies-Bergères, the Lido or the Casino de Paris, rather than the Comédie-Française. But for those who could understand the language, the Parisian theatre in the early autumn of 1949 had a lot of entertainment to offer. Jean Gabin was reputedly brilliant in Henri Bernstein's *La Soif* at Les Ambassadeurs. David Bruce described it as 'a sexy piece, rather old-fashioned in the sense that it is a repetition of all Bernstein plays'.

On Saturday, 1 October, the Ballet de Monte Carlo, produced by the Marquis de Cuevas, opened its season. Tamara Toumanova and Rosella Hightower, one of the American principals whom Cuevas had brought over from the United States, were hailed as superb. George de Cuevas, a Chilean married to a Rockefeller heiress, had taken over the ballet in 1947 from Serge Lifar, with whom he had allegedly fought a duel. Nijinska was Cuevas's *maîtresse de ballet* and he also recruited Lichine and Markova. The capricious and egotistical Cuevas renamed his company 'Le Grand Ballet du Marquis de Cuevas'.

The following month, *Un Tramway nommé Désir* by Tennessee Williams opened and became one of the hits of the year despite hostile reviews. For those who had seen the controversial original in New York with Marlon Brando in his famously ripped tee-shirt, the French version offered a different originality. Jean Cocteau, who adapted it, made many changes. For a start, his evocation of New Orleans was rather curious, 'with some pretty odd erotic Negro dances'. David Bruce went to the first night in a large party with Paule de Beaumont, who had translated the play. The scenery was brilliant: it needed to be, since it was in competition with another European winter. The curtain rose to the sound of crickets to convey a sweltering hot southern night, but the audience was freezing.

Although the critics were unimpressed by the production, Arletty was wonderful in the role of Blanche (which was played by Vivien Leigh at the same time in London). It was her first stage part since she had been banned from acting. Her film, *Portrait d'un assassin*, with Maria Montez and Erich von Stroheim, came out on 25 November, during the play's run.

One night, Arletty had an unexpected visitor in her dressing-room after the performance. Marlon Brando was in Paris for a long holiday after making his name as Kowalski in the original American production. He had several reasons for wanting to see her. *Les Enfants du Paradis* was his favourite film and he had adored Arletty in the role of Garance. In the States, he had been cast as the peasant assassin in *The Eagle Has Two Heads*, a part which Cocteau had written for his lover, Jean Marais. But Brando's 'Method' peasant had been so conspicuously churlish, with nose-picking and crotch-scratching, that Tallulah Bankhead as the Queen with whom the assassin falls in love (the part played by Edwige Feuillère in the Paris production) had taken his crude insouciance as a personal affront. Largely at her insistence, he had not accompanied the production to Broadway.

Brando's notions of diplomacy had not improved. To meet Arletty, he turned up wearing jeans and a tee-shirt. Arletty, a true Parisian in matters of dress, was affronted and gave him an obviously frosty reception. Brando shrugged and transferred his attentions to the Boeuf sur le Toît, that new right-bank colony of the left bank, and spent his time with *Germano-pratins* whose sartorial standards were more relaxed. He found himself a modest Mobylette and Juliette Gréco gave him conducted tours of Paris from the pillion; but the singer he fell for at the Boeuf was Eartha Kitt.

*

The nightclubs in Paris offered a richer variety than anywhere else in the world. The Bal Tabarin was perhaps the most dramatic. Before the show it looked like any other club, with tables and chairs grouped round a dance-floor; but the semi-nude show itself was a breathtaking display, with trap-doors, trapezes, lights, sounds, mirrors and circus animals creating magical effects. The Carrousel, at 40 rue du Colisée, a few doors along from the Boeuf sur le Toît, had female impersonators in beautiful costumes as its main attraction. But the night ended with a can-can danced by the girls from the Folies-Bergères who came over after their performance.

There were any number of male homosexual or lesbian establishments, such as Le Monocle in Montparnasse; but La Vie en Rose, despite its less romantic nickname of '*la salle viande*', or 'the meat parlour', was the most endearingly eccentric. Sir Michael Duff and David Herbert, two eminent English queens, took Louise de Vilmorin, Diana Cooper and her young son, John Julius, there one evening. 'It's a small dancing hall,' wrote Diana, 'with orchestra and couples of middle-aged dentists dancing very well together, not cheek to cheek, as the languorous youth and maiden dance, but briskly and business-like. A "*patron*", with a face painted an inch thick, hangs about waiting for the moment when his shirt and trousers are exchanged for a sequinned Edwardian evening gown and hat, à la Boldini. Then at a beat from the band out troops a corps de ballet of oldish gentlemen en décolletage and maquillage – delight as best they can, while between numbers the male couples go prancing round with here and there a couple of tweedy women.'

Another White Russian nightspot in succession to the Schéhérazade and the Troika was the Dinarzade, run by Alexis de Norgoff and Colonel Tchikacheff, with their staple fare of caviar, shashlik, vodka and champagne. Les Grands Seigneurs in the rue Daunou, near Harry's Bar, otherwise known as Ciro's, had velvet curtains, burgundy walls, huge wine-coolers and gypsy violinists playing in your ear. Like the old Monseigneur in the rue d'Amsterdam which it resembled, it was only for starting a relationship unless you wished to be financially ruined.

Less expensive but also less predictable entertainment was offered by Suzy Solidor at her Club de l'Opéra in the rue Joubert. Solidor had a collection of over a hundred portraits of herself, including works by Christian Bérard, Cocteau, Dufy and Van Dongen. For those who liked tropical rhythm, there was La Cabane Cubaine in Montmartre, or the Martiniquaise Canne à Sucre in Montparnasse. There were informal jazz clubs like that of Honey Johnson, or Chez Inez in the rue Champollion, where Inez Kavanagh from Harlem employed out-of-work musicians; when orders for fried chicken or spare ribs dropped off, Inez herself would 'belt out a number or two'. The Lapin Agile in the rue des Saules in Montmartre, where Koestler had taken Mamaine on their first night together in Paris, was said to be full of penniless painters, but now the tourists had squeezed them out.

For foreigners the most sought-after show in the early summer of 1949 was Josephine Baker's great comeback at the Folie-Bergères in an extravaganza called *Féeries et Folies*. In June, the actor Michael MacLiammoir described taking out a friend in Paris for the first time. The experience began with a dish of snails at the Méditerranée. Then they went to see 'Josephine Baker, appearing in a series of roles that portray the Quest of Love down the ages, from tropical Eve (accompanied by ash-blond Adam, several doves, and misty Jungle of Eden at dawn under gigantic waterfall) through a bevy of startling incarnations that included Greek princesses, Eastern *impératrices*, and Queens of France. After this she dodges about a good deal as the Empress Josephine and as Mary Queen of Scots. This diversion reaches its height in dark purple cathedral where she is publicly executed (in trailing black velvet), after which the lovely headless thing, now robed in dazzling diamanté, sings Gounoud's *Ave Maria* to crashing strains from the organ, and scores of stained-glass saints descend luminously from their windows to celebrate triumph of Mike over Matter, and execute stately saraband in violet-ray. All this *émouvant* in the extreme: we find ourselves far too tired for night-club, put poor tired (but pleased) Paul to bed, and drink cocoa at the Dôme to calm our nerves.'

For the more robust, there was always Les Halles – 'the belly of Paris' in Zola's phrase – to go on to for onion soup just before dawn. After the almost solid soup and a *petit vin blanc*, smartly dressed couples watched beefy-armed and red-nosed porters in blue overalls heaving sides of beef around. Then they would walk slowly through the flower market, buying bunches to take back to the hotel where the night concierge, about to go off-duty, would greet them with an indulgent smile.

At the beginning of July, the municipal council of Paris decided to end the Grande Semaine with a Grande Nuit de Paris as climax. Fountains in the city and at Versailles were turned on and illuminated. The Eiffel Tower was floodlit for the first time, and circus elephants performed at its base. A special supper was organized at 3,000 francs a head, where celebrities – including Edward G. Robinson and Ingrid Bergman – watched the entertainments, which ended in a huge firework display from the Pont d'Iéna. Foreigners were, of course, an important audience, but the exercise was also a political demonstration to the people of Paris that better times were returning.

33
Paris sera toujours Paris

During the most turbulent and difficult periods after the war, Parisians had deliberately kept life as normal as possible. The concierge would swab out the entrance hall in the same way at the same time; the grocer would chalk his prices, however astronomical, with the same circular precision on miniature blackboards; the waiter would produce a menu with his usual nonchalant flourish. Office-workers and bureaucrats would greet each other each morning with the customary handshake, before any mention was made of outside events.

The upper classes especially remained aloof from political turbulence, as if this constituted its own rampart. In the spring of 1948, when France felt threatened by Soviet tank divisions, *vieille France* had refused to be distracted from its priorities. The Duchesse de Vendôme of the French royal family had died, and full consideration was accorded to funeral rites. 'The whole of the 7ème [*arrondissement*],' wrote Nancy Mitford to Evelyn Waugh, 'floats about in crêpe veils looking as if there is a war on.'

Other standards were also firmly maintained, international crisis or not. Adultery in Paris had always been conducted in style, but discretion was *de rigueur*. The conventional times for this recreation were after lunch or between five and seven in the evening, *le cinq à sept*. A private room with a lock on the door and a sofa in the corner could be booked at La Pérouse or, if the couple had time to motor to the outskirts of Paris, there was the aptly named Auberge du Fruit Défendu, where each private room had a bedroom *en suite* with the bed ready turned down. The employees in such establishments guarded their clients' secrets; yet however silent and careful the clandestine couple might be their friends – who guessed what was going on sooner rather than later – were under no such obligation. They followed the affair closely by observing the lovers in public, and discussed progress among themselves.

War and occupation had inevitably loosened some conventions. Well-brought-up young girls may still have been dressed in the style set by Mme Lanvin, or in Jacques Heim's *pour jeunes filles* range, marked by narrow edging, little collars and pastel colours; but chaperoning had become almost entirely obsolete. French girls *de bonne famille*, Susan Mary Patten wrote to a friend in August 1945, 'are having the first good time of their lives, going out every night with French, English or American officers alone or in parties to their friends' houses or to Le Forty-Five, which is a night-club, and to talk to, they are remarkably mature and independent, but retain their old-fashioned good manners, which makes an attractive combination.'

In pre-war years, no girl of good family would have been allowed near a young man whose pedigree was not equal to her own; but things had changed. One mother, on being asked about her daughter's fiancé, said irritably: 'All I know is that he hasn't been in prison, he isn't black, and he's passed his entrance to university. What more do you want?'

Although four years of wartime cloth rationing had at first restricted the wearing of long dresses and black tie to official and grand circles, pre-war standards were soon re-established. The first balls after the Liberation were held in aid of war charities. There were set themes: the Bal du Panache, the Bal des Masques, the Bal des Rubans, the Bal de la Rose. For while people were not yet in the mood for opulent costume balls, they were prepared to devote a little time and imagination to an amusing headdress to enhance their evening clothes. But a ball was still a ball, and incomplete without a décor – of which the best and most memorable were, as likely as not, by one of those two ubiquitous party-goers, Jean Cocteau or Bébé Bérard. French *Vogue* described Bérard's décor for the Bal du Panache in the summer of 1947: 'Christian Bérard's imagination had enhanced the reception rooms of the Maison de l'Amérique Latine with ivy round the windows, asparagus in the chandeliers and ancient armour and helmets with ostrich feather plumes.' Far too many people were invited, and the crush was made worse by the throng of vast tulle gowns; but the headdresses which the ball demanded rose to the occasion.

Artists had designed settings, costumes and celebrations for their patrons throughout European history, but they had not always been guests at the patron's parties, and very rarely were they counted among his close friends. 'Never, since the Age of Enlightenment,' wrote Prince Jean-Louis de Faucigny-Lucinge, 'has society found itself so close to artists.' This gave a dazzling, theatrical quality to grand parties, which made participants both actors and spectators.

The Bal des Oiseaux took place on 24 November 1948 in the Palais Rose – the *fin-de-siècle* copy of the Grand Trianon created by Boni de Castellane with his wife Anna Gould's money. Guests walked up the great staircase of pink and grey marble to the reception rooms, admiring each other's feathered masks, fans and headdresses. Some of the latter were very elaborate, made of great sprays of tropical feathers that rose at least a foot above the wearer's head. The painter Léonore Fini, whose costumes were designed to dramatize her artistic temperament, wore a huge owl mask of dappled feathers which covered most of her head and face, while the same feathers trimmed the very low cut of her dress. According to *Vogue*, which was proud to present photographs of the occasion in colour, many of the guests that evening expressed the wish that Boni de Castellane (who had died in 1932) could see his palace on this occasion: the decorations included pyramids of flowers and gilded branches, among which stuffed birds – taken from their glass domes – were perched like jewels.

These charity balls required hard work from the organizers, but little from those who could afford the ticket. Full costume balls, on the other hand, demanded ingenuity and imagination from both the hosts and their guests. Whenever Comte Étienne de Beaumont gave a ball, he demanded the utmost effort from his guests, rehearsing them for their *entrées* as though they were his private troupe of professional actors. Beaumont was immensely tall and slim, with an aquiline nose and a fastidious, braying voice. He dominated everything, even though the invitations went out in the name of his pious and devoted wife, Edith. Beaumont was very fond of her. She had few artistic ideas of her own, and greatly admired his.

Although he looked like a *belle-époque* dandy out of his time, Beaumont was a friend of Cocteau, Picasso and Derain – each of whom had been commissioned to paint décors for him at one time or another. He also commissioned music for his parties from Francis Poulenc, Henri Sauguet or Georges Auric, as well as ballets by Serge Lifar.

Beaumont's great receptions were held at his eighteenth-century town house which had been built for Prince Masserano. With its grand courtyard, formal garden and vast salons, it was designed for the spectacular parties he liked to give. His pre-war successes included the Bal Colonial, the Bal des Tableaux Célèbres, and the Bal de la Mer. Then, in late 1948, the rumour spread that he was planning his first great post-war costume ball: the Bal des Rois, which would be held on 6 January 1949 – the feast of the Three Kings.

The success of an entertainment on such a scale depended on everyone's burning desire to be invited. Through certain intimate friends Beaumont put the word about, to provoke anxious weeks of waiting for the invitation among those who hoped to be asked. Everyone tried to discover who had received one and who had not, yet few would dare admit that they were not among the select number. Étienne de Beaumont took a malicious pleasure in prolonging the agony. He liked to say that he gave parties for those who were not invited – '*Je donne mes fêtes pour ceux qui ne sont pas conviés.*'

Honoured and much relieved, those fortunate enough to receive an invitation now settled down to the task of thinking up a costume – which was often done in consultation with Beaumont himself. For the high point once again was to be the *entrées*, or presentations, which were set to music and rigorously rehearsed. Costumes for the groups of people entering together might be designed by Cocteau or Marie Laurencin, and made up by Dior or Schiaparelli. People gave parties before the ball, with plenty of food and champagne: Étienne de Beaumont took no interest in food or drink, so little refreshment was on offer at his house.

For the Bal des Rois, each king or queen (plus in some cases consort or entourage) was met by the host, in the role of Grand Chamberlain. He escorted them behind a large curtain, from which they made their *entrée* on to a small stage, magnificently hung in blue damask. There they received the homage of the court, to the sound of an appropriate musical hymn or fanfare. Christian Bérard came as Henry VIII, his lover Boris Kochno as the King of the Crows, and Marie-Laure de Noailles as Louis XIV, whose profile she claimed was identical to her own. Marie-Louise Bousquet came as Queen Marie-Louise of Spain in the portrait by Goya. The Comtesse de Ganay was the Empress Joséphine, dressed by Jacques Fath; while Fath himself and his wife Geneviève represented Charles IX and his Queen, Elizabeth. Christian Dior, the shyest of men, came as the King of the Beasts in a magnificent jewelled cape, and a lion mask that added several inches to his height. The irrepressible Léonore Fini was Persephone, Queen of the Underworld, in a plunging red and black dress with horns on her head; while Elsa Schiaparelli was the Queen of the Bees, crowned with a beehive.

Violet Trefusis came as Queen Victoria (whom she claimed – without justification – as her grandmother) accompanied by Count Mogens Tvede as John Brown; while Tvede's wife, Princess Dolly Radziwill, represented her Radziwill ancestress, Queen Barbara of Poland – accompanied by Nancy Mitford as her husband, King Sigismund August Jagello.

'I went to the ball in black tights and a black beard hoping at last to have a success with the chaps,' wrote Nancy Mitford to Evelyn Waugh, 'but they thought I was Edward James and *fled*.' A very young Claus von Bülow came as Charles XII, on his way to a Turkish jail.

Once the *entrées* were over, this resplendent mixture danced waltzes, cotillions and minuets into the small hours. The success of the Bal des Rois, and the enthusiasm of the participants, inspired other costume balls. Jacques and Geneviève Fath gave a Bal Noir et Blanc, while the Duchesse de Lévis-Mirepoix threw a Bal de la Couleur, in which any article of clothing that was either black or white was forbidden. This was in aid of '*les œuvres sociales de la noblesse française*'. Elsa Schiaparelli gave a dance in the garden of her house in the rue de Berri, with a mass of balloons 'including a large one like the London barrage balloons'.

The Bal des Rois was the last great ball given by Étienne de Beaumont. His wife Edith died soon after, and the Hotel Masseran was sold to Élie de Rothschild. Beaumont continued to live there, but not for long. His funeral service was held at his parish church of Saint-François-Xavier; and of all those who flocked to his parties, less than forty people attended.

His friend Christian Bérard had even less time left to live. In February 1949, during a rehearsal of Molière's *Les Fourberies de Scapin*, he dropped dead on stage – like Molière himself. 'The funeral of Bébé was dreadfully sad,' Nancy Mitford wrote to her sister Diana. 'The huge beautiful church [of Saint-Sulpice] was so full one could hardly get in, [with] everybody I know in Paris from Jean Cocteau to the little girl who makes my hats. In the cortège all the famous people of France as well as the sweet man who runs the bistro he always went to.'

Nancy and her friends clubbed together to adorn his hearse with a six-foot cross made out of violets, which cost £60, a very large sum in those days. Even Jean Galtier-Boissière was impressed by the crowd. 'The world of the theatre' and 'all the *gratin*' were in attendance, but also 'some existentialist sirens [who had] escaped from the cellars of Saint-Germain-des-Prés, wearing red sandals and grey trousers. They smoked in the choir and climbed on each other's backs to take photographs.'

France was starting to see the effects of Marshall aid, which began to fuel economic recovery more rapidly than people had dared hope. Already in 1948 there had been signs of a new attitude emerging. 'There seems to be a change of heart in my community,' the Chief Rabbi told Jacques Dumaine. 'Today fathers no longer choose their sons-in-law from among the ranks of the State civil servants; two years ago the opposite was the case. Is this perhaps a sign that commercial activity is reviving in France?' Janet Flanner noted that for the first time since before the war the shelves in the shops were no longer bare. 'The average Frenchman can now find in the shops nearly everything he wants except the means of paying for it.'

In November of that year, General Marshall visited France to see how the plan was developing. Paul Claudel made a speech of welcome in which he said: 'The word "plan" until now did not sound very good in our ears! It signified for people already exhausted and overburdened the subjection of the human being to distant objectives. But the Marshall Plan, that we can understand straight away, just as we understand the Red Cross.'

The country was on its way to recovery now that the last wave of strikes had crumbled. Despite all the damage caused to the economy, France was in a better position than Great Britain to take advantage of American aid because the Monnet plan to re-shape French industry was in place. Jean Monnet persuaded both the government and David Bruce, then the director in France of the Economic Cooperation Administration responsible for executing the Marshall Plan, to allocate a large proportion of the available funds to industrial regeneration. The priorities – steel, coal, hydro-electric power, tractors and transport – had been established. Little time was wasted. The British government, on the other hand, suffered the illusions of a victor: it did not believe a long-term plan for rebuilding its industry was needed. Investment was channelled towards existing production, not to new factories and new machinery for the future.

From the beginning of 1949, almost everything started to come right for France. In January, only a few weeks after the end of the strikes, a state loan – the first since the Liberation – was fully taken up. Bread rationing came to an end, mainly thanks to Marshall aid, since the drought of 1948 had drastically reduced the harvest. Dairy products were no longer rationed from 15 April 1949, the first anniversary of the European Recovery Programme. Prices became less volatile, wage demands eased and inflation slowed. Even American caution began to relax, as an ambassadorial dispatch to Washington shows. 'While I do not desire to over-emphasize or exaggerate, in my opinion it is safe to say that at last France shows signs of pulling herself together and appears to be on the way to recovery.'

The year proved so calm, in comparison with what had gone before, that foreign journalists based in Paris complained that they no longer had anything to write about. The new mood of inactivity was attributed to the Prime Minister, Dr Henri Queuille, a country doctor and a veteran of the Radicals. Queuille may have been unexciting, but he was cleverer than he appeared and provided the stability that was so desperately needed. His most important appointment was that of Maurice Petsche as Finance Minister, who, without political fanfare, started to free the economy and also the franc by narrowing the rate of exchange between the black market and the official rate.

Imports from the United States had been huge during 1948 as

Marshall Plan produce flooded into the country, 'but by the end of 1949,' Averell Harriman later reported to Washington, 'exports had more than doubled' and the trade gap had narrowed. Coal production was rising. Steel production was close to Monnet's ambitious target of matching the record set in 1929. Car production rose from 5,000 cars in 1947 to over 20,000 by the end of 1949. The rapid increase in traffic, and in the noise of klaxons, produced the most striking change, especially in the centre of Paris, where fewer and fewer bicycles were to be seen.

The Communists no longer dared to attack the Marshall Plan head on, because it only drew attention to the way they had tried to sabotage the country's recovery. Banners at the May Day demonstration concentrated on the peace campaign. Observers from the American Embassy noted with measured satisfaction that the number of marchers was markedly lower than the year before: 'Quietest May Day since Liberation reveals not so much satisfaction of workers with their living conditions as their growing apathy and increasing lack of faith in slogans, formulae and organizations.' On the other side of Paris in the Bois de Boulogne, a crowd of 100,000 Gaullists gathered in an RPF counter-demonstration and then dispersed quietly. The day seemed to underline the fact that political passions were spent, at least for the time being. And as if to confirm the impression that immediate dangers were over, the Soviet forces in Germany lifted the blockade on Berlin later in the month.

The relaxation of international tension coincided with the start of the racing season. On Whit Sunday – 5 June – Duff and Diana Cooper gave their customary lunch at Chantilly before the Prix de Diane. This was the day after the Derby in England, so keen racegoers were able to attend both.

For Diana Cooper, however, that June was memorable for an open-air ballet and party given in her honour. 'There's to be a party given for Diana by all Duffs' mistresses on 24 June,' wrote

Nancy Mitford to Lady Pamela Berry. 'Why not come over for it? I am the only non-mistress on the committee which is Susan Mary [Patten], Alvilde [Chaplin, now Lees-Milne], Maxine [de la Falaise], Ghislaine de Polignac, Barley [Alison] etc. I said what about Loulou [de Vilmorin], and they said no, she would boss everything. Falaise wants us each to spend 40,000 francs on a ballet in which she is to caper around dressed as what she calls a licorne, but you or I a unicorn.' (The unicorn was Diana Cooper's personal emblem.)

As soon as she heard of their plan, Louise de Vilmorin decided to take her revenge on the committee for excluding her. She invited Duff and Diana, as well as 'everybody smart in Paris' to Verrières for the same night. Nancy Mitford, exasperated with most of her fellow committee members, found this pre-emptive strike rather funny. Louise, having made her point, then withdrew, and the party went ahead more or less as planned with Maxine de la Falaise's Unicorn Ballet choreographed by Serge Lifar.

'Well the Mistresses Party,' Nancy reported afterwards to Pam Berry, with her usual exaggeration and glee for the ridiculous: 'Rather nice. The Mistresses made pretty good asses of themselves, all except Susan Mary who was the only person to do any practical work, i.e. glasses, chairs etc. All the others had their heads in the clouds with their idiotic Ballet de la Licorne. The chief idiot was Maxine who lay on the floor at Diana's feet with liver, heart, lights etc (registered customers only) made by Schiaparelli all over the front of her dress – "*la victime éventrée par la licorne*". When the ballet was over, a Frenchwoman next to me said, "*C'était la répétition? Ne dites pas que c'était la performance!*"'

Then on 2 July, the day after the *épuration* officially ended with the final judgement of the Haute Cour de Justice, the Duc and Duchesse de Brissac and Comte Paul de Saint-Sauveur gave the Bal de la Vénerie. Although the political situation was now much less threatening, they felt it would be wiser to make it a *bal payant* for charity, so they chose the most *ancien régime* of charities, the Société Philanthropique, founded by Marie-Antoinette in 1780 and presided over by the Duc de Gramont.

The ball was held at the Château de Chantilly, in the Grandes Écuries. These stables, built in 1719 by the seventh Prince de Condé and known as '*le Palais à loger les chevaux*', looked more like the inside of a cathedral than a palace. Bas-reliefs and antler heads were the only decoration on the pale stone walls that rose thirty feet to a vaulted roof – yet the stables had often been used for great receptions, balls and ceremonies. In the style of the *belle époque*, an *aboyeur*, or barker, announced the names of guests as they arrived, and the men in their hunt tail-coats were as resplendent as the women: red with blue facings for the Rallye Bonnelles, pale yellow and purple for the Caraman-Chimay hunt, black with yellow facings for the Huard. Guests were treated to a demonstration of *haute école* riding by Colonel Jusseaume, fanfares of hunting-horns and a trot-past by the Marquis de Rouälle's famous Saintongeois pack of hounds. The party ended at five in the morning with the dawn light illuminating the Château de Chantilly and the sensation that all was still well with *vieille France*. Twelve days later, on 14 July, the anniversary of the fall of the Bastille, the Pope announced the excommunication of all Communists and fellow-travellers.

The mood of optimism was further reinforced on 18 July, when Odile de Lenoncourt married the Duc de Guiche, eldest son of the Duc de Gramont, at the church of Saint-Louis des Invalides. The right people were still marrying the right people. The church was packed, and the reception that followed took place at the Duc de Gramont's town house. The bride's dress, designed by Christian Dior and very simple, was made of the most sumptuous duchesse satin.

The harvest proved much better than in 1948, with an excellent wheat crop. In September Queuille and his government, furthering their policy of greater currency freedom, allowed the franc to devalue by 20 per cent against the dollar. The British, in a far graver position, were forced to devalue the pound by 30 per cent.

Even the fall of Queuille's government in October – a Socialist manoeuvre to protect themselves from working-class criticism – had little effect on the stock market. There was no threat of a coal strike, and fuel reserves had nearly doubled over the previous year. The biggest cloud was the conflict in Indo-China. Another 16,000 conscripts had been sent out, increasing the army there to 115,000 men.

From the third week of November, Communist energies were directed away from domestic affairs. They were focused on what the party believed to be an event for international rejoicing – Joseph Stalin's seventieth birthday on 21 December. Orders went out from the Central Committee that everyone must contribute towards the event. The run-up to the great day was treated like a presidential campaign, with 30,000 posters depicting the heroic leader and half a million pamphlets printed.

An exhibition of presents, reminiscent of a royal wedding, was held at the metalworkers' union building on the rue Jean-Pierre Timbaud. Twenty-three panels illustrating the life of Stalin decorated the hall where some 4,000 contributions were displayed. They included embroidery and handiwork of all sorts, even a doll's bonnet by a little girl who had died in Auschwitz, the music score of a specially composed '*Chant à Stalin*', scores of poems, including one by Éluard, and works of art almost entirely in the socialist-realist style. One prominent Communist painter was horrified to see that a work which he had proudly presented to Maurice Thorez for his house at Choisy-le-Roi had been included in the pile. This bizarre cargo of bric-à-brac was to be loaded into a railway wagon and dispatched to Moscow. Stalin is unlikely to have bothered to cast an eye over it, or the book of congratulations signed by 40,000 visitors.

On 19 December, the Bruces gave a dinner party for Ernest Hemingway, the ambassador's companion-in-arms during the

Liberation of Paris just over five years before. With Hemingway they invited Duff Cooper, Marie-Louise Bousquet, Pauline de Rothschild and Christian Dior. The high point of the dinner was woodcock accompanied by Romanée Conti. Hemingway boasted of having shot over 8,000 duck with a syndicate of friends near Venice. But this was not a good time for him. He was working on *Across the River and into the Trees*, and suffering from a crisis of impotence which the massacre of ducks had failed to relieve. Like the American colonel in his novel, Hemingway could not come to terms with the fact that the war was over.

The last year of the decade was approaching its end, but Fourth Republic politics continued along the same slippery path. Georges Bidault, who had patched together another ministry at the end of October after the fall of Henri Queuille's government, wondered what he would find in his Christmas stocking. 'Some fruit, I expect, an orange, a banana – or its skin.'

On the left bank there was rejoicing as friends, including Jean-Louis Barrault and Jean Galtier-Boissière, gathered spontaneously to congratulate Jean-Louis Vaudoyer, the belle-lettrist and director of the Comédie-Française during the war, on his election to the 'Immortals'. Laid out on the sofa were the *habits verts* – the green tail-coated uniforms of the Académie Française – which Vaudoyer's grandfather and great-grandfather had also been privileged to wear.

For Galtier-Boissière the most memorable night was Christmas Eve, when he gathered all his friends around him in his apartment overlooking the Place de la Sorbonne. This huge, generous man, with his moustache and '*gros yeux affectueux*', and his face red from many vintages of Bouzy rouge, had a great gift for friendship along with his compulsive irreverence. His long-suffering and devoted wife Charlotte was continually having to tell him off for some misbehaviour or other. At one book-signing session in the provinces, when very drunk, he had written erotic dedications for the women who came forward with copies. Their outraged husbands had promptly torn out the offending page.

Galtier-Boissière's love for the fast-disappearing Paris of brothel, *bal musette* and old-fashioned restaurant was matched only by his loathing of modern political cant. Stalinists like Aragon once again became a favourite target in his monthly satirical magazine *Le Crapouillot*, which he had re-launched in June 1948 with another all-night party of drinking and his favourite songs, like '*Cœur apache*' and '*L'Hirondelle du Faubourg*'. Aragon had already returned the insults from before the war. In his novel *Aurélien*, published just after the Liberation, he had depicted the immensely tall and brave Galtier-Boissière as the miserable little Fuchs, editor of a magazine called *Le Cagna* – a trench-bunker in *poilu* slang, as opposed to a trench-mortar.

That night, Galtier-Boissière and his friends laughed, drank, talked and sang their way through to the last Christmas of the decade. One guest was a brilliant mimic and as the night wore on he went through his '*numéros*' towards his *pièce de résistance*: 'an astonishing ventriloquist act, using as his partner one hand decorated with make-up; the climax was the entry of the famous lioness Saïda into the main cage and the lion-tamer putting her through her tricks . . . Suddenly we noticed that it was seven in the morning.'

34

Recurring Fevers

The close of 1949 marks an obvious end to the immediate post-war period, but the great issues of that time did not of course finish with the decade. The three main ones covered in this book – the Occupation and the *épuration* as part of the *guerre franco-française*; the intelligentsia's admiration for revolutionary ruthlessness; and France's complex relationship with the United States – either continued to affect Parisian life or resurfaced later.

If the Communist Party was the first to suffer from the economic recovery in 1949, Gaullism soon became the first casualty of political calm. 'The General's stock,' wrote Frank Giles, 'like the price of gold, tended to rise in times of trouble and fall when the going became smoother.' Memories of the fatal street-battle in Grenoble, combined with de Gaulle's apocalyptic declarations, now made people uneasy. Despite the renewed instability of government, with few administrations lasting more than six months, his Rassemblement dwindled rapidly in the early 1950s. The majestic '*J'attends*' which de Gaulle had uttered after his resignation in 1946 was to last for twelve years until the crisis over the colonial war in Algeria provided his opportunity.

The greatest beneficiary of political stability in 1949 was economic planning. Jean Monnet did not waste a moment once the Marshall Plan began to achieve its objective of reviving commercial activity. From his desk at the Commissariat du

Plan, his vision had always stretched beyond France's recovery to a united Europe, a project which he had conceived while the war continued. The continent needed strength and unity if it was not to be dominated by the superpowers.

Using as a precedent the joint committees created by the Marshall Plan, Monnet launched a diplomatic offensive in the spring of 1949 to persuade British politicians and civil servants to expand economic cooperation. They, however, were taken aback by French determination: the whole idea made them either uneasy or sceptical. They had already resented Averell Harriman's attempts to push Britain into a closer embrace with European governments. Their lingering attachment to Empire and a world role within the Atlantic alliance meant that Britain's heart was not in Europe.

Convinced by the end of 1949 that Britain could not be a useful partner, Monnet turned his attention to Germany. His main strategic project, a European Coal and Steel Community, was known as the Schuman Plan, after Robert Schuman who had been the most influential Minister of Foreign Affairs on the Continent. Schuman's objective now was to bind France and Germany together 'in an embrace so close that neither could draw back far enough to hit the other'. Konrad Adenauer, then emerging as leader of the nascent Federal Republic, realized immediately the opportunity this plan offered for the rehabilitation of Germany, and became an enthusiastic supporter. Monnet, with Schuman, did not want to allow the British the chance to prevaricate or water down the proposals. He issued an ultimatum to each eligible country, although the prime target was the British government. Those who wished to accept the Schuman Plan in its entirety had to reply by eight o'clock on the morning of 2 June 1950, or stay outside. Bevin was scathing. He refused to believe such a plan could work; the Cabinet and most senior civil servants agreed. The post-war development of Europe was decided. Any British pretension to leadership on the Continent was finished.

*

France had been able to breathe a sigh of relief in 1949, with the Communist threat at home greatly diminished and the end of the Berlin blockade, but a new phase of the Cold War opened in 1950. Mao Tse-tung, the victor of the Chinese civil war, signed a Sino-Soviet Pact in Moscow, and six months later the Korean War began. The fear of atomic war and Soviet tanks on the Place de la Concorde resurged dramatically.

The French Communist Party vigorously continued its peace propaganda and Picasso's dove became the most over-used image of the age. Yet even at this crucial moment, personal rivalries cloaked in ideological nuance seethed in its upper ranks. Doctrinal purity in art soon provided a *casus belli* for the hardliners.

Picasso's decision in 1944 to join a party which still officially condemned non-representational art as decadent had complicated matters for the Communists. At first, the purists of socialist realism had restricted their criticism to coded attacks. But the change in the party line dictated by Moscow in 1947 affected almost everything. 'The fresh air of Soviet art,' declared *Pravda* that summer, 'is polluted by the stale stench of capitalism's artistic bankruptcy.' Picasso and Matisse were held responsible. The main thrust, however, was aimed at the influence of the United States. Abstract art was said to be tainted with American culture. It was 'American imperialism' which controlled 'abstract art like all the rottenness in the world'. This gave Louis Aragon, Picasso's great supporter, the opportunity to deflect the attacks. With a chauvinist twist, he described American modern art as 'the production line imitation of an avant-garde which was born in Paris'.*

French Communism, following the Congress of Intellectuals at Wroclaw in 1948, returned towards a stronger support for

---

*Representatives of the New York school had first exhibited in the Galerie du Luxembourg in 1947, but Jackson Pollock's first show in Paris, organized by the art critic Michel Tapié, only took place in 1951.

socialist realism. Certain distinctions were made clear: Pablo Picasso and Fernand Léger were not Communist painters, but painters who were Communists. At the Salon d'automne of 1949, the socialist-realist painters were all grouped together in the first room; André Fougeron was hailed by Communist critics as the Jacques Louis David of the modern proletariat. For Stalin's seventieth birthday that December, the party chose as their main gift Fougeron's *Hommage à André Houllier*, a portrait of the Houllier family grieving at the spot where their son had been shot by a policeman as he pasted up a Communist poster. Picasso, on the other hand, offered as his present a rapid sketch of a face-like hand holding up a glass with the legend '*Staline à ta santé*'. The compromise solution between the two camps was to declare Fougeron to be the official painter of the party, and Picasso official painter of the peace movement.

The following year, Auguste Lecoeur, whose power base lay in the coalfields of the north, commissioned a series of paintings by Fougeron on miners' lives, known as '*Au Pays des mines*'. In January 1951, without checking dates with anybody else, he announced in *L'Humanité* the opening date of this exhibition. It clashed with the new Picasso exhibition. This was probably a genuine mistake, but intended or not, it brought the battle between the socialist-realist school and the supporters of Picasso out into the open. The vastly greater success of the Picasso exhibition constituted a humiliation for Lecoeur. He had to wait just over two years for his revenge.

When Stalin's death was announced on Friday, 7 March 1953, Aragon called in Pierre Daix and rattled off a shopping-list of features to honour Stalin in a special issue of *Les Lettres Françaises* – 'an article by Joliot, one by me, an article by Courtade, another by Sadoul, one by you. We must have something by Picasso.'

Since Picasso had always refused to do a portrait of Stalin from a photograph, Daix sent a telegram to him at Vallauris saying: 'Do whatever you want', and signed it 'Aragon'. Picasso's drawing of Stalin, which depicted him as a curiously open-eyed young man, arrived at the very moment *Les Lettres Françaises* went to press. Daix took the picture in to Aragon. He admired it and said that the party would appreciate the gesture. While it was being set into the front page, office-boys and typists crowded round the picture. Everyone thought it 'worthy of Stalin'. Daix was overjoyed to be the one who had commissioned Picasso's first portrait of the Soviet leader, and rushed it down to the printers. But a few hours later, when the edition had been run off, the mood in the building had completely changed to one of fear. Journalists from *L'Humanité*, passing by, spotted the drawing and cried out that it was unthinkable that any Communist publication should consider printing such a representation of '*le Grand Staline*'.

Pierre Daix promptly rang Aragon at his apartment: Elsa Triolet answered. She told him angrily that he was mad to have even thought of asking Picasso for such a drawing.

'But, really, Elsa,' Daix broke in, 'Stalin isn't God the Father!'

'Yes he is, Pierre. Nobody's going to reflect much about what this drawing of Picasso signifies. He hasn't even deformed Stalin's face. He's even respected it. But he has dared to touch it. He has actually dared, Pierre, do you understand?'

Aragon rose to the occasion and took full responsibility upon himself. It was almost as if somebody had to face a court martial for treason. But for the staff of *Les Lettres Françaises*, the worst was still to come. Daix found secretaries in tears from the insults screamed down the telephone at them by loyal Communists protesting at the sacrilege. Some even said that it portrayed Stalin as cruel and Asiatic, which was what his enemies wanted.

Those who wished to revenge themselves on Aragon did not waste time. Chief among them was Auguste Lecoeur. He wanted *Les Lettres Françaises* publicly condemned. Aragon prepared a suitably grovelling apology.

*

Communists who found themselves excluded from the party during the frenzy over the Titoist heresy were like lost souls. They had automatically been deprived of the vast majority of their friends – not having made or kept many outside the party. And they had lost all sense of purpose in their lives, along with the sense of comradeship which an embattled community provided. A true Communist used to say that he intended to die with his party membership card in his pocket – '*mourir la carte dans la poche*'.

The wrench was almost as hard for those who took the decision to leave because they could no longer swallow the lies and '*serrer les dents*'. For some this came with the show-trials in Eastern Europe, for many more it came in 1956. Khrushchev denounced Stalin's crimes on 26 February at the Twentieth Congress, yet the French Communist Party, still irredeemably Stalinist, tried to pretend that nothing had happened. The news was entirely suppressed in *L'Humanité* while every other newspaper was full of the story.

Jacqueline Ventadour-Hélion, who had read Khrushchev's speech in *Le Monde*, raised the issue at the next party meeting she attended. There was an embarrassed silence; then the subject was rapidly changed. Afterwards, a cadre told her firmly that 'not all truths should be spoken aloud'. This, for her, was the time to leave. She was already under suspicion for having visited friends in the United States. Communists were not allowed visas – she had in fact obtained one through a friend in the American Embassy who took a more relaxed view of the regulation – so in the party's logic she was therefore a supporter of John Foster Dulles. Unlike those who hated the idea of losing their party card, she felt an immense sense of liberation when it was torn up.

That autumn, during the Suez crisis, Soviet tanks crushed the rising in Hungary. Furious demonstrators attacked the Soviet Embassy. In the crowd, General de Bénouville encountered

Colonel Deglian, the Communist who had come to him on that night in 1948 to warn him to be prepared against an attack.

Crowds also surrounded Communist Party headquarters, where the security guards were ready. A more serious attack was mounted against the offices of *L'Humanité*. Groups climbed over the roofs and threw Molotov cocktails. Inside, staff and other Communist volunteers, who had come in to help defend the place, put out fires and ejected any attackers who managed to break in. They hurled what missiles came to hand, bottles from the canteen, chairs, even a bust of Karl Marx which was said to have flattened one assailant. The most effective were hunks of metal newspaper type. Three Communists were killed in the disorders, and the days of the Resistance were recalled once again. *L'Humanité* claimed afterwards, in an effort to dignify the events, that workers loyal to the party had rushed into Paris from the '*ceinture rouge*' to defend 'their party, their newspaper . . . just as one throws oneself into a fire to save one's wife and children'.

The events of 1956 led to a dramatic decline in the Communist Party's influence on intellectual life in Paris. This did not mean that the left-wing intelligentsia's fascination with revolutionary violence slackened. Over the next decade, new idols and theorists – including Mao, Marcuse and Che Guevara – were raised up to take the place of Stalinism.

Paris continued to be a cultural and literary Mecca for the rest of the world. The *patronnes* of cheap hotels in the *Quartier Latin* still grumbled and failed to prosper. Gabriel García Marquez, who had arranged for his employer, the Colombian newspaper *El Espectador*, to send him to Paris, moved into a maid's attic room on the top floor of the Hotel de Flandre in the rue Cujas. There he lived off cold spaghetti, smoked three packets of Gauloises during the course of a working night, and squeezed sideways against the radiator as he tried to summon up the tropical heat of Colombia's Caribbean coast. The result was *La Mala Hora*, hammered out on an old typewriter. A photograph of his fiancée Mercédès back in Barranquilla pinned to the wall was the only decoration.

He had no radio, or the money to buy newspapers, and his source of information on Castro's revolt against Batista was the poet Nicolas Guillen, who used to yell the latest news from his window. The only luxury was a drink behind the steamed-up windows of La Chope Parisienne amid silent chess-players. On Christmas Night 1957, he saw snow for the first time. He ran out and danced wildly among the large soft flakes.

Madame Lacroix, the *patronne* of the Flandre, was indeed tolerant. Not only did she allow García Marquez credit for a whole year, she permitted the then unknown Peruvian writer Mario Vargas Llosa to stay for two years without paying. At one point García Marquez was reduced to begging in the streets when *El Espectador* went bankrupt. But one day he was encouraged by a curious incident. On the Boulevard Saint-Michel he spotted Hemingway, still his literary idol, across the street. Without thinking, he called out his name: '*Emming-way!*' Ernest Hemingway did not look round, he just raised his hand. Yet the optimistic young South American sensed this gesture as a benediction.

Coincidentally, a new wave of writers from the United States had reached the Latin Quarter at the same time. Several members of the Beat generation, including William Burroughs and Allen Ginsberg, established themselves in what became known as the Beat Hotel at 9 rue Gît-le-Cœur. Their ambition was to meet Louis-Ferdinand Céline, whose novel *Voyage au bout de la nuit* had excited and influenced them. Ginsberg and Burroughs, having arranged an introduction through his editor, went to pay a call on him in the run-down suburb of Meudon. It was to be a visit of homage rather than a literary discussion.

Since his return from Denmark, Céline had not had many visitors, except Arletty, who had corresponded with him during his exile and had remained a faithful friend. She understood his *cafards*; besides, the two had more in common than their origins in Courbevoie. Arletty made a recording of his *Death on the Instalment Plan* and he wrote a scenario for her called *Arletty, jeune fille dauphinoise*, a sort of picaresque adventure in the eighteenth-century manner, rather reminiscent of *Candide*. But Céline did not have long to live: he died on 1 July 1961, the same day as Hemingway.

France's tortuous relationship with the United States was not improved in 1954 when the unwinnable war in Indo-China ended in ignominious defeat at Dien Bien Phu. French dominion over North Africa was also doomed. A fatal combination of bigotry, weakness, wilful short-sightedness, political inconsistency and bad faith was leading to a series of humiliations which together were tantamount to the defeat of 1940. Once again, de Gaulle appeared as the only candidate able to rescue France from the consequences of national pride and then proceed to rebuild it.

The bitter turmoil in Algiers allowed him to return to power in the virtually unopposed *coup d'état* of May 1958. Colonel Passy immediately flew to his old wartime haunt of London as the General's envoy to the intelligence community. Passy arranged a discreet lunch with the former SIS chief of station in Paris, who was now in charge of the European department. He chose the Savoy, where to remind himself of the gastronomic curiosities of London he ordered kippers and a bottle of Bass beer. The purpose of his visit, however, was to ask his old colleagues to spread the message that de Gaulle had come to power only to solve the Algerian crisis. He had absolutely no intention of staying on.

The General, however, had every intention of staying on. His return allowed him to end the Fourth Republic which he had despised from its conception. This time he was able to insist on the Constitution he wanted, with almost all the power concerntrated in the hands of the President. The Fifth Republic, with politicians reduced to rude mechanicals, was patently his creation.

His distrust of the British and the Americans had continued to burn strongly over the years. In 1961, President Kennedy sent a highly secret message for de Gaulle's eyes only to Paris by special courier. The missive informed the French President that the CIA had just started to debrief a Russian defector, and he had produced the names of Soviet moles high in the French administration. If President de Gaulle would like to select a senior English-speaking officer with intelligence experience, his nominee could come to the United States and sit in on the relevant debriefing sessions. De Gaulle promptly summoned General Jean-Louis de Rougemont, who was then head of the army's intelligence staff, to the Élysée Palace. He emphasized to Rougement the great secrecy of the whole affair, and explained in detail what he should do. 'In any case,' said de Gaulle, 'you must see whether this isn't a trap.'

'The Russians?' asked Rougemont.

'No, the Americans!' replied de Gaulle in exasperation.

Because de Gaulle's attitude to the Americans had not changed, neither had the Kremlin's strategy towards France. As mentioned earlier, the Soviet politburo allotted the task of persuading France to leave NATO to Boris Ponomarev.

Ponomarev worked in close liaison with Andrei Gromyko, the Soviet Minister of Foreign Affairs. In 1965 and 1966, Gromyko launched a diplomatic campaign to encourage France to sign as many treaties and agreements as possible on a range of issues. These included a deal by which Russia would take the French colour television system and a Soviet offer to launch French satellites on Soviet rockets. Couve de Murville visited the Soviet Union at the end of October 1965; the subjects to be discussed included the improvement of relations between the two countries, European questions and the German problem. In June

1966, de Gaulle accepted an invitation to visit Moscow not long after an agreement on sharing nuclear research was reached. At the end of September, a Franco-Soviet Chamber of Commerce was established in Paris, and eleven days later a technical collaboration deal was reached between Soviet industry and Renault-Peugeot. All these moves were accompanied by a Franco-Soviet friendship offensive launched in the Soviet and French Communist press.

'A second clandestine channel,' wrote the KGB defector Aleksei Myagkov (a source considered reliable by British intelligence), 'was KGB activity. Using its agents among journalists and officials of the various agencies in France', as well as among members of the Association France–URSS, 'it propagated actively among politicians the theme that the country's political independence suffered from the fact that it was a member of NATO and that foreign troops were stationed on its territory, especially American troops. The same line of thought was canvassed among French citizens recruited in political circles.'

When de Gaulle withdrew France from NATO's military structure on 1 July 1967, the decision was 'received with great satisfaction in Moscow'. The leaders of the KGB 'did not hide their satisfaction at this recognition of the fact that they too had played their part in these events'. It is still impossible to assess how effective that part might have been, but the KGB clearly regarded it as a major success: from 1968 the operation was used as 'an instructive example in KGB officer courses'.

De Gaulle's supporters may have acclaimed him as the Liberator of France, but the General preferred to see himself in the monarchical role as unifier of the country and healer of national wounds. He never forgot that the role of Vichy was potentially more traumatic than the defeat of 1940 or the German occupation, because Vichy was the creation of France itself.

The trials and purges after the Liberation had failed either to satisfy the aggrieved or to convince the population of their fairness. But uneasy consciences about both the Occupation and the *épuration* helped de Gaulle create a myth of national unity – a version of events which took root because it expressed what the majority of the population needed to believe.

The transfer of Jean Moulin's remains to the Panthéon in December 1964 was the apotheosis of the myth that France had liberated herself and thus wiped out the shame of 1940. Once again, de Gaulle managed to manipulate the Resistance into looking like a tolerably well-drilled military unit under his command. The ceremonies took place over two days. On the first, the remains of Jean Moulin lay in state at the Martyrs' Memorial, guarded by relays of *Compagnons de la Libération*. At ten o'clock in the evening the casket was taken in procession through the heart of Paris to the steps of the Panthéon, where it was guarded all night by veterans of the Resistance.

On the following day André Malraux, with de Gaulle and Georges Pompidou beside him, delivered a eulogy from a tribune facing the casket. His speech focused more on General de Gaulle, *le premier résistant*, than on Jean Moulin, his commander in the field. The notion of the Resistance as an army of the state fighting a foreign enemy was the great myth's way of diverting attention away from the aspect of civil war. A march-past followed, with units from the Garde Républicaine and the three services. For this part of the ceremony, de Gaulle, Pompidou and Malraux moved from their tribune to the steps of the Panthéon, beside the casket – so that the parade could 'salute in one single motion both the mortal remains of Jean Moulin and the President of the Republic'.

The myth was not really challenged until after the events of May 1968, when a new generation began to ask uncomfortable questions. Some of them were slanted, some of them made no allowance for the realities of the Occupation, but the process had to be gone through. Marcel Ophuls's documentary *Le Chagrin et la pitié*, released in 1969, was one of the first films to confront the less heroic aspects of the Occupation. This provoked much anger among the older generation. The film was banned from French television. Whatever its flaws, *Le Chagrin et la pitié* was such a powerful piece of documentary cinema that it helped launch a younger generation of researchers into digging, sifting and re-examining material: not an easy task with the archives still firmly closed. Despite the obstacles, it soon became clear that the real shame of the Vichy years was the regime's treatment of Jews.

In 1978, an interview in *L'Express* with the octogenarian Darquier de Pellepoix, the Vichy Commissioner for Jewish Affairs, caused an outcry. Although he had been condemned to death *in absentia* in 1947, the French authorities had never requested his extradition from Spain. Darquier, who was still violently anti-semitic, spoke of his surprise at the hatred against him in France, while the man responsible for the infamous round-up of Jews in Paris – René Bousquet, the former head of the Vichy police – was pursuing a very successful career as a banker.

In 1980, three former SS officers testified that the deportation of Jews from France had received enthusiastic assistance from Vichy officials. Many people still refused to believe it; but the Germans' testimony was proved true by the most determined and successful sleuth of war crimes in France, Serge Klarsfeld. After meticulous research in German archives, Klarsfeld found that the Occupation authorities had kept minutes of meetings with senior Vichy officials helping with the deportation of Jews. The most devastating concerned Adolf Eichmann's visit to Paris at the beginning of July 1942. The Vichy chief of police, René Bousquet, not only agreed that his police should undertake the arrests, but proposed that the deportations should cover non-French Jews throughout the country. Klarsfeld also revealed the telegrams Bousquet had sent to the Prefects of *départements* in the unoccupied zone, ordering them to deport not only Jewish adults but children whose deportation had not even been requested by the Nazis.

Bousquet was an administrator, not an anti-semitic ideologue. He claimed that he acted as he did in order to save French Jews, and it is true that the number sent to Auschwitz was lower than the Germans expected. But the fact remains that he and his men were responsible for the infamous round-up which took nearly 13,000 Jews to the Vélodrome d'Hiver on 16 and 17 July 1942, including 4,000 children.

Bousquet's untroubled and prosperous existence was disturbed by the Darquier interview. He was forced to resign from his various positions and Jewish demonstrations took place outside his apartment building in the Avenue Raphaël. He was not committed for trial, however, until 1989, when he was charged with crimes against humanity. The inquiry was still in progress when, on 8 June 1993, a fifty-year-old mental patient called Christian Didier gained entry to Bousquet's flat and shot him dead.

Information had also emerged about Maurice Papon, the Vichy Prefect of Bordeaux. Papon had suffered remarkably few problems after the Liberation. He became the Prefect of the Paris police soon after de Gaulle's return to power, and in October 1961 he was in charge when 11,000 Algerians were arrested for demonstrating in Paris. Some sixty of these prisoners were said to have been killed over the next few days, and most of the bodies were dumped in the Seine. Papon went on to become Minister of the Budget under President Giscard d'Estaing. His career came to a halt only in 1981, when *Le Canard enchaîné* published documents showing his responsibility for the deportation of 1,690 Jews during the war.

Paul Touvier, the head of the Vichy Milice in Lyons and a close associate of Klaus Barbie, was sentenced to death after the Liberation, but was helped to escape from prison. Traditionalist Catholic groups sheltered him for years. He received a pardon from President Pompidou in 1971, but went back into hiding in 1981 when it became clear that he could be prosecuted for crimes against humanity. He was finally arrested in 1989, but prevarications in the judicial system continued to delay his trial and sentence of life imprisonment in April 1994. Until then, Klaus Barbie – a German – had been the only person tried in France for crimes against humanity.

The civil war among historians is unlikely to end for some time. Older and more conservative writers, who have retained their respect for Marshal Pétain, refuse to accept that Vichy was a fascist regime. In the narrow sense of the term, it cannot be defined as fascist: it was too reactionary and Catholic, despite its lip-service to a National Revolution. But in the broader sense, the personality cult of the Marshal, the anti-Jewish laws, the paramilitary organizations and the total lack of democratic rights could justify the label. This more forgiving school also feels that far too much has been made of the photographs of Pétain's meeting with Hitler at Montoire in 1940. 'Mitterrand,' said one, 'shook the hand of Milosevic – a war criminal – so why should Pétain not have shaken Hitler's hand at Montoire?' Their greatest regret is that Pétain did not protect his reputation by fleeing to North Africa in November 1942 when the Germans invaded the unoccupied zone.

Those on the other side of the fence – mainly the younger historians grouped round the Institut d'Histoire du Temps Présent, and the American historian of Vichy, Robert Paxton – are less preoccupied with the fact that Pétain continued to lend his prestige to collaboration after 1942 than with the responsibility of Vichy for deporting French and foreign Jews to their death. 'The collaboration of the [Vichy] state was appalling,' said Paxton in an interview the day after the assassination of Bousquet. 'Because the orders came from the Ministry of the Interior, the prefects and all parts of the administration obeyed. Without exception. It was a formidable machine for the Nazis who as a result needed only a handful of men to carry out their plans.'

The shame of Vichy – the shame of their parents' generation – clearly played a part in perpetuating the appeal of revolutionary chic among the young, who had only changed their role models. They despised the advanced ossification of the Soviet system, and instead admired guerrilla movements in Latin America.

On the subject of politically engaged intellectuals in France – whether Drieu, Brasillach, Malraux or Sartre – Professor Judt has observed that their fascination with violence contained a 'quasi-erotic charge'. It underlines the fact that while it has long been easy to mock Hemingway, the posturing of French intellectuals, although more sophisticated, demonstrated an arrogant irresponsibility which was far more dangerous and dishonest. Sartre tried to reconcile existentialism with his new phase of revolutionary commitment, but predictably, it failed to be anything more than an exercise in verbose sophistry. By the end of his life he even began to justify terrorist action.

Saint-Germain-des-Prés and the Latin Quarter continued throughout the 1950s and 1960s to be a breeding-ground of *isms*. The *nouveau roman* movement, with the novels of Nathalie Sarraute, Michel Butor and Alain Robbe-Grillet, even produced *chosism* or 'thingism': the exhaustive description of inanimate objects to emphasize how depersonalized the modern world had become. But the materialistic enemy was already within the gates. The Deux Magots sold itself to the tourist trade as the 'Rendez-vous des intellectuels'. Cheap fashion shops and hamburger bars soon stretched the length of the Boulevard Saint-Michel, and in the newspaper kiosks along the Boulevard Saint-Germain *Playboy* magazine had taken over from *Les Temps modernes*. 'It is thus,' wrote Marc Doelnitz, 'that one passes from the cult of the head to the cult of the ass.'

France, like the rest of the world, had started to lose its cultural independence after a spirited rearguard action, a battle fought by Communists and traditionalists for different motives. Yet whether the 'American challenge' started on 6 June 1944 in Normandy, or in 1948 with the final signature on the Marshall Plan, France's cultural purity was bound to be threatened in the long run. The left-wing ideals of the Liberation, along with the intellectual environment in which they had thrived, stood little chance. 'Dirty money', like the industrial warfare of heavy guns, was bound to triumph in the end.

The events of May 1968 in Paris represented the dying flicker of the *guerre franco-française* along with the last great moments of the Parisian intelligentsia's political commitment. This time, however, there was no Stalinist focus, as there had been after the Liberation. Louis Aragon was the only member of the party's Central Committee to go out to address them. They greeted him with cries of '*Shut up, you old fool!*' The party itself, the only serious organization of the left, was loath to become involved in what it saw as Trotskyist or anarchist adventures.

It now seems extraordinary that President de Gaulle and his ministers should have feared that France was again on the brink of civil war. There were also some curiously false echoes of the Liberation twenty-four years before. In an attempt to cow the students, tanks from the 2nd Armoured Division were diverted through Parisian suburbs on what was described as an '*itinéraire psychologique*'.*

Strikes and rioting eroded government confidence to such a degree over the next two weeks that on 29 May de Gaulle left Paris without even warning his closest colleagues. They arrived at the Élysée Palace just before ten o'clock for a meeting of the Council of Ministers and were aghast to hear that the President had left for an undisclosed destination. Rumours spread rapidly that he had retired to Colombey-les-deux-Églises to announce his resignation. Parisians listened to the contradictory reports on their transistor radios in a state of apprehension comparable with that of the uprising in August 1944, when they feared that the Allies would never reach the city in time. There were even rich *paniquards* – those who could obtain fuel for their cars – taking the road to Switzerland with all their valuables.

---

*The newspaper *Combat* on 12 May, following 'the night of the barricades', warned that Paris would become '*Budapest-sur-Seine*'.

De Gaulle had in fact flown to Baden-Baden to meet General Massu at the headquarters of the French army in Germany. His son-in-law, General Alain de Boissieu, had arranged the meeting. The President needed a firm guarantee that he had the full support of the army, which had been discontented since his decision in 1962 to withdraw from Algeria. The price was the release from prison of General Salan, whose *putsch* in that year, with paratroopers emplaned at Algiers ready to seize Paris, had collapsed at the last moment.

The next morning, 30 May, President de Gaulle reappeared at the Élysée Palace after landing by helicopter at Issy-les-Moulineaux. A communiqué was issued. After a meeting of the Council of Ministers, the President would address the nation by radio. Comparisons were immediately made with his radio appeal from London on 18 June 1940. Gaullist supporters, tipped off that their leader was about to fight back, began to gather in central Paris, armed with tricolors and transistors. The General's speech at half past four was brief. He was not resigning. He had decided to dissolve the National Assembly and to appoint Prefects to take on the post-Liberation authority of *Commissaires de la République*. But the underlying message of his text was a challenge to the left. If they wanted civil war instead of constitutional government, they would have it. This was de Gaulle's last dramatic intervention. The next year, following an unfavourable result in a referendum, he resigned as President of the Republic and disappeared to Ireland. The succession was assured with Georges Pompidou as his replacement. The Fifth Republic, with the *dirigiste* Constitution which de Gaulle had wanted in 1945, maintained its stability well beyond the death of its creator eighteen months later.

On that afternoon of his radio broadcast, 30 May 1968, the General's supporters gathered exultantly on the Place de la Concorde and the Champs-Élysées. 'De Gaulle is not alone!' they cried. From crowds nearly a million strong, there emerged a variety of other slogans. The favourite was the chant '*Le communisme ne passera pas!'* No doubt there were many present who had been supporters of Marshal Pétain; but the vast majority now regarded themselves as average Frenchmen, exasperated with political strikes and chaos in the Latin Quarter. The Sartrian road to freedom was at an end. Radical ideas had failed to overcome the bourgeoisie.

References

UNPUBLISHED SOURCES

AN	Archives Nationales, Paris
AVP	Archives de la Ville de Paris
BD	Bruce Diaries, Virginia Historical Society
CDJC	Centre de Documentation Juive Contemporaine, Paris
DCD	Duff Cooper diary
DCP	Duff Cooper papers
DD	Diary of Brigadier Denis Daly, British Military Attaché
ICG	Institut Charles de Gaulle, Paris
IFOP	Institut Français d'Opinion Publique
JO	Journal Officiel
LC–AHP	Library of Congress, Averell Harriman papers
LDCP	Lady Diana Cooper papers
LDCP–CR	Diana Cooper correspondence with Conrad Russell
NARA*	National Archives and Records Administration, Washington, DC
NMP	Nancy Mitford papers
PRO	Public Record Office, Kew
RCCSMHR	Russian Centre for the Conservation and Study of Modern Historical Records, Moscow

*The final digits of the NARA document reference gives the date of receipt by month, day and year: thus dossier No. 851.00/12–448, was received on December 4, 1948.

PREFACE

Page

xi   'recurring fever', Jean Monnet, *Mémoires*, p. 261

CHAPTER I   *The Marshal and the General*

Page

4   'You are a general', Charles de Gaulle, *Mémoires de Guerre*, vol. i,
       p. 53.

5   'Ah! if only I could be sure . . .', *ibid.*, p. 44

6   'poor relations . . .', E. Spears, *Assignment to Catastrophe*, vol. ii, 138

6   '*C'est la dislocation!* ', ibid., p. 143

6   'We would fight on . . .', ibid., p. 150

6   'the destruction of the country . . .', Paul Reynaud, *Au Coeur de la
       mêlée*, p. 743

6   'at the last quarter of an hour', ibid.

7   'with some annoyance . . .', Spears, p. 288

9   'as if it were a commercial company . . .', Peter Novick, *The
       Resistance versus Vichy*, p. 17

10   'Oh, Malraux . . .', Jean Lacouture, *De Gaulle, the Rebel*, p. 212

CHAPTER 2   *The Paths of Collaboration and Resistance*

Page

13   'the gaze fixed . . .', Henri du Moulin de Labarthète, *Le Temps
       des illusions*, p. 50

13   'I collaborate . . .', 22.12.40, AN F/1a/3657

14n   'much surprise was expressed . . .', 23.11.44, PRO FO/371/
       42102/Z8288

15   '*femmes d'une mauvaise vie*', 15.5.43, AN F/1a/3657

15   'I swear to fight . . .', quoted Azéma, 'La Milice', *20ème
       siècle*

15   'This General dares . . .', Emmanuel Le Roy Ladurie, *Paris–
       Montpellier*, p. 14

16   'You are all alone . . .', R. Cassin, *Les Hommes partis de rien*,
       p. 76

21   '*des lendemains* . . .', Gabriel Péri, *Une Vie de combat*, p. 126

CHAPTER 3   *The Resistance of the Interior and the Men of London*

Page

23   'This Admiral knows . . .', Édouard Herriot, *Épisodes 1940–1944*, p. 75

26   '*démietté*', Claude Bouchinet-Serreulles, conversation, 23.11.92

28   'a good idea', Dimitrov to Dekhanazov, Vice People's Commissar for Foreign Affairs, 8.2.43, RCCSMHR 495/74/532

29   'nothing was more like . . .', General de Bénouville, conversation, 21.1.93

30   '*Vichy à la sauce* . . .', Henri Noguères, conversation, 6.10.89

30   'It's our trial', Simone de Beauvoir, *La Force de l'âge*, p. 591

32   'It's pandemonium', Hervé Alphand, *L'Étonnement d'être*, p. 177

33   'Has it occurred . . .', Henri Amouroux, *La Grande Histoire . . .*, vol. viii, p. 546

33   'I do not shake . . .', Charles de Gaulle, *Mémoires de Guerre*, vol. ii, p. 376

33   'the clergy . . .', Gaston Palewski, *Mémoires d'action*, p. 216

CHAPTER 4   *The Race for Paris*

Page

38   'forty Germans were killed . . .', Henri Amouroux, *La Grande Histoire . . .*, vol. viii, p. 650

41   '*Chacun son boche!*', proclamation of 22.8.44, quoted Dansette, p. 508

41   'I arrive . . .', Jean Galtier-Boissière, *Mon Journal pendant l'Occupation*, p. 259

42   'The whole neighbourhood . . .', ibid., p. 261

43   'Horch convertible . . .', AN F/1a/3254

44   'his white habit . . .', Philippe Boegner, *Carnets du Pasteur Boegner*, p. 287

46   'I'll make him talk . . .', John Mowinckel, conversation, 15.10.92

47   'General Hemingway . . .', Jeffrey Myers, *Hemingway*, p. 408

47   'You are lucky', Charles de Gaulle, *Mémoires de guerre*, vol, ii, p. 302

48n   'That day Leclerc's division . . .', Henri Amouroux, *La Grande Histoire*, vol. viii, p. 684

50   'enormous disorder . . .', Simone de Beauvoir, *La Force de l'âge*, pp. 609–10

50   'The greatness of man', *Combat*, 25 August 1944, quoted Gorce, *L'Après Guerre, 1944–1952*, p. 10

50   'on an American flag', Julien Green, *Journal*, p. 669

51   'A vibrant crowd surrounds . . .', Jean Galtier-Boissière, *Mon
      Journal pendant l'Occupation*, p. 276

53   'abandoned by their officers . . .', ibid., p. 280

53   'were mixed up together . . .', Boegner, p. 295

55   'One would have liked . . .', Léonard Rist, quoted Charles Rist,
      Une Saison gâtée, p. 432

56   'The request of Georges Bidault . . .', conversation René Brouillet,
      15.10.92

57   'fifty martini cocktails', 25.8.44, BD

57   '*débauche de fraternité*', Simone de Beauvoir, *La Force des choses*,
      p. 13

CHAPTER 5   *Liberated Paris*

Page
59   'The combination was enough . . .', 25.8.44, BD

60n   '*C'est un plebiscite*', Bulletin No.1, 1.10.44, IFOP

60   'There took place . . .', Charles de Gaulle, *Mémoires de guerre*, vol.
      ii, p. 313

61   'Mixed in the immense crowd . . .', Simone de Beauvoir, *La Force
      de l'âge*, p. 612

62   'cut in half', Jean Cocteau, *Journal 1942–1945*, p. 534

62   'The heroes multiplied', Jean Galtier-Boissière, *Mon Journal pendant
      l'Occupation*, p. 284

63   'The effect was fantastic . . .', Malcolm Muggeridge, *Chronicles of
      Wasted Time*, vol. ii, p. 211

63   'Public order . . .', Philippe Boegner, *Carnets du Pasteur Boegner*,
      p. 301

64   'like a marriage feast', P. Robrieux, *Histoire intérieure . . .*, vol. ii,
      p. 20

64   'For shit's sake . . .', quoted ibid., vol. i, p. 519

66   'the spoken word . . .', Beauvoir, *La Force de l'âge*, p. 599

67   'packed full of types . . .', Jean Galtier-Boissière, *Mon Journal
      depuis la Libération*, p. 43

67   'the short lampshade skirts . . .', Galtier-Boissière, *Mon Journal
      pendant l'Occupation*, p. 251

67   '*les élégantes . . .*', Beauvoir, *La Force de l'âge*, p. 597

68   '*se dédouaner*', Hervé Le Boterf, *La Vie parisienne sous l'Occupation*,
      p. 414
69   'There were only flickering . . .', Muggeridge, p. 211

CHAPTER 6   *The Passage of Exiles*
Page
76   'This is not the occasion . . .', P. G. Wodehouse to Home
      Secretary, 4.9.44, copy included in MI5 report of 28.9.44, DCP
77   'that the best thing . . .', DCD, 1.12.44
78   'a gloomy sort of chap', Malcolm Muggeridge, *Chronicles of Wasted
      Time*, vol. ii, p. 232

CHAPTER 7   *War Tourists and Ritzkrieg*
Page
80   'Hitlers come and go . . .', Malcolm Muggeridge, *Chronicles of
      Wasted Time*, vol. ii, p. 221
81   'Paris was liberated . . .', Georges Brassaï, *Conversations avec Picasso*,
      p. 150
81   'Who's there? . . .', Cleve Gray, conversation, 24.11.92
83   'It was an American enclave . . .', Simone de Beauvoir, *La Force
      des choses*, p. 29
84   'I'm Eric Blair', Paul Potts, *Dante called you Beatrice* (Eyre &
      Spottiswoode, 1960), quoted Bernard Crick, *George Orwell*,
      p. 324
84   '*Vous êtes un général . . .*', Beauvoir, *La Force des choses*, p. 27, and
      Magouche Fielding, conversation, 18.2.92
85   'the impression that members . . .', 5.10.44, DD
86   'beginning a romance', Martha Gellhorn, *A Honeyed Peace*, p. 74
86   'a prudery . . .', 6.2.45, AN F/1a/3255

CHAPTER 8   *The Épuration Sauvage*
Page
88   'At Saint-Sauveur . . .', 28.6.44, BD
89   'My ass . . .', Jean Galtier-Boissière, *Mon Journal depuis la
      Libération*, p. 11

90 'you did not have to be cosy . . .', Sir Isaiah Berlin, conversation, 12.8.93

92 'Considering their youth . . .', Malcolm Muggeridge, *Chronicles of Wasted Time*, vol. ii, p. 217

93 'made incapable . . .', Director General of SNCF, AN F/1a/3208

93 'The BST . . .', Controller-General Robineau to Inspector-General of Police, 23.11.45, AN F/1a/3246

94 'If you take away my braces . . .', Madame du Bouëtiez, French Red Cross representative, Paris prisons, conversation, 29.6.92

97 'It must be acknowledged . . .', Report by Inspector-General of Prisons to Minister of Justice, 21.7.45, AN F/1a/4611

98 'Have you got any customers . . .', Roger Codou, conversation, 13.3.93

99 'violent death of undetermined nature', AVP, Per 55

100 '*de caractère politique*', Direction de Renseignements Généraux, 25.8.45, AN F/1a/3349

101 'France is a country . . .', quoted Galtier-Boissière, *Mon Journal depuis la Libération*, p. 210

101 'the *épuration* in France . . .', Jean-Pierre Rioux, *La France de la Quatrième République*, vol. i, p. 32

101 'French who served in German uniform', Henry Rousso, conversation, 30.6.92

CHAPTER 9 *Provisional Government*

Page

105 'prevent at any price . . .', Kozirev to Ponomarev, International Section of the Central Committee, 9.7.45, RCCSMHR, 17/128/802

105 'De Gaulle . . . is afraid . . .', Dimitrov and Ponomarev, 30.11.44, RCCSMHR 17/128/14

107 'a provoking attitude . . .', Louis Closon, *Commissaire de la République*, p. 69

107 'At the time of the Liberation . . .', quoted M. R. D. Foot, *SOE in France*, p. 420

108 'Toulouse was the soukh . . .', Jacques Baumel, conversation, 6.8.92

109 '*belle brochette de colonels*', quoted Henri Amouroux, *Les Règlements de comptes*, vol. ix, p. 165

113n   'more nicknames . . .', René Serre, *Croisade à coups de poings*, p. 142

113   'This adventure was unexpected . . .', Georges Bidault, *D'une Résistance à l'autre*, p. 70

114   *'peuplé de Vichy'*, Hervé Alphand, *L'Étonnement d'être*, p. 181

114   'He could have helped me . . .', 13.2.47, DCD

115   'There has been snow . . .', NARA 851.00/1–2045

115   *'la Collecte'*, report of 2.2.45 by Direction Générale de la Sûreté Nationale, AN F/1a/3249

116   'the child St Augustine . . .', François Mauriac, *Journal*, vol. iv, p. 8

116   'Milk for our little ones!', AN F/1a/3250

116   'the Siege of Paris', AN F/1a/3249

116   'suitcase-carriers', Yves Farge, *Le Pain de la corruption*, p. 10

117   'In the circumstances . . .', 26.3.45, AN F/1a/3250

117   'We are most unhappy . . .', AN F/1a/3208

118   'The insufficient purge . . .', October 1945. Report on activity of CGT, RCCSMHR, 17/128/16

118   *'un problème délicat'*, Ministre des Travaux Publics, 17.10.44, AN F/1a/3208

118   'The directors of the Renault factories . . .', *L'Humanité*, 22 August 1944, quoted Pierre Assouline, *L'Épuration des intellectuels*, p. 22

119   'fulfilled its duty to the nation . . .', quoted Gaston Palewski, *Mémoires d'action*, p. 228

120   'to put Humpty Dumpty . . .', Grover Smith (ed.), *Letters of Aldous Huxley*, p. 516

CHAPTER 10   *Corps Diplomatique*

Page

122   'He seemed curiously young . . .', 14.9.44, DCD

122   'At *last!*', Sir Alexander Cadogan, *Diaries*, p. 675

123   'extremely frigid and dreary . . .', 24.10.44, DCD

125   'left in disgust . . .', 14.9.44, DD

126   'looking like an old concierge', 21.3.47, DCD

127   'the vodka struggle', 20.11.45, LDCP–CR

128   'The traffic . . .', 7.11.44, DCD

128   'uneasy to conduct . . .', Georges Bidault, *D'une Résistance à l'autre*, p. 72

129   'In Bido Veritas', 24.2.45, DD

129 'Claudel, Alexis Léger . . .', Jacques Dumaine, *Quai d'Orsay 1945–51*, pp. 2–3

130 'was most indignant . . .' 28.11.44, DCD

131 'a curious pair . . .', Malcolm Muggeridge, *Chronicles of Wasted Time*, vol. ii, p. 217

131 'in the happiest of humours', 11.11.44, DCD

131 'for about two hours . . .', 11.11.44, DCD

132n 'Although his outward . . .', RCCSMHR 17/128/14

133 'Communist dressed up as a field marshal . . .', Charles de Gaulle, *Mémoires de guerre*, vol. iii, p. 61

133 'One never ceases to be Polish . . .', Hervé Alphand, *L'Étonnement d'être*, p. 180

134 'France must pay . . .', Foreign Relations of the United States of America, *The Conferences at Cairo and Teheran*, pp. 484–5, quoted Jean Elleinstein, *Goliath contre Goliath*, p. 97

135 'Don't take my . . .', Charles de Gaulle, *Memoires de Guerre*, vol. iii, p. 56

137 'How much is a pint?', Lady Rothschild (Tess Mayor), conversation, 1.12.92

137 'Paris is lugubrious . . .', Alphand, p. 182

137 'It suggested that de Gaulle . . .', 4.1.45, DCD

138 'I felt my brain slowing down . . .', Philippe Boegner, *Carnets du Pasteur Boegner*, p. 324

138 'chased out the Germans . . .', Ponomarev, RCCSMHR 17/128/748

139 'The French authorities . . .', NARA 751.00/5–1245

CHAPTER 11 *Khaki and the Tricolor*

Page

141 'condemned to traffick . . .', Yves Farge, *Le Pain de la corruption*, p. 12

142 'Anyone found in possession . . .', NARA 851.04413/1–545

142 'seize three . . .', 27.6.45, AN F/1a/3249

142 'I am told . . .', Caffery, NARA 851.5017/1–2947

142 'Lise's main sport . . .', Simone de Beauvoir, *La force des choses*, p. 26

143 'The hats in Paris . . .', Corporal Bob Baldrige, letter, 7.3.45

143 'The easy-going manner . . .', Beauvoir, *La Force des choses*, p. 13

143   'ardent and often very enterprising', NARA 711.51/3‑945

143   'juvenile prostitution', Appendix E, SHAEF Mission, Progress Report of 16–31 May 1945

144   'all the Generals at SHAEF . . .', 3.5.45, DCD

144   'did not have a high opinion of Mr Caffery', 3.10.44, DD

145   'full of American businessmen . . .', 21.9.44, DCD

145   'It seems hardly believable', 8.5.45, DCD

145   'a quiet and unostentatious . . .', NARA 851.00/2‑1445

145   'the US is supplying inferior . . .', US Embassy report, NARA 851.00/4‑245.

146   'One couldn't help thinking . . .', 18.6.45, DCD

146   'They do not seem to be taking . . . steps . . .', SHAEF Mission to France, Progress Report No. 19, 1–15 June 1945, NARA 851.00/6‑2145

147   'in a premeditated plan . . .', François Billoux, *Quand nous étions ministres*, p. 39

147   'it appears that they are American deserters . . .', Jean Galtier-Boissière, *Mon Journal depuis la Libération*, p. 136

147   'barbarians . . .', Susan Mary Alsop, *To Marietta from Paris*, p. 53

147   'increase in armed attacks', 15.1.46, F/1a/3349

148   'an army of drivers . . .', Alfred Fabre-Luce, *Journal de la France*, p. 667

149   'America symbolized . . .', Beauvoir, *La Force des choses* p. 28

CHAPTER 12   *Writers and Artists in the Line of Fire*

Page

150   'one could see . . .', Alfred Fabre-Luce, *Journal de la France*, p. 653

151   'the European position of France', Robert Aron, *Histoire de Vichy*, p. 685

151   'He failed with his death . . .', *Franc-Tireur*, 24.8.44

152   'The moral . . . of the story . . .', letter to Victoria Ocampo, 2.4.45., Grover Smith (ed.), *Letters of Aldous Huxley*, p. 518

152   'Paris is beautiful . . .', Robert Brasillach, *Journal d'un homme occupé*, vol. vi, p. 560

153   'On the contrary . . .', Baronne Élie de Rothschild, conversation, 30.10.92

154 'What is this government . . .', Jean Galtier-Boissière, *Mon Journal depuis la Libération*, p. 16

154 'I am the victim . . .', Christian Gilles, *Arletty*, p. 39

154 'France has got what she deserves!', quoted Jean-Louis Faucigny-Lucinge, *Un Gentilhomme cosmopolite*, p. 183

157 'a queue of the damned . . .', Jacques Benoist-Méchin, *À l'Épreuve du temps*, p. 392

157 '*anti-sémite* . . .', 2.11.44, PRO/FO 371/42013/Z7349

157 'I never set foot . . .', Céline, Copenhagen, 6.11.46, NARA 851.00/6-2847

158 '*Paulhan le Juste*', Galtier-Boissière, *Mon Jourbal depuis la Libération*, p. 38

158 'The Nazis . . .', Jean Galtier-Boissière, *Mon Journal pendant l'Occupation*, p. 290

158 'these "intellectuals" had provided . . .', Pierre-Henri Teitgen, *Faites entrer le témoin suivant*, p. 248

159 'one doesn't kill . . .', Benoist-Méchin, *À l'Épreuve du temps*, p. 396

160 'We must get rid of the Jews . . .' quoted Teitgen, p. 250

160 'with eloquence . . .', *Combat*, 20.1.45

161 'Personally, I regret . . .', Gaston Palewski, *Mémoires d'action*, p. 225

162 'Why did you resign?', Celia Goodman (ed.), *Living with Koestler*, p. 60

162 'the screen behind which . . .', Philippe Boegner, *Carnets du Pasteur Boegner*, p. 316

163 'police spy', Annie Cohen-Solal, *Paul Nizan*, p. 253

164 'Not stupid . . .', Galtier-Boissière, *Mon Journal depuis la Libération*, pp. 15-16

CHAPTER 13 *The Return of Exiles*

Page

166 'Any news?', Marguerite Duras, *La Douleur*, p. 15

166n 'The days of tears . . .', quoted ibid., p. 41

167 'Their faces were grey-green . . .', Janet Flanner, *Paris Journal*, p. 26

167 'a greenish, waxen . . .', Jean Galtier-Boissière, *Mon Journal depuis la Libération*, p. 244

167 'Gare de l'Est . . .', Louise Alcan, *Sans armes et sans bagages*, p. 118

167 'You must see this . . .', Mary Vaudoyer, conversation, 23.11.92

169   'the best of the French', Annette Wieviorka, *Déportation et génocide*, p. 88

169   'still dressed in the striped uniform . . .', Galtier-Boissière, *Mon Journal depuis la Libération* p. 231

170   'musulmans', from Dr Dvojetski, *Revue d'histoire de la médecine hébraïque*, Paris, No. 56, July 1962, pp. 55–91, CDJC

170   'Joy did not come . . .', Pierre Daix, *J'ai cru au matin*, p. 143

170   '*univers concentrationnaire*', Dvojetski, CJDC

170   'She had bought me . . .', Raymond Ruffin, *La Vie des Français au jour le jour*, p. 171

172   'All the pictures . . .', Gertrude Stein, *Wars I Have Seen*, p. 174

173   'an Aztec eagle', Anne Chisolm, *Nancy Cunard*, p. 207

173   'a tall lanky Irishman . . .', Deirdre Bair, *Samuel Beckett*, p. 207

174   'It's better not to ask . . .', Julien Green, *Journal*, p. 668

174   'Paris seemed terrifying to me . . .', quoted Susan Mary Alsop, *To Marietta from Paris*, p. 33

174   'The Ritz . . . looked exactly . . .', 22.9.44, DCD

175   'If only I knew . . .', Baronne Élie de Rothschild, conversation, 30.10.92

175   'She's just like her father . . .', Claus von Bülow, conversation, 14.12.92

176   'There was a terrible moment . . .', 10.9.45, LCDCP–CR

177   'the most expensive discomfort . . .', quoted Philip Ziegler, *King Edward VIII*, p. 509

177   'One of the best dinners . . .', 17.10.45, DD

177   'At fifty . . .', Jacques Dumaine, *Quai d'Orsay 1945–51*, p. 42

177   'so anxious to do right', 28.10.45, DCD

CHAPTER 14   *The Great Trials*

Page

180   'his neat, sallow head . . .', Malcolm Muggeridge, *Chronicles of Wasted Time*, vol. ii, p. 220

181   'The purge trials . . .', Susan Mary Alsop, *To Marietta from Paris*, p. 46

181   'it was not possible . . .', Claude Bouchinet-Serreulles, conversation, 23.11.92

181   'One sees more and more . . .', Philippe Boegner, *Carnets du Pasteur Boegner*, p. 335

181 '*la stricte exécution* . . .', Article 3 of Decree of 28.11.44, quoted Jacques Charpentier, *Au Service de la Liberté*, p. 256

182 'silently to surrender . . .', Alsop, op. cit., p. 27

182 '32 per cent', Bulletin 16.8.45, fieldwork 11–25 July, IFOP

183 'furious with de Gaulle . . .', 30.4.45, DD

184 'Why do you not . . .', Charpentier, p. 267

185 'The assembly exploded in anger . . .', stenographic version of Comrade Popova's report to the International Section of the Central Committee, 16.7.45, RCCSMHR, 17/128/748

186 'I made a fine speech', Jacques Isorni, *Philippe Pétain*, p. 477

187 'They are putting the armistice . . .', Charpentier, p. 267

187 'was not a dishonourable . . .', quoted Haute Cour de Justice, *Le Procès du Maréchal Pétain*

189 'The fat of his face . . .', Janet Flanner, *Paris Journal*, p. 39

190 'for several months . . .', quoted Isorni, *Philippe Pétain*, pp. 400–401

190 'For four years . . .', quoted Azéma, 'La Milice', p. 104

191 'I am not . . .', Haute Cour de Justice, p. 257

191 'Each day . . .', quoted Isorni, *Philippe Pétain*, p. 476

191 'Trust me . . .', ibid., p. 393

192 'he was incapable . . .', Comte René de Chambrun, conversation, 16.10.92

193 'The examination procedure . . .', article by Madeleine Jacob, *Franc-Tireur*, 6 October 1945

193 'Like Andalusian . . .', Charpentier, p. 268

193 'The Laval trial . . .', Boegner, p. 352

194 'If Laval is executed . . .', ibid.

195 'The only time . . .', Baronne Élie de Rothschild, conversation, 30.10.92

195 'black-market queens', Alsop, p. 52

CHAPTER 15 *Hunger for the New*

Page

197 'To be twenty . . .', Simone de Beauvoir, *La Force des choses*, p. 19

198 'Oh wonders!' Emmanuel Le Roy Ladurie, *Paris–Montpellier*, p. 25

198 'resistance, black market . . .', Marc Doelnitz, *La Fête à Saint-Germain-des-Prés*, p. 98

201 'We have only to imagine . . .', 25.7.45, DCD

201   'reactionary bourgeois philosophy', A. A. Zhdanov, 11.6.46,
       RCCSMHR 17/125/454

202   'a pretentious metaphysical thesis', A. J. Ayer, *Part of my Life*, p. 284

202   'a charm . . .', Simone de Beauvoir, *La Force de l'âge*, p. 576

203   'overflowing with charm . . .', quoted Saint-Germain-des-Prés,
       p. 14

204   '*désordres amoureux*', Beauvoir, *La Force de l'âge*. p. 589

204   'Sartre had a rather diabolical . . .', quoted Deirdre Bair, *Simone
       de Beauvoir*, p. 345

204   'He discovered . . .', J.-P. Sartre, 'Merleau-Ponty', *Les Temps
       modernes*, October 1961

205   'The impression . . .', Beauvoir, *La Force de l'âge*, p. 586

206   'the Proust of marginal Paris', Edmund White, *Jean Genet*, p.196

206   'a distrustful . . . look . . .', Beauvoir, *La Force de l'âge*, p. 595

206   'a tall, blonde, elegant . . .', Beauvoir, *La Force des choses*, p. 29

207   'he takes himself . . .', Beauvoir, ibid., p. 87

210   'first anti-revolutionary . . .', Jean Cocteau, *Journal*, pp. 554, 565

210   'Joining . . .', *L'Humanité*, 30.10.44

211   'This emaciated . . .', 26.3.47, DCP

211   'I must tell you . . .', Signor to Stepanov, 22.4.46, RCCSMHR
       17/128/967

212   'What did you . . .', Dominique Desanti, *Les Staliniens*, p. 6

213   'Monsieur, I would have you know . . .', Jacques Dumaine, *Quai
       d'Orsay 1945–51*, p. 27

214   'the bourgeois theatre . . .', Jean François Gravier, *Paris, Le Desert
       français*, p. 87

214   'a nostalgia for . . .', Edmund Wilson, *A Literary Chronicle of the
       Forties*, p. 112

CHAPTER 16   *After the Deluge*

Page

215   'You just don't . . .', Nancy Mitford, *The Blessing*, p. 173

216   'One rule here . . .', Susan Mary Alsop, *To Marietta from Paris*, p. 34

217   'expecting to be treated . . .', General Count de Rougemont, as
       told to Susan Mary Alsop, conversation, 2.11.92

217   'One asked nothing . . .', Martha Gellhorn, *A Honeyed Peace*, p. 11

217   'A Free French officer . . .', Guy de Rothschild, *The Whims of
       Fortune*, p. 149

218   'Oh! All that's . . .', Jean-Louis Faucigny-Lucinge, *Un Gentilhomme cosmopolite*, p. 189

218   'Führer of Champagne', Odette Pol Roger, conversation, 10.10.89

218   'the house smelled . . .', Alsop, p. 27

220   'We were told . . .', Popova's report to Ponomarev, 16.7.45, RCCSMHR 17/128/748

220   'has more orders . . .', 29.11.45, LDCP–CR

220   'They crouch . . .', Alsop, p. 35

220   'Today . . . I heard an old . . .', to Evelyn Waugh, 2.4.48, NMP

221   'Monsieur le duc . . .', Duc de Brissac, *Mémoires*, p. 151

221   'The French . . .', Alsop, p. 5

221   'a Scandinavian student . . .', Claus von Bülow, conversation, 14.12.92

222   'He can do no good . . .', to Lascelles, 26.11.45, DCP

222   'to entertain official personages . . .', to Lascelles, 5.11.45, DCP

222   'Wally drew me aside . . .', 12.12.45, DD

222   'I told him . . .', 15.12.45, DD

222   'The famous charm . . .', Lascelles, letter, 17.11.45, DCP

223   'You ought to marry . . .', to Diana Mosley, 15.6.46, NMP

223   'the rights of passion . . .', Charlotte Mosley (ed.), *Love from Nancy*, p. 218

224   'I end up . . .', ibid., p. 215

224   'we hadn't been there two minutes . . .', 5.6.46, NMP

224   'Does it not occur to you . . .', quoted Selina Hastings, *Nancy Mitford*, p. 179

CHAPTER 17   *The Salons*

Page

225   'Well, as somebody . . .', to Randolph Churchill, 8.10.45, NMP

226   'his luxury peasant accent', Jean-Louis Faucigny-Lucinge, *Un Gentilhomme cosmopolite*, p. 102

228   'Oh, the objects . . .', to Lady Pamela Berry, 29.10.49, NMP

228   'I think, ladies and gentlemen . . .', Jean Galtier-Boissière, *Mon Journal depuis la Libération*, p. 31

229   'I have forgotten . . .', Jean Galtier-Boissière, *Mon Journal dans la grande pagaïe*, p. 160

229   'a French *gratin-académie* . . .', to Evelyn Waugh, 21.4.46, NMP

230   'Marie-Louise can never have been . . .', Faucigny-Lucinge,
        p. 90

230   'a strange combination . . .', Cyrus L. Sulzberger, *A Long Row of
        Candles*, p. 258

231   'looking like a little mongoose . . .', conversation Cleve Gray,
        24.11.92

232   'a cross between a chapel . . .', Truman Capote, interview, *Paris
        Review*, No. 61, Spring 1975, quoted George Wickes, *The Amazon
        of Letters*, p. 256

232   'to meet somebody . . .', ibid.

232   'In England . . .', quoted Wickes, p. 45

233   '*le goût de la tendresse*', Denise Tual, conversation, 20.10.92

233   'his lips had . . .', Bettina Ballard, *In My Fashion*, p. 23

234   'In four strokes . . .', Marc Doelnitz, *La Fête à Saint-Germain-des-
        Prés*, p. 112

235   'to find Picasso . . .', Malcolm Muggeridge, *Chronicles of Wasted
        Time*, vol. ii, p. 235

235   'a desperate fear . . .', Louise de Vilmorin to Diana Cooper: a
        letter surviving only in DC's translation, undated, *c.* 1959

235   'Hungarian countess . . .', Evelyn Waugh to Nancy Mitford,
        7.8.46; Mark Amory (ed.), *The Letters of Evelyn Waugh*, p. 232

236   '*le coup de pistolet* . . .', Jean Cocteau, *Journal 1942–1945*, p. 597

237   'Not much to eat . . .', Louise de Vilmorin to Diana Cooper, op.
        cit.

237   'We had just reached the coffee . . .', 7.11.44, DCD

CHAPTER 18   *Communists in Government*

Page

238   'I've seen this man . . .', Jean Galtier-Boissière, *Mon Journal depuis
        la Libération*, pp. 254–5

240   'at least one girl . . .', Susan Mary Alsop, *To Marietta from Paris*,
        p. 31

240   'This victory had been far away . . .', Simone de Beauvoir,
        La Force des choses, p. 42

240   'too exhausted . . .', Galtier-Boissière, *Mon Journal depuis la
        Libération*, p. 252

241   'the principal reason . . .', Stepanov for Dimitrov, received 2.2.45,
        RCCSMHR, 17/128/43

242   'Every week . . .', NARA 851.00/2–1445

244   '*tristement petit-bourgeois*', Dominique Desanti, *Les Staliniens*, p. 53

245   'efforts to bring about . . .', NARA 851.00/6–2245

246   'No word . . .', NARA 851.00/6–1445

246   'cynical Hitlerian . . .', Musée des Deux Guerres, Buton, p. 154

246   'For the whole period . . .', 15.6.45, RCCSMHR 17/128/748

CHAPTER 19   *The Abdication of Charles XI*

Page

248   'De Gaulle is much blamed . . .', 9.6.45, DCD

248   'When I asked him . . .', NARA 851.00/6–1545

248   'When people . . .', Claude Bouchinet-Serreulles, conversation, 23.11.92

248   'a hypersensitive loner . . .', Philippe Boegner, *Carnets du Pasteur Boegner*, p. 343

249   'England was preparing . . .', Charles de Gaulle, *Mémoires de guerre*, vol. iii, p. 181

250   'owing to recent events . . .', 28.6.45, DCD

250   'intended to retire . . .', 27.6.45, DCD

251   '*l'intendance suivra*', quoted Frank Giles, *The Locust Years*, p. 20

251   'with de Gaulle . . .', Winant to Secretary of State, NARA 851.00/6–1845

252   'why France saw the world . . .', de Gaulle, *Mémoires de guerre*, vol. iii, p. 210

252   'A country which . . .', General Impression of France, NARA 851.00/8–2445

254   'I never liked or admired . . .', 13.11.45, DCD

255   '*le caractère national* . . .', quoted Jean Lacouture, *De Gaulle, Le Politique*, p. 217

255   'It's de Gaulle . . .', Luizet's report to Ministry of the Interior, 20.11.45, AN F/1a/3201

257   'Yesterday we were tricked . . .', Directeur des RG au DG de SN, 21.11.43, AN F/1a/3201

257   'that the Communists . . .', 3.12.45, DCD

258   'There are only two real . . .', Caffery, secret telegram to Secretary of State, 6 December 1945, NARA 851.00/12–745

259   'You talk of greatness . . .', Jean Monnet, *Mémoires*, p. 270

260   'De Gaulle "was looking ill . . ."', 1.1.46, DD

260   'their games . . .', A. Astoux, *L'Oubli*, p. 79
260   'felt bound up . . .', Claude Bouchinet-Serreulles, conversation, 23.11.92
261   'On January 20th . . .', Duff Cooper, *Old Men Forget*, p. 365
261   'Gentlemen, I have decided . . .', 21.1.46, DD
261   'was as usual very interesting . . .', 22.1.46, DCD
261   'a political crisis . . .', NARA 851.00/1–2046
262   'caused hardly a ripple . . .', NARA 851.00/2–2546
262   'demonstrated their satisfaction . . .', AN F/1a/3201
263   'You cannot imagine . . .', Hervé Alphand, *L'Étonnement d' être*, p. 192
263   'His stomach . . .', Malcolm Muggeridge, *Chronicles of Wasted Time*, p. 213
264   'Passy . . . said that . . .', Brigadier Daly, Top Secret to Deputy Director Military Intelligence, 21.4.46, DD

CHAPTER 20   *The Shadow-Theatre – Plots and Counter-Plots*

Page

267   '*cette femme*' . . . 'Very well indeed', 4.4.46, DD
267   'The severe judgements . . .', Philippe Boegner, *Carnets du Pasteur Boegner*, p. 323
268   'unemployed' ['*en chômage*'], 22.11.45, DCD
268   'the Communist Party had paid . . .', 17.12.45, DD
269   'How many pupils . . .', quoted letter to Deputy Director Military Intelligence, 4.4.46, DD
270   'new political movement . . .', 4.2.46 DCD
270   'I have the honour to report . . .', NARA 851.00/2–2546
271   'favourable to chaos . . .', NARA 851.011/5–146
272   'all highly dangerous . . .', 7.5.46, DD
273   'I have just been accused . . .', 7.5.46, DD
275   'the Communists would create incidents . . .', 15.3.46, DD
275   'The circulation . . .', NARA 851.00/3–1446
275   'Clement Fried . . .', NARA 751.61/5–146
276   'While it is difficult to state . . .', NARA 851.00/3–1446
276   'to effect movement . . .', War Department, Top Secret to General MacNarney, NARA 851.00/5–346
277   'General MacNarney should not be given . . .', NARA 851.00/5–346

278   'As you may already know . . .', NARA 851.00/3–1247

CHAPTER 21   *Politics and Letters*

Page

279   'the nation's perfect baby . . .', Jean Galtier-Boissière, *Mon Journal dans la drôle de paix*, p. 251

279   'competent source', Caffery, NARA 851.00/4–2046

280   'plebiscite for or against Communism', NARA 851.011/5–146

280   'the Cossacks . . .', NARA 851.00/5–846

280   'I managed to . . .', Claude Mauriac, *Un Autre de Gaulle*, p. 190

281   'They imagine that France . . .', Jacques Dumaine, *Quai d'Orsay 1945–51*, p. 59

282   'We have discovered . . .', André Dewavrin, conversation 20.11.92

283   'You've been poisoned', ibid.

283   'It appears that the more the affair . . .', NARA 851.00/6–1846

285   'made a good speech . . .', 12.5.46, DCD

285   'I will perhaps . . .', C. Mauriac, p. 194

285   'will be President . . .', 11.5.46, DCD

286   'intensive anti-Communist . . .', Robert Murphy, Top Secret to Secretary of State, NARA 851.00/5–2446

286   'deeply chagrined', NARA 851.00/5–2546

287   'the worst catastrophe . . .', Robert Murphy, Top Secret to Secretary of State, NARA 851.00/5–2566

288   'struck a more responsive . . .', NARA 851.00/6–2046

CHAPTER 22   *The Diplomatic Battleground*

Page

290   'We do not know . . .', Jacques Dumaine, *Quai d'Orsay 1945–51*, p. 47

290   'After twenty-four hours . . .', ibid., p. 55

291   'The next item . . .', 1.5.46, DCD

291   'Agreement was reached . . .', 2.5.46, DCD

291   'Tell Duff . . .', 30.4.46, DCD

291   'Thorez was dimpling prettily . . .', Dumaine, p. 60

292   'Ernie is aggressively real . . .', 25.4.46, LDCP–CR

292   'Whisky improved his temper . . .', Dumaine, op. cit., p. 58

292   'I had Mme Duhamel . . .', 9.5.46, DCD

293   'Luce is a queer duck . . .', 16.5.49, BD

293   'madly in love . . .', 1.5.46, DCD

293   'She is as pretty as ever . . .', 2.12.44, DCD

293   'Mrs O.R. is a . . .', 4.5.46, DCD

293   'Dicky, portly, fine-looking . . .', 3.6.46, LDCP–CR

294   'This made a deep . . .', 4.6.46, DCD

294   'was an irretrievable . . .', 17.5.46, DCD

295   'a strong Germany to fight . . .', 26.5.46, DCD

295   '*une certaine nevrosité*', 27.5.46, AN F/1a/3364

260   'has not taken any steps . . .', Ponomarev to Molotov and
        Malenkov, 16.2.46, RCCSMHR 17/128/967

297   'I'm told the . . .', to Diana Mosley, 9.8.46, NMP

297   'more class distinction than ever', 10.8.46, LDCP–CR

298   '"Old Tawm" . . .', Cyrus Sulzberger, *A Long Row of Candles*,
        p. 295

298   'Senator Vandenberg beside me . . .', Dumaine, op. cit.,
        p. 60

298   'It is odd . . .', 25.9.46, DCD

299   'France is on the verge . . .', 21.10.46, NMP

299   'Bogomolov, the Soviet ambassador . . .', Princesse Ghislaine de
        Polignac, conversation, 1.7.92

300n   'the French Communist Party . . .', Mamaine Paget, quoted
        Celia Goodman (ed.), *Living with Koestler*, p. 36

301   'He subordinated . . .', Simone de Beauvoir, *La Force de choses*,
        p. 126

303   'a true fighter', ibid., p. 129

303   'The Communists are right . . .', ibid., p. 13

CHAPTER 23   *The Fashionable World*

Page

304   'Yes, true Parisiennes . . .', Lise Deharme in *Les Lettres Françaises*,
        21.10.44, quoted Jean-Pierre Bernard, *Paris Rouge*, p. 102

306   'I finally had the idea . . .', Susan Train (ed.), *Le Théâtre de la
        mode*, p. 64

307   'Paris always has . . .', Bettina Ballard, *In My Fashion*, p. 211

308   'a child's idea . . .', 1.4.46, LDCP–CR

308   'any more complications', 5.4.45, DCD

308   'No one is going to come . . .', Susan Mary Alsop, *To Marietta from Paris*, pp. 83–4

310   'the paddock is overrun . . .', 6.2.46, AN F/1a 3255

310   'the owner of . . .', Guy de Rothschild, *The Whims of Fortune*, p. 101

311   '*L'intoxiqué* . . .', François Billoux, *Quand nous étions ministres*, p. 75

311   'Allow me . . .', quoted Georgette Elgey, *La République des illusions*, p. 245

314   '*on ne parle* . . .', to Violet Hammersley, 6.7.48; Charlotte Mosley (ed.), *Love from Nancy*, p. 217

314   'Neither Balmain nor I . . .', Christian Dior, *Dior by Dior*, p. 210

314   'Gertrude Stein with her . . .', Ballard, p. 229

314   'WHERE is Miss . . .', Alsop, p. 93

314   'She is living . . .', 27.2.47, DCD

315   'People shout . . .', 6.12.47, Mosley (ed.), p. 196

315   'a strange woman . . .', to Diana Mosley, 29.10.47, NMP

316   'The London New Look . . .', to Violet Hammersley, 6.7.48; Mosley (ed.), p. 217

CHAPTER 24   *A Tale of Two Cities*

Page

316   'There is the Paris . . .', Paul Laurent, *L'Avant-Garde*, 20.12.50; quoted Jean-Pierre Bernard, *Paris Rouge*, p. 10

317   'architecture is nothing else . . .', Jean François Gravier, *Paris, Le Desert français*, p. 171

318   'slums which ruin . . .', Préfet de la Seine au Conseil Municipal, AVP 51 Db

318   'One cannot . . .', Gravier, p. 191

321   'Perhaps this year . . .', Jean Gager, conversation, 14.3.93

322   'the food position . . .', SHAEF mission, Progress Report No. 19, 1–15.6.45, NARA 851.00/6–2145

323   'The dead generally take . . .', quoted Georgette Elgey, *La République des illusions*, p. 181

325   'I'm suffering today . . .', 1.1.46, LDCP–CR

325   'I gave them a delicious dinner . . .', Graham Payne and Sheridan Morley (eds.), *The Noël Coward Diaries*, London: Weidenfeld & Nicolson, 1982, 6.4.46, p. 55

326   'two pheasants . . .', Janet Flanner, *Paris Journal*, p. 48

326   'caressed the cans . . .', Susan Mary Alsop, *To Marietta from Paris*,
         p. 24

327   'the women come to work . . .', AN F/1a/3255

327   'It's the foundation . . .', Jean Galtier-Boissière, *Mon Journal dans
         la grande pagaïe*, p. 18

328   'In most of these brothels . . .', Jean Oberlé, *La Vie d'artiste*,
         p. 93

329   'Every breath . . .', to Diana Mosley, 26.12.46, NMP

329   'I never saw anything . . .', ibid.

330   'It's a triumph . . .', 15.3.46, LDCP–CR

CHAPTER 25   *Fighting Back against the Communists*

Page

331   'It looks as though . . .', 12.4.46, DCD

331   'through the CGT . . .', Suslov to Zhdanov, report on meeting
         19.6.46, RCCSMHR 17/128/967

331   'After the CGT . . .', Alain Signor to Stepanov, 22.4.46,
         RCCSMHR 17/128/967

332   'very weak', ibid.

332   'Such a compromise . . .', quoted A. Astoux, *L'Oubli*, p. 93

333   'I'd prefer to . . .', André Philip, quoted Georgette Elgey, *La
         République des illusions*, p. 231

333   'a man who has stood . . .', quoted Jean Galtier-Boissière, *Mon
         Journal dans la grande pagaïe*, p. 36

334   'align France with the Soviets . . .', NARA 751.61/3–447

334   'The French enjoyed . . .', Susan Mary Alsop, *To Marietta from
         Paris*, p. 92

335   'brutal candour . . .', Dean Acheson, *Present at the Creation*, p. 213

335   'When we were convened . . .', ibid., p. 219

336   'I believe that it must be . . .', ibid., p. 222

337   'very effective administrator', NARA 851.105/5–2147

338   'At the same time . . .', NARA 851.00/7–947

340   'Madame de Gaulle clicked away . . .', Jacques Soustelle, *Vingt-
         huit ans de Gaullisme*, p. 45

341   'ladies in mink . . .', ibid., p. 48

342   'Sister of Hitler's mistress . . .', Charlotte Mosley (ed.), *Love from
         Nancy*, p. 180

342   'Like the Archangel . . .', to Gaston Palewski, 12.4.47, NMP

344   'Churchill, his tail-coat . . .', Jacques Dumaine, *Quai d'Orsay 1945–51*, p. 120

344   'Make no mistake . . .', quoted Claude Mauriac, *Un Autre de Gaulle*, p. 283

345   'he was suddenly transfigured', ibid. p. 289

CHAPTER 26   *The Self-Fulfilling Prophecy*

Page

347   'Examples of such solidarity . . .', Hervé Alphand, *L'Étonnement d'être*, p. 198

347   'There was almost entire agreement . . .', 17.6.47, DCD

348   *'flagrante et obstinée'*, Georges Bidault, *D'une Résistance à l'autre*, p. 152

348   'impressed upon him . . .', 30.6.47, DCD

348   'go straight ahead . . .', 1.7.47, DCD

348   'seeing Molotov . . .', Alphand, p. 201

349   'All is going well . . .', 7.7.47, DCD

349   'lofty and demanding . . . If we do not get . . .', Sir Isaiah Berlin, conversation, 12.8.93

350   'strongly objected . . .', 16.7.47, DCD

350   'it was very badly received', 17.7.47, DCD

351   'The season here . . .', to Mark Ogilvie-Grant, 10.7.47, NMP

351   'Rita Hayworth is very pretty . . .', 25.8.47, DCD

352   'as though it were a treasure', Edmund White, *Jean Genet*, p. 344

352   'a surrealist meal . . .', quoted Henri Béhar, *André Breton*, p. 382

352   'We're ruined!', quoted James Lord, *Giacometti*, p. 311

353   'It's wonderful . . .', Béhar, p. 383

354   'such a separation . . .', RCCSMHR 77/3/94

354   'France has sacrificed . . .', ibid.

355   'Comrade Stalin has said . . .', RCCSMHR 77/3/95

356   'to avoid problems', Duclos, RCCSMHR 77/3c/98

356   'lie', Thorez 1.10.47., RCCSMHR 17/128/265

356   'Information on attack groups . . .', RCCSMHR 77/3/95

356   'full of glamorous . . .', Celia Goodman (ed.), *Living with Koestler*, p. 58

357   'anti-semitic . . .', quoted ibid. p. 60

357   'received in return a long letter . . .', Arthur and Cynthia Koestler, *Stranger on the Square*, pp. 68–9

357   'At times she reminded me . . .', ibid., p. 72

358   'in which Le Petit . . .', Mamaine Paget, letter 4.11.47, quoted Goodman (ed.), p. 62. This was published in the magazine *Occident* in 1948 under the title 'Les Temps héroïques'.

358   '*On n'embastille pas Voltaire*', conversation Philippe Dechartre, 1.7.92

358   '*égocentrisme vertigineux*', Claude Mauriac, *Un Autre de Gaulle*, p. 286

358   'a spectacular success', NARA 851.00/10–647

358   'a wonderful new tease . . .', 23.10.47, NMP

359   'very pleased with the story . . .', 25.10.47, DCD

359   'People talk only . . .', André Gide and Matin du Gard, *Correspondance*, p. 391

360   'when supposedly responsible . . .', Top Secret to Bevin, 13.11.47, DCP

CHAPTER 27   *The Republic at Bay*

Page

361   'It was a remarkable . . .', 28.10.47, DCD

362   'to pull the rug . . .', Caffery, 24.10.47, NARA 851.00/10–2447

362   'that would bring de Gaulle . . .', NARA 851.00/10–2947

364   'a sensitive man . . .', E. Depreux, *Souvenirs d'un militant*, p. 248

364   'Do you realize . . .', Roger Pannequin, *Adieu camarades*, p. 92

366   'The strikes were called . . .', US Embassy translation of Political Orientation Instruction No. 1 of 26.12.47, NARA 851.00/1–948

366   '*Le Populaire*', Henri Noguères, conversation, 6.10.89

366   'The Colonel . . .', to Lady Redesdale, 25.11.47, NMP

367   'The whole population . . .', to Diana Mosley, 1.12.47, NMP

368   'The train is jammed . . .', Susan Mary Alsop, *To Marietta from Paris*, p. 119

369   'All seems quiet . . .', 30.11.47, DCD

370   'I told the *Times* man . . .', to Diana Mosley, 1.12.47, NMP

372   'Under these circumstances . . .', US Embassy translation of Political Orientation Instruction No. 1, 26.12.47, NARA 851.00/1–948

372   'All Leclerc's boys . . .', to Diana Mosley, 5.12.47, NMP

373   'gala occasion . . .', Alsop, p. 120

373   'in spite of the fact . . .', 2.12.47, NMP

373   'conspicuous exceptions . . .', 10.12.47, DCD

374   'heavy ivory grosgrain . . .', Alsop, pp. 121–2

374   "courageous and energetic . . .', NARA 851.00/3–1247

375   'the psychological and political . . .', NARA 851.00/4–1048

CHAPTER 28   *The Great Boom of Saint-Germain-des-Prés*

Page

376   'people would come in . . .', quoted Saint-Germain-des-Prés, p. 58

377   'From that moment . . .', Paul Boubal, quoted in 'Night and Day' by Vincent Gille, ibid., p. 57

380   'He was a great one for jokes . . .', Juliette Gréco, conversation, 30.10.93

380   'she pushed gossip . . .', Simone de Beauvoir, *La Force des choses*, p. 158

380   'full of inventive ideas . . .', Juliette Gréco, conversation, 30.10.93

380   '*C'était une période* . . .', ibid.

383   'To be part of the very fabric . . .', Marc Doelnitz, *La Fête à Saint-Germain-des-Prés*, p. 163.

383   'THIS IS HOW . . .', ibid., p. 165

383   'a violent form of exercise . . .', Anne-Marie Cazalis, *Les Mémoires d'une Anne*, p. 83

384   'These poverty-stricken . . .', quoted *Samedi-Soir*, 15.1.49

385   'a drugstore . . .', Janet Flanner, *Paris Journal 1944–65*, p. 92

386   'Astruc was the only one . . .', Juliette Gréco, conversation, 30.10.93

386   'I don't know how to sing . . .', Juliette Gréco, *Jujube*, p. 139

CHAPTER 29   *The Curious Triangle*

Page

388   'Unable to be angry . . .', 2.3.48, NMP

390   'they had to engage . . .', quoted Georgette Elgey, *La République des illusions*, p. 380

390   'the dissolution . . .', NARA 851.00/4–1048

390   'that we had the strength . . .', Raymond Aron, *Mémoires*, p. 230

390   'have given very careful thought . . .', NARA 851.00/3–2448

391   'as proof of . . .', NARA 851.00/5–1248

392   'the formation of a Reich . . .', PRO/FO 371/72947/ Z4745

393   'You're following a very bad policy . . .', quoted Hervé Alphand,
       L'Étonnement d'être, p. 210

394   'Don't ask why . . .', General de Bénouville, conversation, 21.1.93

394   'some forty Communists . . .', NARA 851.00/8–948

395   'As seen from Moscow . . .', NARA 851.00B/10-1448

396   'in the present situation . . .', RCCSMHR 17/128/595

396   'the arrest of . . .', NARA 851.00/1-1749

396   'unhappily he hasn't got . . .' Susan Mary Alsop, *To Marietta
       from Paris*, p. 133

397   'France is the present front line . . .', 2.11.48, PRO/FO 371/
       72953/Z8941

398   'The government has decided . . .', 20.11.48 to Secretary of State
       for Information, AN F/1a 4745

398   'any sort of negotiation . . .', AN F/1a/4745

398   'import licences . . .', 17.11.48, ibid.

398   'six months of strikes . . .', Alsop, p. 131

398   'accepted a place . . .', NARA 851.00/12-2948

398   'main target . . .', Aleksei Myagkov, *Inside the KGB*, p. 23

CHAPTER 30   *The Treason of the Intellectuals*

Page

401   'The ignoble word . . .', 12.3.47, quoted Jean Galtier-Boissière,
       Mon Journal dans la grande pagaïe, p. 212

401   'talk for hours . . .', Emmanuel Le Roy Ladurie, *Paris–Montpellier*,
       p. 46

402   'Are you sure . . .', Jean Gager, conversation, 14.3.93

402   'even though he was against . . .', Soria to Kamenov, 16.9.48,
       RCCSMHR 17/128/595

403   'hiding White Russian . . .', Baranov report for *Pravda*, 18.4.49,
       RCCSMHR 17/128/1186

403   'they're going to accuse you. . .', Louis Teuléry, conversation,
       15.3.93

403   'You've got to know . . .', Pierre Daix, *J'ai cru au matin*, p. 216

404   'Zoltán Szabó', letter to Rudolf Fischer, 15.3.92; and Ivan
       Boldizsar, 'On Zoltán Szabó', *New Hungarian Quarterly*, vol.xxx,
       No. 114, Summer 1989

404   'Trotskyist and *provocateur*', Fitin to Suslov, 27.6.46,
       RCCSMHR 17/128/967

404   'There are two ideological . . .', 16.9.48, RCCSMHR 17/128/595

405   'bourgeois reactionary philosophy', 11.6.46, RCCSMHR 17/125/454

405   'lived in a bubble', Annie Cohen-Solal, *Sartre, 1905–1980*, p. 310

410   'She's a prepossessing blonde . . .', Nina Berberova, *L'Affaire Kravtchenko*, p. 77

411   'They're not the public . . .', ibid., p. 96

411   'She did not come . . .', ibid., p. 79

412   'Kuibyshev', A. Solzhenitsyn, *Gulag Archipelago*, vol. iii, London: Collins & Harvill, 1978, p. 48

413   'At first when K. . . .', Celia Goodman (ed.), *Living with Koestler*, p. 100

414   'On that evening . . .', Arthur and Cynthia Koestler, *Stranger on the Square*, p. 72

415   'the intellectual method . . .', *Les Temps modernes*, No. 81, July 1952

416   'Such a polemic . . .', Raymond Aron, *L'Opium des intellectuels*, p. 70

416   'With his eyes shining . . .', Simone de Beauvoir, *La Force des choses*, p. 189

CHAPTER 31   *Americans in Paris*

Page

419   'like Christmas morning . . .', Susan Mary Alsop, *To Marietta from Paris*, p. 125

419   'lobster and young turkey . . .', 23.12.46, LDCP–CR

420   'burst upon Paris . . .', ibid.

420   '*anti-charme*', Jean-Louis Faucigny-Lucinge, *Un Gentilhomme cosmopolite*, p. 88

420   'dime-store maharani', Truman Capote, *Answered Prayers*, p. 78

420   'The sun never . . .', Arthur Miller, *Time Bends*, pp. 157–9

421   'Despite the waterfall . . .', Capote, p. 74

421   'leathery little basement bar', ibid., p. 37

422   'he was the victim . . .', John Malcolm Brinnin, *Truman Capote*, London: Sidgwick, 1987, p. 41

422   'white mushroom', Deirdre Bair, *Simone de Beauvoir*, p. 403

422   'Wall-eyed . . .', Capote, p. 38

422   'Miss Stein's widow', ibid., p. 41

423   'For God's sake . . .', quoted Christopher Sawyer-Lauçanno, *The Continual Pilgrimage*, p. 69

425   'We hope to hold . . .', 13.5.48, LC–AHP 271

425   'We have developed . . .', Seattle, 18.8.47, LC–AHP 273

425   'unwarranted interference . . .', Department of State Bulletin, 16.11.47, p. 937, quoted Rudi Abramson, *Spanning the Century*, p. 419

427   '*La 5e Colonne* . . .', headline in *L'Humanité*, 10.12.48

427   'The boys had all been . . .', Letitia Baldrige, *Diamonds and Diplomats*, p. 4

428   'the need to send . . .', 29.12.48, AN F/1a/4745

428   'At times . . .', Tom Wilson, conversation, 14.11.92

429   'I think I've found . . .', Evangeline Bruce, conversation, 12.11.92

429   'The Embassy flag . . .', 14.5.49, BD

430   'simple Sunday night dinner', 5.6.49, BD

430   'Boni de Castellane's . . .', 1.6.49, BD

430   'What a fine man . . .', 28.5.49, BD

430   'My boy' . . . 'Dean dear', Lucius Battle, conversation, 6.11.92

430   'Haven't they got . . .', ibid.

431   'after a steady . . .', 18.6.49, BD; and Evangeline Bruce, conversation, 7.11.92

431   'I want to drink a toast . . .', Lucius Battle, conversation, 6.11.92

432   'As usual, there is a financial crisis . . .', 16.6.49, BD

433   '*la Coca-colonisation* . . .', 19.10.49, BD

433   'It is a clear case of discrimination . . .', 3.12.49, BD

434   'the pederasts of . . .', *Action*, 6.10.49, quoted Jean-Pierre Bernard, *Paris Rouge*, p. 71

434   'Each evening . . .', *L'Humanité*, 15.5.52, quoted Bernard, p. 93

434   'a deeply civilized man . . .', Jean Monnet, *Mémoires*, p. 319

434   'everyone was struck . . .', Baldrige, p. 12

435   'Drunks were plentiful . . .', 5.7.49, BD

CHAPTER 32   *The Tourist Invasion*

Page

436   '*une véritable* . . .', copy of letter from F. Roger to Pomméry & Greno Champagne, 29.9.45, DCP

437   'We are informed . . .', 14.4.49, NMP

437   'You should have seen them . . .', 31.8.49, NMP

437   'gold swizzle sticks . . .', Art Buchwald, *Paris after Dark*, p. 67
438   'like a young Scott Fitzgerald . . .', Susan Mary Alsop, *To Marietta from Paris*, p. 163
438   'to have her mattress . . .', 9.6.49, BD
440   'a sexy piece . . .', 20.9.49, BD
440   'with some pretty odd . . .', Alsop, p. 154
442   'It's a small . . .', 18.2.47, LDCP–CR
443   'belt out a number or two', Buchwald, p. 83
443   'Josephine Baker . . .', Michael MacLiammoir, *Put Money in Thy Purse*, London: Columbus, 1976, pp. 81–2

CHAPTER 33   Paris sera toujours Paris

Page

445   'The whole of . . .', to Evelyn Waugh, 2.4.48, NMP
446   'are having the first good time . . .', Susan Mary Alsop, *To Marietta from Paris*, p. 39
446   'All I know . . .', Comte Jean de Ricaumont, conversation, 3.7.92
447   'Never, since the Age of Enlightenment . . .', Jean-Louis Faucigny-Lucinge, *Un Gentilhomme cosmopolite*, p. 104
450   'I went to the ball . . .', Charlotte Mosley (ed.), *Love from Nancy*, p. 224
450   'including a large one . . .', 1.7.49, BD
450   'The funeral of Bébé . . .', Mosely (ed.), p. 227
451   'some existentialist sirens . . .', Jean Galtier-Boissière, *Mon Journal dans la grande pagaïe*, p. 225
451   'There seems to be a change of heart . . .', Jacques Dumaine, *Quai d'Orsay 1945–51*, p. 151
451   'The average Frenchman . . .', Janet Flanner, *Paris Journal 1944–65*, p. 82
451   'The word "plan" . . .', NARA 711.51/11–848
452   'While I do not desire . . .', NARA 851.00/2–1049
453   'but by the end of 1949 . . .', 954, LC–AHP
453   'Quietest May Day . . .', NARA 851.00(W)/5–649
453   'There's to be a party . . .', 25.5.49, NMP
454   'Well the Mistresses Party . . .', 28.6.49, NMP
457   'Some fruit . . .', Frank Giles, *The Locust Years*, p. 112
458   'an astonishing . . .', Galtier-Boissière, *Mon Journal dans la grande pagaïe*, pp. 278–9

CHAPTER 34 *Recurring Fevers*

Page

459   'The General's stock . . .', Frank Giles, *The Locust Years*, p. 111

460   'in an embrace . . .', Schuman to Sir Oliver Franks, quoted Peter Hennessy, *Never Again*, p. 399

461   'The fresh air of Soviet art . . .', quoted Jean Galtier-Boissière, *Mon Journal dans la grande pagaïe*, p. 135

461   'American imperialism . . .', Pierre Daix, *L'Ordre et l'aventure*, pp. 233–4

461   'the production line . . .', ibid.

462   'an article by Joliot . . .', Pierre Daix, *Aragon*, p. 372

464   'not all truths . . .', Jacqueline Ventadour-Hélion, conversation, 22.1.93

465   'their party . . .', *L'Humanité*, 9.11.56, quoted Jean-Pierre Bernard, *Paris Rouge*, p. 54

468   'In any case . . .', unpublished manuscript of General Jean-Louis du Temple de Rougemont

469   'A second clandestine . . .', Aleksei Myagkov, *Inside the KGB*, pp. 23–4

470   'salute in one single motion . . .', from the Military Governor of Paris, quoted Henry Rousso, *The Vichy Syndrome*, p. 89

473   'Mitterrand . . . shook the hand . . .', Henri Amouroux, conversation, 12.3.93

473   'The collaboration . . .', Paxton, interview in *Libération*, 9.6.93

474   'quasi-erotic charge', Tony Judt, *Un Passé imparfait*, p. 352

474   'It is thus . . .', Marc Doelnitz, *La Fête à Saint-Germain-des-Prés*, p. 11

Bibliography

Abramson, Rudi, *Spanning the Century: The Life of W. Averell Harriman*, New York: Morrow, 1992

Acheson, Dean, *Present at the Creation*, London: Hamish Hamilton, 1970

Alcan, Louise, *Sans armes et sans bagages*, Limoges: Les Imprimés d'art, 1946

Alphand, Hervé, *L'Étonnement d'être*, Paris: Fayard, 1977

Alsop, Susan Mary, *To Marietta from Paris*, New York: Doubleday, 1975

Ambrose, Stephen, *Eisenhower, 1890–1952*, vol. i, London: Allen & Unwin, 1984

Amory, Mark (ed.), *The Letters of Evelyn Waugh*, London: Weidenfeld & Nicolson, 1980

Amouroux, Henri, *La Grande Histoire des Français sous l'Occupation, Joies et douleurs du peuple libéré*, vol. viii, Paris: Laffont, 1988

——, *Les Règlements de comptes*, vol. ix, Paris: Laffont, 1991

Apuleyo Mendoza, Plinio, 'García Marquez à Paris', *Silex* No. 11, Grenoble: 1982

Ariotti, Philippe, *Arletty*, Paris: Henri Veyrier, 1990

Aron, Raymond, *Mémoires*, Paris: Julliard, 1983

——, *L'Opium des intellectuels*, Paris: Calmann-Lévy, 1986

Aron, Robert, *Histoire de Vichy*, Paris: Fayard, 1954

——, *Histoire de la libération de la France*, Paris: Fayard, 1959

——, *Fragments d'une vie*, Paris: Plon, 1981

——, *Histoire de l'épuration*, 6 vols., Paris: Tallandier, 1977

——, *Les Grands Dossiers de l'Histoire Contemporaine*, Paris: Perrin, 1969

Assouline, Pierre, *L'Épuration des intellectuels*, Brussels: Complexe, 1990

Astoux, A., *L'Oubli*, Paris: Lattès, 1974

Auriol, Vincent, *Hier . . . Demain*, Paris: Armand Colin, 1945

Ayer, A. J., *Part of my Life*, London: Collins, 1977

Azéma, Jean-Pierre, *De Munich à la Libération*, Paris: Seuil, 1979

——, 'La Milice', *20ème siècle*, No. 28, December 1990

Bair, Deirdre, *Samuel Beckett*, London: Cape, 1978

——, *Simone de Beauvoir*, London: Cape, 1990

Baldrige, Letitia, *Diamonds and Diplomats*, London: Robert Hale, 1969

Ballard, Bettina, *In My Fashion*; New York: David McKay, 1960

Barrault, Jean-Louis, *Memories for Tomorrow*, London: Thames & Hudson, 1974

Baumann, Denise, *La Mémoire des oubliés*, Paris: Albin Michel, 1988

Beach, Sylvia, *Shakespeare & Company*, New York: Harcourt Brace, 1959

Beauvoir, Simone de, *La Force de l'âge*, Paris: Gallimard, 1960

——, *La Force des choses*, Paris: Gallimard, 1963

Béhar, Henri, *André Breton: Le Grand Indésirable*, Paris: Calmann-Lévy, 1990

Benoist-Méchin, Jacques, *De la défaite au désastre*, vols. i and ii, Paris: Albin Michel, 1984, 1985

——, *A l'Épreuve du temps*, vol. ii, Paris: Julliard, 1989

Berberova, Nina, *L'Affaire Kravtchenko*, Paris: Actes Sud, 1990

Bergeron, André, *Tant qu'il y aura du grain à moudre*, Paris: Laffont, 1988

Bernard, Jean-Pierre, *Paris Rouge: Les Communistes Français dans la capitale*, Paris: Champ Vallon, 1991

Bidault, Georges, *D'une Résistance à l'autre*, Paris: Presses du siècle, 1965

Billoux, François, *Quand nous étions ministres*, Paris: Éditions sociales, 1972

Boegner, Philippe (ed.), *Carnets du Pasteur Boegner, 1945*, Paris: Fayard, 1992

Bohlen, Charles, *Witness to History*, New York: Norton, 1973

Boissieu, Alain de, *Pour combattre avec de Gaulle*, Paris: Plon, 1982

——, *Pour servir le Général*, Paris: Plon, 1982

Bonnefous, Édouard, *La Vie de 1940 à 1970*, Paris: Nathan, 1987

Bothorel, Jean, *Louise – la vie de Louise de Vilmorin*, Paris: Grasset, 1993

Bouchinet-Serreulles, Claude, 'Pour accompagner mon Général', *La Revue des Deux Mondes*, October–November 1980

Bourdrel, Philippe, *L'Épuration sauvage: 1944–1945*, Paris: Perrin, 1988

Bourget, Pierre, *Paris Année 1944*, Paris: Plon, 1984

Brasillach, Robert, *Journal d'un homme occupé*, *Œuvres complètes*, vol. vi, Paris: Club de l'honnête homme, 1964

Brassaï, *Conversations avec Picasso*, Paris: Gallimard, 1964

Brinkley, Douglas, and Clifford Hackett (eds.) *Jean Monnet, The Path to European Unity*, New York: St Martin's Press, 1991

Brissac, Duc de, *Mémoires, La Suite des Temps (1939–1958)*, Paris: Grasset, 1974

Bruce, David K., *OSS against the Reich: The World War II Diaries of Colonel David K.E. Bruce*, Kent, Ohio: Kent State University Press, 1991

Buchwald, Art, *Paris after Dark*, Paris: Herald Tribune, 1950

Buton, Philippe, 'Le PCF, l'armée et le pouvoir à la Libération', in *Communisme*, Paris: Presses Universitaires de France, 1983

——, *La France et les Français de la Libération: 1944–1945*, Paris: Le Musée, 1984

——, *Le Couteau entre les dents*, Paris: Chêne, 1989

Cadogan, Sir Alexander, *Diaries*, London: Cassell, 1971

Capote, Truman, *Answered Prayers*, New York: Random House, 1987

Cassin, R., *Les Hommes partis de rien*, Paris: Plon, 1987

Caute, David, *Communism and the French Intellectuals*, London: Deutsch, 1964

Cazalis, Anne-Marie, *Les Mémoires d'une Anne*, Paris: Stock, 1976

Chalon, Jean, *Florence et Louise les Magnifiques*, Paris: Le Rocher, 1987

Chambrun, René de, *Pierre Laval devant l'Histoire*, Paris: France-Empire, 1983

Charbonneau, Henry, *Mémoires de Porthos*, Paris: Éditions du Clan, 1967

Charles-Roux, Edmonde, *Le Temps Chanel*, Paris: Grasset, 1980

Charlot, J., *Le Gaullisme d'opposition*, Paris: Fayard, 1983

Charpentier, Jacques, *Au Service de la Liberté*, Paris: Fayard, 1949

Chastenet, Jacques, *De Pétain à de Gaulle*, Paris: Fayard, 1970

Chebel d'Appollonia, Ariane, *Histoire politique des intellectuels en France 1944–1954*, vols. i and ii, Brussels: Complexe, 1991

Chisolm, Anne, *Nancy Cunard*, London: Sidgwick & Jackson, 1979

Closon, Louis, *Le Temps des passions*, Paris: Presses de la Cité, 1974

——, *Commissaire de la République*, Paris: Presses de la Cité, 1980

Cocteau, Jean, *Journal 1942–1945*, Paris: Gallimard, 1989

Codou, Roger, *Le Cabochard: Mémoires d'un communiste*, Paris: Maspéro, 1983

Cohen-Solal, Annie, *Sartre, 1905–1980*, Paris: Gallimard, 1985

——, with Henriette Nizan, *Paul Nizan, Communiste impossible*, Paris: Grasset, 1980

Colette, *Autobiographie*, Paris: Fayard, 1968

Colville, John, *The Fringes of Power*, London: Hodder & Stoughton, 1985
Cooper, Duff, *Old Men Forget*, London: Hart-Davis, 1953
Cotta, Michèle, *La Collaboration, 1940–1944*, Paris: Armand Colin, 1963
Courtois, Stephane, *Le PCF et la guerre*, Paris: Ramsay, 1980
Coutau-Bégarie, Hervé, and Claude Huan, *Darlan*, Paris: Fayard, 1989
Crick, Bernard, *George Orwell – A Life*, London: Secker & Warburg, 1980

Daix, Pierre, *Aragon, une vie à changer*, Paris: Seuil, 1975
——, *J'ai cru au matin*, Paris: Laffont, 1976
——, *L'Ordre et l'aventure*, Paris: Arthaud, 1984
Dansette, Adrien, *Histoire de la Libération de Paris*, Paris: Fayard, 1946
Debré, Michel, *Trois Républiques pour une France*, Paris: Albin Michel, 1985
De Gaulle, Charles, *Lettres, notes et carnets (mai 45 – juin 51)*, vol. vi, Paris: Plon, 1984
——, *Mémoires de guerre, 3 vols. (L'Appel, 1940–1942; L'Unité, 1942–1944; Le Salut, 1944–1946)*, Paris: Plon, 1962
De Jouvenal, Bertrand, *L'Amérique en Europe*, Paris: Plon, 1948
Depreux, E., *Souvenirs d'un militant*, Paris: Fayard, 1972
Desanti, Dominique, *Les Staliniens: une expérience politique, 1944–1956*, Paris: Fayard, 1975
——, *Sacha Guitry*, Paris: Grasset, 1982
——, *Drieu la Rochelle*, Paris: Flammarion, 1978
Desjardins, Thierry, *François Mitterrand, un socialiste gaullien*, Paris: Hachette, 1978
Dior, Christian, *Dior by Dior*, London: Weidenfeld, 1974
Dodds-Parker, Douglas, *Setting Europe Ablaze*, London: Springwood, 1983
Doelnitz, Marc, *La Fête à Saint-Germain-des-Prés*, Paris: Laffont, 1979
Dronne, Raymond, *La Libération de Paris*, Paris: Presses de la Cité, 1970
Duclos, Jacques, *Mémoires, 1945–1952, Sur la brèche*, Paris: Fayard, 1971
Dumaine, Jacques, *Quai d'Orsay 1945–51*, London: Chapman & Hall, 1958
Duras, Marguerite, *La Douleur*, Paris: P.O.L., 1985

Egen, Jean, *Messieurs du Canard*, Paris: Stock, 1973
Elgey, Georgette, *La République des illusions, 1945–51*, Paris: Fayard, 1965
Elleinstein, Jean, *Histoire du phénomène stalinien*, Paris: Grasset, 1975
——, *Goliath contre Goliath: Histoire des relations américano-sovietiques*, Paris: Fayard, 1986

Fabre-Luce, Alfred, *Deux Crimes d'Alger*, Paris: Julliard, 1979

——, *Journal de la France*, Geneva: Éditions du Cheval Ailé, 1946

Farge, Yves, *Le Pain de la corruption*, Paris: Éditions du Mail, 1947

Faucigny-Lucinge, Prince Jean-Louis, *Un Gentilhomme cosmopolite*, Paris: Perrin, 1990

Fauvet, J., *La IVe République*, Paris: Fayard, 1959

——, *La France déchirée*, Paris: Fayard, 1957

Flanner, Janet, *Paris Journal 1944–65*, London: Gollancz, 1966

Foot, M.R.D., *SOE in France*, London: HMSO, 1966

Frenay, Henri, *La Nuit finira*, Paris: Abélard-Schuman, 1983

Funk, Arthur, *The Politics of Torch*, Lawrence: University Press of Kansas, 1974

Galtier-Boissière, Jean, *Mon Journal pendant l'Occupation*, Paris: La Jeune Parque, 1944

——, *Mon Journal depuis la Libération*, Paris: La Jeune Parque, 1945

——, *Mon Journal dans la drôle de paix*, Paris: La Jeune Parque, 1947

——, *Mon Journal dans la grande pagaïe*, Paris: La Jeune Parque, 1950

Gellhorn, Martha, *A Honeyed Peace*, London: André Deutsch, 1954

Gerbet, Pierre, *Le Relèvement, 1944–1949*, Paris: Imprimerie Nationale, 1991

Gide, André, *Correspondance 1895–1950*, vol. ii, Lyons: Presses Universitaires de Lyon, 1990

——, *Journal, 1939–1949*, Paris: Gallimard, 1954

——, and Roger Martin du Gard, *Correspondance, 1935–1951*, Paris: Gallimard, 1968

Giles, Frank, *Sundry Times*, London: John Murray, 1986

——, *The Locust Years, The Story of the Fourth Republic*, London: Secker, 1991

Gilles, Christian, *Arletty ou la liberté d'être*, Paris: Seguier, 1988

Giraud, Henri-Christian, *De Gaulle et les Communistes*, vol. ii, Paris: Albin Michel, 1988

Goodman, Celia (ed.), *Living with Koestler, Mamaine Koestler's Letters, 1945–1951*, New York: St Martin's Press, 1985

Gorce, Paul Marie de la, *L'Après Guerre, 1944–1952*, Paris: Grasset, 1978

Gravier, Jean François, *Paris, Le Desert français*, Paris: Le Portulan, 1947

Gréco, Juliette, *Jujube*, Paris: Stock, 1982

Green, Julien, *Journal, 1928–1949*, Paris: Plon, 1969

Groussard, G., *Service Secret 1940–45*, Paris: La Table Ronde, 1964

Guitry, Sacha, *Si j'ai bonne mémoire*, Paris: Perrin, 1980
——, *Soixante jours de prison*, Paris: Perrin, 1964
——, *Quatre ans de l'occupation*, vol. ii, Paris: Solar, 1954
Gun, Nerin, *Pétain, Laval, de Gaulle*, Paris: Albin Michel, 1979

Hamilton, Peter, *Doisneau*, London: Tauris Parke, 1992
Hamon, Hervé, and Patrick Rotman, *Tu vois, je n'ai pas oublié*, Paris: Seuil/Fayard, 1990
d'Harcourt, Duc, *Regards sur un passé*, Paris: Laffont, 1989
d'Harcourt, Pierre, *The Real Enemy*, London: Longmans, 1967
Hastings, Selina, *Nancy Mitford*, London: Hamish Hamilton, 1985
Haut Cour de Justice, *Les Procès de la Collaboration*, Paris: Albin Michel, 1948
——, *Le Procès du Maréchal Pétain*, Paris: Albin Michel, 1976
Hennessy, Peter, *Never Again: Britain 1945–1951*, London: Cape, 1992
Herriot, Édouard, *Épisodes, 1940–1944*, Paris; Flammarion, 1950
Hobhouse, Janet, *Everybody who was Anybody*, London: Weidenfeld & Nicolson, 1975
Hoffman, Michael, *Gertrude Stein*, London: Prior, 1976
Hogan, Michael, *The Marshall Plan 1947–1952*, Cambridge: Cambridge University Press, 1987
Holban, Boris, *Testament*, Paris: Calmann-Lévy, 1989
Hostache, René, *De Gaulle 1944: victoire de la légitimité*, Paris: Plon, 1978

Isorni, Jacques, *Mémoires*, vols. i and ii, Paris: Laffont, 1984, 1986
——, *Philippe Pétain*, Paris: La Table Ronde, 1973
——, *Le Procès de Robert Brasillach*, Paris: Flammarion, 1946

Jeannelle, Sophie (ed.), 'Jean Chaintron, le PCF et le 70e anniversaire de Staline', in *Communisme*, Paris: P.U.F., 1983
Joxe, L., *Victoire sur la nuit*, Paris: Flammarion, 1981
Judt, Tony, *Un Passé imparfait: les intellectuels en France, 1944–1956*, Paris: Fayard, 1992
——, *Marxism and the French Left*, Oxford: Clarendon Press, 1986
——, *Resistance and Revolution in Mediterranean Europe, 1939–1948*, London: Routledge, 1989
Jünger, Ernst, *Premier journal parisien*, Paris: Christian Bourgois, 1980
——, *Second journal parisien*, Paris: Christian Bourgois, 1980

Kennan, George, *Memoirs 1925–1950*, New York: Little Brown, 1967

Kersaudy, F., *Churchill and de Gaulle*, New York: Athenaeum, 1981

Kochno, Boris, *Christian Bérard*, Paris: Herscher, 1987

Koestler, Arthur and Cynthia, *Stranger on the Square*, London: Hutchinson, 1983

Kravchenko, Victor, *I Chose Freedom*, New York: Scribner, 1946

——, *I Chose Justice*, London: Robert Hale, 1951

Kriegel, Annie, *Ce que j'ai cru comprendre*, Paris: Laffont, 1991

——, *Communismes au miroir français*, Paris: Gallimard, 1974

Kupferman, F., *Pierre Laval*, Paris: Balland, 1987

——, *Les Procès de Vichy*, Brussels: Complexe, 1980

——, *Les Premiers beaux jours, 1944–1946*, Paris: Calmann-Lévy, 1985

Lacouture, Jean, *De Gaulle, the Rebel*, London: Collins-Harvill, 1990

——, *The Ruler*, London: Collins-Harvill, 1991

——, *De Gaulle, Le Politique*, Paris: Seuil, 1985

——, *François Mauriac*, Paris: Seuil, 1980

——, *André Malraux*, Paris: Seuil, 1973

Ladurie, Emmanuel Le Roy, *Paris–Montpellier*, Paris: Gallimard, 1982

Laloy, Jean, *Yalta*, Paris: Laffont, 1988

Latour, Anny, *La Résistance Juive en France*, Paris: Stock, 1970

Lattre de Tassigny, J., *Ne pas subir*, Paris: Plon, 1984

Laval, Michel, *Brasillach ou la trahison du clerc*, Paris: Hachette, 1992

Le Boterf, Hervé, *La Vie parisienne sous l'Occupation*, Paris: France-Empire, 1974

Lecoeur, Auguste, *Le Partisan*, Paris: L'Actuel, 1963

Lewin, Christophe, *Le Retour des prisonniers de guerre français*, Paris: Sorbonne, 1987

Lifar, Serge, *Les Mémoires d'Icare*, Paris: Filipacchi, 1989

Lippmann, Walter, *The Cold War*, London: Hamish Hamilton, 1947

Lord, James, *Giacometti*, London: Faber, 1983

Lottman, Herbert, *The Left Bank*, London: Heinemann, 1982

——, *Camus*, Paris: Seuil, 1978

Mackinnon, Lachlan, *The Lives of Elsa Triolet*, London: Chatto, 1992

Malaurie, G., *L'Affaire Kravchenko*, Paris: Laffont, 1982

Malraux, André, *Antimémoires*, Paris: Gallimard, 1967

——, *De Gaulle par Malraux*, Paris: Club du Livre, 1980

Marnham, Patrick, *The Man Who Wasn't Maigret*, London: Bloomsbury, 1992

Marwick, Arthur (ed.), *Total War and Social Change in France*, London: Macmillan, 1988

Mauriac, Claude, *Un Autre de Gaulle: Journal 1944–1954*, Paris: Hachette, 1970

Mauriac, François, *Journal*, vol. iv, Paris: Flammarion, 1950

——, *Journal*, vol. v, Paris: Flammarion, 1953

——, *De Gaulle*, Paris: Grasset, 1964

——, *Mémoires Politiques*, Paris: Grasset, 1967

Merleau-Ponty, Maurice, *Signes*, Paris: Gallimard, 1960

Michel, Henri, *Paris Résistant*, Paris: Albin Michel, 1982

——, *Les Courants de pensée de la Résistance*, Paris: P.U.F., 1962

——, *Paris Allemand*, Paris: Albin Michel, 1981

Miller, Arthur, *Time Bends*, London: Methuen, 1987

Milward, Alan, *The Reconstruction of Western Europe, 1945–51*, London: Methuen, 1984

Mioche, Philippe, *Le Plan Monnet: Genèse et élaboration*, Paris: Sorbonne, 1985

Mitford, Nancy, *The Blessing*, London: Hamish Hamilton, 1951

Monnet, Jean, *Mémoires*, Paris: Fayard, 1976

Morand, Paul, *Lettres du voyageur*, Paris: Le Rocher, 1988

Mosley, Charlotte (ed.), *Love from Nancy: The Letters of Nancy Mitford*, London: Hodder & Stoughton, 1993

Moulin de Labarthète, Henri du, *Le Temps des illusions*, Geneva: Éditions du Cheval ailé, 1947

Muggeridge, Malcolm, *Chronicles of Wasted Time*, vol. ii, *The Infernal Grove*, London: Collins, 1973

Murphy, Robert, *Diplomat Among Warriors*, New York: Doubleday, 1964

Myagkov, Aleksei, *Inside the KGB – An Exposé by an Officer of the Third Directorate*, London: Foreign Affairs Publishing, 1976

Myers, David, *George Kennan and the Dilemmas of US Foreign Policy*, Oxford: Oxford University Press, 1988

Myers, Jeffrey, *Hemingway*, London: Macmillan, 1986

Neave, Airey, *Saturday at MI9*, London: Hodder, 1969

Noguères, Henri, *Histoire de la Résistance*, vol. 5, Paris: Laffont, 1981

——, *La vie quotidienne des Résistants*, Paris: Laffont, 1984

Noirot, Paul, *La Mémoire ouverte*, Paris: Stock, 1976

Novick, Peter, *The Resistance versus Vichy*, London: Chatto & Windus, 1968

——, *L'Épuration française, 1944–1949*, Paris: Balland, 1985

Oberlé, Jean, *La Vie d'artiste*, Paris: Denoël, 1956

Ostrovsky, Erika, *Céline and his Vision*, New York: New York University Press, 1967

Palewski, Gaston, *Mémoires d'action 1924–1974*, Paris: Plon, 1988

Pannequin, Roger, *Ami, si tu tombes*, Paris: Le Sagittaire, 1976

——, *Adieu camarades*, Paris: Le Sagittaire, 1977

Passy, Colonel (Dewavrin, André), *2e Bureau Londres, Souvenirs*, Paris: Solar, 1947

——, *10 Duke Street, Souvenirs*, Paris: Solar, 1947

Paulhan, Jean, *Lettre au directeurs de la Résistance*, Paris: Éditions de Minuit, 1951

Paxton, Robert, *Vichy France: Old Guard and New Order, 1940–44*, New York: Columbia University Press, 1982

——, (ed.), *Fragments de mémoire [Pierre Drieu La Rochelle]*, Paris: Gallimard, 1982

Penrose, Antony, *The Lives of Lee Miller*, London: Thames & Hudson, 1985

Péri, Gabriel, *Une Vie de combat*, Paris: Éditions sociales, 1947

Perrault, Gilles, *Paris sous l'Occupation*, Paris: Belfond, 1987

Pompidou, Georges, *Pour rétablir une vérité*, Paris: Flammarion, 1982

Pryce-Jones, David, *Paris in the Third Reich*, London: Collins, 1981

Purtschet, C., *Le Rassemblement du peuple français, 1947–1953*, Paris: Cujas, 1965

Ragache, Jean Robert, *La Vie quotidienne des écrivains et des artistes sous l'Occupation, 1940–1944*, Paris: Hachette, 1988

Rebatet, Lucien, *Mémoires d'un fasciste*, Paris: Société Nouvelle des Editions J.-J. Pauvert, 1976

Reynaud, Paul, *Au Cœur de la mêlée: 1930–1945*, Paris: Flammarion, 1951

Rioux, Jean-Pierre, *La France de la Quatrième République*, vol. i: *L'Ardeur et la nécessité, 1944–1952*, Paris: Le Seuil, 1980

—— (ed.), *La Vie culturelle sous Vichy*, Brussels: Complexe, 1990

Rist, Charles, *Une Saison gâtée*, Paris: Fayard, 1983

Robrieux, P., *Histoire intérieure du parti communiste*, vols. i and ii, Paris: Fayard, 1980–84

——, *Maurice Thorez*, Paris: Fayard, 1975

——, *L'Affaire Manouchian*, Paris: Fayard, 1986

Rothschild, Guy de, *The Whims of Fortune*, London: Granada, 1985

Rousso, Henry, *Un Château en Allemagne, La France de Pétain en exil –
Sigmaringen, 1944–1945*, Paris: Ramsay, 1980
——, *The Vichy Syndrome*, Cambridge, Mass.: Harvard, 1991
——, 'L'Épuration en France: une histoire inachevée', *Vingtième Siècle
revue d'histoire*, No. 33, January–March 1992
——, and Claude Roy, *Somme Toute*, Paris: Gallimard, 1969
Ruffin, Raymond, *La Vie des Français au jour le jour, de la Libération à la
Victoire*, Paris: Presses de la Cité, 1986
——, *Journal d'un J3*, Paris: Presses de la Cité, 1979

Saint-Germain-des-Prés, catalogue to exhibition *Saint-Germain-des-Prés,
1945–1950*, Pavillon de Marsan 1989–1990, Paris: Pavillon des Arts,
1989
Sawyer-Lauçanno, Christopher, *The Continual Pilgrimage: American Writers
in Paris*, London: Bloomsbury, 1992
Schoenbrun, D., *Maquis*, London: Hale, 1990
Serre, René, *Croisade à coups de poings*, Paris: Martel, 1954
Signoret, Simone, *La Nostalgie n'est plus ce qu'elle était*, Paris: Seuil, 1976
Smith, Grover (ed.), *Letters of Aldous Huxley*, London: Chatto & Windus,
1969
Soustelle, Jacques, *Vingt-huit ans de Gaullisme*, Paris: J'ai lu, 1971
Spears, E., *Assignment to Catastrophe*, vol. ii, *The Fall of France*, London:
Heinemann, 1954
Stein, Gertrude, *Paris France*, London: Batsford, 1940
——, *Wars I Have Seen*, New York: Random House, 1945
——, *Brewsie and Willie*, New York: Random House, 1946
Stéphane, Roger, *Tout est bien*, Paris: Quai Voltaire, 1989
——, *Fin d'une jeunesse*, Paris: La Table Ronde, 1954
——, *André Malraux, entretiens et précisions*, Paris: Gallimard, 1984
Strauss, D., *Menace in the West: The Rise of French Anti-Americanism in
Modern Times*, Westport, Conn.: Greenwood Press, 1978
Sulzberger, Cyrus L., *A Long Row of Candles*, London: Macdonald, 1969
Sulzberger, Marina, *Letters and Diaries of Marina Sulzberger*, New York:
Crown, 1978

Teitgen, Pierre-Henri, *Faites entrer le témoin suivant*, Paris: Ouest
France, 1988
Thorez, *Fils du peuple*, Paris: Éditions Sociales, 1949
Tillon, C., *On chantait rouge*, Paris: Laffont, 1976

Train, Susan (ed.), *Le Théâtre de la mode*, Paris: Le May, 1990

Triboulet, Raymond, *Un Gaulliste de la IVe*, Paris: Plon, 1958

Veillon, Dominique, *Le Franc-Tireur*, Paris: Flammarion, 1978

——, *La Mode sous l'Occupation*, Paris: Payot, 1990

Vendroux, J., *Souvenirs de famille et journal politique*, Paris: Plon, 1974

Verdès-Leroux, Jeannine, *Au Service du parti – Le parti communiste, les intellectuels et la culture (1944–1956)*, Paris: Fayard-Minuit, 1983

Vernier, Claude, *Tendre Exil*, Paris: La Découverte-Maspéro, 1983

Vian, Boris, *Manuel de Saint-Germain-des-Prés*, Paris: Chêne, 1974

Villon, P., *Résistant de la première heure*, Paris: Éditions sociales, 1983

Voldman, Danielle, *Attention Mines, 1944–46*, Paris: France-Empire, 1985

Wall, Irwin, *French Communism in the Era of Stalin*, Westport, Conn.: Greenwood Press, 1983

——, *The United States and the Making of Post-War France (1945–1954)*, Cambridge: Cambridge University Press, 1991

White, Edmund, *Jean Genet*, London: Chatto & Windus, 1993

White, Sam, *Sam White's Paris*, London: New English Library, 1983

Wickes, George, *The Amazon of Letters: The Life and Loves of Nathalie Barney*, London: W.H. Allen, 1977

Wieviorka, Annette, *Ils étaient juifs, résistants, communistes*, Paris: Denoël, 1986

——, *Déportation et génocide*, Paris: Plon, 1992

Wilson, Edmund, *A Literary Chronicle of the Forties*, London: W.H. Allen, 1951

Wurmser, André, *Fidèlement vôtre. Soixante ans de vie politique et littéraire*, Paris: Grasset, 1979

Ziegler, Philip, *King Edward VIII*, London: Collins, 1990

Photographic
Acknowledgements

Illustrations 4, 5, 6 and 13 are reproduced by permission of Roger-Viollet; numbers 1 and 2 by Robert Doisneau, permission of Rapho; and numbers 12 and 16 by Willy Ronis, permission of Rapho. Number 3 is reproduced by permission of the Brassaï estate; 8 by permission of the Horst estate; 9 by permission of Keystone; 10 by permission of the Christian Dior Archive © ADAGP, Paris and DACS, London 1994; 11 by permission of *Paris Match;* 17 by permission of the André Ostier estate; and 19 by permission of the Service des Musées © DACS 1994.

We are extremely grateful to Mrs David Bruce for kindly lending illustration 18. The remainder come from the albums of Lady Diana Cooper and her family, and if any photographer or archive owns the copyright of any of them, they should contact the publisher.

Index